THE MARRIAGE OF CADMUS AND HARMONY

THE MARRIAGE
OF CADMUS AND
HARMONY

ROBERTO CALASSO

Translated from the Italian by Tim Parks

Alfred A. Knopf   New York   1993

This Is a Borzoi Book Published by Alfred A. Knopf, Inc.

Copyright © 1993 by Alfred A. Knopf, Inc.
All rights reserved under International and Pan-American Copyright
Conventions. Published in the United States by Alfred A. Knopf, Inc.,
New York, and simultaneously in Canada by Random House of Canada
Limited, Toronto. Distributed by Random House, Inc., New York.

Originally published in Italy as *Le nozze di Cadmo e Armonia*
by Adelphi Edizioni S.p.A., Milan, in 1988. Copyright © 1988
by Adelphi Edizioni S.p.A.

Library of Congress Cataloging-in-Publication Data
Calasso, Roberto.
[Nozze di Cadmo e Armonia. English]
The marriage of Cadmus and Harmony / Roberto Calasso ; translated
from the Italian by Tim Parks.
p. cm.
Translation of: Le nozze di Cadmo e Armonia.
ISBN 0-394-58154-7
1. Cadmus (Greek mythology)—Fiction. 2. Harmonia (Greek
mythology)—Fiction. I. Title.
PQ4863.A3818N6913 1993
853'.914—dc20   92-2820   CIP

Manufactured in the United States of America
First American Edition

These things never happened, but are always

Sallust, *Of Gods and of the World*

I

ON A BEACH IN SIDON A BULL WAS APING a lover's coo. It was Zeus. He shuddered, the way he did when a gadfly got him. But this time it was a sweet shuddering. Eros was lifting a girl onto his back: Europa. Then the white beast dived into the sea, his majestic body rising just far enough above the water to keep the girl from getting wet. There were plenty of witnesses. Triton answered the amorous bellowing with a burst on his conch. Trembling, Europa hung on to one of the bull's long horns. Boreas spotted them too as they plowed through the waves. Sly and jealous, he whistled when he saw the young breasts his breath had uncovered. High above, Athena blushed at the sight of her father bestraddled by a girl. An Achaean sailor saw them and gasped. Could it be Tethys, eager to see the sky? Or just some Nereid with clothes on her back for a change? Or was it that trickster Poseidon carrying off another wench?

Europa, meantime, could see no end to this crazy sea crossing. But she guessed what would happen to her when they hit land again. And she shouted to wind and water: "Tell my father Europa has been carried off by a bull—my kidnapper, my sailor, my future bedmate, I imagine. Please, give this necklace to my mother." She was going to call to Boreas too, ask him to lift her up on his wings, the way he'd done with his own bride, Oreithyia, from Athens. But she bit her tongue: why swap one abductor for another?

. . .

But how did it all begin? A group of girls were playing by the river, picking flowers. Again and again such scenes were to prove irresistible to the gods. Persephone was carried off "while playing with the girls with the deep cleavages." She too had been gathering flowers: roses, crocuses, violets, irises, hyacinths, narcissi. But mainly narcissi, "that wondrous, radiant flower, awesome to the sight of gods and mortals alike." Thalia was playing ball in a field of flowers on the mountainside when she was clutched by an eagle's claws: Zeus again. Creusa felt Apollo's hands lock around her wrists as she bent to pick saffron on the slopes of the Athens Acropolis. Europa and her friends were likewise gathering narcissi, hyacinths, violets, roses, thyme.

All of a sudden they find themselves surrounded by a herd of bulls. And one of those bulls is dazzling white, his small horns flashing like jewels. There's nothing in the least threatening about him. So much so that, though shy at first, Europa now brings her flowers to his white muzzle. The bull whines with pleasure, like a puppy, slumps down on the grass, and offers his little horns to the garlands. The princess makes so bold as to climb, like an Amazon, on his back. At which, the herd moves discreetly away from the dry riverbed and off toward the beach. With a show of nervousness, the bull approaches the water. And then it's too late: the white beast is already breasting the waves with Europa up on top. She turns to look back, right hand hanging on to a horn, left leaning on the animal's hide. As they move, the breeze flutters her clothes.

But how did it all begin? Shortly before dawn, asleep in her room on the first floor of the royal palace, Europa had had a strange dream: she was caught between two women; one was Asia, the other was the land facing her, and she had no name. The two women were fighting over her, violently. Each wanted her for herself. Asia looked like a woman from Europa's own country, whereas the other was a total stranger. And in the end it was the stranger whose powerful hands dragged her off. It was the will of Zeus, she said: Europa was to be an Asian girl carried off by a stranger. The dream was extremely vivid, as though happening in broad daylight, and on waking Europa was afraid and sat silent on her bed for a long time. Then she went out, the way she always did, with her friends. They walked down to the mouth of the river, and Europa wandered about between the roses and the breaking waves, her golden basket in one hand.

A blondish bull appeared in the meadow, a white circle on his forehead. The animal had a sweet scent, which drowned the smell of the flowers. He came up to Europa and licked her neck. She stroked him, at the same time drying the saliva that dribbled freely from the animal's mouth. The bull knelt down in front of her, offering her his back. And the moment she climbed up, he made a dash for the sea. Terrified, Europa looked back toward the beach, shouted to her friends, one arm waving in the air. Then, already out in the waves, she hung on to a big horn with one hand and held the hem of her tunic up tight against her breast with the other. Behind her, the tunic billowed out in a purple sail.

But how did it all begin? Europa was out walking with her friends, a shining gold basket in her hand. Hephaestus had made it two generations before to give to Libye. And Libye had given it to her daughter Telephassa, who had given it to her daughter Europa. It was the family talisman. On the side, embossed in gold, was a stray heifer apparently swimming in an enamel sea. Two mysterious men were standing on the shore watching. And there was a golden Zeus too, his hand just skimming the bronze-colored animal. In the background, a silver Nile. The heifer was Io, Europa's great-great-grandmother.

Her story too was one of abduction and metamorphosis. Tormented by a gadfly, she crossed and recrossed sea after sea in a state of constant mental anguish. She even gave her name to the sea that led to Italy. Zeus's love for her had brought her to madness and disaster. It all began with some strange dreams, when Io was priestess in the Heraion near Argos, the oldest of all shrines and the place that gave the Greeks their way of measuring time; for centuries they numbered their years with reference to the succession of priestesses in the Heraion. Io's dreams whispered of Zeus's passionate love for her and told her to go to the fields of Lerna, where her father's sheep and oxen grazed. From now on she would no longer be a priestess consecrated to the goddess but an animal consecrated to the god, like the ones that wandered freely about the sanctuary grounds. Thus her dreams insisted. And so it was.

But one day the sanctuary grounds would expand to become the whole world, with its boundless seas, which she was to ford one after the other without respite, forever goaded by that relentless gadfly. And the vaster the landscape about her, the more intense her suffering became. By the time she came across another victim, Prometheus, what she wanted most of all was to die, not realizing that she had found another sufferer like herself who could not hope to die. But for Io, as for Prometheus, release from obsession did come at last. One day, after she had crossed to Egypt, Zeus skimmed his hand lightly over her. At which the crazed young cow became a girl again and was united with the god. In memory of that moment she called her son Epaphus, which means "a hand's light touch." Epaphus later became king of Egypt, and rumor had it he was also the ox called Apis.

As she walked down toward the flowery meadows near the sea, what Europa was carrying, embossed in precious metals, was her destiny. As in a piece of music, her own tune was the melodic inversion of her ancestor, Io's. A bull would carry her off from Asia toward the continent that was to be called Europe, just as years before the desperate sea wandering of a young cow who had first grazed in Greek pastures was to end in Egypt with the light touch of Zeus's hand. And one day the gift of the golden basket would be handed down to Europa. She carried it along, without thinking.

But how did it all begin? If it is history we want, then it is
a history of conflict. And the conflict begins with the abduction of a girl, or with the sacrifice of a girl. And the one
is continually becoming the other. It was the "merchant
wolves," arriving by ship from Phoenicia, who carried off
the *tauropárthenos* from Argos. *Tauropárthenos* means
"the virgin dedicated to the bull." Her name was Io. Like a
beacon signaling from mountain to mountain, this rape lit
the bonfire of hatred between the two continents. From that
moment on, Europe and Asia never stopped fighting each
other, blow answering blow. Thus the Cretans, "the boars
of Ida," carried off Europa from Asia. They sailed back to
their home country in a ship shaped like a bull, offering
Europa as a bride to their king, Asterius. One of Europa's
grandchildren was to have the same celestial name. He was
a young man with a bull's head, and he lived in the middle
of a labyrinth, awaiting his victims. What they usually
called him, though, was the Minotaur.

But how did it all begin? When they arrived in Argos, the
Phoenician merchants spent five or six days selling the wares
they'd brought from the Red Sea, Egypt, and Assyria. Their
ship lay at anchor while on the shore the local people gazed
at, touched, and bargained over those objects from so far
away. There were still some last things to be sold when a
group of women arrived. One of them was Io, the king's
daughter. The bargaining and buying went on. Until all of
a sudden, the seafaring merchants leaped on the women.
Some of them managed to escape. But Io and a number of
others were carried off. This was the abduction the Cretans
were revenging when they carried off the Phoenician king's
daughter, Europa. But the Phoenicians have a different version: Io was in fact in love with the captain of the foreign
ship. She was already pregnant and ashamed, and so left
with the Phoenicians of her own free will.

Out of these events history itself was born: the abduction

of Helen, the Trojan War, and, before that, the Argonauts' expedition and the abduction of Medea—all are links in the same chain. A call to arms goes back and forth between Asia and Europe, and every back and forth is a woman, a woman and a swarm of predators, going from one shore to the other. Nevertheless, Herodotus did note a difference between the two sides in the dispute: "To abduct women," he writes, "is considered the action of scoundrels, but to worry about abducted women is the reaction of fools. The wise man does not give a moment's thought to the women who have been abducted, because it is clear that, had they not wanted to be abducted, they would not have been." The Greeks did not behave wisely: "For one Spartan woman they gathered together a great army and, arriving in Asia, laid low the power of Priam." Since then, the war between Europe and Asia has never ceased.

They landed on a large island but didn't stop. Instead they pushed on into the hills. Only when they'd reached Gortyn, under a huge, shady plane tree, did Zeus and Europa make love. Zeus was an eagle. Afterward he disappeared. But left his loved one with a guardian. In the silent heat, Europa heard the clopping of bronze hooves coming from far away. Someone was riding flat out. It must be a machine, or a being from another age, a child of the ash nymphs. It was both: Talos, another bull, the guardian bull, sentry of the island; or alternatively, as some said, a mechanical giant put together by Hephaestus. A long vein stood out on his body, running from neck to hooves—or perhaps feet. And there a bronze nail stopped the gush of blood and sent it bubbling back inside. That nail was the secret of the creature's life, and likewise of the art of casting. Talos would gallop about and hurl stones all over the place: at nothing mostly, or at approaching strangers. Back in the Palace of Sidon, Europa had been used to waking to the sound of friendly voices, the companions she went down to the sea with; here she woke to silence, and in the depth of that silence a distant sound, which would gradually become deafening. But she saw no one. She knew that Talos went on running up and down the coasts of the large island: Crete, Europe.

Io, Telephassa, Europa, Argiope, Pasiphaë, Ariadne, Phaedra: the names evoke a broad, pure, shining face that lights things up at a distance, that lights up all of us, like the moon. "Huge, pale figures, tremendous, lonely, dark and desolate, fatal, mysterious lovers condemned to titanic infamies. What will become of you? What will your destiny be? Where can you hide your fearful passions? What terrors, what compassion you inspire, what immense and awesome sadness you arouse in those mortals called to contemplate so much shame and horror, so many crimes, such great misfortune." So said Gustave Moreau.

Diodorus Siculus: "They also say that the honors given to the gods and the sacrifices and rites of the mysteries originally came down to other men from Crete, and in making this claim they offer what they believe is an extremely strong argument. The initiation rite that the Athenians celebrate in Eleusis, the most illustrious, one might say, of all rites, and again the Samothracians' rite and the rite begun by Orpheus in Thrace among the Cicones, all these rites are passed on from one initiate to another in secret. But in Cnossos, Crete, it has always been the custom to practice such initiation rites in broad daylight and to let everybody know about them. What is considered unnameable among other peoples is available for all who want to hear in Crete."

Mystery, in Crete, was made plain to all, no one tried to hide it. The "unnameable things" that abounded in Attica were laid open to everybody. But there was no sense of challenge about this. Crete, with its hundred cities and not a single defensive wall around them, looked like a huge plaything.

Only a tidal wave, or dark raiders striking from the sea, could have been its doom, not the recklessness of the sort of civilization that seeks self-knowledge, and in so doing destroys itself.

A few thousand years later, a famous morphologist of civilization was to be baffled by Crete, for, having studied the whole multitude of Cretan remains, he could find not a single indication of any historical, political, or even biographical consciousness, such as had always dominated Egyptian thought. For a man who hungered after the signs of great civilizations, Crete had something childish about it, something elusive, something below par.

The Linear B Tablets include many names of gods: about half were to go on living as Olympian gods, the other half were lost. We know nothing about them: they are mere names that appear alongside those of Zeus, Poseidon, Hera. As if the Olympian gods had once been far more numerous and now carried around with them the shadows of their lost brothers and sisters.

Crete: pots of grain numbered in the storehouses, seals showing beasts half one thing half another, delicate frescoes, ivory knots, lists of offerings, honey, inscribed poppy pods, ox skulls, double-edged axes. Columns of cypress wood, palaces with stairways and shafts of light, nameless tombstones. Tiny idols heaped in piles, not statues, not doubles made of stone. Nothing of the verticality of the divine, no sign of the hallucinatory presence of upright stone.

Stories never live alone: they are the branches of a family that we have to trace back, and forward. In the rapture of her sea crossing on the back of a white bull, Europa conceals within herself, like still undiscovered powers, the destinies of her love-crazed granddaughters Phaedra and Ariadne, who would one day hang themselves out of shame and desperation. And down among the celestial roots of this story tree we come across the wanderings of the mad heifer, the ancestral Io, who again holds within herself the image of another mad heifer, mother of Phaedra and Ariadne: Pasiphaë. And she too hung herself in shame.

From a rock, Ariadne watches Phaedra on a swing. Lost in thought, she waits. Both are young princesses, in Cnossos. Daughters of Minos and Pasiphaë. They have lots of brothers and sisters. And a half brother too, Asterius. Asterius has a bull's head, because his father was the big white bull Pasiphaë fell in love with. Asterius has been shut up in a building designed by an Athenian inventor who is on the run because, so rumor has it, he killed somebody. That covered building is strange indeed. The princesses were already familiar with the labyrinth, but in the past it had been out in the open for everybody to see, a broad space for the dance. They didn't realize—nobody would have told them—that, when their father, Minos, set out to conquer the continent and the Cretans began to have too many dealings with the Greeks, the moment had come for them to cover up their secrets, and ultimately to be ashamed of them. Daedalus, the Athenian, designs a building in Crete that hides behind stone walls both mystery (the pattern of the dance) and shame (Asterius, the Minotaur). From that day on, the mystery is also the thing you are ashamed of.

This development depended, in turn, on the developing history of metamorphoses. Forms would become manifest insofar as they underwent metamorphosis. Each form had its own perfect sharpness, so long as it retained that form, but everybody knew that a moment later it might become something else. At the time of Europa and Io, the veil of epiphany was still operating. The bellowing bull, the crazed cow, would once again appear as god and girl. But as generation followed generation, metamorphosis became more difficult, and the fatal nature of reality, its irreversibility, all the more evident. Only a generation after Europa, Pasiphaë would have to crouch inside a wooden cow, a big toy on wheels, and have herself pushed as far as the meadows of Gortyn, where the bull she desired was grazing. And from their union was born a creature who would never be able to go back to being either beast or man. He would be a hybrid, forever. And just as the craftsman Daedalus had had to invent an inanimate object to allow the mother to love the bull, so now he had to invent another object, the labyrinth, to conceal the son. The Minotaur would be slain, Pasiphaë was to die in captivity and shame. Humans could no longer gain access to other forms and return from them. The veil of epiphany was rent and tattered now. If the power of metamorphosis was to be maintained, there was no alternative but to invent objects and generate monsters.

"Since it is the custom in Crete for the women to take part in the games, Ariadne was there with the others, and she was amazed when she saw Theseus, and admired his skill as, one after another, he overcame all adversaries." While Ariadne gazes at the Stranger, Crete crumbles. Before being betrayed herself, Ariadne chose to betray her island.

Dionysus courts her, then accuses her, then kills her, then rediscovers her, then transforms her into the crown of the northern sky, Corona Borealis. But this is a different Dionysus from the one Ariadne knew in her childhood. He wasn't even called Dionysus then. He was the Bull: the total Bull, who descends from the heavens like Zeus, rises from the sea like Poseidon, grazes under the plane trees of Gortyn. He encompassed all things: he was in the honey and blood offered to the gods, he was in the slender horns at each side of the altars, in the ox skulls painted along the walls of the palace. Youths with armbands, loincloths, and wavy hair gripped him by the horns at a run. The Bull had always followed Ariadne about, right from the start, always accompanied her, always kept his eye on her.

Now the Bull steps aside and the Athenian hero moves in.

They would appear to be enemies, but they swap places very smoothly. The scene is already set. No more monster business now, but sordid affairs. That is Ariadne's destiny. No more the childish, the regal palace, but the porticoes and public squares where tough, clever men take the first opportunity to stab each other in the back, where the word, which in Crete had served to take inventories of goods in warehouses, would become sovereign, vibrant, revered. Ariadne would not live to see all this: she stopped halfway, caught on another island, rocky and inhospitable. She closed her eyes, so as never to have to see again either the god or the man who of their natures could do nothing more than appear and disappear.

Theseus transformed the divine habit of carrying off young maidens into a human pastime. Every adventure he sets out on he carries off a woman, whether it be the Cretan Ariadne when he goes south or the Amazon Antiope when he heads north. There was always something playful and even reckless about these adventures. And some of them hardly finished in noble fashion, for no sooner had Theseus conquered a trophy than he was in a hurry to be rid of it, so as to go after another. At fifty he was still at it, carrying off a certain Helen who danced in the shrine of Artemis Orthia. On that occasion he was assisted by the only being to whom he would be faithful to the end: his friend Peirithous.

They first met as enemies and were supposed to fight to the death. But, when they saw each other, just as they were about to fight their duel, each found he was admiring his adversary. Each was attracted to the beauty and strength of the other. From that moment they became companions in adventure. And Theseus was never so happy as when he was with Peirithous, inventing irreverent adventures, going through with them, talking about them afterward. They knew the world, these two, they had seen it all, had killed mythical beasts, carried off princesses. Nothing could separate them, least of all a woman.

One day Peirithous felt lonely; his wife, Hippodamia, had recently died. He thought he'd go and see his friend Theseus in Athens. And the widower found another widower: Phaedra had hung herself. As so often before, they talked and talked, and pretty soon they fell to talking about new adventures. There was a girl in Sparta, Peirithous said, ten years old and more beautiful than any woman. Her name was Helen. Why not carry her off? When they had captured her, they shook a die to see who would have her. Theseus won.

And one day, together as always, during one of those coded conversations that were their greatest pleasure in life (neither the women nor the adventures in themselves could offer so much in the end)—one day it occurred to them that, having roamed more or less the whole world, the only thing left for them to do was to violate the underworld. They had carried off earthly princesses, so why not carry off divine queens? They'd managed to trick living kings, so why couldn't they do the same in the kingdom of the dead? Thus Peirithous and Theseus went down to Hades to carry off its queen.

Theseus is he who gets up and goes. Not even Helen can hold him, happy prisoner as she is. And, while fears of reprisals are mounting and the abductor's friends are closing ranks to protect her, Peirithous comes up with his idea: head off even farther down the Peloponnese, as far as Cape Taenarum, where you can climb down into Hades, and carry off the most powerful of queens. And off Theseus goes. This time it isn't a question of abducting a twelve-year-old (or had she been ten?), dancing in the shrine of Artemis, nor is it a matter of learning the dances of the labyrinth from a ravishing girl. This time the project is tougher: "these two tried to snatch Dis's bride from her marriage bed."

. . .

The punishment reserved for Theseus by the king of the underworld is a subtle one, answering mockery with mockery. Hades listens to the two friends politely. He asks how he can help them, he invites them to make themselves comfortable on two golden chairs set into the rock. But an invisible bond glues the friends to those chairs. They can't get up. Peirithous, "he who wanders in circles," and Theseus, the abductor, must forget their very selves, sitting still in the kingdom of the dead. When Heracles saves Theseus, dragging him from the chair by force, he leaves strips of flesh behind. Which is why, they say, Athenian boys have such small, lean buttocks.

All around Athens, before it was called Athens, the country was full of brigands and wild beasts who attacked and tormented travelers. One day a herald arrived from the sea with the news that a young man had made the rounds of all the roads and slain all the troublemakers: Sinis and Phaea, Sciron, Cercyon, and Procrustes, to name but a few. But what was this young man like? people asked. He had a sword with an ivory hilt slung over one shoulder and two shining javelins, one in each hand. He wore a Spartan cap over tawny curls and a purple jersey on his chest under a woolen cloak from Thessaly. A wicked light flashed in his eyes.

Theseus wore his hair short in front—so that nobody could grab it in a fight, he said—and long and plaited behind. The curls that fell on his forehead he had dedicated to Apollo in Delphi. When first he appeared in the vicinity of Athens, he was sixteen years old and wore a long Ionian tunic. His hair had been twisted into a handsome plait behind. The laborers working on the temple of Delphinian Apollo—they only had the roof to go—jeered and shouted jokes. What on earth was a marriageable young girl doing wandering about beneath the Acropolis on her own? Theseus didn't answer them. He went up to a cart with a bull yoked to it, freed the bull, and tossed it in the air. They saw it fly up above their still un-finished roof. It was the first time Theseus had had dealings with a bull.

But how many more were to cross his path! The Minotaur in Crete, into whose boy's body he would bury his sword. The bull he would capture at Marathon to the joy of the Athenians. Then a bull would rise from the sea to kill his son, Hippolytus. And on many other and more obscure oc-casions Theseus would find himself up against the bull. So close was his relationship with the beast that he put a bull's head on the first coins he minted in his city, the sacred Athens. It was Theseus who chose the name.

There is something blasphemous about Theseus, an indom-itable insolence that looks forward to Alcibiades. When he and his friend Peirithous embark on their trip to the under-world to snatch back Persephone, an adventure that smacks of parody, one thinks of Alcibiades, whose critics accused him of celebrating religious mysteries with prostitutes and vagabonds. And just as Alcibiades would one day with great solemnity lead a procession along the Sacred Way toward Eleusis, so Theseus presided over the city's most secret rites. He played with those secrets because he knew them so well, because they had belonged to him from birth.

Theseus has no particular reason for deserting Ariadne. There wasn't another woman. It was just that she slipped his mind for a moment, a moment that might be any mo-ment. And when Theseus gets distracted, someone is lost. Ariadne had helped the Stranger kill her half brother with the bull's head, she had left the family palace, she was ready to wash Theseus's feet in Athens, like a slave. But Theseus has forgotten, he is already thinking of something else. And the place where Ariadne gets left behind becomes, once and for all, the landscape of abandoned love. Theseus isn't cruel because he leaves Ariadne. If that were the case, his cruelty would be no different from that of so many others. No, Theseus is cruel because he leaves Ariadne on the island of Naxos. Not the home where she was born, and certainly not the home she hoped to be welcomed in, nor even some country in between. Just a beach lashed by thundering waves, an abstract place where only the seaweed moves. It is the island where no one lives, the place where obsession turns round and round on itself, with no way out. A constant flaunting of death. This is a place of the soul.

Ariadne has been left behind. The clothes fall from her body one by one. It is a scene of mourning. Awake now, but still as the statue of a Bacchant, Minos's daughter gazes into the distance toward the eternal absentee, for Theseus's swift ship has already disappeared over the horizon, and her mind rises and falls with the waves. The thin ribbon that held her blond hair slips off, her cloak falls away leaving her chest bare, her breasts are no longer supported by their sash. One after another, the clothes in which she left Crete forever fall and scatter at her feet. The waves toy with them in the sand and seaweed.

As Ariadne gazed naked into the empty distance and thought how much she would like to be in Athens, as Theseus's bride, and to prepare his bed for him, though she would never lie in it, and to serve another who would lie in it, and to offer Theseus a bowl of water to wash his hands in after the banquet—as, in short, she was making a mental inventory of all the most minute demonstrations of servility she would have liked to show her vanished lover, a new thought occurred to her: perhaps another woman had had feelings like her own; her dedication and degradation were not unique, as she had at first liked to think. But who was that other woman? The queen, the all-splendid, shameless Pasiphaë, her mother. In the end she too, shut up in her wooden cow, that awkward, clumsy, colored toy on wheels, had agreed to play servant to a mere herdsman. She had bent her neck to let them put her in the yoke, she had whispered words of love to a dumb bull chomping grass. Hidden in the suffocating dark, in the smell of the wood, the herdsman's pipes got on her nerves, because there was only one sound she wanted to hear: the lowing of that white bull.

Then another thought occurred to Ariadne, a thought that followed from the first: if she, Ariadne, had done nothing more than repeat the passion of her mother, Pasiphaë, if she herself was Pasiphaë, then Theseus was the bull. But Theseus had killed the bull, her half brother, and killed him with her help. So had she been helping Theseus to kill himself? Or were the only people to get killed in this story themselves: Pasiphaë, who hung herself, Ariadne, who was preparing to hang herself, and her sister, Phaedra, who would hang herself some time later. While the bulls and their victors just seem to swap places, over and over, as if for them the process of killing and being killed was as simple an alternation as undressing and getting dressed again. The bull didn't experience the ultimate perpendicular death of hanging, the being lifted away from this earth.

When the enamel blue prow of the Athenian ship arrived in Crete, when Theseus stopped King Minos from laying his hands, as he always would, on one of the Athenian girls, when during the games Theseus beat the hateful, imposing General Bull, who used to trounce everybody, then Ariadne began to think that this irreverent stranger might be strong enough to break the bull-obsessed circle in which her family was imprisoned. So she betrayed the divine bull who had dazzled her in a cave, betrayed her brother bull, the Minotaur, betrayed her mother, who had gone mad for a bull, and betrayed her father, who had chosen not to sacrifice the white bull from the sea but to put it out to pasture because it was too beautiful to be killed. At the end of all these betrayals, she found herself on a deserted beach, abandoned by Theseus. But she hadn't managed to escape the bull.

When Dionysus appeared, sham and seductive, too punctual, too merry, Ariadne sensed that somehow Dionysus and Theseus weren't rivals at all, but accomplices. Amid the clamor of flutes and tambourines, Dionysus suffocated such thoughts. Ariadne was dazzled by the divine glory the god offered her. And secretly she sneered at Theseus, who had brought that glory on her by his very treachery. She sensed the deviousness of the affair: if Theseus hadn't broken his word (but he had taken an oath to Athena, she remembered with a start, and Athena scorned marriage), Dionysus wouldn't have raised her to himself. No point in crying like a peasant girl, when you have a god next to you. But Dionysus doesn't stay next to anyone. A god is never a constant presence. And off Dionysus went with his noisy followers, to India. Ariadne was alone again.

When the god reappeared, loaded with treasures and slaves, Ariadne observed his triumph and caught the passionate glance Dionysus threw at a young Indian girl, a princess, just one among his many Oriental spoils. Soon Ariadne would find herself crying on a beach again, her hair loose in the wind. With his overwhelming lightness, Dionysus had saved her from what Theseus had done to her, only to repeat the crime himself a short while later, thus making it at once more awful and more splendid. The Indian concubine polluted their bed. Ariadne cried and was constantly obsessed by the fear that Theseus should never come to hear of it! But how ingenuous . . . Hadn't she realized yet that Dionysus and Theseus were not really enemies? Those two opposed figures were both manifestations of the same man who went on betraying her, while she went on letting herself be betrayed. "I have grown used to loving the same man forever." That capacity to love forever was her death sentence, it destroyed any hope of escaping from her obsessive circle, her resplendent crown.

From first to last Ariadne's story is woven into a crown. "My cousin's arriving," the young princess thought when they told her Dionysus had landed on the island. She had never seen this relative, born from his mother's death pyre and rumored to be so handsome. When he appeared, Dionysus didn't want to stay in the palace. He gripped her wrist and led her to one of Crete's many caves. And there the darkness was rent by a dazzling crown. Fiery gold and Indian jewels. Dionysus offered Ariadne the crown as a gift on the occasion of this, their first embrace. Sign of perfection, "herald of propitious silence," the crown was a circle of seduction. But *to seduce* also means "to destroy" in Greek: *phtheírein*. The crown is the perfection of deceit, it is the deceit that circles in on itself, it is that perfection which includes deceit within it.

By the time Ariadne turned her gaze on the handsome Theseus, she was no longer a girl playing with her sisters in the palace of Cnossos. She was a god's bride, even if no one knew of their union. The only witness had been that shining crown. But when Theseus came up from his father Poseidon's underwater palace, he too had been holding a crown. It was made of small apple blossoms, dripping water and radiating light. He gave it to Ariadne, as Dionysus had given her his crown. And at the same time Ariadne gave Theseus Dionysus's crown. For his part, Theseus was repeating the god's gesture; for hers, Ariadne was betraying the god, so as to enable the Stranger to kill the Minotaur, who belonged to the bull god. When he set off into the dark passages of the labyrinth, Theseus was led by the light of the resplendent crown. His sword sparkled in that light before he buried it in the body of the youth with the bull's head. So Ariadne brought deception to a higher level: she betrayed her divine partner and at the same time offered his love gift to the man who was taking his place.

But wasn't the deception already there from the beginning, in the god's gift to her? Ariadne is deceived precisely as she deceives: she imagines Theseus is the god's opposite; she sees him as the man who will take her as his bride to Athens, beyond the vicious circle of the bull. When he reappeared in Naxos, Dionysus was waving a shining crown. Ariadne looked at it and thought of the other crowns that had been behind the other deceptions in her life. She realized now that that crown was the same crown and always had been. Her story really was over now; Ariadne would be forever alone, prisoner of that radiant crown in the sky: Corona Borealis.

In any Cretan story, there's a bull at the beginning and a bull at the end. At the beginning Minos summons Poseidon's white bull up out of the sea. If it appears, he promises, he will sacrifice it to the god. The bull does appear, but Minos doesn't keep his promise. The bull is too beautiful, he doesn't want to kill it, he wants it for his own. It is for that bull that Minos's wife Pasiphaë will develop her fatal passion.

At the end, Theseus captures a bull at Marathon, and once again it's the Cretan bull risen from the sea. After its couplings with Pasiphaë the bull had turned wild, and Minos had called for Heracles to capture it. The hero caught the bull and took it away to the mainland. For a long time the bull wandered about the Peloponnese before turning up in Attica. Where nobody had been able to get the better of it, not even Androgeus, Minos's son, who used to beat all the Athenians in their games. Theseus captured it, at Marathon. He offered it to his father, Aegeus, who sacrificed it to Apollo. Everything between that beginning and that end, which is to say Ariadne's destiny, takes place within the displacement of a sacrifice: from Poseidon to Apollo, from Crete to Athens. That passage is strewn with corpses. The mute, the sacrificial victim is part and parcel of the religious rite. But the myth claims other victims for itself, those who fall around the place of sacrifice, iron filings in the magnetic field. Out of the sacrifice, together with the blood, stream the stories. Thus the characters in the tragedy emerge. In the Cretan stories these characters are Pasiphaë, the Minotaur, Ariadne, Phaedra, Minos, Hippolytus, and Aegeus himself. Returning from Crete, Theseus forgets to lower the black sails, and Aegeus kills himself by leaping from the Acropolis. It's the last footnote to the displacement of the sacrifice.

"Finally, some people in Naxos have their own version of the story. They claim that there were two Minoses and two Ariadnes: one was Dionysus's bride in Naxos and mother of Staphylus and his brother; the other, who lived some time later, was first abducted then abandoned by Theseus, arriving afterward on the island with a nurse called Corcyne, whose grave these people will take you to. The second Ariadne, who also died on the island, was not granted the same honors as the first: the festival to commemorate the earlier Ariadne takes place amid games and fun, whereas for the second there are only sacrifices mingled with mourning and sadness."

Ariadne's is a dual destiny right from the start, and the rites held on Naxos celebrated that duality, without looking for relief in notions of death and resurrection. She who becomes Dionysus's "bride," the only one chosen from the crowd of women surrounding him, she who even receives a new name from him when he calls her Libera, is also the woman Dionysus has killed. He asks Artemis to do it. The goddess was always ready to draw her bow. Dionysus asks her to transfix Ariadne with an arrow. And he wants to watch too. Then time turns all to euphemism. All that will remain on the walls of Pompeii is an image of celestial love.

Mythical figures live many lives, die many deaths, and in this they differ from the characters we find in novels, who can never go beyond the single gesture. But in each of these lives and deaths all the others are present, and we can hear their echo. Only when we become aware of a sudden consistency between incompatibles can we say we have crossed the threshold of myth. Abandoned in Naxos, Ariadne was shot dead by Artemis's arrow; Dionysus ordered the killing and stood watching, motionless. Or: Ariadne hung herself in Naxos, after being left by Theseus. Or: pregnant by Theseus and shipwrecked in Cyprus, she died there in childbirth. Or: Dionysus came to Ariadne in Naxos, together with his band of followers; they celebrated a divine marriage, after which she rose into the sky, where we still see her today amid the northern constellations. Or: Dionysus came to Ariadne in Naxos, after which she followed him around on his adventures, sharing his bed and fighting with his soldiers; when Dionysus attacked Perseus in the country near Argos, Ariadne went with him, armed to fight amid the ranks of the crazed Bacchants, until Perseus shook the deadly face of Medusa in front of her and Ariadne was turned to stone. And there she stayed, a stone in a field.

No other woman, or goddess, had so many deaths as Ariadne. That stone in Argos, that constellation in the sky, that hanging corpse, that death by childbirth, that girl with an arrow through her breast: Ariadne was all of this.

But would the story have ever been set in motion without the gadfly, instrument of Hera's revenge? Wherever we look, among the lives of the heroes, we are met by the unwavering, implacable gaze of the goddess, that bovine eye that never seems to close. The very name Heracles ("glory of Hera") tells us right from the start that glory is neither more nor less than a by-product of Hera's revenge.

But how did it all begin? As children, Zeus and his sister Hera quickly discovered secret love. "Unbeknown to their dear parents, they embraced in bed," says Homer. They enjoyed the most extravagantly drawn out amorous childhood of all time. "Then Zeus petted [with Hera] for three hundred years." In their ears they could hear the endless thunder of the Imbrasus, the river of Samos. They embraced between the river and the sea. They never grew weary, they forgot the world beyond those waters—and Zeus put off the moment when he would rule over it. Thousands of years later, in the wet sand of the Imbraso, a stone relief that must once have stood on a wooden bed was found. It shows Zeus, standing, moving toward Hera. Her chest is bare, and he is taking her right breast in his hand.

Hera is goddess of the bed—she even worries if old Oceanus and Tethys, who brought her up as a girl, are depriving themselves of it. For her, the veil, the first veil, is the *pastós*, the nuptial curtain that surrounds the *thálamos*. In Paestum, in Samos there is still evidence that the bed was a central devotional object of the cult. And when Hera makes love to Zeus on top of Mount Gargaron, the earth sprouts a carpet of flowers for the occasion. "Thick and soft, it lifted them up off the ground." The pseudo-bed is then surrounded by a golden cloud, to substitute for the *pastós*. The bed, for Hera, was the primordial place par excellence, the playpen of erotic devotion. In her most majestic shrine, the Heraion in Argos, the worshiper could see, placed on a votive table, an image of Hera's mouth closing amorously around Zeus's erect phallus. No other goddess, not even Aphrodite, had allowed an image like that in her shrine.

And it was in the Heraion that the story of Zeus's first betrayal, origin of all vendettas, began. To betray Hera, Zeus chose one of her priestesses, the human being closest to her, since it was she held the keys to the shrine. Her name was Io. In looks and dress it was Io's duty to re-create the image of the goddess she served. She was a copy endeavoring to imitate a statue. But Zeus chose the copy; he wanted that minimal difference which is enough to overturn order and generate the new, generate meaning. And he wanted it *because* it was a difference, and her *because* she was a copy. The more negligible the difference, the more terrible and violent the revenge. All Zeus's other adventures, all Hera's other vendettas, would be nothing more than further heaves on that same wheel of necessity Hera set rolling to punish the woman most like herself.

II

THERE IS A GIVE-AND-TAKE AMONG THE gods, a strict accountancy that takes on new ramifications with every passing age. Artemis came in useful as a murderer when Dionysus wanted to kill Ariadne. But the day would come when Artemis too, proud virgin that she was, would find to her amazement that she needed the help of that impure and promiscuous god. She too would need to ask someone to kill for her, leaving him the choice of weapon. And she asked Dionysus.

A mortal had made a fool of her. Aura, a tall mountain girl with clean limbs and feet that could run like the wind. She would take on boars and lions single-handed, disdaining weaker prey. And she likewise disdained Aphrodite and all her doings. All she wanted was virginity and strength, nothing else. One hot, sultry day, while sleeping on some laurel twigs, Aura had a disturbing dream: a barbaric, whirling Eros was offering Aphrodite and Adonis a lioness he had caught with an enchanted girdle (Aphrodite's perhaps? Had this erotic ornament become a weapon for capturing wild beasts?). In the dream, Aura saw herself standing next to Aphrodite and Adonis, her arms around their shoulders. It was a sinuous, flourishing group they made! Eros approached with his lioness and presented the animal with these words: "Goddess of garlands, I bring you Aura, the girl whose only love is her virginity. See, the enchanted girdle has bent the stubborn will of the invincible lioness." Aura woke up with a sense of anxiety. For the first time she had seen herself split in two: she was the prey, and she was also the huntress watching her prey. She was furious with the laurel leaves she'd slept on, and hence with Daphne: why had a virgin sent her a dream worthy of a slut? Then she forgot all about it.

On another hot, sultry day, Aura was leading Artemis's chariot toward the Sangarius waterfalls, where the goddess planned to bathe. Running beside the chariot, the goddess's maids had taken their bands from their foreheads and were lifting up the hems of their tunics, showing their knees. They were the Hyperborean virgins. Opis lifted Artemis's bow from her shoulders, and Hekaerge took her quiver. Loxo untied her boots. Artemis stepped carefully into the water. She kept her legs tight together, lifting her tunic off only as the water began to lap at it. Aura watched her with a cruel, inquisitive eye. She studied her mistress's body. Then she swam around her, stretching right out in the water. She stopped next to the goddess, shook a few drops from her breasts, and said: "Artemis, why are your breasts soft and swollen, why have your cheeks got that rosy bloom? You're not like Athena: her chest is tight as a boy's. Or look at my body with its sweet smell of strength. My breasts are round as shields. My skin is taut as a bowstring. Perhaps you'd be better suited to shooting and suffering Eros's arrows. No one looking at you would ever think of inviolable virginity." Artemis listened in silence. "Her eyes flashed murderous glints." She leapt out of the water, put on her tunic and girdle, and disappeared without saying another word.

She went straight to Nemesis, high up in the Taurus Mountains, to ask her advice. She found her, as ever, sitting in front of her wheel. A griffin was squatting on her throne. Nemesis could remember Artemis coming in for all kinds of insults. But always from men, or at most from a mother with children, Niobe, for example, now transformed to a damp rock in the mountains here. Or was it the old matrimonial comedy business? Had Zeus gone and teased her again about it being time to get married? No, said Artemis, this time it was a virgin, Lelanto's daughter. She couldn't even bring herself to repeat the insulting things Aura had dared to say about her body and breasts. Nemesis decided she wouldn't turn Aura to stone, as she had Niobe. Apart from anything else, they were related; the girl belonged to the ancient family of the Titans, as did Nemesis herself. But she would rob her of her virginity, a punishment no less cruel perhaps. And this time it would be Dionysus who would take care of the matter. Artemis agreed. As if to give her a foretaste of her destiny, Nemesis got on her griffin-drawn chariot and went off to see Aura. To make the stubborn girl bow her head, she cracked her whip of snakes on her neck. And Aura's body went under the wheel of necessity.

Now Dionysus could get moving. In his last adventure he had come across another girl warrior: Pallene. Something he'd never experienced before in all his amorous adventures had happened with her. He'd had to agree to a wrestling match with the girl. The match took place in front of a crowd of spectators, and, most important, in front of the girl's incestuous father. Pallene appeared in the sand-covered ring with her long tresses around her neck and a red sash around her breasts. A piece of white cloth barely covered her crotch. Her skin was shiny with oil. The match was a long one. Sometimes Dionysus would find himself squeezing the palm of a deliciously white hand. And, rather than overcome that body, he wanted to touch it. He wanted to put off his voluptuous victory, but meanwhile he realized that he was breathing hard like a mere mortal. A moment's distraction, no more, and Pallene was struggling to lift Dionysus and throw him. That was too much. Dionysus slipped out of her grasp and managed to lift her instead. But then he ended up laying her down quite softly, his furtive eyes straying over her body, her thick hair in the dust. And already Pallene was back on her feet again. So Dionysus decided to throw her properly. He gripped her by the neck and tried to make her knee give. But he judged the move badly and lost his balance. Down he went on his back in the dust, Pallene astride his stomach. A second later, Pallene slipped away, leaving Dionysus on the ground. But just another moment and Dionysus had managed to throw her. The score was even, and Pallene wanted to go on. But her father, Sithon, intervened, giving Dionysus the victory. Drenched in sweat, the god looked up at the king coming over to give him his prize and speared him with his thyrsus. The man was a murderer and destined to die in any event. As a love gift Dionysus gave Pallene the thyrsus dripping with her father's blood. The next thing was the wedding.

Amid the hubbub of the celebrations, Pallene wept for Sithon. He may have been cruel, but he was still her father. Gently, Dionysus pointed to the rat-gnawed heads of her twenty previous suitors on display in front of the palace doors like the first fruits of the harvest. And to soothe her he said she couldn't possibly be the daughter of such a terrible man. Maybe her real father was a god, Hermes, for example, or Ares. But, even as he spoke, Dionysus was already beginning to feel vaguely impatient. He had beaten Pallene. She was his lover now. Soon she would become a faithful follower like so many others. Yet only that once had Dionysus experienced the excitement of finding himself wrestling in the dust with a woman he desired but couldn't dominate. And he yearned for an unattainable body.

He went off alone into the mountains. He couldn't stop fantasizing a strong, elusive woman, a woman as capable of hurting him as he was of hurting her. The time was ripe for Eros to have him longing for an even more unattainable body. He sensed in a sudden gust of wind that a woman even stronger, even more beautiful, and even more hostile than the wrestler Pallene was hiding right there in the woods: Aura. And already he knew that she would flee from him; she would never surrender. For once Dionysus decided to go it alone and in silence, free from the clamor of his Bacchants. Crouching behind a bush, he caught a glimpse of Aura's white thigh thrusting through the dark undergrowth. Dogs bayed all around. And Dionysus found himself melting like a woman. He had never felt so powerless. The idea of talking to the girl seemed as pointless as talking to an oak tree. But a hamadryad living in the roots of a pine told him what he needed to know: he would never lie down with Aura in a bed. Only in the forest and only if he bound her hands and feet would he ever be able to possess her. And he should remember not to leave her any gifts.

While the exhausted Dionysus was sleeping, Ariadne appeared to him again. Why did he always desert his women the same way he had deserted her? Why, having desired the girl so much when they were rolling about together in the sand, was he now completely forgetting Pallene? In the end Theseus had been the better of the two. And, before she went, Ariadne made an ironic gesture. She gave him a spindle and asked him to give it to his next victim as a gift so that one day people would say, She gave Theseus the thread and Dionysus the spindle.

Again the weather was fiercely hot, and Aura was looking for a stream. Dionysus decided that only one of his weapons could work: wine. When Aura brought her lips down to the stream, she found a strange-tasting liquid. She had never experienced anything like it. Numbed and stupefied, she lay down in the shadow of a huge tree. And slept. Barefoot, making no noise, Dionysus approached. Moving quickly, he slipped off her bow and quiver and hid them behind a rock. He couldn't get over his nervousness. For days now he just couldn't stop thinking of another huntress he had known, Nikaia, a girl so beautiful it was as if her body had plundered all the beauties of Olympus. She too had steered clear of men, and when Hymnos, a herdsman, came to tell her of his passion and devotion, Nikaia had cut him short with an arrow through the throat. At which the woods had echoed with a chant that recalled a nursery rhyme: "The handsome herdsman is gone, the beautiful maiden has won." The lines echoed again now in Dionysus's mind as his wary hands tied a rope around Aura's feet. Then he looped another rope around her wrists. Aura was still asleep, in a state of cloying intoxication, and Dionysus took her like that, bound hand and foot. Her body was completely relaxed, dozing on the bare earth, but the ground itself rose and fell to celebrate their union, and the hamadryad shook the branches of the pine tree. While Dionysus was taking immense pleasure in her body, a pleasure intensified by the baseness of it all, the huntress had a heady, disturbing dream, which followed on from her other dream. Gently linked to those of Aphrodite and Adonis, her arms had become entwined to form a single knot with that alien flesh, and her wrists were writhing in the terrifying spasm of a pleasure that was not hers, but theirs, and yet was being passed on to her through the joined veins in their wrists. At the same time Aura saw her head bowed like that of the captured lioness. She was consenting to her own ruin. Dionysus withdrew. Still making no noise, walking on tiptoe, he recovered Aura's bow and quiver and laid them next to her naked body. He freed her hands and feet. Then he went back to the forest.

When she woke up, Aura saw her naked thighs, saw that the girdle covering her breasts had been untied. She felt she would go mad. She went down into the valley, yelling. Just as she had once shot lions and boars, she now loosed her arrows at herdsmen and shepherds. Everywhere she went, she left streams of blood. Any hunters she saw, she shot. Walking into a vineyard, she killed the farmers working there, because she knew they were followers of Dionysus, an enemy god, even though she thought she had never met him. When she found a temple to Aphrodite, she took a whip to the goddess's statue. Then she lifted it from its pedestal and hurled it into the waters of the river Sangarius, the whip still wrapped around its marble flanks. Then she hid in her forest again. She tried to think which of the gods might have raped her, and she cursed them one by one. She would shoot her arrows into their shrines. She would kill the gods themselves. The first to go would be Aphrodite and Dionysus. As for Artemis, she deserved nothing but scorn: the virgin goddess hadn't been able to protect her, just as she hadn't known how to answer those few teasing and rather funny comments about her heavy, swollen breasts. Aura wanted to cut open her womb and scrape out the stranger's semen. She stood defenseless in front of a lioness, but the lioness didn't consider her a worthy victim. She wanted to find out who her lover had been, so she could make him eat their child.

Then Artemis appeared with a sneer. She mocked Aura for walking slowly and heavily, the way pregnant women do. Where was that swift, light step she'd had? And where would Aura be without her speed? She asked her what gifts her lover, Dionysus, had left her. Had he given her some rattles by any chance, for their children to play with? Then she disappeared. Aura continued to wander about. Soon she felt the first birth pains. They went on and on. While Aura was suffering, Artemis appeared again to mock her. She gave birth to twins. Dionysus was proud but afraid that Aura might kill them. He called the huntress Nikaia. He had played the wine trick on her too, raped her in her sleep and deserted her just as he had Aura. And she too had borne him a child, a daughter, Teleté, which means "initiation," "ultimate achievement."

Repetition, for a god, is a sign of majesty, necessity's seal. Nikaia, the magnificent girl who had once had blood gushing from the throat of a harmless herdsman merely because he'd dared speak a few words of love to her, was now working at a loom like any poor woman. (Should Dionysus have given her Ariadne's spindle perhaps?) But now Nikaia would be able to see that another huntress had come to the same sorry end. Now she could take comfort, Dionysus said, in the thought that she formed part of a divine order. But her role did not end there: she must become the god's accomplice, help him save at least one of those twins Aura was about to kill. The world, the whole world, the world far away from the woods, the world of temples, ships, and markets, was awaiting the arrival of two new creatures: one was Nikaia's own daughter, Teleté; the other was one of those twins now in the hands of a pain-crazed Aura.

Aura lifted the two newborn babies to the sky, to the wind that had carried her through life when she ran, and dedicated them to the breeze. She wanted them dashed to pieces. She offered them to a lioness, to have them gobbled up. But a panther came into the lair: tenderly, the animal licked the two infant bodies and fed them, while two snakes protected the entrance to the cave. Then Aura took one of the twins in her hands, threw him in the air, and, when he fell in the dust, leaped on him to tear him to pieces. Terrified, Artemis intervened: she took the other child and, holding a baby in her arms for the first time in her life, fled into the forest.

Aura was alone again. She went down to the banks of the Sangarius, threw her bow and quiver into the river, then dived in herself. The waves covered her body. Water squirted from her breasts. Artemis gave the surviving child to Dionysus. The father took the two babies born from the two girls he had raped in their sleep and brought them to the place where the rites of the mysteries were celebrated. Even Athena clutched the little boy to her virgin breast. Then she handed the child to the Bacchants of Eleusis. In Attica they lit torches in his honor. He was called Iacchus, "the new being who appeared in Eleusis." Those who had the fortune to see him became happy. Those who didn't, didn't even know what happiness means.

But Dionysus's wanderings and conquests were over now. It was time for him to climb up to Olympus. He would still find himself thinking of Ariadne sometimes. He took a garland of flowers up the mountain in remembrance. Then he sat down at the table of the Twelve. His seat was next to Apollo's.

Dionysus's first love was a boy. His name was Ampelos. He played with the young god and the satyrs on the banks of the Pactolus in Lydia. Dionysus noticed the way his long hair fell on his neck, the light that glowed from his body as he climbed out of the water. When he saw him wrestling with a satyr and their feet became knotted together, he was jealous. He wanted to be the only one to fight with Ampelos. They were "erotic athletes." They threw each other to the ground, and Dionysus loved it when Ampelos got him down and sat on his naked belly. Then they would wash the dust and sweat from their skins, swimming in the river. They invented new games. Ampelos always won. He plaited a crown of snakes and put it on his head the way he'd seen his friend do. He also imitated Dionysus by wearing a mottled tunic. He learned to talk to bears, lions, and tigers. Dionysus encouraged him, but there came the day when he warned him too: you needn't fear any wild beast, he said, but watch out for the horns of the cruel bull.

Dionysus was alone one day when he witnessed a scene he felt must be an omen. A horned dragon appeared among the rocks. On his back he was carrying a deer. He tipped the creature off onto a stone altar and plunged a horn into its defenseless body. A pool of blood formed on the stone. Dionysus watched and felt grieved, but along with his grieving came an overwhelming desire to laugh, as if his heart were being split in two. Then he found Ampelos again, and they went on wandering about and hunting together as usual. Ampelos used to like playing his reed pipes, and he played badly. But Dionysus never tired of praising him, because while he praised he would watch him. Sometimes Ampelos would remember Dionysus's warning about the bull, but it made less and less sense. By now he knew all the wild animals, and they were all his friends: why on earth shouldn't the bull be a friend too? And one day, when he was out on his own, he met a bull among the rocks. The animal was thirsty, its tongue hanging out. The bull drank, then stared at the boy, then belched, and a stream of saliva dribbled from his mouth. Ampelos tried to stroke his horns. He made himself a rush whip and a sort of bridle. He arranged a mottled pelt over the bull's back and mounted it. For a few moments he experienced a sense of elation no other animal had ever given him. But Selene was jealous. She saw him from on high and sent a gadfly. Irritated, the bull began to gallop, trying to escape that awful sting. Ampelos could no longer control the beast. A last jolt threw him to the ground. There was a dry, cracking sound as his neck snapped. The bull dragged him on, its horn sinking deeper and deeper into the boy's flesh.

Dionysus found Ampelos in the dust, covered in blood,

but still beautiful. Gathered in a circle, the satyrs began to mourn over him. But Dionysus couldn't join in with them. It wasn't in his nature to weep. And he realized that he wouldn't be able to follow Ampelos into Hades, because he was immortal. Over and over he promised himself he'd kill the whole bull species with his thyrsus. Eros, who had disguised himself as a shaggy satyr, came over to console him. He told him a love sting could only be cured by the sting of another love. So he should look elsewhere. When a flower has been cut, the gardener plants another one. But now Dionysus was crying for Ampelos. It was a sign that something had happened that would change his nature, and the nature of the world.

At that moment the Hours were hurrying toward the house of Helios, the sun. There was a sense that something new was about to take place on the celestial wheel. It was time to consult the tablets of Harmony, where Phanes' primordial hand had inscribed the events of this world in their order. Helios pointed to them where they hung on a wall of his house. The Hours looked at the fourth tablet: it showed the Lion and the Virgin, and Ganymede holding a cup. They interpreted the image: Ampelos would become the vine. He who had brought tears to the god who never wept would also bring delight to the world. Upon hearing which, Dionysus recovered. When the grapes born from Ampelos's body were mature, he picked the first bunches and, with a gesture he seemed to know of old, squeezed them gently in his hands. He watched as a red stain spread across his fingers. Then he licked them. He thought, Ampelos your end demonstrates the splendor of your body. Even in death you haven't lost your rosy color.

No other god, let alone Athena with her sober olive, or Demeter with her nourishing bread, had ever had anything that could vie with that liquor. It was exactly what had been missing from life, what life had been waiting for: intoxication.

. . .

Bursting with youth, his Bacchants buzzing all around him, Dionysus stormed over to Naxos to appear before the abandoned Ariadne. Eros was darting about him like a sweet hornet. The women following the god were holding leafy thyrsi, bloody shreds of young bull's flesh, baskets of sacred objects. Dionysus had come from Attica, where he had done something no one would ever forget: he had revealed the secret of wine to man. Behind him he was leaving an extraordinary new drink and the body of another abandoned girl. On his departure, Erigone had hung herself from a tree. But there was no royal frame to put her story in, and it was not to be handed down from one rhyme to the next by a chain of poets. Erigone wouldn't find her poets until much later, two scholars of the latter days of the ancient world, who, oppressed like others by the times in which they lived, felt almost obliged to write about secrets hitherto left untold. They were Eratosthenes and Nonnus, two Egyptians.

The secret of bread had been revealed by Demeter in Attica, and a holy place, Eleusis, had been established to celebrate the event. The secret of wine had been revealed in Attica by Dionysus, to common people, but that day was to be commemorated only by a ceremony with masks, dolls, and swings. There was something very obscure about the whole business, and the ritual commemoration suggested an aura of playfulness at once childish and sinister.

Dionysus had turned up in the role of Unknown Guest in the house of an old Attican gardener, Icarius, who lived with his daughter Erigone and loved to plant new types of trees. His house was a poor one. All the same, he welcomed the Stranger with the same gesture with which Abraham welcomed the angel, by keeping a place in his mind empty and ready for his guest. It was from that gesture that every other gift would derive. Erigone immediately went off to milk their goat for the guest. Sweetly, Dionysus stopped her from making what a philologist would one day describe as "an adorable faux pas." He was about to reveal to her father, "as a reward for his fair-mindedness and devotion," something that no one had ever known before: wine. And now Erigone was pouring cup after cup of the new drink for her father. Icarius felt good. Then Dionysus explained that this new drink was perhaps even more powerful than the bread Demeter had revealed to other farmers, because it could both wake a man up and put him to sleep, dissolve the pains that afflicted the heart and make them liquid and fleeting. Now it was Icarius's job to pass this revelation on to others, as Triptolemus had passed on the revelation of grain.

Was it then that Dionysus seduced Erigone? We don't know. Like a piece of flotsam from a shipwreck, the only mention that has survived of the affair is a single line in Ovid. Arachne had the effrontery to challenge Athena to a tapestry competition. The cloth she wove showed Europa being carried off by the bull: you could see the girl's feet drawing back fearfully from the water. It showed Leda beneath the wings of the swan. It showed Danaë under a shower of gold. It showed Asteria in the clutches of an eagle. And it also showed Erigone, who Dionysus tricked with his grapes (*falsa deceperit uva*). Not a word more does Ovid give us. But out of a sense of defiance, Arachne's cloth included only stories that would bring shame to the gods. Erigone, then, was deceived and seduced by that powerful fruit. Other authors tell us that Dionysus and Erigone had a child: his name was Staphylus, "bunch of grapes," but this was also the name of the child other writers attribute to Dionysus and Ariadne.

Icarius obeyed Dionysus's orders. He got onto his cart and set off around Attica to show people this plant with the wondrous juice. One evening he was drinking with a few shepherds. Some of them fell into a deep sleep. It seemed they would never wake up. The shepherds began to suspect Icarius was up to something. Maybe he'd come to poison them and steal their sheep? They felt the impulse to kill. They surrounded Icarius. One picked up a sickle, another a spade, a third an ax, a fourth a big stone. They all hit out at the old man. Then, to finish the job, they ran him through with their cooking spit.

As he lay dying, Icarius remembered something that had happened not long before. Dionysus had taught him how to plant the vines and look after them. Icarius watched over their growth with the same love he had for his trees, waiting for the moment when he would be able to squeeze the grapes with his own hands. One day he caught a goat eating some vine leaves. He was overcome by anger and killed the animal on the spot. Now he realized the goat had been himself.

But something else had happened that had to do with that goat. Icarius had skinned it, put on its pelt, and, with some other peasants, improvised a dance around the beast's mangled corpse. Icarius didn't appreciate, as he lay dying, that the gesture had been the origin of tragedy, but he did sense that the death of the goat was connected with what was happening to him, the shepherds circling him, each one hitting him with a different weapon, until he saw the spit that would pierce his heart.

As to the origin of tragedy, all reconstructions ultimately come up against this contradiction. On the one hand there is Eratosthenes' remark: "It was then that the inhabitants of Icarius danced around a goat for the first time." Here tragedy seems to involve singing and dancing *around* the goat. But then Aristotle says that early tragedy was the singing and dancing *of* the goats. An ancient and pointless dispute was to go on for generations around this contradiction, which isn't actually a contradiction at all. "If one wishes to dress up as a satyr [a goat], one first has to kill a goat and skin it." Eratosthenes and Aristotle were saying the same thing, except that Aristotle omits the first and decisive part of the process: the slaying of the goat. Thus it is to Eratosthenes that, along with the first extremely accurate estimate of the circumference of the earth, we owe an extremely concise definition of the process from which tragedy developed. There are three phases: Icarius kills the goat; Icarius skins the goat and stretches part of the pelt into a wineskin; Icarius and his friends dance around the goat and stamp on the wineskin while wearing strips of the pelt. Thus the dance *around* the goat is also the dance *of* the goats. It is as if a long, tortuous, and obscure process were suddenly reduced before our very eyes to a few shabby elements which are nevertheless capable of releasing an enormous power.

Of all the women who ascended to the heavens, Erigone was the poorest, the one we know least about. They called her Atletis: the wanderer, the roving spirit, the beggar. And yet this woman's dog, Maera, was to assume an important position in the night sky, a place central to every calamity, every blessing: he was to become Sirius. One day Erigone was woken up by Maera's whimpering. Her father had disappeared some months ago. His daughter had searched for him far and wide, wandering about speechless. She felt Maera tugging at her tunic. The dog wanted to take her somewhere. He led her to a well beneath a big tree where they had thrown Icarius's body. Erigone buried him. Then she climbed high into the tree and hanged herself. Maera stayed there to watch over the two bodies and starved himself to death.

Attica was soon in the thrall of an extraordinary epidemic of suicides: as in Wedekind's Germany, where the schoolchildren killed themselves with the coming of spring, in Athens young girls began to hang themselves for no apparent reason. Apollo's oracle proposed a remedy: they must introduce a ceremony in honor of the peasant's daughter to be found hanging from a branch of the big tree above the well. In the middle of the ceremony was a swing. Then dolls and masks were hung on trees, to sway back and forth in the wind.

Meanwhile, Icarius's murderers had escaped to the island of Ceos. These were the dog days of the year with Sirius ascendant; the island was suffering from a devastating heat wave. Everything had burned up and died. This time Apollo spoke through his son Aristaeus, who was king of the island. Icarius's murderers must be punished. As soon as they had been killed, a cool northwesterly wind began to blow, the *meltemi* which makes life possible in Greece and which would reappear every year from then on, along with the dog days.

From a rock, Ariadne watches Phaedra on her swing. Their mother, Pasiphaë, hangs herself. Ariadne hangs herself. Phaedra hangs herself. Erigone hangs herself. Erigone is not a princess, but it is she who ascends to the heavens as the hanged woman. Her celestial home is the constellation of Virgo. Ariadne is nearby, in the sky, but as Dionysus's bride. With Erigone we come to the first of the hanged women. And we also come back to the swing. Behind the swing is the image of "the golden swing in the sky," mentioned in the *Rig Veda*. Every time the sun approaches the solstices, it risks going out of control; the world trembles; its star may just go on along its trajectory, carried away by its momentum, rather than turning back. And it is precisely here, at the solstice, that we have that curve which forms the golden swing in the sky. Having reached the limit of its oscillation, the sun turns back, as does the Athenian girl on her swing, pushed by a satyr. But, for this to happen, people have to die. Some of the victims are guilty, like Icarius's murderers. But, before them, we must have a perfectly innocent victim: Erigone. The swinging stops in the perpendicular jerk of the hanged woman.

The tree where Erigone's body was to remain hanging is not just large, it is immense: it covers the whole earth, and its branches stretch away among the constellations. In the sky, Erigone holds an ear of corn in her hand. She has rejected a bunch of those grapes that brought death to her father and herself. Icarius's last words were "The sweet [Dionysus] is Erigone's enemy." That hanged orphan reminds us of the death that is not assimilated back into life, the death that wanders about continually in the air, with the spirits of the dead, the dolls and masks hung from a tree.

Erigone is an Isis flung by the mystical law of inversion to a point exactly opposite that of the celestial queen: in terrestrial terms Erigone represents the total impotence of the poor and vagrant orphan girl. But Isis too had been a beggar in the world when looking for the body of Osiris. In the heavens, Isis and Erigone find themselves together in the same constellation: Virgo. In Sirius they see the dog that helped them: Anubis in the case of Isis, Maera in the case of Erigone. After Osiris's death, Isis tore out a lock of her hair. Erigone too tore out a lock of her hair after Icarius's death. Not far from Virgo and from the Dog, we find the locks placed on top of each other in Berenice's Hair, also known as the Lock, and even Ariadne's Lock. And Nonnus uses the same word, *bótrys*, to mean either a lock of hair or a bunch of grapes. Dionysus didn't let Erigone escape him, even in the heavens. He is there in the gift of mourning.

Dionysus would arrive in Athens for the Anthesteria with the spirits of the dead, then disappear with them. The big sealed jars were opened, the new wine flowed. They carried it in carts pulled by donkeys to Dionysus's shrine in the Marshes, and there they worshiped the god. It was an enigmatic place: there were no marshes where the small shrine stood, nor had there ever been any. But the gods inhabit a different world from our own, and the marsh from which Dionysus was supposed to emerge belonged to that world. Farmers, slaves, and the laborers of large landowners all gathered together. They danced and waited for the feast.

The shrine opened at sundown and would stay open only for that one day of the year. It was an unclean day. The fresh pitch on the doors of the houses reminded people of the spirits roaming about who would eventually be chased off. All the other shrines were closed, their doors tied tight with ropes. Paralysis seized the very heart of the city.

In the evening, a trumpet blast marked the beginning of a drinking contest. "The King drinks, the Queen laughs." But they drank without talking, without singing, without praying. There were hundreds of them, under many roofs, each with his big pitcher. Yet there was the same silence the herald commanded during sacrifices. Even the children had their own tables, their own pitchers, and sat silent. An invisible guest was among them: Orestes, the impure, who had once sought refuge in Athens. Nobody had dared take him into their homes, but nor had anyone dared send him away. Athens loves the guilty. Sitting alone at a table, a pitcher all to himself, the man who had killed his mother drank in silence. And that had been the first day of this feast, the Choes. Wine and blood ran together, as they had when Icarius was killed by the shepherds. In opening the big jugs, the worshipers had released not only the wine but also the dead, and now they stalked about disguised with masks. Often they were women: Nymphs or others of Dionysus's creatures. They asked for food and wine, begging as Erigone had. None of them must be left unsatisfied. When it was over, everybody took their jugs and heather crowns back to Dionysus's shrine like broken toys. They arrived, staggering in the evening torchlight, as the fourteen dames of honor chosen by the king took their secret oaths over the baskets. Then there was another procession, from the shrine to the house of the king-archon, in the agorá, the marketplace. And there, in the king's very bed, Dionysus would take the man's place and possess the queen, the Basilinna. This wasn't a temple but the house of an important public official, and the Basilinna was not one of the god's priestesses. For one night Dionysus imposed his presence in the bed of an important citizen. He had arrived in Piraeus that very

day, a sailor from far away. His ship had been solemnly
hauled as far as the city. Now he was demanding a night of
passion, surrounded by secrecy. A still damp prow forced
its way through the door of a bedroom in the city center.

This is Dionysus. He arrives, unexpected, and possesses.
There was a considerable scandal when on one occasion the
Basilinna happened to be the daughter of a notorious hetaera, and not even an Athenian at that. The mother's name
was Neaera; she had sold her body time and again and all
too soon had arranged to sell her daughter's too, until her
husband, a pander and sycophant, managed to marry the
girl off to an Athenian from an old family, one of the Co-
roinids, who later became the king-archon. Thus the god
found himself being welcomed by a girl already used to
dealing with customers and pimps.

Summoned by the women of Argos as a bull rising from the
sea, Dionysus, of all the gods, is the one who feels most su-
premely at ease with women. His enemies "used to say that
he revealed the religious mysteries and initiations so as to
seduce other men's women." If the Charites make him a gift,
it will be a peplos, a woman's tunic. Dionysus doesn't descend on women like a predator, clutch them to his chest,
then suddenly let go and disappear. He is constantly in the
process of seducing them, because their life forces come together in him. The juice of the vine is his, and likewise the
many juices of life. "Sovereign of all that is moist," Dionysus
himself is liquid, a stream that surrounds us. "Mad for the
women," Nonnus, the last poet to celebrate the god, frequently calls him, "mad for the girls." And with Christian malice Clement of Alexandria speaks of Dionysus as
choiropsálēs, "the one who touches the vulva": the one
whose fingers could make it vibrate like the strings of a lyre.
The Sicyonians worshiped him as "lord of the female sex."
Dionysus is the only god who doesn't need to demonstrate
his virility, not even in war. When his army sets out for India, it looks like a gaggle of noisy girls.

Dionysus's phallus is more hallucinogenic than coercive. It is close to a fungus, or a parasite in nature, or to the toxic grass stuffed in the cavity of the thyrsus. It has none of the faithfulness of the farmer's crop, it won't stretch out in the plowed furrow where Iasion made love to Demeter, nor does it push its way up amid flourishing harvest fields, but rather in the most intractable woodland. It is a metallic tip concealed beneath innocuous green leaves. It doesn't intoxicate to promote growth; yet, growth sustains intoxication, as the stem of a goblet holds up the wine. Dionysus is not a useful god who helps weave or knot things together, but a god who loosens and unties. The weavers are his enemies. Yet there comes a moment when the weavers will abandon their looms to dash off after him into the mountains. Dionysus is the river we hear flowing by in the distance, an incessant booming from far away; then one day it rises and floods everything, as if the normal above-water state of things, the sober delimitation of our existence, were but a brief parenthesis overwhelmed in an instant.

For centuries poets, philosophers, and mythographers recounted and expounded all the many variations of the scene where a goddess is seen while bathing: whether it be Artemis spied on by Actaeon, Athena watched by Tiresias, or Persephone under the all-seeing eyes of Zeus. But it is not until we arrive at the death knells of the pagan world, a century after Constantine, that the poet Nonnus at last reveals what happened before the goddess went off to bathe. For it wasn't just the noon heat that sent those mythical bodies running to the water. In the case of Semele it was, more than anything else, the need to wash away blood, streams of blood.

But how did it all begin? Princess Semele was leading her mules along the streets of Thebes, wielding a silver whip. Suddenly she remembered a strange dream from the night before. There was a huge tree and sticking out from among its leaves a big, as yet unripe piece of fruit, covered with a beading of dew. A flash of lightning from above burned up the tree trunk, but the piece of fruit remained untouched. She just glimpsed the wings of a bird snatching the fruit up into the sky. Then high above, tearing through the canvas backdrop of the heavens, a male thigh appeared, and a hand sewed the piece of fruit into the thigh, shutting it away under golden buckles. Then the swelling burst open, and a figure with a man's body and a bull's head appeared. Semele knew that she was the tree.

She told her father about the dream. Cadmus sent for Tiresias. Semele guessed what his answer would be: a sacrifice. Whenever something strange and frightening came up, you killed an animal. But what animal? A bull, said Tiresias. And Semele would have to sacrifice it with her own hands. She lit the fire on the altar herself. She was standing very close to the animal, and when it was killed a jet of blood spurted across her stomach. Touching her plaited hair, she found it was sticky. And looking down she saw her whole tunic was sodden with blood. So she ran, through the cover of the high reeds, toward the river Asopus. A few moments later and the blood was forgotten. She had bathed in this water since earliest childhood and swam with her head up, against the stream, shaking off the night's terror in the wind.

Stung by love, Zeus watched Semele swimming from on high. He forgot the earth spread out beneath his feet to stare at that pool of water and the girl swimming. Patiently waiting for their mistress, her mules looked on, and likewise Zeus. The god's eyes slithered over her wet skin, from toes to bare neck, refraining only from the mysteries of the groin. They lingered over her chest, glistening like armor. The tips of her breasts sent sharp javelins flying into the wound Eros had opened. For a moment Zeus thought he was seeing another princess, Europa, who he had carried off from Sidon. But no, it wasn't Europa, though there was a blood relation, since Cadmus was Europa's brother—and above all they shared the same splendor, the same resplendent sheen. In his mind Zeus left the heavens to swim at Semele's side. He watched the sun impatiently. He wouldn't be able to go to her bed till nightfall.

The bars defending the palace of Thebes rose silently in the dark. Zeus stretched out on Semele's bed in the form of a bull with human limbs. Then he was a panther. Then a young man with vine shoots in his curls. Finally he settled into that most perfect of shapes: the serpent. Zeus prolonged their union like some story without end, a rehearsal of the life of the god about to be generated. The snake slithered over Semele's trembling body and gently licked her neck. Then, gripping her bust in one of his coils, wrapping her breasts in a scaly sash, he sprinkled her not with poison but with liquid honey. Now the snake was pressing his mouth against Semele's mouth, a dribble of nectar trickling down onto her lips intoxicated her, and all the while vine leaves were sprouting up on the bed and there was a sound of drums beating in the darkness. The earth laughed. Dionysus was conceived just as Zeus shouted the name with which for centuries he was to be evoked: "Evoe!"

III

DELOS WAS A HUMP OF DESERTED ROCK, drifting about the sea like a stalk of asphodel. It was here that Apollo was born, in a place not even wretched slave girls would come to hide their shame. Before Leda, the only creatures to give birth on that godforsaken rock had been the seals. But there was a palm tree, and the mother clutched it, alone, bracing her knees in the thin grass. Then Apollo emerged, and everything turned to gold, from top to bottom. Even the water in the river turned to gold and the leaves on the olive tree likewise. And the gold must have stretched downward into the depths, because it anchored Delos to the seabed. From that day on, the island drifted no more.

If Olympus differs from every other celestial home, it is thanks to the presence of three unnatural divinities: Apollo, Artemis, Athena. More than mere functions, these imperious custodians of the unique stripped away that thin, shrouding curtain which nature weaves about its forces. The bright enameled surface and the void, the sharp outline, the arrow. These, and not water or earth, are their elements. There is something autistic about Olympus's unnatural gods. Apollo, Artemis, Athena march forward cloaked in their own auras. They look down at the world when they plan to strike it, but otherwise their eyes are elsewhere, as if gazing at an invisible mirror, where they find their own images detached from all else. When Apollo and Artemis draw their bows to kill, they are serene, abstracted, their eyes steady on the arrow. All around, Niobe's children lie dying, slumped over rocks, or on the bare earth. The folds of Artemis's tunic don't so much as flutter: all her vitality is concentrated in the left arm holding the bow and the right arm reaching behind the shoulder as her fingers select another mortal arrow from her quiver.

The infant Artemis sat on Zeus's lap. She knew what she wanted for the future and told her father all her wishes one by one: to remain forever a virgin, to have many names, to rival her brother, to possess a bow and arrow, to carry a torch and wear a tunic with a fringe down to the knee, to hunt wild beasts, to have sixty Oceanides as an escort and twenty Amnisian Nymphs as maids to look after her sandals and dogs, to hold sway over all mountains; she could get by without the cities. As she spoke, she tried, but failed, to grab her father's beard. Zeus laughed and agreed. He would give her everything she wanted. Artemis left him; she knew where she was headed: first to the dense forests of Crete, then to the ocean. There she chose her sixty Nymphs. They were all nine years old.

The perennial virginity young Artemis demanded as a first gift from her father Zeus is the indomitable sign of detachment. Copulation, *mixis*, means "mingling" with the world. Virgo, the virgin, is an isolated, sovereign sign. Its counterpart, when the divine reaches down to touch the world, is rape. The image of rape establishes the canonical relationship the divine now has with a world matured and softened by sacrifices: contact is still possible, but it is no longer the contact of a shared meal; rather it is the sudden, obsessive invasion that plucks away the flower of thought.

Man's relationship with the gods passed through two regimes: first conviviality, then rape. The third regime, the

modern one, is that of indifference, but with the implication
that the gods have already withdrawn, and, hence, if they
are indifferent in our regard, we can be indifferent as to
their existence or otherwise. Such is the peculiar situation
of the modern world. But returning to earlier times: there
was an age when the gods would sit down alongside mortals,
as they did at Cadmus and Harmony's wedding feast in
Thebes. At this point gods and men had no difficulty recognizing each other; sometimes they were even companions
in adventure, as were Zeus and Cadmus, when the man
proved of vital help to the god. Relative roles in the cosmos
were not disputed, since they had already been assigned;
hence gods and men met simply to share some feast before
returning each to his own business. Then came another
phase, during which a god might *not* be recognized. As a
result the god had to assume the role he has never abandoned since, right down to our own times, that of the Unknown Guest, the Stranger. One day the sons of Lycaon,
king of Arcadia, invited to their table an unknown laborer
who was in fact Zeus. "Eager to know whether they were
speaking to a real god, they sacrificed a child and mixed his
flesh with that of the sacred victims, thinking that if the
stranger was a god he would discover what they had done."
Furious, Zeus pushed over the table. That table was the
ecliptic plane, which from that day on would be forever
tilted. There followed the most tremendous flood.

After that banquet, Zeus made only rare appearances as
the Unknown Guest. The role passed, for the most part, to
other gods. Now, when Zeus chose to tread the earth, his
usual manifestation was through rape. This is the sign of
the overwhelming power of the divine, of the residual capacity of distant gods to invade mortal minds and bodies.
Rape is at once possessing and possession. With the old con-
vivial familiarity between god and man lost, with ceremonial contact through sacrifice impoverished, man's soul was
left exposed to a gusting violence, an amorous persecution,
an obsessional goad. Such are the stories of which mythology is woven: they tell how mortal mind and body are still

subject to the divine, even when they are no longer seeking it out, even when the ritual approaches to the divine have become confused.

The twelve gods of Olympus agreed to appear as entirely human. It was the first time a group of divinities had renounced abstraction and animal heads. No more the unrepresentable behind the flower or the swastika, no more the monstrous creature, the stone fallen from heaven, the whirlpool. Now the gods took on a cool, polished skin, or an unreal warmth, and a body where you could see the ripple of muscles, the long veins.

The change brought with it a new exhilaration and a new terror. All previous manifestations seemed tentative and cautious by comparison; they hadn't risked the boldest of adventures, which was precisely that of the gods' disguising themselves as human in a human world, having passed through the whole gamut of metamorphoses. Then this last disguise was more exciting than any of the others. More exciting and more dangerous. For it might well be that the gods' divinity would no longer be grasped in its fullness. On earth they would meet people who treated them with too much familiarity, maybe even provoked them. The unnatural gods, Apollo, Artemis, and Athena, whose very identity depended on detachment, were more subject to this danger than the others. Any old shepherd might claim he played his pipes better than Apollo; whereas it was unlikely that a mere hetaera would try to tell Aphrodite how to do her job. The people of earth were a temptation: alluring because full of stories and intrigues, or sometimes because isolated in their own stubborn perfection that asked nothing from heaven. But they were also treacherous, ready to stab a god in the back, to disfigure the hermae. A new state of mind emerged, something unknown in the past, that of the god who is misunderstood, mocked, belittled. The result was a string of vendettas and punishments, dispatches issued from an ever busy office.

. . .

That Theseus was a creature of Apollo one can gather from
all kinds of signs and gestures of homage scattered throughout his adventures. Theseus is always coming up against
monsters, and the first slayer of monsters was Apollo. In Delphi the young hero offers the curl that fell across his forehead to Apollo. When he arrives in Athens, Theseus hurls a
bull up in the air. But it is important that this takes place
in a temple to Delphinian Apollo. Theseus will go back to
the same temple before setting off for Crete, this time bringing a branch of the sacred olive tree wrapped in wool, a
request for the god to help him. When he catches the bull
at Marathon, and the Athenians go wild with joy, Theseus
has it sacrificed to Apollo. After killing the Minotaur, Theseus goes to Delos and performs the dance of the cranes. A
code within the dance contains the secret of the labyrinth.
And Delos was Apollo's birthplace.

But Apollo makes no comment. All Theseus's life, the
only thing Apollo ever says to him is "Take Aphrodite as
your guide." The order is decisive. All Theseus's adventures are cloaked in an erotic aura. During the Cretan expedition, it is Apollo who pulls the strings, but from the
shadows. The mission is too delicate an affair for him to be
seen to be involved. What we see on the stage is the struggle
between Dionysus and the hero Theseus, but, in the darkness behind, Apollo and Dionysus have struck up a pact.
What that involved was the *translatio imperii* from Crete
to Athens: one god took over from another; power passed
from the secret twists of the labyrinth to the frontal evidence
of the acropolis. And all of this came about courtesy of
Theseus, because the stories had to tell of other things: of
young girls being sacrificed, of love affairs, duels, desertions, suicides. The human melodrama with its songs and
chatter must cover up for the silent substance of the divine
pact.

. . .

This changing of the guard, which occurs with Theseus's expedition to Crete, implies an affinity between Apollo and Dionysus behind their apparent opposition. But it is an affinity they are not eager to bring out into the open, if only because it is not something to be proud of. First and foremost, what these gods have in common in this story is their having been betrayed by mortal women. Ariadne betrays Dionysus for Theseus; Coronis betrays Apollo with the mortal Ischys. To kill the women who loved and betrayed them, Apollo and Dionysus call on Artemis, the divine assassin, with her bow and arrows. And both of them watch in silence as their women are slain. There could be no greater complicity for the two gods than this having both turned, with the same gesture, to the same assassin, to put to death the women they loved.

Coronis was washing her feet in Lake Boebeis. Apollo saw her and desired her. Desire came as a sudden shock, it caught him by surprise, and immediately he wanted to have done with it. He descended on Coronis like the night. Their coupling was violent, exhilarating, and fast. In Apollo's mind the clutch of a body and the shooting of an arrow were superimposed. The meeting of their bodies was not a mingling, as for Dionysus, but a collision. In the same way, Apollo had once killed Hyacinthus, the boy he loved most: they were playing together, and the god let fly a discus.

Coronis was pregnant by Apollo when she found herself attracted to a stranger. He came from Arcadia, and his name was Ischys. A white crow watched over her. Apollo had told the bird to guard the woman he loved, "so that no one might violate her purity." The crow saw Coronis give herself to Ischys. So off it flew to Delphi and its master to tell the tale. It said it had discovered Coronis's "secret doings." In his fury, Apollo threw down his plectrum. His laurel crown fell in the dust. Looking at the crow, his eyes were full of hatred, and the creature's feathers turned black as pitch. Then Apollo asked his sister Artemis to go and kill Coronis, in

Lacereia Artemis's arrow pierced the faithless woman's breast. Along with her, the goddess killed many other women by the rugged shores of Lake Boebeis. Before dying, Coronis whispered to the god that he had killed his own son too. At which Apollo tried to save her. In vain. His medical skills were not up to it. But when the woman's sweet-smelling body was stretched on a pyre high as a wall, the flames parted before the god's grasping hand, and from the dead mother's belly, safe and sound, he pulled out Asclepius, the healer.

Ariadne, Coronis: two stories that call to each other, that answer each other. Not only was the killer the same in both cases—Artemis—but perhaps the mortal seducer was likewise the same—Theseus. Ischys is a shadowy figure, of whom we know nothing apart from his name. But of Theseus we know a great deal: we know that in one version he left Ariadne the moment "he fell desperately in love with Aigle, daughter of Panopeus." So wrote Hesiod; but Pisistratus chose to delete this very line. Why? Did it reveal too much about the hero? A marble stele found in Epidaurus and signed by Isyllus, explains that Aigle (or Aegla) "was so beautiful that people would also call her Coronis," and that she had a child called Asclepius. Aigle means "splendor," as Ariadne-Aridela means "the resplendent one." Coronis (crown) suggests a beauty that goes beyond diffuse brilliance, involves the etching of a form. But who was "Aigle, daughter of Panopeus"? Her father was the king of a small Phocian town with the same name, Panopeus: "Panopeus with its lovely open space for dancing," says Homer. And in that square danced the Thyiades, initiates of Dionysus. It was one of the places they stopped in the long procession that took them from Athens to Delphi to "enact secret rites for Dionysus." And already we are reminded of the open space where Ariadne danced out the labyrinth. What's more, Pausanias explains that the inhabitants of Panopeus "are not Phocians; originally they were

Phlegyans." And already we are reminded that Coronis was the daughter of Phlegyas, from Thessaly, a hero who took the same name as his people. It was with those people that Phlegyas migrated to Phocis, where he reigned as king.

Coronis, Aigle: daughters of a king of Phocis, living near an open square where the initiates of Dionysus danced, along the road that would take them to the temple of Apollo. There is a twinning between Coronis and Aigle, just as there is a twinning between Coronis-Aigle and Ariadne, and both point us in the direction of a more obscure parallel between these women's divine lovers: Dionysus and Apollo. Wasn't Coronis the name of one of the Nymphs who brought up Dionysus in Naxos? And, checking through Dionysus's other nurses, we come across, yes, another by the name of Aigle. And wasn't Coronis also the name of one of the girls on the ship Theseus came back from Crete on? *Koróne* means "the curved beak of the crow," but it also means "a garland, a crown." And wasn't Ariadne's story a story of crowns? *Koróne* also means "the stern of a ship" and "the high point of a feast." *Koronís* means "the wavy flourish that used to mark the end of a book, a seal of completion." On an Athenian jar we see Theseus carrying off a girl called Corone, while two of his other women, Helen and the Amazon Antiope, try in vain to stop him. Corone is being lifted up in the air, tightly held in the circle of the hero's arms, yet still three fingers of her left hand find time to toy, delicately, with the curls of Theseus's little ponytail. Casting a sharp glance behind, Peirithous protects the abductor's back. "I saw, let's run," the anonymous artist's hand has written beside the scene. The style is unmistakably that of Euthymides.

Ariadne and Coronis each preferred a foreign man to a god. For them the Stranger is "strength," which is what the name Ischys means. And Theseus is the strong man par excellence. Of all the women to whom the gods made love, Coronis is the most brazenly irreverent. Already pregnant by Apollo's "pure seed," elegant in her tunics as Pindar describes her, she nevertheless felt "that passion for things far away" and went off to bed with the stranger who came from Arcadia. Pindar comments proverbially: "The craziest type of people are those who scorn what they have around them and look elsewhere / vainly searching for what cannot exist." In Coronis's case, what she had around her was a god, a god whose child, Asclepius, she was already bearing. It is as if, out of sheer caprice, the fullness of the Greek heaven were fractured here. The stranger from Arcadia was even more of a stranger than the god, and hence more attractive. The bright enamel of divine apparition is scarred by sudden cracks. But this allows it to breathe with the naturalness of literature, which rejects the coercion of the sacred text.

All that was left of Coronis was a heap of ashes. But years later Asclepius too would be reduced to ashes. He had dared to bring a dead man back to life, so Zeus struck him with a thunderbolt. And, just that once, Apollo cried, "wept countless tears as he approached his sacred people, the Hyperboreans." The tears were drops of amber, and they rolled down into the Eridanus, that river at once earthly and celestial where Phaethon had fallen. All around, the stench of his corpse lingered on. And tall black poplars rustled to mourn his passing. Those poplars were the daughters of the sun.

The destiny of death by burning runs through the stories of Apollo and Dionysus like a scar. Semele is burned to death, and she is Dionysus's mother; Coronis and Asclepius are reduced to ashes, and they are Apollo's lover and son. The divine fire devours those venturing outside the human sphere, whether they be betraying a god, bringing a man back to life, or seeing a god bereft of the cloaking veil of epiphany. Beyond the limit laid down for what is acceptable, burns the fire. Apollo and Dionysus are often to be found along the edges of that borderline, on the divine side and the human; they provoke that back-and-forth in men, that desire to go beyond oneself, which we seem to cling to even more than to our humanity, even more than to life itself. And sometimes this dangerous game rebounds on the two gods who play it. Apollo hid his tears among the Hyperboreans while driving his swan-drawn chariot through the air. Likewise silhouetted against the sky, the enchanter Abaris, emissary of Apollo, would one day arrive in Greece from the North. Riding the immense arrow of ecstasy.

The lives of Theseus and Heracles were intertwined from beginning to end. On seeing Heracles in a lionskin, the infant Theseus had thrown an ax at him. Thinking he was a lion. The gesture suggests a secret hostility later to be submerged in admiration. When he was a youth, Theseus "would dream of Heracles' deeds by night and burn with ambition to emulate him by day." He never tired of hearing stories about the hero, "especially from those who had seen him and been present when he had done some deed or made a speech." Apart from anything else, the two heroes were cousins. When he was old enough, Theseus left his home in Troezen and set off on his travels. From then on, and for years and years, Theseus and Heracles would perform similar exploits, sometimes doing exactly the same thing, as if in a competition. When the two heroes ran into each other, in foreign countries, they were like mercenaries who inevitably meet where blood is flowing. And if one day Heracles went down into the underworld to free Theseus, you would say it was no more than his duty as an old comrade in arms. Yet the distance between the two is immense. Their postures might seem similar, but in reality they were quite opposite, the way some archaic *koûroi* might seem similar to archaic Egyptian statues of the same period, while in fact a crucial divergence in internal time sets them apart: the Egyptian statues looked back to an irrecoverable past, which their rigidity strived hopelessly to regain; the Greek figures expressed tension the very moment before it relaxes, as if wishing to hold at bay for one last time the Alexandrian suppleness that was about to overwhelm them.

Heracles is obliged to follow the zodiac wheel of his labors to the very ends of the earth. As a hero he is too human, blinded like everybody else, albeit stronger and more able than everybody else. Catapulted into the heavens as a result of celestial exigencies, he is never to know what purpose his labors really served, and the pretext the events of his life offer him smacks of mockery. All on account of a spiteful king. Theseus operates between Argos and Epirus, sails to Crete and the Black Sea, but he does have a base: Athens. His deeds are those of an adventurer who responds to a sense of challenge, to whimsy, to curiosity, and to pleasure. And if the step that most determines a life is initiation, it will be Theseus who introduces Heracles to Eleusis, not vice versa, despite the fact that he is the younger and less well known among the the gods. On his own Heracles would never have been admitted, would have remained forever a stranger, a profane outsider. Why? The life of the hero, like the process of initiation, has different levels. On a first level Theseus and Heracles are similar: this is the moment at which someone finally emerges from the blazing circle of force. As Plutarch remarks with the dispatch of the great Greek writers: "It appears that at that time there were men who, for deftness of hand, speed of legs, and strength of muscles, transcended normal human nature and were tireless. They never used their physical capacities to do good or to help others, but reveled in their own brutal arrogance and enjoyed exploiting their strength to commit savage, ferocious deeds, conquering, ill-treating, and murdering whosoever fell into their hands. For them, respect, justice, fairness, and magnanimity were virtues prized only by such as lacked the courage to do harm and were afraid of suffering it themselves; for those who had the strength to impose themselves, such qualities could have no meaning." It is Theseus and Heracles who first use force to a different end than that of merely crushing their opponents. They become "athletes on behalf of men." And, rather than strength itself, what they care about is the art of applying it: "Theseus invented the art of wrestling, and later teaching of the sport took the basic moves from him. Before Theseus, it was merely a question of height and brute force."

This is only the first level of a hero's life. It is the level at which he competes with other men. But there is a higher level, a much greater dimension to conquer, where even the combination of force and intelligence is not enough: this is the dimension where men meet and clash with gods. Once again we are in a kingdom where force is supreme, but this time it is divine force. If the hero is alone and can count on nothing but his own strength, he will never be able to enter this kingdom. He needs a woman's help. And this is where the paths of Theseus and Heracles divide, forever. Women, for Heracles, are part of the fate he must suffer. He may rape them, as he does with Auge; he may impregnate fifty in a single night, as he does with Thespius's daughters; he may become their slave, as with Omphale. But he is never able to appropriate their wisdom. He doesn't even realize that it is they who possess the wisdom he lacks. Deep down, he harbors a grim suspicion of them, as if foreseeing how it will be a woman's gift that will bring him to his death, and an excruciating death at that. Heracles is "the irreconcilable enemy of female sovereignty," because he senses that he will never be able to grasp it for himself. When the Argonauts land on the island of Lemnos and, without realizing it, find themselves caught up with the women who have murdered their husbands, Heracles is the only one who stays on board ship.

Nothing could be further from the spirit of Theseus, who sets sail all on his own to go and find the Amazons. And immediately Theseus tricks their queen, Antiope. He invites her onto his ship, abducts her, has her fall in love with him, makes her his wife and the mother of his son, Hippolytus. What's more, and this is what really marks Theseus out, in the end Antiope would "die a heroine's death," fighting beside Theseus to save Athens. And she was fighting against her own comrades, who had pitched camp beneath the Acropolis and were attacking Athens precisely to avenge her abduction. Theseus knows that woman is the repository of the secret he lacks; hence he uses her to the utmost, until she has betrayed everything: her country, her people, her sex, her secret. Thus, when Heracles arrived in Eleusis, an unclean stranger, he was accepted only because Theseus "had vouched for him." The saying "Nothing without Theseus," which the Athenians were to repeat for centuries, alludes to this: apart from being a hero, Theseus also initiates heroes; without him the rough-and-ready hero could never achieve that initiatory completeness which is *teleíōsis*, *teleté*.

Heracles is contaminated by the sacred, it persecutes him his whole life. It drives him mad, and in the end it destroys him. Theseus, in contrast, seems to wash the blood from his hands after every adventure, to shrug off the violence and the many deaths. Heracles becomes a pretext for the gods to play out a long game. Theseus dares to use the gods to play his own game. But it would be churlish to see him as someone who knows how to turn everything to his advantage. The hero who founded Athens was also to have the privilege of being the first to be expelled from it. "After Theseus had given the Athenians democracy, a certain Lycus denounced him and managed to have the hero ostracized." In the end, even Theseus will be killed. He dies in exile, dashed to pieces at the foot of a cliff. Somebody pushed him from behind. "At the time, nobody paid any attention to the fact that Theseus was dead." But his game is still played in the city Theseus himself named: Athens, the most sacred, the most blasphemous of cities.

Heracles deserves the compassion of the moderns, because he was one of the last victims of the Zodiac. And the moderns no longer really appreciate what that means. They are no longer in the habit of calculating a man's deeds in terms of the measures of the heavens. As a hero, Heracles is a beast of burden: he has to plow the immense plain of the heavens in every one of its twelve segments. As a result he never manages to achieve that detachment from self which the modern demands and which Theseus achieves so gloriously. Such detachment entails the hero's mingling and alternating the deeds he is obliged to do with his own personal acts of caprice and defiance. But for Heracles everything is obligation, right up to the atrocious burns that kill him. A pitiful seriousness weighs him down. All too rarely does he laugh. And sometimes he finds himself having to suffer the laughter of others.

Heracles' buttocks were like an old leather shield, blackened by long exposure to the sun and by the fiery breaths of Cacus and of the Cretan bull. When Heracles caught the mocking Cercopes, who came in the form of two annoying gadflies to rob him and deprive him of his sleep, first he forced them to return to their human form, then he hung them both by their feet on a beam and lifted them on his shoulders, balancing out the weight on both sides. The heads of the two tiny rascals thus dangled at the level of the hero's powerful buttocks, left uncovered by his lionskin. At which the Cercops remembered the prophetic words of their mother: "My little White Asses, beware of the moment when you meet the great Black Ass." Hanging upside down, the two thieves shook with laughter, while the hero's buttocks continued to rise and fall as he marched steadily on. And, as he walked, the hero heard their muffled sneering behind his back. He was sad. Even the people he thrashed didn't take him seriously. He let the two rascals down and started laughing with them. Others say he killed them.

A mythical event can mean a change of landscape. The Rock of Argos once looked out over a countryside famous for its droughts. And from dry dust one went straight into the mud of the Lerna marshes. So Argos lacked a clean supply of fresh running water. Before it could have one, the bloody affair of the Danaids must take place. A fifty-oared galley arrived from Egypt. With a girl at every oar. They were the fifty daughters of Danaus, the Danaids, with their father. Driven by "an innate repulsion for men," they were fleeing forced marriages with their fifty cousins, sons of Aegyptus. And, having fled, they had chosen to return to their family's ancestral home, the place where the wanderings of their forebear Io had begun. They spoke a foreign language, and their skin had been darkened by the African sun. The old king of Argos, Pelasgus, immediately saw their arrival as an unmanageable invasion. Coming toward him were fifty women with extravagant, barbaric clothes and nomadic desert eyes, but from the left arm hole of each Danaid protruded an olive branch wound in white wool. It was the only recognizably Greek sign they carried, but it was a clear one: they were asking for asylum. And they added that, if they were not granted it, they would hang themselves. They were more specific: they would hang themselves from the statues in the temple, using the girdles from their tunics. Fifty women hanging themselves from fifty statues! What a pestilence, dense and poisonous as the muggy airs of Egypt! Better risk a war than that.

Pelasgus gave asylum to this crowd of beautiful barbarians and took them into the town. He was a shade embarrassed: he didn't know whether to have them sleep in the houses of his subjects or apart, in buildings placed at their disposition. He sensed he was risking his kingdom for these unknown foreigners, who had arrived only the day before. But he didn't dare send them away. Every time he wavered, he would see fifty statues with fifty women hanging from them. From the Rock of Argos, the ships of the defiant cousins were spotted on the horizon, coming to get their women. They were Egyptians and respected only Egyptian gods; there wasn't a shrine in the whole of Greece could stop them. Pelasgus had always hoped some sort of compromise might be reached. What if the piratical abduction were dressed up as a series of peaceful marriages? Fifty couples reunited in a huge party? In the end the Danaids gave in. But each went to her marriage bed concealing a knife. And forty-nine times that night a woman's hand plunged its blade into the body of the man who lay beside her. Only the eldest sister broke the pact: Hypermestra. She let her husband, Lynceus, escape. Throughout the bloody night, torch signals were exchanged among the hills. Hypermestra's sisters cut off forty-nine heads and went to toss them into the Lerna marshes. Then they heaped up the headless corpses before the gates of Argos.

What happened to the Danaids after that is far from clear. We do know that they were purified by Athena and Hermes. And we know that around the scorching Argos they discovered springs of the purest water. This, together with the massacre of their husbands, was their greatest achievement. Then their father decided they should marry again. Not an easy matter. Nobody came forward with any nuptial gifts. So the deal was turned on its head: the Danaids would be given away to the winners of a series of races. Only Hypermestra, who had run off with Lynceus, and Amymone, abducted by the god Poseidon, were missing. Lined up like a chorus in a play, Danaus gave away the forty-eight remaining girls at the finish line. Whoever touched the tunic of a Danaid first could have her as his bride. "The fastest matchmaking ever," Pindar remarked. By noon it was all over.

And they're lined up again the next time we see them, with all their enchanting names—Autonoe, Automate, Cleopatra, Pirene, Iphimedusa, Asteria, Gorge, Hyperippe, Clite—but this time in the underworld, not far from where Sisyphus is pushing his rock. Each is holding a jar. They are taking turns pouring water into a big, leaky pitcher. The water flows out and runs away. For many commentators this became an image of the unhappiness related to something that can never be achieved. But Bachofen sees the forty-eight girls differently. He doesn't place them in the underworld but in a primordial landscape of reeds and marshes, where the Nile splits up into its delta and sinks into the thirsty soil. The Danaids had come from Africa to the driest place in the Peloponnese, bringing with them the gift of water. Their ancestor Io also liked to appear with a reed in her hand, a creature of the marshes. As Bachofen saw it, that constant pouring of water into a bottomless container had nothing futile or despairing about it. On the contrary, it was almost an image of happiness. He recalled another mythical girl: Iphimedeia. She had fallen in love with Poseidon, as had Io with Zeus. So she would often walk along the beach, go down into the sea, raise the water from the waves and pour it over her breasts. A gesture of love. Then one day Poseidon appeared, wrapped himself around her, and generated two children. Iphimedeia's gesture has something blissful and timeless about it; it is the motion of feminine substance toward the other, toward any other. A motion that cannot be satisfied, satisfied only in its unfailing repetition.

The Greeks welcomed the gift of water, but rejected the Danaids. *Lérnē kakôn*, "Lerna, place of evil," became a proverbial saying recalling another: *Lémnia kaká*, which evoked the crime of the women of Lemnos. The two massacres had much in common. On both occasions the murderers were Amazons. On both occasions all the men but one got their throats cut. On Lemnos, Hypsipyle took pity on her father, Thoas. In Argos, Hypermestra took pity on her husband, Lynceus. "Of all crimes, that of the women of Lemnos was the worst," says Aeschylus. It was the utmost iniquity. With time, from the forty-nine putrefied heads of the sons of Aegyptus, a countless-headed hydra was born. It would take Heracles, scourge of the Amazons and descendant of Hypermestra, the only Danaid who broke the pact, to kill that monster.

Aeschylus wrote two trilogies that take absolution as their theme: the *Oresteia* and the *Danaides*. The first has come down to us complete; of the second we have only the first tragedy, the *Supplices*, and a few fragments. In the first trilogy, Athena absolves Orestes of a crime he has indeed committed, matricide. In the second, Aphrodite absolves Hypermestra of the charge of not having committed a crime, not having killed her husband. It was upon these two absolutions that classical Athens was founded.

The *Oresteia* has survived the centuries intact, and its story is common knowledge; the *Danaides* has been forgotten, and few think of the fifty sisters as an exemplary subject for tragedy. But one may assume that to Aeschylus's mind the two absolutions were mirror images of each other and the two trilogies had the same weight, the one counterbalancing the other. One absolved a man, the other a woman. Everybody feels that Orestes' guilt is the more obvious, Hypermestra's the more paradoxical: how can one consider it a crime to back out of a premeditated and traitorous murder? But Aeschylus has weighed his crimes well. Hypermestra's real crime is her betrayal of her sisters. She is the African Amazon breaking away from her tribe. And this is the kind of crime that Athens understands, makes its own, just as it will make Antiope, queen of the Amazons, its own once she has become Theseus's bride. It is a mysteriously fecund crime. Antiope will give birth to Hippolytus, the handsome Orphic, dressed in white linen, who flees the girls; one of Hypermestra's descendants will be Heracles, enemy of the Amazons. The Amazon graft is a precious one, a delicate one, producing useful, antidotal fruits. Just as Athena defends Orestes, so does Aphrodite Hypermestra, and with the same high eloquence: "The pure sky loves to violate the land, / and the land is seized by desire for this embrace; / the teeming rain from the sky / makes the earth fecund, so that for mortals it generates / the pastures for their flocks and the sap of Demeter / and the fruit on the trees. From these moist embraces / everything which is comes into being. And I am the cause of this." Greece was a nuptial land of sexual union, attracted by divine virginity. But it feared those Amazons with neither home nor husband. Hypermestra had betrayed them. For that she deserved to be saved.

Apollo was the first slayer of monsters; then came Cadmus, Perseus, Bellerophon, Heracles, Jason, Theseus. Alongside this list of monster slayers we could place a list of traitors, of women: Hypermestra, Hypsipyle, Medea, Ariadne, Antiope, Helen, Antigone. These women don't have a god as their forebear, but a priestess: Io, who betrayed her goddess, Hera, in whose sanctuary she lived as "guardian of the keys." "Io illustrates the awakening of woman from the long sleep of an untroubled infancy, a happiness that was ignorant but perfect, to a tormenting love that will be at once the delight and sorrow of her life, forever. She has been dazzled by the divinity of Zeus."

The heroic gesture of woman is betrayal: its influence on the course of events is just as great as the slaying of monsters. With the monster slain, an impurity lingers on to dog the hero. There will also be the withered remains of the foe whose power the hero turns to his advantage. Heracles clothes himself in the skin of the Nemean lion; Perseus brandishes the petrifying face of the Gorgon as he goes into battle. Leave only emptiness and the chatter of human voices. The isthmus becomes practicable, people trade, and write poems recalling monsters.

The effects of woman's betrayal are more subtle and less immediate perhaps, but equally devastating. Helen provokes a war that wipes out the entire race of heroes, ushering in a completely new age, when the heroes will merely be remembered in verse. And as a civilizing gesture, woman's betrayal is no less effective than man's monster slaying. The monster is an enemy beaten in a duel; in her betrayal, the traitor suppresses her own roots, detaching her life from its natural context. Ariadne is the ruin of Crete, where she was born; Antiope dies fighting the Amazons, her own subjects who were faithfully rallying to her aid; Helen leads the heroes she has loved to their downfall; Medea forsakes the country of sorcery to arrive, at the end of her adventures, in the country of law, Athens; Antigone betrays the law of her city to make a gesture of mercy toward a dead man who does not belong to that city. Like a spiral, woman's betrayal twists around on itself, forever rejecting that which is given. It is not the negation that comes into play in the frontal and mortal collision of forces but the negation that amounts to

a gradual breaking away from ourselves, opposition to ourselves, effacement of ourselves, in a game that may exalt or
destroy and which generally both exalts and destroys.

The slaying of monsters and woman's betrayal are two
ways in which negation can operate. The first clears a space,
leaves an evocative vacuum where before there was a clut-
ter, thick with heads and tentacles, a scaly arabesque. Woman's betrayal does not alter the elements in space but
rearranges them. The influence of certain pieces on the
chessboard is inverted. White attacks white. Black attacks
black. The effect is confusing, above all disturbing. For the
first time roles have been reversed. And it is always a woman
who reverses them. There's an obstinacy about the hero that
obliges him to keep on and on, following just the one path
and no other. Hence his need to be complemented, his need
of another form of negation. The woman with her betrayal
completes the hero's work: she brings it to its conclusion and
winds up the story. This is done in agreement with the hero.
It is part of the hero's civilizing work to suppress himself,
because the hero is monstrous. Immediately after the monsters, die the heroes.

With the heroes, man takes his first step beyond the necessary: into the realm of risk, defiance, shrewdness, deceit,
art. And with the heroes a new world of love is disclosed.
The woman helps the hero to slay monsters and capture talismans. A shining initiator into religious mystagogue, she
has a splendor that ranges from the glimmering radiance of
Ariadne to the dazzle of Medea. But the heroes also ushered
in a new kind of love: that between man and man. Heracles
and Iolaus, Theseus and Peirithous, Achilles and Patroclus,
Orestes and Pylades—all enjoyed what Aeschylus calls "the
sacred communion of thighs," a communion Achilles chided
Patroclus for having forgotten merely because he was dead.

The love of one man for another appears with the heroes
and immediately reaches its perfect expression. Only the
heroes—and precisely because they were heroes—could have

overcome what so far for the Greeks had been an insurmountable obstacle to such a love: the rigid distinction between separate roles, the obstinate asymmetry between *erastés* and *erómenos*, lover and beloved, which had condemned love relationships to being painfully short and stifled by the strictest rules. The cruelest of these rules was that, while the lover was granted his swift and predatory pleasure, the beloved was not to enjoy any sexual pleasure at all but must submit himself to the other only reluctantly, in something like the way nineteenth-century wives were encouraged to submit to their husbands. And the lover could not look into the eyes of his beloved as he ravished him, so as to avoid embarrassment. The heroes swept all these rules aside. Their relationships were long lasting—only death could end them—and their love didn't fade merely because the beloved grew hairs on his legs or because his skin, hardened by a life of adventure, lost its youthful smoothness. Thus the heroes achieved that most yearned for of states, in which the distinction between lover and beloved begins to blur. Between Orestes and Pylades, "it would have been difficult to say which of the two was the lover, since the lover's tenderness found its reflection in the other's face as in a mirror." In the same way, these words from the Pseudo-Lucian hold up a late mirror to what was the most constant erotic wish of Greek men, and the most vain.

When it came to slaying monsters, the hero's model was Apollo killing Python; when it came to making love to young boys it was Apollo's love for Hyacinthus and Cyparissus. But there is an episode in the god's life that hints at something even more arcane than those often fatal love affairs. It is the story of how Apollo became a servant to Admetus, king of Pherae in Thessaly. Of Admetus we know that he was handsome, that he was famous for his herds of cattle, that he loved sumptuous feasts, and that he possessed the gift of hospitality. So much and no more. But we know a great deal about what people did for him. Out of love for Admetus,

Apollo was willing to pass as a hireling. For a long time, "inflamed by love for the young Admetus," this proudest of gods became a mere herdsman, taking a provincial king's cattle out to graze. In so doing, he left his shock of dazzling hair unkempt and even forsook his lyre, making music on nothing better than a reed pipe.

His sister Artemis blushed with shame. And out of love for Admetus, his Alcestis, the most beautiful of Pelias's daughters, agreed to die like a stranger, unthreatened by anybody, taking the place of a hostage condemned to death. For love of Admetus, Apollo got the Fates drunk: it must have been the wildest party ever, although we know nothing about it except that it happened. In Plutarch's vision of things, the Fates, those young girls whose beautiful arms spin the thread of every life on earth, were "the daughters of Ananke," Necessity. And Necessity, as Euripides reminds us, having met her, "as he wandered among Muse and mountaintop," without ever "discovering anything more powerful," is the only power that has neither altars nor statues. Ananke is the only divinity who pays no heed to sacrifices. Her daughters can only be fooled by drunkenness. And very rarely does drink get the better of them. It was a hard task, but Apollo managed it, merely out of love for Admetus, because he wanted to delay the man's death.

Apollo has an old feud with death. Zeus had forced him to become a servant—oh blessed servitude—to Admetus because Asclepius, son of Apollo and the faithless Coronis, had dared to bring a man back from the dead. Zeus shriveled Asclepius with a thunderbolt, and in revenge Apollo killed the Cyclopes who forged the thunderbolts. Zeus responded by planning a terrible punishment for Apollo. He had meant to hurl him down into Tartarus, and it was only when Leto, his old mistress, begged him not to that he decided to send the god to Thessaly, condemned to be a servant to Admetus. With Apollo's other lovers, Hyacinthus for example, and Cyparissus, love had always ended in death. Accidents they may have been, and they caused him pain, but the fact was that Apollo himself had killed them. While playing with Hyacinthus, the god hurled a discus that shattered the boy's skull. Cyparissus fled from Apollo's advances and in desperation turned himself into a cypress. With Admetus the pattern was reversed. Apollo's love was so great that in trying to snatch Admetus from death he himself again risked what for a god is the equivalent of death: exile. Yet another thing Apollo did out of love for Admetus, and perhaps it was the most momentous of all, was to accept payment from his beloved, like a *pórnos*, a merest prostitute, unprotected by any rights, a stranger in his own city, despised first and foremost by his own lovers. It was the first example ever of *bonheur dans l'esclavage*. That it should have been Apollo who submitted to it made the adventure all the more astounding.

Thus Apollo, lover par excellence, took his love to an extreme where no human after him could follow. Not only did he confound the roles of lover and beloved, as would Orestes and Pylades, Achilles and Patroclus, but he went so far as to become the prostitute of his beloved, and hence one of those beings, "considered the worst of all perverts," in whose defense no one in Greece ever ventured to speak so much as a word. And, as servant to his beloved, he attempted to roll back the borders of death, something not even Zeus himself had dared interfere with, not even for his own son Sarpedon.

But who was Admetus? When he heard from Apollo that his death could be delayed if somebody else were ready to die in his place, Admetus began to make the rounds of friends and relations. He asked all of them if they were willing to take his place. No one would. So Admetus went to his two old parents, sure they would agree. But even they said no. Next it was the turn of his young and beautiful bride. And Alcestis said yes. The Greeks questioned whether woman was capable of *philía* in a man's regard, capable that is of that friendship which grows out of love ("*philía dià tòn érōta*," as Plato puts it), and which only men were supposed to experience. But Alcestis actually lifted *philía* to a higher plane by making the ultimate sacrifice. Even Plato was forced to admit that in comparison with Admetus's wife, Orpheus "seems weak spirited, nothing more than a zither strummer," because he went into the underworld alive in his search for Eurydice rather than simply agreeing to die, as Alcestis did, without any hope of return or salvation. True, Alcestis remains the only feminine example of *philía* the Greeks ever quote, but it is an awesome example. So much so that the gods themselves allowed Heracles to snatch her back just as the young woman was about to cross the calm waters of the lake of the dead. So Alcestis was brought back among the living, back to the grief-stricken Admetus. The king of Pherae had been saved on three occasions: by a god, by a woman, and by a hero. And all this merely because he had shown himself hospitable.

In this elusive, because supernatural, story, the point of maximum impenetrability is the object of love: Admetus. Euripides has Alcestis die onstage like a heroine out of Ibsen, and before dying she bares her heart to us. Ancient literature offers plenty of eloquent references to Apollo's passion, although texts never connect his having been Admetus's lover to his having been paid as the king's servant. The two images of Apollo are always kept separate. Of Admetus we know only that he insulted his old father for refusing to die in his place. All else is obscure, no less so than the way gods are obscure to mortals. Only one character trait shines through the ancient texts: Admetus was hospitable.

But who is Admetus? Dazzled by Alcestis and Apollo, who loved him to the point of self-denial, we might choose to leave the object of their love in the shadows. But let's stop awhile and take a good look at him: let's scan the landscape and the names. And we shall discover that Admetus belongs to the shadows as of right.

The landscape is Thessaly, a land that "in olden times was a lake surrounded by mountains high as the sky itself" (one of them was Olympus); a land that preserved its familiarity

with the deep waters which periodically burst forth to flood
it from a hundred springs and rivers; a fertile country, yellow, rugged, with plenty of horses, cattle, witches. The pre-
siding divinity is not the cool, transparent Athena but a
great goddess who looms from the darkness, Pheraia. She
holds a torch in each hand and is rarely mentioned. And this
too is typical of the spirit of Thessaly, a land where divinity
is closer to the primordial anonymity, where the gods rarely
assume a human face, and where the Olympians are loath
to descend. When a god does appear, he bursts forth,
brusque and wild, like the horse Scapheus, whose mane
leaps out from the rock split open by his own hooves. The
horses that gallop around Thessaly are creatures of the deep,
shooting out of the cracks in the ground, the cracks from
which Poseidon's wave rises to flood the plain. They are the
dead, brilliantly white, brilliantly black. And Pheraia is a
local name for Hecate, the night-roaming, underworld goddess who rends the dark with her torches. As a goddess, she
is horse, bull, lioness, dog, but she is also she who appears
on the back of bull, horse, or lion. A nurse to boys, a mul-
tiplier of cattle. In Thessaly she is *Brimó*, the strong one,
who unites with Hermes, son of Ischys, also the strong one,
the lover Coronis preferred to Apollo. And *strength* (*alké*)
also forms part of the name Alcestis. In the land of Thessaly, rather than as a person divinity presents itself as pure
force. But Pheraia, says Hesychius's dictionary, is also the
"daughter [*kóre*] of Admetus." Is it possible that before becoming a pair of provincial rulers, Alcestis and Admetus
were already sitting side by side as sovereigns of the
underworld?

Now the landscape yields up its secret. It is the luxuriant
country of the dead, this Thessaly where Apollo must be
slave for a "great year," until the stars return to their original positions—that is, for nine years. Apollo's stay in Thessaly is a time cycle in Hades. The fact that Zeus chose this
place instead of Tartarus as a punishment for Apollo itself
suggests that this is a land of death. The name *Admetus*
means "indomitable." And who is more indomitable than

the lord of the dead? Now the few things we know about Admetus take on new meaning: who could be more hospitable than the king of the dead? His is the inn that closes its doors to no one, at no hour of the day or night. And no one has such numerous herds as the king of the dead. When Admetus invites friends and relations to die for him, he is scarcely doing anything unusual: it's what he does all the time. And the reason Admetus fully expects others to substitute for him in death is now clear: he is the lord of death, he greets the arriving corpses, sorts them and spreads them out across his extensive domains.

Now we see how truly extreme Apollo's love is, more so even than it had seemed: out of love, Apollo tries to save the king of the dead from death. Now the love of both Apollo and Alcestis reveals itself as thoroughly provocative: it is a love for the shadow that steals all away. From Alcestis we discover what the *kórē*, snatched by Hades while gathering narcissi, never told us: that the god of the invisible is not just an abductor but a lover too.

The texts have little to say about Apollo's period of servitude because it would mean touching on matters best kept secret. About Heracles' servitude under Omphale the poets chose to be ironic. But, when it came to Apollo's under Admetus, no one wanted to risk it. All that remains is the exemplum of a love so great as to compensate for any amount of shame and suffering. According to Apollonius Rhodius, after killing the Cyclopes, Apollo was punished by being sent not to Thessaly but to the Hyperboreans in the far North. There he wept tears of amber, even though a god cannot weep. But what really put the story out of bounds was not just the scandalous suffering (and scandalously servile passion) of the "pure god in flight from the heavens." There was something else behind it. An ancient prophecy, the secret of Prometheus: the prediction that Zeus would one day see his throne usurped, by his most luminous son.

Apollo often plays around the borders of death. But Zeus

is watching from on high. He knows that, if ignored, his son's game will bring about the advent of a new age, the collapse of the Olympian order. Within the secret that lies behind this, and it's a secret rarely even alluded to, Apollo is to Zeus what Zeus had been to Kronos. And the place where the powers of the two gods always collide is death. Even beneath the sun of the dead, among the herds of Thessaly, Apollo doesn't forget his challenge to his father and chooses to snatch, if only for a short while, his indomitable beloved, Admetus, from that moment when "the established day does him violence." The never-mentioned dispute between father and son is left forever unsettled at that point.

The admirable asymmetry on which the Athenian man's love for the younger boy is based is described in minute detail by that surveyor of all matters erotic, Plato. The entire metaphysics of love is concentrated in the gesture with which the beloved grants his grace (*cháris*) to the lover. This gesture, still echoed in the Italian expression *concedere le proprie grazie*, and again in the passionate intertwining drawn tight by the French verb *agréer* (and derivations: *agréments*, *agréable*, and so on), is the very core of erotic drama and mystery. How should we think of it? How achieve it? For the Barbarians it is something to condemn; for the more lascivious Greeks and those incapable of expressing themselves, such as the Spartans or the Boeotians, it is simply something enjoyable, and as such obligatory: to give way to a lover becomes a state directive. But as ever the Athenians are a little more complicated and multifarious (*poikíloi*) than their neighbors, even when it comes to "the law of love." They are not so impudent as to speak of a "grace" that actually turns out to be an obligation. What could they come up with, then, to achieve the beloved's grace, without ever being sure of it? The word.

As warriors besieging a fortress will try one ruse after another to have that object so long before their eyes fall at last into their hands, so the Athenian lover engages in a war of words, surrounds his beloved with arguments that hem him in like soldiers. And the things he says are not just crude gallantries but the first blazing precursors of what one day, using a Greek word without remembering its origin, will be called metaphysics. The notion that thought derives from erotic dialogue is, for the great Athenians, true in the most straightforward, literal sense. Indeed, that link between a body to be captured like a fortress and the flight of metaphysics is, for Plato, the very image of eros. The rest of the world are mere Barbarians who simply don't understand, or other Greeks with no talent for language, in other words, suffering from "mental sloth." They too are excluded from that finest of wars, which is the war of love.

As far as the lover was concerned, Athens invented a perfect duplicity, which uplifted him while leaving his undertaking forever uncertain. On the one hand, there is nothing the lover may not do; he is forgiven any and every excess. He alone can break his oath without the gods punishing him, since "there are no oaths in the affairs of Aphrodite." And again, the lover may get wildly excited, or choose to sleep the night outside the barred door of his beloved's house, and nobody will take it upon himself to criticize him. On the other hand, endless difficulties are placed in his way: his beloved will go to the gymnasium accompanied by a lynx-eyed pedagogue hired by the boy's father precisely to prevent him from listening to the advances of any would-be lover lying in wait. And the boy's friends are worse still: they watch him carefully, and if ever he shows signs of giving way, they taunt him and make him feel ashamed of that first hint of a passion that, encouraged by the lover's alluring words, could lead to the desired exchange of graces, to the moment when the lover will breathe "intelligence and every other virtue" into the mouth and body of his beloved, while the latter submits to his lover's advances because he wishes to gain "education and knowledge of every kind." (*Eis-pneîn*, "breathe into," is first and foremost the lover's prerogative, and *eíspnēlos*, "he who breathes into another," was another word for "lover.") This is the only and arduous "meeting point" admitted between the two asymmetrical laws that govern the lives of the lover and his beloved. Thus, at that fleeting and paradoxical point, "it is good for the young beloved to surrender himself to his lover; but only at that point and at no other." So says Plato. And such was the life of the lover, the most precarious, the most risky, and the most provocative of all the roles the Athenians invented.

After slaughtering their men, the women of Lemnos were struck by a kind of revenge the gods had never used before nor would again: they began to smell. And in this revenge we glimpse the grievance that Greece nursed against womankind. Greek men thought of women as of a perfume that is too strong, a perfume that breaks down to become a suffocating stench, a sorcery, "sparkling with desire, laden with aromas, glorious," but stupefying, something that must be shaken off. It is an attitude betrayed by small gestures, like that passage in the Pseudo-Lucian where we hear of a man climbing out of bed, "saturated with femininity," and immediately wanting to dive into cold water. When it comes to women, Greek sensibility brings together both fear and repugnance: on the one hand, there is the horror at the woman without her makeup who "gets up in the morning uglier than a monkey"; on the other, there is the suspicion that makeup is being used as a weapon of *apátè*, of irresistible deceit. Makeup and female smells combine to generate a softness that bewitches and exhausts. Better for men the sweat and dust of the gymnasium. "Boys' sweat has a finer smell than anything in a woman's makeup box."

One gets a sense, in these reactions to womankind, of something remote being revealed as though through nervous reflex. In the later, more private and idiosyncratic writers, we pick up echoes that take us back to a time long, long before, to the terror roused by the invasion of the Amazons, to the loathsome crime of the women of Lemnos.

For the Greeks, the unnameable aspect of eros was passivity during coitus. If the male beloved (*erómenos*) has to be so careful and to observe so many rules in order to distinguish his behavior beyond any shadow of a doubt from that of the male prostitute, who, "despite having a man's body, sins a woman's sins," it is not simply because of the indignity attached to whoever accepts the woman's part, thus debasing his own sexual status. Rather, it is the very pleasure of the woman, the pleasure of passivity, that is suspect and perhaps conceals a profound malignancy. This treacherous pleasure incites the Greek man to rage against the grossness inherent in the physiology and anatomy of these aesthetically inferior beings, obliged to parade "prominent, shapeless breasts, which they keep bound up like prisoners." But he rages precisely because he senses that this grossness might conceal a mocking power that eludes male control. The Athenians were extremely evasive on this question, although they never tired of mentioning cases of male love for boys.

As for what women might get up to when alone and unobserved by masculine eyes, a reverent and ominous silence appears to reign. And when it comes to love between women, the writers sometimes daren't even use the word. In fact it is pathetic to see how in certain passages on the subject, modern translators will translate that forbidden word as *lesbianism*, without even sensing any incongruousness. The word *lesbianism* meant nothing to the Greeks, whereas the verb *lesbiázein* meant "licking the sexual organs," and the word *tribádes*, "the rubbers," referred to women who had sex with other women, as though in the fury of their embrace they wanted to consume each other's vulvas.

But it wasn't so much love between women that scandalized the Greeks—to their credit they were not easily scandalized—as the suspicion, which had taken root in their minds, that women might have their own indecipherable

erotic self-sufficiency, and that those rites and mysteries
they celebrated, and in which they refused to let men participate, might be the proof of this. And, behind it all, their
most serious suspicion had to do with pleasure in coitus.
Only Tiresias had been able to glimpse the truth, and that
was precisely why he was blinded.

One day Zeus and Hera were quarreling. They called Tiresias and asked him which of the two, man or woman, got
the most pleasure from sex. Tiresias answered that if the
pleasure were divided into ten parts, the woman enjoyed
nine and the man only one. On hearing this, Hera got mad
and blinded Tiresias. But why did Hera get mad? Couldn't
she glory in her own superiority, something that set her
above even Zeus? No, because here Tiresias was trespassing
on a secret, one of those secrets sages are called upon to
safeguard rather than reveal. This sexual tittle-tattle continued to make the rounds, however. Centuries later it was
still being bandied about, though, as always, with distor-
tions: now they were saying that a woman's pleasure was
only twice that of the man. But it was enough: it confirmed
an antique doubt, a fear at least as old as the ruttish daughters of the sun. Perhaps woman, that creature shut away in
the gynaeceum, where "not a single particle of true eros
penetrates," knew a great deal more than her master, who
was always cruising about gymnasiums and porticoes.

"Make up your minds who you think are better, those who
love boys, or those who like women. I, in fact, who have
enjoyed both kinds of passion, am like balanced scales with
the two plates either side at exactly the same height." So
says Theomnestus. Since time immemorial the question as
to which took the erotic prize, love with boys or with
women, had been a real thorn in the flesh for the Greeks.
Some even maintained that Orpheus was torn apart by
women because he had been the first to declare the superiority of love with boys. Later on, even though the debate
had been settled before it started in favor of the boys, the

rule was that one wasn't to say so too openly. Finally, in the late and loquacious years of the Pseudo-Lucian, we hear a cackle of voices—spiteful or mellifluous, uncertain or arrogant—still debating the issue. Licinus answers Theomnestus's question in the best way possible: with a story. One day, walking beneath the porticoes of Rhodes, he met two old acquaintances: Caricles, a young man from Corinth, and the impetuous Callicratides, an Athenian. Caricles was wearing, as always, a little makeup. He thought it made him more attractive to women. And there was never any shortage of those around him. His house was full of dancers and singers. The only voices heard there were women's voices, except, that is, for one old cook, past it now, and a few very young slave boys. Quite the opposite of Callicratides' house. Callicratides did the rounds of the gymnasiums and surrounded himself exclusively with attractive and as yet hairless boys. When the first suspicion of a beard began to scratch their skin, he would move them on to administrative work and bring in others. The three friends decided to spend a few lazy days together taking turns discussing that old chestnut: who takes the erotic palm, boys or women?

For Callicratides, women were "an abyss," like the great ravines in the rocks around Athens where criminals were thrown. Caricles, however, couldn't respond to boys at all and thought incessantly about women. Having taken a boat to Cnidos, the three friends were eager to see the famous Aphrodite by Praxiteles. Even before they went into Aphrodite's temple, they could feel a light breeze blowing from it. It was the aura. The courtyard of the sanctuary wasn't paved with the usual austere slabs of gray stone but was full of plants and fruit trees. In the garden all around them they saw myrtles with their berries and other shrubs associated with the goddess. Plants typical of Dionysus were also in abundance, since "Aphrodite is even more delightful when she is with Dionysus, and their gifts are sweeter if mixed together." Finally the three friends went into the temple. In the center they saw the Parian marble of Praxiteles' Aphrodite, naked, a faint lift to the corners of her lips, a faint hint of arrogance. Caricles immediately began to rave over the stunning frontal view. One could suffer anything for a woman like that, and so saying he stretched up to kiss her. Callicratides watched in silence. There was a door behind the statue, and the three friends asked one of the temple guardians if she had the keys to it. It was then that Callicratides was stunned by the beauty of Aphrodite's buttocks. He yelled his admiration, and Caricles' eyes were wet with tears.

Then the three fell silent as they continued to contemplate that marble body. Behind a thigh they noticed a mark, like a stain on a tunic. Licinus assumed it was a defect in the marble and remarked on this as yet another reason for admiring Praxiteles: how clever of him to hide this blemish in one of the least visible parts of the statue. But the guardian who had opened the door and was standing beside the visitors told them that the real story behind the stain was rather different.

She explained that a young man from a prominent family had once been in the habit of visiting the temple and had fallen in love with the goddess. He would spend whole days parading his devotion. He got up at dawn to go to the sanctuary and went home only reluctantly after sundown. Standing before the statue, he would whisper on and on in some secret lover's conversation, breaking off every now and then to consult the oracle by tossing a few Libyan gazelle bones. He was waiting anxiously for Aphrodite's throw to come up. That was when every face of the bones bore a different number. One evening, when the guardians came to close the temple, the young man hid behind the door where the three visitors were now standing and spent "an unspeakable night" with the statue. The fruits of his lovemaking had stained the statue. That mark on the white marble demonstrated the indignity the image of the goddess had suffered. The young man was never seen again. Rumor had it that he drowned himself in the sea. When the guardian had finished, Caricles immediately exclaimed: "So, men love women even when they are made out of stone. Just imagine if she had been alive . . ." But Callicratides smiled and said that actually the story supported his side of the argument. For despite being alone a whole night with the statue, and completely free to do whatever he wanted, the young man had embraced the marble as if it were a boy and hadn't wanted to take the woman from the front. The two antagonists began arguing again, and Licinus was hard put to persuade them to leave the temple and continue elsewhere. In the meantime the worshipers were beginning to arrive.

To a considerable extent classical morality developed around reflections on the nature of men's love for boys; basically such reflections stressed the quality of *areté* and played down something self-evident: pleasure. *Areté* means an "excellence" that is also "virtue." The word always had a moral meaning attached; the morality wasn't just something added by mischievous latecomers. In any event, *areté* is incandescent whenever manifest in a man's love for a boy. In its Kantian, unattached isolation, the Greeks would scarcely have appreciated the quality at all. The last and ultimate image of *areté* Greece offers us is a field strewn with the corpses of young Thebans after the battle of Chaeronea. The corpses were found lying in pairs: they were all couples, lovers, who had gone into battle together against the Macedonians. It was to be Greece's last stand. Afterward, Philip II and Alexander set about turning the country into a museum.

"Nothing beautiful or charming ever comes to a man except through the Charites," says Theocritus. But how did the Charites come down to man? As three rough stones that fell from heaven in Orchomenus. Only much later were statues placed next to those stones. What falls from heaven is indomitable, forever. Yet man is obliged to conquer those stones, or girls with fine tresses, if he wants his singing to be "full of the breath of the Charites." How to go about it? From the *Chárites*, one passes to *cháris*, from the Graces to grace. And it is Plutarch who tells us what the relationship is: "The ancients, Protogenes, used the word *cháris* to mean the spontaneous consent of the woman to the man." Grace, then, the inconquerable, surrenders itself only to he who strives to conquer it through erotic siege, even though he knows he can never enter the citadel if the citadel doesn't open, grace-fully, for him.

The relationship between *erastés* and *erómenos*, lover and beloved, was highly formalized and to a certain extent followed the rules of a ritual. In Sparta and Crete, the main centers of love between men, one could still find clear evidence of these rites. In Crete, each boy's parents knew that one day they would be forewarned of their son's imminent abduction. The lover would then arrive and, if the parents considered him worthy, would be free to carry off the boy and disappear into the country with him. Their whereabouts unknown, they would live together in complete privacy for two months. Finally the beloved would reappear in the city with "a piece of armor, an ox, and a cup," ceremonial gifts from his lover. Athens, with its vocation for modernity, was less rigid than Crete but equally tough below the surface. Here the rite was transformed into set behavior patterns that, though immersed in the buzz and chatter of the city square, remained as recognizable as dance steps. The lovers would cruise around the gymnasiums with a fake air of abstraction, their eyes running over the youngsters working out in the dust. It was the primordial setting for desire. The lovers would watch the boys, throwing furtive glances at "hips and thighs, the way sacrificing priests and seers size up their victims." They would sneak glances at the prints their genitals left in the sand. They would wait till midday, when, with the combination of oil, sweat, and sand, "dew and down would bloom on the boys' genitals as on the skin of a peach." The place was drenched with pleasure, but the word *pleasure* couldn't be mentioned, because pleasure was common property—even slaves and immigrants could enjoy it—whereas the amorous journey undertaken that morning aimed at an excellence, a splendor and glory, that belonged to one and one alone: an Athenian, the chosen one, the boy who, through subterfuge and gifts of garlands, would become the beloved.

That reluctance to admit the pleasure involved would never be dropped, not even in the ultimate intimacy: "in the act of love the boy does not share in the man's pleasure, as does the woman; but contemplates, in a state of sobriety, the excitement of the other drunken with Aphrodite." When the lover approaches, the beloved stands upright and looks straight ahead, his eyes not meeting those of his lover, who bends down and almost doubles up over him, greedily. The vase painters generally show thigh-to-thigh contact rather than anal penetration: this allows the beloved to maintain his erect, indifferent, detached position. But all too soon the whole situation would be reversed. The first facial hair marked the beginning of the end of the boy's period as beloved. The hairs were called Harmodius and Aristogiton because they freed the boy from this erotic tyranny. Then, as though in need of a little time out, the boy escapes "from the tempest and torment of male love." But very soon he is back in that tempest, and in a new role: instead of being eyed, nude in the gymnasium, he is himself cruising around younger boys, in the same places, nosing out his prey. Transformed from *erómenos* into *erastés*, he would finally discover, as a lover, what it means to be possessed by love. Only the lover is *éntheos*, says Plato. Only the lover is "full of god."

IV

O F THE OLYMPIANS, THE FIRST THING WE can say is that they were *new* gods. They had names and shapes. But Herodotus assures us that "before yesterday" no one knew "where any of these gods had come from, nor whether they had existed eternally, nor what they looked like." When Herodotus says "yesterday," he means Homer and Hesiod, whom he calculated as having lived four centuries before himself. And to his mind it was they who "gave the gods their names, shared out arts and honors among them, and revealed what they looked like." But in Hesiod we can still sense the effort involved in establishing a cosmogony, the slow detachment of the gods from what is either too abstract or too concrete. Only at the end, after the cosmos had quaked again and again, did Zeus "divide the honors among them."

But Homer is the real scandal, his indifference toward the origin of things, the total absence of pomposity, his presumption in beginning not at the beginning of his tale but at the end, at the last of those ten disastrous years of war beneath the walls of Troy, years that had served, above all else, to wipe out the whole race of the heroes. The heroes were themselves a recent phenomenon, and here was the poet already celebrating their passing. The Olympians had quickly established a constant rhythm to their lives and seemed intent on maintaining it forever, as if it were the obvious choice. The earth was there for raids, whims, intrigues, experiments. But what happened before Olympus?

Here and there Homer does give us hints, but fleeting ones. No one is interested in going into details. While the destiny of a Trojan warrior can be most engrossing.

There is something assumed in Homer but never mentioned, something that lies behind both silences and eloquence. It is the idea of perfection. What is perfect is its own origin and does not wish to dwell on how it came into being. What is perfect severs all ties with its surroundings, because sufficient unto itself. Perfection doesn't explain its own history but offers its completion. In the long history of divinities, the inhabitants of Olympus were the first who wished to be perfect rather than powerful. Like an obsidian blade, the aesthetic for the first time cut away all ties, connections, devotions. What remained was a group of figures, isolated in the air, complete, initiated, perfect—three words that Greek covers in just one: *téleios*. Even though it would not appear until much later, the statue was the beginning, the way in which these new beings would manifest themselves.

When the Greeks needed to appeal to an ultimate authority, it wasn't a sacred text but Homer that they went to. Greece was founded on the *Iliad*. And the *Iliad* was founded on a play of words, the substitution of a couple of letters in a name. Briseis, Chryseis. The bone of contention that triggers the poem is Briseis *kallipáreos*, Briseis "of the lovely cheeks": Agamemnon wants her exchanged with, or substituted for, Chryseis *kallipáreos*, Chryseis "of the lovely cheeks." In Greek only two letters separate the two girls. And it was not "because of the girl," Achilles childishly insists, that the whole quarrel began but because of the substitution, as if the hero sensed that it was this notion of exchange that had tightened the noose that no hero, nor any generation that came after the heroes, would be able to loosen.

It is the power of exchange in all its manifestations that looms over the opening of the *Iliad*: there is the woman, or rather the two women, each with lovely cheeks, almost indistinguishable, like coins from the same mint; there are the words of Agamemnon and Achilles, which oppose each other as one force opposes another (*antibíosi epéessin*); there is the "immense," the "splendid ransom," offered by the priest Chryses for his daughter Chryseis, and "the holy hecatomb" the Achaeans offer the priest. On each occasion, the elements of the exchange are presented in pairs: the women, the words, the offerings. The only thing missing is money, which will eventually be composed from the mixing of these elements. But, for money to emerge in its purest form, the heroes must first kill each other off. As early as Thucydides we have the observation that precisely what was lacking during the Trojan War was money. That "lack of money" (*achrēmatía*) made the whole mixture less potent than it would later be, but far more glorious.

"Helen is the only woman in Homer who clearly has distinctive epithets of her own," observes Milman Parry. *Kallipáreos*—"of the lovely cheeks"—is applied to eight women and thus used more than any other female epithet. The *Iliad* tells the story of two quarrels: the quarrel over Helen, the unique Helen, who no one would dare to substitute; and the quarrel over Briseis "of the lovely cheeks," who Agamemnon would like to substitute with Chryseis "of the lovely cheeks." Between uniqueness unassailable and unassailable substitution, a war flares up on the Trojan plain, a war that can never end.

If we are to give credence to his spouse-sister, Hera, Zeus "was interested in only one thing, going to bed with women, mortal and immortal alike." But at least one woman rejected him, and, what was worse, an immortal: Thetis. Resentful, Zeus went on "spying on her from on high, against her will." And, given that she had refused him, he resorted to the most solemn of oaths to make sure she would never have an immortal companion. As Hera saw it, Thetis didn't

yield to Zeus because she was "at once respectful and secretly afraid" of his celestial partner, herself. So the two of
them became friends. But here, as elsewhere, Hera's vision
of events is too self-centered. There was a more serious mo-
tive behind Thetis's rejection, indeed the most serious mo-
tive possible: her union with Zeus would have led to the
birth of the son destined to displace his father: "a son
stronger than his father," say both Pindar and Aeschylus,
using exactly the same words.

The primordial Themis revealed the danger to a general
assembly of Zeus and the other Olympians. Only then did
Zeus really give up on Thetis, because he wanted to "preserve his own power forever." Perhaps Thetis already knew
the secret, perhaps that was why she had rejected the god
of gods. Or at least one might conclude as much by analogy,
since there was another occasion when Thetis was the only
woman who protected Zeus's sovereignty. This was when
various other Olympians, including Athena, who was born
from the god's own temple, wanted to put him in chains.
Upon which Thetis, a marine goddess who never went to
Olympus, called Briareos, a hundred-headed Titan, to the
rescue, and Zeus was saved. Zeus was thus indebted to Thetis for her support, "in both word and deed," and she would
exploit that indebtedness to defend her son, Achilles.

As for the motives behind the Olympian plot to bind Zeus
in a thousand knots, Homer's lips are sealed. But a god in
chains is a god dethroned: that, and nothing less than that,
was what the Olympians had been plotting. Thus the need
for a woman's help was not limited to the heroes but also
applied to the greatest of the gods. Even Zeus, in his un-
scathed Olympian stability, knew that his reign must end
one day. As early as Homer's time, he already owed his con-
tinuing reign to expediency, since on one occasion he had
repressed his desire for a woman to avoid the birth of a more
powerful son and on another he had been saved only because that same woman had called on the help of Briareos,
one of those rough-hewn, primordial creatures the Olympians would generally rather not have mentioned. Even

Zeus, then, had opposed cunning to destiny; even the supreme god had put off his own end. The game was not over yet.

Before revealing her secret to the Olympians, Themis had told her son Prometheus. Chained to a rock, Prometheus thought of Zeus endlessly pursuing his "empty-headed" philandering, never knowing which of his conquests might prove fatal to him. Those frivolous adventures were becoming rather like a game of Russian roulette. And Prometheus kept his mouth shut.

Thus Zeus's womanizing takes on a new light. Each affair might conceal the supreme danger. Every time he approached a woman, Zeus knew he might be about to provoke his own downfall. Thus far the stories take us: but for every myth told, there is another, unnameable, that is not told, another which beckons from the shadows, surfacing only through allusions, fragments, coincidences, with nobody ever daring to tell all in a single story. And here the "son stronger than his father" is not to be born yet, because he is already present: he is Apollo. Over the never-ending Olympian banquet, a father and son are watching each other, while between them, invisible to all but themselves, sparkles the serrated sickle Kronos used to slice off the testicles of his father, Uranus.

Whenever their lives were set aflame, through desire or suffering, or even reflection, the Homeric heroes knew that a god was at work. They endured the god, and observed him, but what actually happened as a result was a surprise most of all for themselves. Thus dispossessed of their emotion, their shame, and their glory too, they were more cautious than anybody when it came to attributing to themselves the origin of their actions. "To me, you are not the cause, only the gods can be causes," says old Priam, looking at Helen on the Scaean Gate. He couldn't bring himself to hate her, nor to see her as guilty for nine bloody years' fighting, even though Helen's body had become the very image of a war about to end in massacre.

No psychology since has ever gone beyond this; all we have done is invent, for those powers that act upon us, longer, more numerous, more awkward names, which are less effective, less closely aligned to the gain of our experience, whether that be pleasure or terror. The moderns are proud above all of their responsibility, but in being so they presume to respond with a voice that they are not even sure is theirs. The Homeric heroes knew nothing of that cumbersome word *responsibility*, nor would they have believed in it if they had. For them, it was as if every crime were committed in a state of mental infirmity. But such infirmity meant that a god was present and at work. What we consider infirmity they saw as "divine infatuation" (*átē*). They knew that this invisible incursion often brought ruin: so much so that the word *átē* would gradually come to mean "ruin." But they also knew, and it was Sophocles who said it, that "mortal life can never have anything grandiose about it except through *átē*."

Thus a people obsessed with the idea of hubris were also a people who dismissed with the utmost skepticism an agent's claim actually to *do* anything. When we know for sure that a person is the agent of some action, then that action is mediocre; as soon as there is a hint of greatness, of whatever kind, be it shameful or virtuous, it is no longer that person acting. The agent sags and flops, like a medium when his voices desert him. For the Homeric heroes there was no guilty party, only guilt, immense guilt. That was the miasma that impregnated blood, dust, and tears. With an intuition the moderns jettisoned and have never recovered, the heroes did not distinguish between the evil of the mind and the evil of the deed, murder and death. Guilt for them is like a boulder blocking the road; it is palpable, it looms. Perhaps the guilty party is as much a sufferer as the victim. In confronting guilt, all we can do is make a ruthless computation of the forces involved. And, when considering the guilty party, there will always be an element of uncertainty. We can never establish just how far he really is guilty, because the guilty party is part and parcel of the guilt and obeys its mechanics. Until eventually he is crushed by it perhaps, perhaps abandoned, perhaps freed, while the guilt rolls on to threaten others, to create new stories, new victims.

Every sudden heightening of intensity brought you into a god's sphere of influence. And, within that sphere, the god in question would fight against or ally himself with other gods on a second stage alive with presences. From that moment on, every event, every encounter occurred in parallel, in two places. To tell a story meant to weave those two series of parallel events together, to make both worlds visible.

Agamemnon and Achilles quarrel over the *géras*, that part of the spoils of war which is divided, though not in equal portions, among the prestigious members of the army. Zeus, talking to the other gods assembled on the golden paving of Olympus, reminds them that he is fond of the Trojans because they have never forgotten to give him his *géras*, that part of the sacrifice dedicated to him through sacrifices. And he makes the point while discussing the fate of Agamemnon, Achilles, and their enemies. Every word in human terminology takes on another meaning in a divine context, but the words themselves frequently remain the same, and every story unfolds simultaneously on earth and in heaven. With Olympian conjuring, it will sometimes even seem that everything is happening on the same stage. When Helen goes to Paris's bedroom to visit the warrior, just returned from the battlefield "as though from a dance," it is Aphrodite who gets a chair for her. But this closeness and familiarity doesn't diminish the distance in the slightest. These beings blessed with the power of speech may be aware of sometimes possessing divine beauty or strength or grace, yet there will always be something they lack: the inextinguishable reserves of the Olympians, their "inextinguishable laughter" when they see Hephaestus limping through their banqueting hall, that capacity for "living easily" which is the hallmark of those few beings who know that they will live forever.

Ate has bright tresses and a light step. She doesn't even touch the ground. She alights on men's heads and traps them in a net. "She tramples whatever is weak," then moves on to the next head. She doesn't even flinch before the gods. On one occasion Zeus was foolish enough to start boasting that Alcmene was about to bear him a son, Heracles. The words burst forth happily from his mind, but silent Ate had already slipped in there. The infatuated god swore an oath that his next descendant would reign over all his neighbors. With a single bound, Hera was down in Argos: she delayed Heracles' birth and speeded up that of another child descended from Zeus, Eurystheus. Thus for years and years Heracles would have to toil in the service of Eurystheus, who reigned over all his neighbors.

Homeric fairness doesn't distinguish between the fatal infatuations that befall the gods and those that befall men. The imperceptible tread of Ate's foot may alight on anyone's head. On this occasion, when Zeus discovered the trick, "a sharp pain stabbed into the depths of his mind," and he grabbed Ate by her tresses and hurled her to earth. Ate plunged down on top of a hill in Phrygia. There one day Troy would rise.

Anake, Necessity, who stands above everything in ancient Greece, even Olympus and its gods, was never to have a face. Homer does not personify her, but he does describe her three daughters, the Fates with their spindles; or the Erinyes, her emissaries; or Ate with her light feet. All female figures. There was only one place of worship dedicated to Ananke: on the slopes of the Acrocorinth, the mountain belonging to Aphrodite and her sacred prostitutes, stood a sanctuary to

Ananke and Bia, goddess of violence. "But there is a tradition not to enter the temple," remarks Pausanias. And, indeed, what could one ask of she who does not listen? The difference between gods and men can be grasped above all in their relationship to Ananke. The gods endure her and use her; men merely endure her.

While Achaeans and Trojans do battle, Zeus and Poseidon, the gods who rule sky and sea, are invisibly at work all around them. But what are they up to? "They are tightening that knot that cannot be broken or loosened, but which has loosened the knees of many." The warriors wave their swords in the empty air until they meet the obstacle that is their enemy. All move, caught in the same net, where innumerable threads are close to being tightened. When the knot is drawn tight, the warrior dies, even before the lethal metal touches him. What Zeus and Poseidon do on the plains of Troy is no different from what Hephaestus did to Ares and Aphrodite when he caught them in bed together, or even what Oceanus does in hugging the earth. Hephaestus's net was gold, as befitted an object in Olympus, but it was thin as a spider's web too, and invisible even to the gods who laughed as they watched the embarrassment of the captive lovers. Oceanus wraps the earth in nine liquid coils.

According to Parmenides, being itself is trapped by the "bonds of powerful Ananke's net." And in the Platonic vision of things, we find an immense light, "bound to the sky and embracing its whole circumference, the way hempen ropes are bound around the hulls of galleys." In each case knots and bonds are essential. Necessity is a bond that curves back on itself, a knotted rope (*peírar*) that holds everything within its limits (*péras*). *Deî*, a key word, meaning "it is necessary," appears for the first time in the *Iliad*: "Why is it necessary (*deî*) for the Argives to make war on the Trojans?" That verb form, governed by an impersonal subject, the *es* of everything that escapes an agent's will, is traced back by Onians to *déō*, "to bind," and not to *déō*, "to lack," as other philologists would have it. It is the same image, observes Onians, "that, without being aware of its meaning in the dark history of the race, we find in a common expression of our own language: 'it is bound to happen.'"

Let's put some pressure now on this word *anánkē*. Chantraine concludes that "no etymology grasps the real sense of *anánkē* and its derivations: 'constriction' and at the same time 'kinship.' The underlying notion that might justify this double semantic development would be that of the *bond*." Others see the word as being close to the idea of "taking in one's arms." When speaking of Heracles caught in the horrendous shirt of Nessus, the chorus in the *Trachiniae* begin: "If in the Centaur's murderous net, a *dolopoiòs anánkē* torments him . . ." But how are we to understand that *dolopoiòs anánkē*? A "deceitful embrace"? Or "deceitful necessity"? Or both? Once again we have the net, and necessity seen as a lethal embrace. With wonderful monotony, the net, its knots ever ready to tighten, is always there. It falls over Aphrodite's adulterous bed, over the battlefield beneath the walls of Troy, over being itself, and the cosmos, and the blistered body of Heracles. Whatever the situation, that one weapon is more than enough for Ananke. There were many in Greece who doubted the existence of the gods, but none ever expressed a doubt about that net, at once invisible and more powerful than the gods.

When Alexander arrived in Gordium, he went to the acropolis and found the cart that was tied to its yoke with a knot that no one had been able to undo. There was a legend about that cart, "which said that whoever untied the knot that bound the cart to its yoke would rule over all of Asia. The knot was tied with cornel bark, and it was impossible to find either beginning or end. Unable to untie the knot and not wanting to leave it as it was, in case his failure should spread disquiet through his army, some say that he sliced the knot cleanly with his sword and then claimed that he had untied it." But there's another version to the story, according to which Alexander "removed the belaying pin from the drawbar [this was a wooden pin forced into the drawbar and around which the knot was secured] and thus removed the yoke from the drawbar." Then Alexander and his followers "went away from the cart convinced that the oracle's predictions about the untying of the knot had been fulfilled." Thus, "the knot that can be neither broken nor loosened," the knot that Zeus and Poseidon tightened around the heads of the warriors beneath the walls of Troy, was not to be untied even by Alexander. Alexander, however, had come up with what would later be the obvious solution: to get around necessity by removing the pin in the drawbar. And as Alexander thus did what countless others would do after him, Greece itself fell apart. Alexander left, the knot remained intact, "with neither beginning nor end," but the cart had been separated from its yoke.

In the late pagan era we can still find this in Macrobius: "*amor osculo significatur, necessitas nodo*": "love is represented with a kiss, necessity with a knot." Two circular images, the mouth and the noose, embrace everything that is. Eros, "born when Ananke was lord and everything bowed before her gloomy will," once boasted that he had gained possession of the "Ogygian scepter," primordial as the waters of the Styx itself. He could now force "his own decrees upon the gods." But Eros said nothing of Ananke, who had come before him. There is a hostility between Eros and Ananke, a hostility that springs from an obscure likeness, as between the kiss and the knot.

Ananke belongs to the world of Kronos. Indeed she is his companion and sits with him on their polar throne as Zeus sits beside Hera in Olympus. That is why Ananke has no face, just as her divine spouse has no face. The figure, the mobile shape, will make its appearance only with the world that comes after theirs. The Olympian gods know that the law of Kronos has not been abrogated, nor can it ever be. But they don't want to feel it weighing down on them every second of every day. Olympus is a rebellion of lightness against the precision of the law, which at that time was referred to as *pondus et mensura*, "weight and measure." A vain rebellion, but divine. Kronos's chains become Hephaestus's golden web. The gods know that the two imprisoning nets are the same; what has changed is the aesthetic appearance. And it is on this that life on Olympus is based. Of the two, they prefer to submit to Eros rather than Ananke, even though they know that Eros is just a dazzling cover for Ananke. And cover in the literal sense: Ananke's inflexible bond, which tightens in a great circle around the world, is covered by a speckled belt, which we see in the sky as the Milky Way. But we can also see it, in perfect miniature, on the body of Aphrodite when the goddess wears her "many-hued, embroidered girdle in which all charms and spells reside: tenderness and desire are there, and softly whispered words, the seduction that has stolen the intellect even from those of sound mind."

Unraveled across the darkness of the sky, that belt denotes not deceit but the splendor of the world. Worn by Aphrodite, the girdle becomes both splendor and deceit. But perhaps this was precisely what the Olympians wanted: that a soft, deceiving sash should cover the inflexible bond of necessity. So it was that, when the time was ripe, Zeus overthrew Kronos with deceit: and now that girdle adorned the waist of Aphrodite.

Why did the Olympians prefer the girdle of deceit to the serpent of necessity, coiled around the cosmos? They were looking for a more colorful life, a life with more play. After millennia of astral submission, they preferred to make believe that they were subject to Eros just as much as to Ananke, though all the time aware that in fact this was just a blasphemous fraud. Sophocles' Deianira says as much, as if it were obvious: "The gods bow to Eros's every whim, and so must I."

If Ananke commands alone, life becomes rigid and ritualistic. And the Olympians were not fond of Mesopotamian gravity, although they did enjoy their sacrifices. What they wanted for themselves was not just eternal life but childish insouciance. When the time had come to be rid of the heroes, a plague would have been quite enough to settle the matter. But a war, a long, complicated war, was far more attractive. So the gods set about starting it off and then making it last. Zeus, from his vantage point in the sky, wouldn't have been interested in watching the ravages of a plague. But when Trojans and Achaeans return to the battlefield, he is eager to watch them, and sometimes even to suffer with them: he sees Sarpedon, for him "the dearest of men," come to the end of the role that "had been assigned him of old," and he can do nothing to spare him the mortal blows of Patroclus. For a moment Zeus imagines he might be able to "snatch him alive" from the battle. It is a moment of sublime Olympian childishness, which Hera immediately crushes. And as she does so we hear Ananke, disguised as a wise administrator, speaking through her.

But war is a spectacle for all the Olympians, not just for Zeus. As the battle approached, "Athena and Apollo, with their silver bows, alighted like vultures on the tall oak of Zeus, who holds the aegis, and enjoyed the sight of the men in their serried ranks, a shiver trembling across shields, helmets, and javelins."

The Achaean warriors advance, legs and thighs white with dust. The heavy hooves of their horses churn up clouds of it into a bronze sky. Here and there the terrain is sandy. Mydon crashes from his chariot and sticks for a moment, head in the sand, legs in the air, until his own horses trample him into the dust. Two female figures move about in the din of battle. They are Eris, Strife, and Enyo, the War Cry. Eris wears a long, dark, checkered tunic with a pattern of circles and crosses. The same color is picked up in her broad, soft wings. Her arms are naked and white. Enyo is glistening with sweat. Hers is the "shameless uproar of the slaughter." She delights, they say, in "the blood-sodden clay."

. . .

There is a moment in which the peculiarly Greek breaks
away from the Asian continent, like one of those islands off
the Anatolian coast whose jagged cliffs still follow the line
of the vast maternal mainland. That moment is the Greek
discovery of outline, of a new sharpness, a clean, dry daylight. It is the moment when man enters into Zeus, into the
clear light of noon. *Éndios* is what we have when "the earth
warmed up / And the sky glittered more brilliantly than
crystal." By the time of the tragedians, *dîos* has come to
mean nothing more than "divine," insofar as it is a "property of Zeus." But in the Homeric age *dîos* means first and
foremost "clear," "brilliant," "glorious." To appear in Zeus
is to glow with light against the background of the sky. Light
on light. When Homer gives the epithet *dîos* to his characters, the word does not refer first of all to what they may
have of "divine," but to the clarity, the splendor that is always with them and against which they stand out. The
leaden eyes of the Sumers are the eyes of nocturnal birds;
they sink away into the darkness. With foot arched, and the
corners of his mouth upturned in an inexplicable smile, the
Homeric hero pushes on toward the smoking earth, and his
folly is the Pan-inspired madness of high noon. Before the
hour strikes, he achieves a vision of things as sharply separate from one another and complete in themselves as
though scissored from the sky by cosmic shears and thrust
out into a light from which there is no escape.

In its dark age, after four hundred years with neither writing
nor cultural center, Greece rediscovered splendor. In Homer
whatever is good and beautiful is also dazzling. Breastplates
shine from afar, bodies from close up. Yet around them,
while the bards were chanting the *Iliad*, the Greeks had very
little that was splendid to enjoy. Gone the high-vaulted palaces, all burned, all ravaged. Gone the Asian jewels. Gone
the embossed gold goblets. Gone the grand chariots of war.
The splendor was all in the mind. Among the objects they
handled were jars and vases where the same geometric fig-

ures were stubbornly repeated over and over, as if all at once
the Greeks had decided there was only one thing that mattered: outline, the sharp, the angular profile, separation. On
the immense urn found in the Dipylon, one band of geometric patterns follows hard on another, until framed between them we find a scene with human figures. It is a
funeral, and the men are black, faceless silhouettes, their
muscles in sharp relief. The corpse lies on a long coffin, like
a dangerous insect. The Homeric radiance and the sharp
profile of that insect presuppose each other, balance each
other off. In all surviving evidence of archaic Greece, the one
is included in the other.

Every notion of progress is refuted by the existence of the
Iliad. The perfection of the first step makes any idea of progressive ascension ridiculous. But at the same time the *Iliad*
is an act of provocation as far as forms and shapes are concerned; it defies them and draws them into a fan that has
yet to be fully opened. And this state is thanks precisely to
the commanding sharpness with which the poem excludes,
even expels from within itself, what for centuries to come
would be articulated in language. That perfect beginning,
through its very appearance, evokes absent counterweights:
Mallarmé.

Odysseus stands out among the Achaean leaders because he
"can think." The others revere his complex mind the way
they revere the fleet foot of Achilles. But this doesn't make
Odysseus feel any more independent of the gods than his
peers. He doesn't have the solid eloquence of Diomedes, or
the rounded periods of Nestor, but he looks for the propitious moment, when he can get the gods' attention with a
word, and not a word too many. Odysseus is he who can
"escape from a burning brazier." In the word that gives us
that "escape" (*nostésaimen*) we get close to the meaning of
"coming back" (*nóstos*): to escape unharmed is to come

back. And no one is capable of coming back like Odysseus. There is something firm, solid, but never mentioned, on which the hero knows he can always fall back and put his weight, even when his wanderings take him far from home. That this is only a small island in the mind gives us a sense of the spatial relationship between that rocky splinter and the vast surrounding seascape. Yet that small, tough mental outcrop, like the hero's broad chest, is something that will resist, a constant support. Odysseus experiences fire, faces it, defies it. But more than that, and unlike so many other men and women who live close to the divine, Odysseus *is able to escape* the fire. That is why the powerful Diomedes feels safer in the dark if he has Odysseus beside him, like a watchful shadow.

In what is the darkest of all nights for the Achaeans, when they have been pushed back to their ships by a counter-attack from the besieged Trojans and when, with Diomedes, he is about to set out on a dangerous mission to steal secrets from the enemy camp, Odysseus hears the cry of a heron unseen in the night. It's Athena alerting him to her presence. And Odysseus speaks to the goddess, who has always been at his side. He speaks just a few brief, intimate words, less than half of what Diomedes will say immediately afterward. Odysseus doesn't remind her of paternal precedents, nor does he promise sacrifices. He says to the goddess: "One more time, Athena, love me, as much as you can."

Between the ingenuous ostentation of Diomedes and the spare directness of Odysseus a story would open up that was to take centuries of repetitions and subversions to work itself out. But that night the two are still united, just as the "awesome weapons" the heroes only a moment ago belted on are still brushing against each other. And the goddess is still equally present to each of them. They communicate with her before they talk to each other. She is "the fire of heaven," in which the Greeks share, before the sobriety of Odysseus crosses it, unharmed, before that sobriety is left to survive alone, with no memory of the fire it once crossed, no memory of its antique familiarity with a goddess who once let the hero insist that she love him, "one more time, as much as you can."

Achilles is unique, and hence also an only child, "nature's *enfant gâté.*" Six brothers before him died thanks to their mother Thetis's attempts to render them immortal. They did not survive her trial by fire. The flames that licked Achilles made him *almost* immortal. And what that meant was more mortal than other mortals. He was destined to have a shorter life than others because, for Thetis, he took the place of the son who was supposed to overthrow Zeus and who was never born. Instead of a god who would live longer than other gods, he became a man who would have a shorter life than other men. And yet, of all men, he was the closest to being a god. Because he had taken the place of he who should have put an end to Zeus, his own end was forcibly etched into his flesh. Achilles is time in its purest state, drumming hooves galloping away. Compressed into the piercing fraction of a mortal life span, he came closest to having the qualities the Olympians lived and breathed: intensity and facility. His furious temper, which sets the *Iliad* moving, is more intense than that of any other warrior, and the fleetness of his foot is that of one who cleaves the air without meeting resistance.

No hero was on more intimate terms with women than Achilles. At nine he was playing in Scyros as a girl among other girls, and it was only the blast of Odysseus's trumpet that woke him from his girlish dream. Born of a sea goddess, brought up by two Naiads, Achilles' girl companions nicknamed him Pyrrha, the Blonde, the tawny blonde. Thus he enjoyed a bliss never granted to any other male: that of being at once a girl and a seducer of girls. Ostensibly, he was a foreign girl playing with the daughters of Lycomedes, but the oldest of those daughters, Deidameia, soon gave birth to the child of their "secret passion": Neoptolemus.

There was a meadow on windswept Scyros, beneath a tower, and here Lycomedes' daughters would gather armfuls of flowers. They had an open expression in their eyes, round cheeks, a dashing gait. Playing with them, Achilles could be distinguished only by the brusque way he would toss back his hair.

His boyhood loves behind him, women would come to spell death for Achilles. And death would be with him always. The dog days dragged on in Aulis, and the restless heroes exercised outside their tents to kill the time. Achilles was fantasizing "a thousand girls" came "hunting to his bed" when the girl who claimed she was destined to share his marriage bed appeared: Iphigenia.

It was an appalling equivocation: her father, Agamemnon, had used the marriage as a bait to lure her to her death as a sacrificial victim. Upon which Clytemnestra said to Achilles: "It would be a woeful omen for your future marriage if my daughter were to be killed." The omen remained suspended in the air, intact.

From then on, Achilles' passions, which had begun as child's play, would be framed and smothered in blood. And, like Iphigenia, Achilles himself would be killed with a fake nuptial crown on his head. Agamemnon's trick prefigured something nobody had imagined, least of all Agamemnon himself, something that linked Iphigenia to Achilles. One writer even claims they had a child. If so, they must have had it without ever having been together, except in the sense that they were both lured into the same fatal trap.

There was a time when hierogamy and sacrifice were the same thing. In the course of history, this unnameable unity gradually split into two. In the beginning, the primordial god would copulate and kill himself at the same time. Men recalling this feat could hardly emulate it if they wanted to survive and were thus forced to divide it into two phases:

killing and copulation, sacrifice and marriage. But the flavor
of marriage lingers on in the sacrifice, just as the flavor of
the sacrifice lingers on in marriage. A tangible object unites
the two events: the crown. One is crowned whether going to
the altar as a victim or going as a bride. And the ambiguity
of that crown is the constant, never articulated heart of tragedy: the misunderstandings, recognitions, and double
meanings that tense the tragic nerve all derive from the primordial double meaning contained within the crown.

It would be ingenuous to suppose that only the moderns
have been able to appreciate all this, as if in classical tragedy
it had always remained implicit and unconscious. On the
contrary, this notion seems to have formed the canonical
background underlying tragedy. Otherwise, to quote just
one example, why would Euripides' chorus in *Iphigenia in
Aulis* move so abruptly from the evocation of Peleus and
Thetis's marriage, at which the gods are among the guests,
to the description of Iphigenia as a "spotted heifer" from
whose "mortal throat blood will be made to flow" in Aulis,
where her father claims to be bringing her to her marriage.
That truncated passage, split into two dismembered parts,
marriage and sacrifice, is, as Euripides saw it, one single
speech: and we pass from one part to the other of necessity,
because they belong together. In the same way, the ancient
texts make perfectly clear that the tension of tragedy is the
tension between murder and sacrifice, the crushing of the
one against the other or, alternatively, the splitting apart of
the two terms. In fact, all the surviving tragedies could be
classified according to the angle of impact between murder
and sacrifice or according to the varying densities of ambiguity in the way the two phenomena are presented. In
Iphigenia in Aulis we are hammered time after time with the
verb *kteínein*, "to kill," while *thúein*, "to sacrifice," is used
only rarely, the distance between the two being spanned by
spházein, "to slit a throat." Yet the plot to this tragedy
hinges on a sacrifice, not a murder. Whereas *Agamemnon*,
which tells the story of a murder, is saturated in the terminology of sacrifice.

When Iphigenia agrees to her own sacrifice, agrees, as she puts it, "to this wicked spilling of blood by a wicked father," because "the whole of Greece is looking to her" and her death will allow "the Greeks to reign over the barbarians rather than the barbarians over the Greeks," for "the barbarians stand for slavery, the Greeks for freedom"—when a speech like this pours rapidly, confidently, from the mouth of the virgin of Mycenae, it's clear that any cosmic vision of sacrifice has already foundered. Sacrifice here no longer has to do with the equilibrium between gods and men but between men and other men, between "the kings of men" and that dangerous multitude milling around the tents.

But here comes the outrageous enigma: man now discovers that sacrifice is just as effective as a tool of social manipulation as it was to appease the gods. Any cosmic tension evaporates. What we're left with is an unsuspecting girl whose throat is to be cut before an army mad with the lust to be setting sail for an almighty bloodletting (it's Aphrodite, not Ares, who's goading them on). And that killing turns out to be very useful. It is the first *pro patria mori*, and it stands apart from all the others and dwarfs them, just as Pericles' speech on democracy dwarfs thousands of later speeches on the subject. Even before the Achaeans hoisted their sails for Troy, Iphigenia's body had been used as the medium for a radical secularization of the practice of sacrifice. The gods were still there, intact, but man's relationship with them was now taking on the same spareness and pathos as that between daughter and father, servant and master, lover and beloved, husband and wife. The only thing that separated heaven and earth now was an immense inequality in terms of power. Not an inequality of mind, or heart, or ceremony at all. With all the cosmic scaffolding that had stood between gods and men having thus collapsed, life seemed the more buoyant and resplendent, but lonely too, fleeting and irretrievable. Such is the dominant sentiment that runs through the lucid age of Greece from Homer to Euripides. Everything is reduced to a few simple elements that can be reduced no further. Life is no longer a

series of trade-offs between invisible powers but "the sweetness of looking at the light." Thus speaks the *philopsychia*
in Iphigenia, that last "clutching at life." And her conclusion is brusque: "To look into the light is the sweetest thing
for a mortal; what lies beneath the earth is nothingness."

This brazen speech, the daring claim that the whole world
of spirits is "nothingness," points to the affinity that predestined the girl to be Achilles' bride. For the defiant words
she hurls at Agamemnon as she is about to die prefigure
Achilles' answer to Odysseus in the underworld, his scorn
for any vain sovereignty over the dead and his heartrending
desire for a part, however miserable, in the life above.

The whole classical world, from the Minoan frescoes to the
Roman banquets, is strewn with leafy crowns. To be a *co-
ronarius* in Rome was to have a profitable business, since
crowns were used on all kinds of occasions. "In the olden
times," Pliny recalls, "crowns were used to show respect for
the gods and the Lares, public and private, the tombs and
the Manes." Then there were crowns for the statues of the
gods, for sacrificial victims, and for brides and bridegrooms.
Crowns for the winning athletes at the games. Crowns for
poets and soldiers who excelled. Crowns worn for fun at
banquets. Lovers would hang crowns on their beloveds'
doors. And Cleopatra even had the idea of poisoning Antony
with the petals of a crown. From the Egyptian mummies to
the Christian polemicists, who tried to avoid this pagan
usage but lapsed back into it just the same, you could say
that the Mediterranean world lived and moved for centuries
within that circular image, those symbolic but ephemeral
flowers, different for every occasion. Such was the ubiqui-
tousness of the crown that a whole literature sprang up
around it. Few other subjects seemed so well suited to con-
tests of erudition between sophists at banquets. But, if we
look behind their relaxed chatter to the origin of the crown,
what do we find?

The first crown was a gift from Zeus to Prometheus. It

thus came from the gods as homage to a man whose relationship with them was anything but clear, at once a threat
and a means of salvation. The crown in fact was supposed
to compensate for the fetters in which Zeus himself had long
imprisoned Prometheus. The cold grip of the metal was thus
transformed into what Aeschylus calls "the best of all fetters": a circular weave of leaves, twigs, and flowers. It was
the same process by which Aphrodite's many-colored girdle
had come to be superimposed over Ate's suffocating net.
And, just as deceit was woven into Aphrodite's girdle, in the
crown of Prometheus we can see deceit throwing down its
ultimate challenge. Hyginus writes: "*Nonnulli etiam coronam habuisse dixerunt, ut se victorem impune peccasse
diceret*": "Some say that [Prometheus] got hold of a crown,
so that he could claim to have triumphed, unpunished for
his crime." Like the girdle of Aphrodite, Prometheus's
crown is the fetter of necessity. Except that now, dispersed
in petals and transformed by beauty, that fetter approaches
the delicate superfluousness of ornament. The veil of aesthetic appearance can conceal beneath it even the gamble
of the man who attempts to elude necessity, the man who
still seeks an impunity *anánkē* does not concede. Or so Hyginus insinuates.

Aeschylus, however, has a different vision of events. He
describes the crown given to Prometheus as an *antípoina*, a
"retribution," which is also a ransom. Prometheus had
earned his ransom by revealing to Zeus that, if he had a
child with Thetis, it would overthrow him. Hence, having
first deceived the god, Prometheus had then saved him. And
now he was to remain among men and bring them a second
revelation, after that of fire: the crown. From chain to
crown: it was still a fetter of a kind; anything strong that
grips us is a fetter. But now the fetter had been lightened;
it became fragile and soft, gently encircling the head, for
"all our feelings are in our heads." What did that vegetable
weave conceal, then, that was so precious? Perfection. It was
the Greek gift par excellence, the goal this people always
sought.

It would be a long time before crowns were being handed out at banquets. In the beginning, it was the idea of separation that was essential. Forerunner of the magic circle, the crown divided the world in two: there was the sacred fragment within the crown (sacrificial victim, spouse, or statue) and everything else outside. "Everything that belonged to the cult, whether people, animals, victims, or symbols, would be marked out by a crown or a band, as a sign of consecration, and often by both crown and band." At this point the crown was "herald of the holy silence," prelude to the sacrificial killing. But, having begun with this cult use, the Greeks developed the crown in a way all their own. The sacred is something that impregnates, it pours into the young girl, the animal, the statue, and fills them. Hence the sacred comes to partake of fullness, and fullness with perfection, since as Aristotle puts it, "we offer to the gods only that which is perfect and whole." The *Iliad* speaks of "youths who filled [or crowned: *epestépsanto*] the bowls with wine." The crown was the rim of the goblet, the point at which fullness becomes excess. The crown was a mobile *templum*, bringing together election and danger. The perfect brings death upon itself, since one can't have fullness without spillage, and what spills out is the excess that sacrifice claims for itself. "What is full, is perfect, and coronation signifies perfection of some kind." So says Athenaeus. Animals for sacrifice would only be crowned once it was clear that they were perfect, "so as not to kill something that was not useful."

At first the crown enclosed the sacred, separating it off from the profane world. In the end, it enclosed the perfect in its self-sufficient fullness. With a deft and unspoken shifting of contexts, the Greeks removed the crown from blood and sacrifice. They wanted it to celebrate what was perfect in its own right. From now on it would not form part of a ceremony that was acted out but would celebrate something that simply existed in itself. The crown is nothing less than the highest, the most exposed level of existence. Sappho says to Dika: "Weave stems of anise with your soft hands and top your curls with sweet crowns; for the blessed Charites prefer to look at those adorned with flowers, and turn away from whoever is without a crown to wear." By this point, Dika is perfection itself, attracting the benevolent gaze of the Charites. We've come a long way from Iphigenia, who believed she was wearing her crown as a bride, whereas in fact that crown singled her out as the victim to be slain on the altar.

The Greeks escaped from the sacred to the perfect, trusting in the sovereignty of the aesthetic. It would be a desperately brief escape, one that lasted only as long as the tension between sacred and perfect could be maintained, only as long as the sacred and perfect were able to live side by side without taking anything away from each other. But no other people had attempted so much. If it is in Sappho that we first find a crown that seems to attract the gaze of the Charites purely for itself, if it is with her that the ritual use first appears to become a pretext for aesthetic polish, then we owe this carefree immediacy not to *tò kalón*, too serious a matter altogether, but to *habrosýnē*, a word that did not catch on among philosophers and which one can only translate today by mixing notions such as delicacy and splendor, grace and luxury. "I love *habrosýnē*," says Sappho in another line, and perhaps it is the only one of her confessions we have no cause to doubt.

Crown, necklace, garland: they all have the same shape, and often the one will become the other. When Amphiaraus left his palace in Corinth to fight beneath the walls of Thebes, he knew perfectly well, clairvoyant as he was, that the adventure would end in his death. It was only the treachery of his wife, Eriphyle, that had managed to winkle him out of concealment and force him to go to the field of Polynices: in return for her betrayal, Polynices gave Eriphyle the necklace that had once been Aphrodite's gift to Harmony. In the courtyard of the palace, as the horses tugged at their reins, impatient to be off, with helmet already on his head and sword pointing heavenward, Amphiaraus turned to look back one last time. And what he looked at most of all was his young son, Alcmaeon. He had already patiently explained to the child how one day he would have to kill his mother to avenge the father who was now saying good-bye forever. The boy hadn't seemed to be paying attention, laughing and fooling about as he listened, but his father's words would haunt his memory like a refrain from a nursery rhyme. Amphiaraus looked at him now, naked, healthy, arms raised to wave good-bye, against a backdrop of women. Behind him other arms were waving, white arms, Demonassa and Eurydice, his daughters. Then the bony arms of the old wet nurse. And behind them all, head wrapped in a shawl, Eriphyle: Amphiaraus met her cold stare, which rivaled his own in its hatred. One of her arms was hidden: she didn't lift it to wave, and, from the fingers of that hand, huge and brilliant, hung Harmony's necklace, a garland of golden light dangling almost to the ground.

In scenes like these, which mark the beginning of the end of a noble house, each respects his own role, as if everything were perfectly normal, even though all are aware of the impending disaster. But outside the group there will always be one person crouching down, a hand lifted to his head. It is he who sees but cannot act. One day he will become the tragic poet, he will tell these stories. But for the moment he is silent. To the unpracticed eye there is nothing out of the ordinary about the scene: the head of a family is riding off to war, a common enough event. Only the observer who kept his eyes on the ground would have realized that something terrible was happening. For the courtyard is swarming with animals: fearless lizards slither between people's legs; a hedgehog is in danger of being crushed under Amphiaraus's heel; a majestically large scorpion is climbing slowly along the groove of one of the columns of the atrium; a nervous, trembling hare rubs its flank along the chariot; an owl has alighted on a horse's mane; and, amid the stones outside the courtyard, a snake lifts its head, motionless, and watches.

Many generations passed, and the story of Amphiaraus

and Eryphyle was turned into verse and widely discussed. Now, after all the trouble it had caused, Harmony's necklace, like the necklace Menelaus gave to Helen, was kept in the temple of Delphi. During the second Sacred War, the Phocians sacked the temple and their leaders decided to share out the famous jewels among their wives. They drew lots to see who got what. Eryphyle's necklace went to "a woman who looked sad and resentful, though deeply serious, while Helen's went to a woman of outstanding beauty and loose morals. The latter fell in love with a young man from Epirus and ran off with him, while the other hatched a plot to kill her husband." The woman who eloped later sank to prostitution, "throwing her beauty at anyone who wished to abuse her." The woman who killed her husband was burned alive in her own home. The fire was started by her eldest son, who had gone crazy.

The necklace, the crown, the garland. As the years passed the leaves and petals of beauty fell away, leaving only the cold fetter of the circle, unadorned necessity; and what once had given rise to whole cycles of stories, the Theban cycle, the Trojan cycle, now shrank back into the stuff of commonplace crime where the protagonists remain nameless and only the bare events are remembered: an elopement, a murder, in a Greece that had nothing to look forward to now but its capitulation to Alexander and wanted only to forget the past. But all of this, and no less than this, was of the nature of the crown, the necklace, the garland.

In the girdle of Aphrodite, in the crown, in the body of Helen and of her phantom, beauty is superimposed over necessity, cloaking it in deceit. The necessary has a certain splendor, and behind any splendor one senses a metallic coldness, as though of a weapon poised to strike. The real split in Greek consciousness, like all the other irreversible steps it took, comes when Plato for the first time affirms, "How very different is the nature of the necessary from the nature of the good." And he means an immense, an unbridgeable distance—the same distance that made atheists of "those who study astronomy and other sciences of the necessary, when they see that what is, is so out of necessity and not out of any plan conceived by some will to accomplish the good." The Beautiful, in this scenario, must either be quickly reabsorbed into the Good—as its agent, instrument, and pedagogue—or left up in the air, like a malignant spell (*goéteuma*) bewitching the mind only to subject it even more helplessly to the fiat of necessity. With Homer we are still at a stage when the Good isn't even mentioned: happy and unhappy, the poet's warriors know only the many-colored weave of necessity and sate themselves with its splendor, which at the end of the day will destroy them. "The mortal cannot go intrepid through these many-colored beauties," says Agamemnon, a few seconds before falling beneath Clytemnestra's ax.

Agamemnon, *ánax andrôn*, "king of men," is kingship itself. As such, he must preside over relations with heaven and with earth. It is on him that all exchanges converge. And at the origin of exchange there is always a death of some kind. Such is the shove that sets the wheel moving, that breaks "the silence of the winds." For Agamemnon, this becomes clear with the sacrifice of his daughter Iphigenia. The person who controls the mechanism of exchange, the king, is that unique person who must sacrifice the uniqueness of every other, including his daughter. But this one master of exchanges, prince of substitutions, may in turn be attacked by uniqueness. When the priest Chryses asks to ransom his daughter Chryseis and, to replace her, Agamemnon demands that Achilles hand over Briseis, uniqueness rises in rebellion against exchange.

Achilles is kingship without a kingdom. He carries his grace within himself and does not need a hierarchical order to sustain it. It is in his grace, not his power, that Achilles is more kingly than the others. And that is precisely why Agamemnon is so determined to show him who is really king, as Nestor explains with near pedantic exactness: "Son of Peleus, don't be so stubborn as to clash head on with a king: no prestige can equal that of a king who holds the scepter, a king to whom Zeus has granted glory. You are strong, your mother is a goddess; but he is even stronger than you, because he commands more men." On the one hand, we have a king who is considered such because a whole society converges on his person; on the other hand, we have an individual who is kingly in his very isolation, in the uniqueness of his gift. With Achilles we witness, in Homeric radiance, the emergence of a quality that Vedic mathematics never guessed at: the unique, unsustained by the sacred, precarious, fleeting, irreplaceable, not exchangeable, entrusted to a brief appearance ending in death, and for this very reason incommensurable. That which exists only once, and for only a short time, cannot be measured against any other commodity.

Shut away in his tent, furious with Agamemnon, Achilles sleeps with Diomeda "of the lovely cheeks," just as Briseis had been "of the lovely cheeks." But still Achilles refuses to accept the substitution of Briseis. The elderly Phoenix, who loves Achilles as only an old servant whose chest the baby hero once belched wine over can, simply does not understand this absurd insistence. How can Achilles, "for just one girl!" turn down the seven girls of Lesbos, plus "some even better ones," together with a host of other gifts Agamemnon is offering to keep him sweet. Phoenix, in his tribal devotion, can't even conceive of the claim to uniqueness. But it is precisely to Achilles that the poem gives the speech that for the first time announces this discovery, this emotion that will put its stamp on history from that moment on and has survived intact to this very day: a foothold in the vast shipwreck of ideas, the only thing still self-evident to everybody, blasphemous and devout alike, in this age that no longer manages to be either blasphemous or devout. This is what Achilles says: "Fat sheep and oxen you can steal; cooking pots and golden-maned horses you can buy; but once it has left the circle of his teeth, the life of a man [*andròs psyché*] can be neither replaced, nor stolen, nor bought." Not only have these words never been confuted with the passing centuries, but they have gathered further intensity and urgency, as beliefs and principles withered away all around to leave them standing alone. Today, whenever somebody who doesn't belong to any creed refuses to kill, Achilles' words live on in him.

The aesthetic justification of existence was not an invention of the young Nietzsche. He was just the first to give it a name. Earlier, it had been the tacit premise of life in Greece under the Olympians. Perfection of the outward appearance was indissolubly linked to the acceptance of a life without redemption, without salvation, without hope of repetition, circumscribed by the precarious wonder of its brief apparition. Achilles is the son of a goddess, and this fact gives him a strength and grace unknown to others, but he chooses a brief and resplendent life, which is irrecoverable.

Rather than the life of one individual, the life Achilles chooses is an image of all life as Homer understood it. Later, in the underworld, Achilles comes out with a speech that offers a mirror image of the one he made when refusing Agamemnon's gifts. The hero now appears as just one among many, "unfeeling shades of exhausted mortals." All that's left of life is a long weariness. Odysseus tries to call him "happy," even among the dead, and claims to admire him because even here he has preserved his "great power." But once again Achilles is ready with words that will prove unanswerable: "Don't try to prettify death for me, noble Odysseus. I would rather live as a cowherd in the service of a poor peasant, with barely enough to eat, than reign over all these wasted dead." It is only because life is irretrievable and irrepeatable that the glory of appearance can reach such intensity. Here there is no hidden meaning, no reference to, nor hint of, anything else, such as the Platonic tyranny will later impose. Here appearance is everything, is the essential integrity of what exists only for the brief period when it is present and visible. It is a fleeting figure briefly capturing the perfection of those other figures who live on unhindered, on Olympus.

On two occasions, before the beginning and after the end of the Trojan War, Agamemnon finds himself obliged to preside over the sacrifice of a virgin. The first time it is his daughter Iphigenia, whom he lures to Aulis by pretending to offer her in marriage to Achilles. The second time it is the Trojan Polyxena, who Achilles thought he was going to meet and marry in the temple where, hiding behind a column, treacherous Apollo kills him. Iphigenia is sacrificed because the long, windless calm is preventing the Achaean ships from leaving; Polyxena is sacrificed because the long, windless calm is preventing the Achaean ships from returning. In the case of Iphigenia, the deceived bride, Achilles tries to oppose the sacrifice; in the case of Polyxena, Achilles, the deceived groom, reappears as a ghost to claim his victim.

Right from the beginning, the lives of Agamemnon and Achilles run in perfect parallel. Agamemnon is never the cause of the sacrifice, but it is always he who carries it out, with a watchful eye on the multitude who obey him and who are kept under control by these gestures. His concern is that murder should be sufficiently well camouflaged as sacrifice, until he himself is murdered like a sacrificial beast by Clytemnestra. There is a circularity in his destiny that allows of no deviation. Achilles opposes him every step of the way: it is he who is about to marry the victim of both sacrifices. The first time, alive, he rejects the sacrifice; the second, dead, he demands it. Agamemnon carries out the law of men; Achilles wants to escape the will of the gods, or to assume their role himself. Agamemnon does not touch the victim but gives orders for her to be killed; it will be Neoptolemus, Achilles' son, who actually plunges his knife into Polyxena's throat. Agamemnon is death's administrator; for Achilles, death is always either too attractive or too repugnant. At the two extremes of the stage stand the two heroes. In the center, in ceremonial silence, the two sacrifices that open and close the Trojan War are consummated.

This is how Iphigenia is sacrificed: "After the prayer, Agamemnon made a sign to the servants officiating with him to seize his daughter Iphigenia just as she was falling to the ground wrapped in her tunics, then to lift her on top of the altar like a goat and with mute violence stop her mouth with its fine line like the prow of a ship, using a gag [or a horse bit?], so that she might not curse her family. Her saffrondyed tunic having slithered to the ground, Iphigenia's eyes darted arrows at each of her sacrificers, moving them to pity, as though she were a painting that wanted to speak, she who had so often sung at banquets in the beautiful halls of her father's palace, lovingly intoning in her pure virgin voice the third good-luck paean to her beloved father."

This is how Polyxena is sacrificed: "The people cheered her, and King Agamemnon told the young men to let go of the virgin. . . . When she heard the king's words, Polyxena grabbed her tunic and tore it from her shoulder right down to her waist, near her navel, so that everybody could see her beautiful breasts and torso. She was like a statue. And sinking to one knee, she spoke the boldest and saddest speech of all: 'Look, young man, here is my breast; if you want to strike here, then strike; if you would prefer the neck, then here is my throat, ready.' And he, Neoptolemus, both wishing and, out of pity for the girl, not wishing to, cut her windpipe with his knife. The blood gushed out. Yet, even as she died, she was most careful to fall in proper fashion, hiding what must be hidden from the eyes of men." After which some of the warriors scattered leaves on the girl. A scholiast notes in the margin: "They throw leaves over Polyxena, as if she had won an event at the games: for this was the way they congratulated the winners."

Achilles always seeks out the woman who is hostile and distant. He fell in love with Polyxena when he saw her on the walls of Troy throwing down buckles and earrings as ransom for the return of Hector's body. This was the woman Achilles was to die for. The nuptial crown on his head, he went into the temple of Apollo Thymbraeus, the same temple where he had killed one of Polyxena's brothers, Troilus. Apollo was supposed to be a witness to the marriage. Instead, hidden behind a column, the god let fly the arrow that struck Achilles' heel. It was a story of intertwining betrayals. How could Achilles have imagined that the god who had always been opposed to him would now be a benevolent witness at his marriage to one of Priam's daughters? And what were his Achaean comrades supposed to make of his decision? Achilles is capable of betrayal but not of reflecting on it: his actions are impulsive surges, changing direction unexpectedly. Thus he rains a frenzy of blows onto the body of Penthesilea, convinced he is slaying a mighty Trojan warrior not even Ajax had been able to handle. Then he lifts the helm of the dying Amazon. He looks Penthesilea in the eye for the first time, precisely as he plunges his sword into her breast. And in that instant he is overwhelmed by passion. He had pinned the Amazon to her horse. Now he takes the virgin warrior in his arms with loving care. In the dust and blood, Achilles made love to Penthesilea, lifeless in her armor.

The hideous Thersites was fool enough to laugh over that rape. Achilles slew him with a punch. He insisted that Penthesilea have the same funeral honors as Patroclus. He crossed the battlefield with the Amazon's body on his back. And once again the Achaeans were against him. Furious over the death of his relative Thersites, Diomedes tried to throw Penthesilea's body into the river Scamander, dragging her away by one foot. The others, shouting and screaming, wanted to toss her to the dogs. That woman was the closest thing to himself Achilles had ever come across. But he didn't find out until a moment after he had killed her. She was hostile, and dead: everything Achilles loved in a woman.

.　.　.

Beneath the walls of Troy, Achilles loved Briseis, Penthesilea, Polyxena. And each time his love met with a sorry end. But there was another woman constantly on his mind, a woman he had never even seen: Helen. As he camped in his pine hut on the plain of Ilium, he thought of Helen as the woman who "sends shivers down the spine." But at night he dreamed of her, "tossing and turning on his bed at the apparition of her imagined face." There are those who claim that, like two crafty pimps, Tethys and Aphrodite arranged a meeting between Achilles and Helen during one of the truces. But most believe that the two only saw each other after Achilles' death. Helen was a phantom as she always had been. Achilles became her fifth husband.

On leaving the Danube for the open sea, sailors must pass by Leuke, the White Island. They see a coastline of dunes, rocks, and woods. It's an island for castaways and people who want to offer up a sacrifice. No one has ever dared stay there after sundown. And no woman has ever trod its sandy beaches. The only building on the island is a temple with two statues: Achilles and Helen. Piled inside are heaps of precious votive gifts. The temple guards are sea gulls. Every morning they wet their wings in the sea and sprinkle water on the stones. And with their wings they sweep the floor. Achilles lives on the island as Helen's fifth husband. Some have seen him appear in the dazzling armor that once blinded Homer with its brilliance. Around the statues, visitors have seen Ajax Telamonius and Ajax Oileus, Patroclus and Antilochus. At night they chant the poetry of Homer in high, clear voices. Sometimes, when boats drop anchor off the beach, the sailors hear a drumming of horses' hooves, the clashing of weapons, and cries of warriors.

Helen ends in whiteness, as in whiteness she began. The foam of the waves from which Aphrodite was born dried and hardened to become the white shell of a swan's egg, which was then tossed "into a swampy place." The mobile immensity of the sea had shrunk to a patch of stagnant water, surrounded by reeds. When that egg hatched in the swamp, Helen appeared. Some authors say the Dioscuri were huddled in the same egg. So right from the start, Helen, the unique one, is linked to the notion of twinship and division. The unique one appears as the Double. When people speak of Helen, we can never know whether they are referring to her body or her phantom copy.

Like the young Spartan women, she used to play outside with the boys, "thighs naked and tunics lifting in the wind, around the racetrack and in the gymnasium." One day an Athenian was passing by with a friend, and stopped to look at her. "At that the all-knowing Theseus quite rightly became excited, and even to so great a man you seemed a worthy prey (*digna rapina*) to carry off, as you sported in the gymnasium, glistening with oil, a nude girl among nude boys, as was the custom among your people." Helen had met her first man. She was twelve years old, Theseus was fifty. He sodomized her and shut her away on the rock of Aphidna. Theseus's mother, Aethra, lived there, and Helen was soon entrusted to her, because Theseus was impatient to be off on his adventures with Peirithous again. They were planning to go down to Hades this time. The twins Castor and Pollux were furious and promptly set off in search of their sister. When they arrived on Aphidna, Theseus had already gone. They besieged the rock and got Helen back. Among the slaves they took away was Aethra.

Back in Sparta, the hero's mother became Helen's maid. She saw thirty-eight suitors turn up at the palace to ask for the princess's hand. She saw Helen choose Menelaus, and she saw the marriage and the birth of Hermione. One day an Asian prince arrived, a man more handsome than any other and loaded with precious things that nobody in Sparta had ever seen before. On meeting him, Helen asked in a whisper whether he was Dionysus or Eros and immediately became tongue-tied. The prince galloped about Laconia with Menelaus, who took pride in being a good host and showing off everything interesting his kingdom could boast.

Helen only saw the guest over the dinner table. The prince recounted adventures, some of them amorous. Hiding behind his cup, he kept looking at her. Sometimes he couldn't keep from sighing. Helen laughed in his face. One evening, Helen's tunic fell open for a second, leaving "free passage for his eyes" to her white breasts. The prince was lifting a cup to his lips, and the decorated handle slipped from his fingers. The cup shattered on the floor. Menelaus went on talking men's talk. Helen said nothing, looking after little Hermione.

Of all times to go away, the prince chuckled to himself, Menelaus had chosen these very days. He was going off to Crete, for his grandfather Catreus's funeral. As he left, Menelaus, serious as ever, told Helen to look after their guest. After that, there were absolutely no other men about. Helen and the prince were each sleeping alone in the same palace. In the emptiness of the palace halls, Aphrodite assembled those archons of desire Himeros and Pothos, and the Charites too. But on the visible plane, the person who acted as pimp was Aethra. Paris gripped Helen's wrist. The Trojan's escorts loaded up her riches and the things the prince had pretended were gifts. Paris stood tall on a chariot drawn by four horses. Helen was next to him, tunic tossed back over her shoulders, offering her body half naked to the night, where nothing could be seen but Eros's dazzling torch twisting and turning in front of them. Behind the fleeing couple, another Eros was waving a torch. The two lovers and their escorts raced across the open space of red earth and scattered olive trees that led down from Sparta to the coast. Unnoticed among the Trojans, Aethra was with them too. On reaching the water, they saw a tiny island, a toy almost, just a few yards from the shore. On that island, as though on a huge bed covered with a green canopy of pine trees and surrounded by deep water, Helen spent her first night with her third lover.

Helen is the power of the phantom, the simulacrum—and the simulacrum is that place where absence is sovereign. Of her five husbands, the ones she loved most were Paris and Achilles. And, for both Paris and Achilles, Helen was a phantom before she was a woman. Ever since Aphrodite promised the shepherd of Ida that he would possess Helen of Sparta, that pure name had canceled out the powers and kingdoms Athena and Hera were offering him. Despite grim omens, the shepherd of Ida, now recognized as a prince, set off with galleys full of treasure toward that name.

As for Achilles, he was the only one of the Achaean leaders who hadn't rushed off to Sparta to ask for Helen's hand. He thus set off to a war he knew would end in death for him, for a woman about whom he knew nothing but her name. In nine years of siege, Achilles could have said no more about Helen than did Paris himself before he left Troy to find her: "*Te vigilans oculis, animo te nocte videbam.*" So much the longer, indeed never ending, would be their life together as phantoms on Leuke, island of white splendor.

Adrasteia, Moira, Tyche, Ananke, Ate, Aisa, Dike, Nemesis, Erinyes, Heimarmene: such are the names that embody necessity. And they are all women. While Kronos dreams, deep in ambrosia, and in his dreams calculates the measures of the universe, these women keep watch, making sure that every being plays his part, no more and no less, so that nothing and no one may exceed their established bounds. Yet all life is excess. That is why we find these women on the prowl everywhere. They are wet nurses, helmswomen, weavers, flitting, towering. They are all related: Dike and Ananke are daughters of Kronos. Dike is a priestess to Adrasteia. The Moirai and the Erinyes are sisters. They share a family resemblance, the family of destiny. They hail from that distant past when the only powers that existed were abstract and faceless or at most hybrid, compound creatures. They move "in the fog, in black cloud," women's torsos looming from balconies of smoke. And even these strange bodies come and go: Moira has temples, but without statues, where worshipers practice her cult; or sometimes she has statues, but without temples, where no cult is practiced. The more all-encompassing they are, like Ananke, the less they are represented. While the emissaries of necessity—the Erinyes, the Moirai, or Ate—are regular guests among men, beautiful even, when the nature of their work doesn't make them terrifying, and they only talk among themselves.

One of these women did have a body that was both stable and very beautiful: Nemesis. Rich, thick hair, white clothes. She always had a friend with her, Aidós. One day their names would be translated as Vengeance and Shame, but at the time we're talking of, when they had only just emerged from the black cloud, their natures were far more complex and variegated. What did they have in common? The notion of offense. Aidós held people back from offending. Nemesis represented the ineluctable consequences of offending. They were united in a vision of life as something that gets wounded and then, as it writhes, wounds in its turn. Zeus began to watch Nemesis. Nothing like this had ever happened with the women of necessity: never had Zeus felt any desire for the bodies of Adrasteia, Moira, Tyche, Ananke, Aisa, or the Erinyes. And once, in his anger, he had even hurled Ate down from heaven. When it came to his amorous adventures, Zeus found mortal women far more attractive. He wasn't interested in bothering those figures of fate; they were too similar to one another, disturbing the way twins can be, too ancient, and, in the end, hostile. But with Nemesis it was different. Something tremendous must have been at stake in that erotic conquest.

Never, for a woman, had Zeus traveled so far, crossing country after country, sea after sea, "beneath the earth, beneath the black, unfished waters," and on and on to "the ends of the earth," the watery snake, Oceanus. Stubborn and desperate, Nemesis transformed herself into all kinds of animals, while Zeus never let up following her. And when all the feather flapping was finally done, when atlas and zoology were exhausted, what was left? A wild goose and a swan. The swan settled on the goose and forced her to yield. Zeus "passionately united himself with her, out of powerful necessity." But how bizarre! Nemesis, a figure of necessity, is overcome by necessity. And, as the swan assaults her, Nemesis, friend of Aidós, is "mentally torn apart *aidoî kaì nemései*" (which in too modern a translation might be rendered as "by shame and vengeance"). Thus, Nemesis is torn apart by herself. Offending us as it does with such paradoxes, this can hardly be one of Zeus's usual adventures. But whenever his adventures are too grandiose, Zeus allows them to be repeated with variations, so that each version may possess a shining fragment of the truth. Such was the case with Nemesis.

Zeus spent half a night of love with Leda, leaving the other half to her husband, Tyndareos. During that night, Leda conceived four children, divided between heaven and earth: Helen and Pollux by Zeus, Clytemnestra and Castor by Tyndareos. That night was the delicate cameo and repetition of another night, at once dangerous and sublime, that Zeus had spent with Nemesis, as that other night with Nemesis was a delicate cameo and repetition of the long chase across the entire face of the earth that had ended in the violent coupling of swan and wild goose.

To seduce necessity: it had to be the most difficult of amorous undertakings. It was what men would later call a contradiction. And in fact Nemesis wasn't interested in Zeus and rejected his imploring advances. What was needed was a trick, a divine trick. Zeus asked Aphrodite to help him. Together they agreed that Zeus would turn himself into a swan while Aphrodite, in the guise of an eagle, would pretend to follow him. Nemesis was making a sacrifice when she saw a splendid swan flapping toward her, exhausted. From the top of a nearby rock, an eagle was watching them, motionless and threatening, ready to spread its wings and dive on its prey. The frightened swan huddled against Nemesis's lap. She didn't reject the animal. She wanted to protect it from that menacing eagle. She fell asleep with the creature, squeezing it between her thighs. They slept. And Nem-

esis was still sleeping when the swan raped her. Then from
Nemesis' womb a white egg appeared. Hermes took it, carried it to Sparta, and placed it in Leda's womb. When the
big egg hatched, from inside the shell emerged a tiny, perfect female figure: Helen.

The life of Helen marked a moment of precarious, fleeting
equilibrium, when, thanks to the deceitful cunning of Zeus,
necessity and beauty were superimposed the one over the
other. The rape of Nemesis was the most formidable theo-
logical gamble of Zeus's reign. To provoke a forced convergence of beauty and necessity was to challenge the law
of heaven. Only Olympus could have sustained such a thing,
certainly not the earth, where that challenge blazed uncon-
trollably throughout Helen's lifetime. It was a time marked
from beginning to end by calamity. But it was also the time
men would go on dreaming of, long after that fire had gone
out.

On their wedding night, when the bride and groom retired
to their bedroom where the whitewash was still damp on the
walls, Menelaus found his legs sluggish and his mind dazed.
The long, nerve-racking courtship, the oath over the quar-
tered horse, the honors, the festivals, the banquets—everything fused in one powerful impulse to flop down on his bed
and sleep. Helen lay awake and thought of the friends who
until a short while ago had been singing and dancing for her
in the palace. They were a "band of young women," two
hundred and forty girls, who exercised along the river Eurotas, their bodies greased with oil like boys'. And now they
would be thinking of her, as she, Helen, shared her bed with
Menelaus for the first time.

The next morning, at dawn, those girls would gather
water lilies near the meadows where they always went and
weave them into a crown. Then they would go and hang the
crown from the branches of a big plane tree, raising to the

sky and abandoning to the breeze those flowers that had grown from slime. One of them would take out a golden cruet and, drop by drop, pour an oil used in funeral sacrifices over the tree. Others of them would carve on the bark "Worship me: I am Helen's tree." So Helen lay awake, through the night, fantasizing.

After the flight from Sparta, after the years of war in Troy, after the eventful return trip to Sparta, after the death of Menelaus, Helen found herself caught between two stepsons who loathed her: Nicostratus and Megapenthe. So she decided to run off again, alone this time, to seek refuge with a childhood friend. She sailed as far as Rhodes, which was ruled by Polyxo, a widow now, one of the many widows the Trojan War had left scattered across these islands. Helen was finally seeking refuge in a woman, in her memories of girlhood. Polyxo wanted to avenge her husband, Tlepolemus. Like so many other women, she blamed Helen for his death. But she greeted her with kindness.

For the first time in her life, Helen was not being pestered by men. One day she was lying, daydreaming, in the bath when some of Polisso's serving maids burst in disguised as Erinyes. They seized her, naked, fingernails digging into her flesh, dragged her dripping from the water, and carried her off. Outside they hung her from a tree. The big plane tree near Sparta would still bear the carved inscription "Worship me: I am Helen's tree" when the people of Rhodes founded their temple to Helen Dendritis, Helen of the Tree, next to the plane tree where they had found her body hanging.

While they were fleeing Sparta, gusting winds forced Helen and Paris to land on the beach in Sidon. Thus it was that Leda's white daughter and her lover came to seek refuge on the very beach where Europa had been carried off by the white bull. They then sailed on as far as Egypt, to the Canopic mouth of the Nile. "On that shore there was, and still is, a sanctuary to Heracles: if even the merest servant takes refuge there and marks himself with the sacred signs, thereby consecrating himself to the god, it is forbidden to touch him." The two lovers felt they were safe. But there are people who always get to know everything, and look on unmoved: the Egyptian priests. Even as he interrogated the stranger, and Paris ducked his questions, Proteus, king of Memphis, had already heard the true story of the wandering lovers from the temple priests. At the end of his interrogation he passed judgment: he couldn't have this criminal, Paris, killed, as he would have liked, because he was a foreigner and untouchable. But he would keep Helen and her riches. Paris could go back to Troy, but only with a phantom copy of her.

The way Herodotus saw it, Homer was perfectly aware of this episode in Helen's story and lets us know as much when he speaks of "the Sidon women's embroidered veils, which godlike Paris brought back across the vast sea from Sidon, on that voyage when he carried off the noble Helen." But then why doesn't the poet ever mention it? Especially when one considers how essential an element it is, because it means that the Trojans knew they didn't have Helen within their walls at all, but only a phantom. For ten years the war had raged around an absent woman, whom the Trojans would have been more than happy to hand over to the Achaeans, if only they had actually had her. Why on earth did Homer keep quiet about that extraordinary fact in the events leading up to the war? Herodotus answers: "because this story was not suitable for epic composition." It is an explanation that leaves us dumbfounded. So the centuries-old accusation against Homer, that he was a craftsman of deceit, turns out to be true, does it? For overridingly literary motives, Homer kept quiet about the supreme scandal of the Trojan War: that blood had been spilled for a woman who was not actually there, for an impalpable ghost. For hundreds, even thousands of years, the poet's story would be repeated, prolonging to the end of time the deceit that took the heroes to their deaths beneath the walls of Troy.

What treachery could have prompted Homer to do such a thing?

The epos, the epic poem, is a compact, reflecting surface, where the building bricks of formulaic locutions are laid one after the other. Homer did not want to reveal the secret about the nature of Helen, the fact that she was a phantom, because this would have created a vacuum in the surface of his poem. The name Helen must designate a being no less solid than the towering Diomedes. And it is precisely in this way that the phantom is sovereign, when it is hidden away, eating into the bodies from inside.

Homer foresaw his great future enemy: Plato, evoker of copies, of unstoppable cascades of copies that would flood the world. And illuminating those copies with the art of reason, Plato would try to dissolve Helen's enchantment, the enchantment of the unique, in their profusion. But the unique Helen shines more brightly than any other, precisely because she hides the simulacrum within herself, her phantom and the twins she was born with. Faced with the flood of copies Plato released upon the world, the eye would retreat, overcome by an ultimate sense of bewilderment. After which, it would turn elsewhere, toward something invisible and secure, *beyond*, where the bodiless prototypes are at rest: the ideas. For the unique woman, Plato's idea is a disaster, because it aims to replace her. The two look at each other sidelong, like rivals, ready for anything, each examining the other's makeup. To defend herself, Helen relies on the brilliant surface, makes it throb as no other figure, however fleshy, could, since other figures had no doubles, and indeed as no idea ever could, since ideas have no pores: this is the supreme level of existence, mocking every other. The object of the dispute between Homer and Plato is the body of Helen. Both men won. When we see the goddess reproduced thousands upon thousands of times, the Platonic curse of the copy triumphs. But the goddess is a star and occupies a unique, unassailable place, in the sky.

The Trojan War remains unique among all wars, "not just for the great passion involved, but likewise for how long it lasted and how much effort went into it." Unique not just on earth but in heaven too. For the Twelve Olympians the war was "a greater and more terrible struggle than their fight with the Giants." Thus writes Isocrates, spokesman for the mainstream of Athenian thought.

But how could a cosmic event such as the Gigantomachy have troubled the gods less than a war between men? As the up and coming celestial generation, the Olympians had presented a united front against the giants. Yet, when they looked down at what was happening on the plains of Troy, a kind of civil war broke out among them: "they fought among themselves over that woman [Helen]." Unbearable to men, Helen's beauty was likewise dangerous for the gods. The risk they ran was that of becoming too like men, to the point of engaging in that ultimate and peculiarly human of horrors, the civil war. Isocrates has a wonderful way of prettifying the truth. Hence he has nothing to add to this remark, which, however, stands out all the more coming from him.

If the Trojan War was a dangerous business for gods as well as men, this was because it served to generate that mighty "upheaval" which once and for all shifted the civilized world's center of gravity to Greece and the Greek city of Athens, the city of Theseus, the man who first *recognized* Helen, when she was a prepubescent girl and immediately decided that he couldn't live without "her intimacy." In the Athenian twilight, Helen appeared as the *felix culpa* that had allowed Greece to see off the opulent barbarians. Behind Greece's transformation into the dominant civilization, which Isocrates was so proud of, stood not a founding hero, nor a king, nor a warrior, but an adulterous woman of whom only two qualities have been obsessively documented: her flair for betrayal and her beauty.

In the vaster historical perspective, the adulteries disappeared but not the beauty. Helen had been the living proof of the Athenian theorem, according to which "beauty, by nature, rules over strength." It is a sovereignty that comes into its own only when strength has pushed itself to the limit, in the slaughter of the heroes. It was then that beauty finally asserted itself, as it asserted itself over Theseus, that champion of physical strength, "sovereign of himself," who left in Athenian customs a "trace of his sweetness."

More than acts of worship, it was beauty that offered a firm link between the life of the city and that of the Olympians. Mortals and immortals communicated through beauty, without any need for ceremonies. Even Zeus agreed to renounce the use of force and "humble himself" only when he found himself before the beauty of a mortal woman. And he agreed "always to hunt that nature with art and not with violence." So highly did the Olympians value beauty that they even forgave "their own women when they were overcome by it." When beauty seduced her into an earthly adventure, no goddess "ever tried to hide what had happened, as though it were something to be ashamed of." On the contrary, rather than have people keep quiet about it, they wanted it to be celebrated. And this distinguishes the gods sharply from mortals, who have never been able to forgive their beautiful women. Helen lived surrounded by the love of a few men and the hate of both innumerable other men and all women. For centuries she would be subjected to insults and blasphemy. Yet she would always remain "the only woman Zeus allowed to call him father." Thus Helen behaved with the same shamelessness as the Olympian goddesses when "she appeared one night to Homer and ordered him to write a poem about the warriors of Troy, wishing to make their deaths more enviable than those of other men; and it was partly thanks to Homer's artfulness, but above all because of her, that that poem became so seductive [*epa-phróditon*] and famous everywhere." Rather than weep over her crimes, Helen, like a sovereign, commissioned the *Iliad* from Homer to celebrate them. And literature obeyed her command, assimilating Helen's Aphrodite-like charm.

These were the last years of freedom for Athens, and through Isocrates the city recounted its history. His speech on Helen seems to go straight on into the Panathenaicus, that grandiose celebration of the declining Athens. Isocrates, "the most modest of orators," was ninety-four years old when he started writing it, and he worked on it for three years, fighting illness all the while. Then, when news of the defeat at Chaeronea came, he decided to starve himself to death. The Macedonians would soon have conquered Attica, as the peninsula's eastern enemies had so often tried to do and failed. "Some say that he died on the ninth day of his abstinence from food; others say on the fourth, the day they held the funerals for those who had fallen at Chaeronea."

Behind what the Greeks called *heídōlon*, which is at once the idol, the statue, the simulacrum, the phantom, lies the mental image. This fanciful and insubstantial creature imitates the world and at the same time subjects it to a frenzy of different combinations, confounding its forms in inexhaustible proliferation. It emanates a prodigious strength, our awe in the face of what we see in the invisible. It has all the features of the arbitrary, of what is born in the dark, from formlessness, the way our world was perhaps once born. But this time the chaos is the vast shadowy canvas that lies behind our eyes and on which phosphenic patterns constantly merge and fade. Such constant formation of images occurs in each one of us in every instant. But these are not the only peculiarities of the phenomenon. When the phantom, the mental image, takes over our minds, when it begins to join with other similar or alien figures, then little by little it fills the whole space of the mind in an ever more detailed and ever richer concatenation. What initially presented itself as the prodigy of appearance, cut off from everything, is now linked, from one phantom to another, to everything.

At one extreme of the mental image lies our amazement

at form, at its self-sufficient and sovereign existence. At the other lies our amazement at the chain of connections that reproduce in the mind the necessity of the material world. It is hard to see those two opposite points in the phantom's spectrum. To see them simultaneously would be unbearable. For the Greeks, Helen was the embodiment of that vision, beauty hatched from the egg of necessity.

The tension between Helen's body and Helen's phantom was too strong: after Homer the Greeks were no longer able to hold the two together. The first sign of breakdown came with Stesichorus: after writing his *Helen*, in which she is presented as "bigamous and trigamous, a betrayer of men," he had to produce a poem in her defense after she blinded him in revenge. In Homer, body and phantom existed tacitly side by side: after Homer, the knot that held them together in a single being was gradually loosened, until finally it came apart. On the one hand, there would be the guilty woman, "with her many lovers," "sold over and over for her beauty," like the commonest hetaera. On the other, a Helen who had been the victim of divine malice and who waited in Egypt for the return of Menelaus while rejecting the advances of the local king, another Penelope almost.

Euripides dedicated two tragedies—*Helen* and *The Trojan Women*—to this two-faced heroine, illuminating first one side, then the other. The plays mark the earliest emergence of that grim matrimonial morality on which all melodrama would later be based. Helen's ill-omened adultery, with its wildly disproportionate consequences, would thus go on and on gripping audiences right to the end, right up to Debussy's *Pelléas et Mélisande* and Hofmannsthal-Strauss's *Die Frau ohne Schatten*.

Helen resembled her two brothers, Castor and Pollux. She had a "simple spirit" (whatever that might mean), mild manners, splendid hair, a beauty spot between her eyebrows, a small mouth, perfect breasts. In Lindos she consecrated an amber cup that exactly covered one of them. When he burst into Troy to kill her, "they say that no sooner had he glimpsed Helen's naked breasts than Menelaus dropped his sword."

All her life Helen did nothing but show herself off and betray. We know little about how she felt, and what we do know is subject to doubt, because she had such a talent for mimicry (another of Aphrodite's gifts) that they used to call her Echo. So she could easily have faked anything she wanted to. She brought nothing new to mankind, not even the disasters she caused. As Horace says, with the dismissive dispatch of the Quirites: "the cunt had been a terrible provoker of wars long before Helen came on the scene." So even though some do grant her "skill in tapestry," and even if she did (like a host of others) learn "many doctrines" from the learned Egyptians, Helen nevertheless remains the least virtuous of beings one could imagine. Maybe she had no psychology. And maybe it was impossible for her to have one. If she weeps, as she does on the Scaean Gate, a veil, dazzling as Zeus's thunderbolts, hides her tears. The only thing she cared about was appearance, and hence poetry too. When she arrived in Mycenae with Menelaus and found the corpse of her sister, Clytemnestra, throat freshly slashed by Orestes, Helen did, as a sign of grief, cut the ends of her hair, but not so much as to risk making herself ugly. Not only did she compel Homer to write about her but, as one charming Byzantine author would later claim, she actually composed a poem about the Trojan War herself, which Homer then used for his own.

Napoleon began as a novelist: Helen wished to end up as the narrator of her own life. In any event, there must have been a profound affinity between her and poetry, for no woman in literature has ever been so exalted and so savaged. The chorus of Euripides' *Cyclops* speaks of her thus: "So then, when you'd got your hands on the girl, did you take turns at balling her, seeing that she likes swapping husbands?"

Nemesis fled to the ends of the earth to escape Zeus, transforming herself into one animal after another, just as the
manifest flees and scatters before being caught and pinned
down by its principle. The same sequence of flight with
metamorphoses followed by rape is repeated when Peleus
chases Thetis and finally couples with her in the form of a
cuttlefish. The repetition of a mythical event, with its play
of variations, tells us that something remote is beckoning to
us. There is no such thing as the isolated mythical event,
just as there is no such thing as the isolated word. Myth, like
language, gives all of itself in each of its fragments. When
a myth brings into play repetition and variants, the skeleton
of the system emerges for a while, the latent order, covered
in seaweed.

Those two marine rapes, preceded by animal metamorphoses, stand out among hundreds of amorous adventures,
just as the solitary children born from them stand out amid
all others: Helen and Achilles, the two unique ones. Helen
was unique in being Zeus's only daughter on an earth
swarming with the god's bastard sons. Achilles was unique
in that he was born to substitute for the truly unique one:
that son Thetis never bore who would have replaced Zeus.
And if Achilles, the unique one, is also a substitute for the
unique one, this points to the fact that the realm of substitutions contains within itself the realm of the unique, without which, however, it could have neither meaning nor
intensity. The most archaic form of the amorous chase, still
close to the realm of perennial metamorphosis, was thus
only a hairbreadth away from the most modern of dangers,
that of the dawning of a post-Olympian era.

Having brought about the existence of Helen and Achilles,
Zeus realized that he had already stretched the potential of
his realm to the limit. Helen and Achilles had made their
appearance; now nothing could prevent the consequences.
But the apparition was to be a darting flash and no more.
The blaze of Troy would consume them. After that, they

could safely be allowed to proceed to the innocuous Blessed Isles. Or maybe they could get together on Leuke, as phantoms. But the world would never again know that tension, so insidious to the gods and for mortals unbearable, except in their memories, their poetry. We have mentioned four realms here: the realm of perennial metamorphosis is that of every beginning, when the word has not yet detached itself from the thing, nor the mind from the matter; the realm of substitution is the world of the digit, above all the digit as sign, as incessant substitution; the realm of the unique is the world that always eludes the clutches of language, the very appearing of the irrepeatable; the realm of Zeus is that of the Greek stories, of which we are still a part.

In Eratosthenes' version, Nemesis's long flight came to an end in the sea off Rhamnus in Attica, when Zeus the swan settled on the wild duck. That was the only time Nemesis would ever play a passive role. From then on, and for hundreds, thousands of years, she would appear as a young woman, of calm and grave expression, roaming all over the earth, treading, as often as not, on lifeless corpses. That remote animal scene in a wilderness of sea, unwatched by any eye, is the only episode of her life we know about. It was also the greatest exploit of Zeus's reign: that of having forced necessity to bring forth beauty.

When the inhabitants of Rhamnus decided to consecrate a sanctuary to Nemesis, they commissioned Phidias to sculpt a giant statue of the goddess. Some claim that the Rhamnus Nemesis was in fact an Aphrodite sculpted by Agoracritus, Phidias's pupil and lover. Others say that Phidias allowed the sculpture to be passed off as the work of his lover. Either way, the statue would be famous for centuries. Varro preferred it above all others. A fragment of the head has been discovered; the rest we must reconstruct from descriptions and coins. So the base of the statue showed Leda leading a reluctant Helen toward her real mother, Nemesis. But what was the relationship between mother and daughter? We

know a great deal about Helen, whereas only a few details
have come down to us about the divine figure of Nemesis,
and even these are often enigmatic. This goddess of the offense that boomerangs back on its perpetrator must have
been very beautiful if people could mistake her for Aphrodite. Herself the great enemy of hubris, she gave birth to a
daughter whose very body was an offense and in doing so
provoked the most magnificent unfolding of hubris in all of
Greek history: the Trojan War.

In one hand Nemesis held a designer's square, or a pair
of reins, or an apple branch. The wheel of destiny stood beside her and could become the wheel of her griffin-drawn
chariot. She also held the urn of destiny. "Queen of motives
and arbitress of all things," she had always possessed the
power to bind men in the "never-to-be-loosened net of necessity" (*necessitatis insolubili retinaculo vinciens*). Often
Nemesis would lift a hand to her shoulder, as if to adjust
her tunic. And often she bowed her head, eyes on her breast,
as though deep in thought. Some of the ancients said that
when she did this she was spitting into her tunic to ward off
bad luck. Phidias (or Agoracritus) sculpted a handsome
crown on her head with representations of stags and of Nike,
goddess of victory. She held a decorated goblet in her hand
showing figures of Negroes. When Pausanias saw the statue,
he was puzzled by this goblet. He wasn't convinced by the
explanations people gave him, that it showed a group of
Ethiopians, because Nemesis's father was Oceanus and the
Ethiopians lived near Oceanus. In a doggedly determined
digression on the Ethiopians, he demonstrates that such a
supposition was baseless. But he didn't dare to suggest an
alternative and moved on. Other classical authors found it
equally difficult to account for all Nemesis's attributes. The
designer's square stood for the notion of measure, the
cosmic rule that punishes every excess, but what was that
aphrodisian apple branch about? And the impressive stags
around her forehead? And why that frequently repeated
gesture of raising a hand to one shoulder, where she had a
buckle in the shape of a griffin, her favorite animal? Was it
to cover herself better, or to undo the buckle?

Nemesis came from Asia Minor. Before arriving in Rhamnus, she was worshiped in Smyrna. Above the cult's statues were hung the three golden Charites, by Bupalus. And in Smyrna we find that Nemesis was not just one figure. Here the faithful worshiped two identical Nemeses. One day Alexander the Great went hunting on Mount Pagus. On his way back, he stopped to rest under a large plane tree near the sanctuary of the two Nemeses. And two identical women appeared to him in a dream. They were looking at each other, and each had a hand on her tunic buckle, one the left hand, the other the right, as though in a mirror. They told him to found a new Smyrna beyond the Meles, the river "with the finest water of all, rising in a cavern where it is said Homer composed his poems." Alexander obeyed.

But why should Nemesis, this guardian of the cosmic law, which is intrinsically indivisible, appear as two figures? Perhaps here we have found our way back to the place where the phantom began its long journey. Helen was born with the Dioscuri twins. She was the unique one; she brought together in a single body all the beauty that in the normal way of things would have been shared out equally among everybody in obedience to the *némein* that many of the ancients had even then linked to Nemesis. But right from the egg she hatched out of, Helen was also pursued by duplication, which reigns within the phantom. And it wasn't just a question of her twin brothers; her mother was also split into two figures. Now, as her mother, Leda, took her toward her other mother, her real mother, Helen realized that Nemesis too had a double. Not only beauty itself, but likewise the destiny of being double, the realm of the phantom, all these things can be traced back to that Asiatic mother with the mysterious gesture, the woman Zeus chose to generate his only daughter to live among men.

V

HEROPHILE, DEMOPHILE, SABBE: SUCH are the names of the Sibyls that have come down to us. From Palestine to the Troad they left a few scattered remains, and sometimes verses. One day, converging from every corner of the Mediterranean, they all climbed toward Delphi, which was "difficult to get to even for a strong man." Herophile prophesied the coming of Helen, "how she would grow up in Sparta to be the ruination of Asia and Europe." In her verses she sometimes calls herself Artemis, and she also claimed to be Apollo's sister, or his daughter. Some permanent bond linked her to Apollo Smintheus, the Apollo of the Rat, harbinger of the plague. You can still find Herophile's tomb in the Troad, among the trees of the wood sacred to Apollo Smintheus, and the epitaph says: "I lie close to the Nymphs and to Hermes, / I have not lost my sovereignty."

In the latter days of Delphi, the Pythia was selected the same way a priest's housekeeper is: that is, she had to be over fifty. But originally she had been a young girl chosen from among all the girls of Delphi, and she had worn a simple girl's tunic without a gold hem. One day Echecrates, the Thessalian, saw the virgin prophesying, was seized by passion, carried the girl off, and raped her. After which the people of Delphi introduced the age limit for the prophetess, although she continued to dress as a little girl. But the situation had been very different in more ancient times. Then the Sibyls came from far away and chanted their prophesies from a rock, later to be hemmed in between the Bouleuterion and the Portico of the Athenians.

In a state of divine possession, they spoke in impeccable verse. In fact, it was only now that men realized what perfect speech could be, since the hexameter was Apollo's gift to Phemonoe, his daughter, his mountain Nymph, his first Pythia. The god knew that power came from possession, from the snake coiled around the water spring. But that wasn't enough for Apollo: his women, his soothsaying daughters, must reveal not only the enigmas of the future but verse itself. Poetry thus arrived on the scene as the form structuring those ambiguous words that people came to hear to help them make decisions about their lives, words whose meaning they often appreciated only when it was too late. And Apollo didn't want slovenly shamans but young virgins from the grottoes of Parnassus, girls still close to the Nymphs, and speaking in well-turned verse.

The moderns have often imagined the operation of the oracle as some kind of collaboration between a team of Madame Sosostris and cold Parnassian priests who polished up the metrics of the Pythia's groans (and of course derailed her meaning to suit their own dark designs). But the Sibyls, the first women ever to prophesy at Delphi, had no need of prompters. The notion—seemingly self-evident to the moderns—that possession and formal excellence are incompatible would never have occurred to them. Into the impervious history of Delphi, Orpheus and Musaeus arrive almost as parvenus, at least when compared with the Sibyls: "They say that Orpheus put on such airs about his mysteries and was generally so presumptuous that both he and Musaeus, who imitated him in everything, refused to submit themselves to the test and take part in any musical competition." This was when they were in Delphi. And perhaps Orpheus and Musaeus weren't avoiding that competition out of arrogance, nor for fear of being beaten, but because right there for all to see, as it still is today, was the rock where Phemonoe pronounced the very first hexameters.

. . .

Apollo and Dionysus are false friends, and likewise false enemies. Behind the charade of their clashes, their encounters,
their overlapping, there is something that forever unites
them, forever distinguishes them from their divine peers:
possession. Both Apollo and Dionysus know that possession
is the highest form of knowledge, the greatest power. And
this is the knowledge, this the power they seek. Zeus too, of
course, is practiced in the art of possession, in fact he need
only listen to the rustling oaks of Dodona to generate it. But
Zeus is everything and hence gives pride of place to nothing.
Apollo and Dionysus, in contrast, choose possession as their
peculiar weapon and are loath to let others mess with it. For
Dionysus, possession is an immediate, unassailable reality;
it is with him in all his wanderings, whether in the houses
of the city or out on the rugged mountains. If someone refuses to acknowledge it, Dionysus is ready to unleash that
possession like a terrifying beast. And it is then that the
Proetides, the weaver sisters who were reluctant to follow the
call of the god, dash off and race furiously about the mountains. Soon they are killing people, sometimes innocent travelers. This is how Dionysus punishes those who don't accept
his possession, which is like a perennial spring gushing from
his body, or the dark liquid that he revealed to men.

For Apollo, possession is a conquest. And, like every conquest, it must be defended by an imperious hand. Like every
conquest, it also tends to obliterate whatever power came
before it. But the possession that attracted Apollo was very
different from the possession that had always been the territory of Dionysus. Apollo wants his possession to be articulated by meter; he wants to stamp the seal of form on the
flow of enthusiasm, at the very moment it occurs. Apollo is
responsible for imposing logic too: a restraining meter in the
flux of thought. When faced with the darting, disordered,
furtive intelligence of Hermes, Apollo drew a dividing line;
on the one side Hermes could preside over divination by dice
and bones, could even have the Thriai, the honey maidens,
despite his elder brother's once having loved them, but the

supreme, the invincible oracle of the word, Apollo kept for himself.

In the thick of the stones, marble, and metal at Delphi, the visitor would think of other ghosts, of the first temples to Apollo, now no more. The first, a hut of laurel branches broken from trees in the valley of Tempe; the second, made of wax and feathers; the third, built in bronze by Hephaestus and Athena. Pindar could still wonder: "Oh Muses, with what patterns did the able hands of Hephaestus and Athena decorate the temple?" We shall never know, but Pindar thought he could recall fragments of an image: "Bronze the walls and bronze too rose the columns; golden above the pediment chanted six Enchantresses." These words were already sounding obscure by the time Pausanias heard them. At most, he supposed, the Enchantresses might have been an "imitation of Homer's Sirens." Yet they held the secret to a long story, the story of the origins of possession.

Iynx was a girl sorceress. She made up love potions. Not for herself, but because she wanted love to make the rounds. One day she offered a drink to Zeus. The god drank it, and the first girl he saw was Io, wandering about in the grounds of Hera's sanctuary in Argos. Zeus was possessed by love for Io. And so began history on earth, a history of flight, persecution, metamorphosis. The first victim was the sorceress herself. In revenge, Hera turned her into a bird known as the wryneck, because of the way it twists its neck with a sudden jerking movement. When Jason reached Colchis, he knew that if he wanted to get the Golden Fleece he would have to win over the young sorceress Medea. Aphrodite looked down from heaven and decided to help him. A sorceress can only be overcome by a more potent sorcery. So Aphrodite took the wryneck, the "delirious, multicolored bird," and fixed it with bonds that could not be untied to a little wheel with four spokes. Now the circular motion of the wheel would forever accompany the jerky twisting of the bird's neck. That small object, that plaything, becomes the mechanism, the artifice of possession. It imposes an obsessive circular motion on the mind, a motion that uproots it from its inertia and hooks it onto the divine wheel, which turns incessantly like the spheres. Even the thoughts of the gods get caught on that wheel.

Jason learned to use Aphrodite's gift. Medea immediately lost all consideration for her parents. The girl's mind was obsessed by desire for a distant country, for a name, Greece, which she confused with Jason's presence. Thus, drawing on her sorcery, her herbs and ointments, Medea saved the Stranger and ruined her own family. It wasn't Apollo or Dionysus, then, lords of possession that they were, who invented the *íynx*, this strange object that is the only visible artifact of possession. Aphrodite, goddess of "the swiftest arrows," got there first; for erotic possession is the starting point for any possession. What at Delphi is an enigma, for Aphrodite is a plaything. The worshipers at Apollo's temple in Delphi would see small wheels hanging from the ceiling, small wheels with the bodies of birds attached. It was said that those wheels produced a voice, a seductive call. They were the Enchantresses Pindar spoke of, linking the human mind to the circular motion of the heavens.

The boy Apollo straightens in his mother Leto's arms and lets fly an arrow at an enormous snake wrapped in huge coils around the dappled slopes of Delphi. The youth Apollo, wavy, blond hair falling on his shoulders, chases after a young girl. Just as he is about to catch her, the girl turns herself into a laurel tree. Each of these actions is the shadow of the other. If we look carefully at Python, we can see the delicate Daphne in the snake. Looking at the laurel leaves, we can see the scales of Python.

No sooner have you grabbed hold of it than myth opens out into a fan of a thousand segments. Here the variant is the origin. Everything that happens, happens this way, or that way, or this other way. And in each of these diverging stories all the others are reflected, all brush by us like folds of the same cloth. If, out of some perversity of tradition, only one version of some mythical event has come down to us, it is like a body without a shadow, and we must do our best to trace out that invisible shadow in our minds. Apollo slays the monster, he is the first slayer of monsters. But what is this monster? It is Python's skin, camouflaging itself among bushes and rock, and it is the soft skin of Daphne, already turning into laurel and marble.

Apollo doesn't manage to possess the Nymph, and maybe he doesn't even want to. What he is looking for in the Nymph is the crown of laurel left in his hand as her body dissolves: he wants representation. No Nymph could ever reject or escape Dionysus, because the Nymph is part of himself. There is only one exception, Aura, who has her double in Nikaia. But the rape of Aura would introduce Iacchus to the Eleusinian mysteries. Hence it could not be other than unique, in its initial duality.

The Nymph *is* possession, and a *nymphólēptos* is a person who becomes delirious on being captured by the Nymphs. Apollo does not possess the Nymphs, he does not possess possession, but he educates it, governs it. The Muses were wild young girls from Helicon. It was Apollo made them move over to the mountain opposite, Parnassus; it was he trained them in the gifts that made that band of wild girls the Muses, and hence those women who took possession of the mind, but each imposing the laws of an art.

Plutarch, priest of Delphic Apollo, claimed that Dionysus was just as important in Delphi as Apollo. In the freezing winter months, the months when the dead rise and torches wander about the slopes of Parnassus, Dionysus is lord of Delphi. But then Apollo returns from his nordic quest among the Hyperboreans, and for the other nine months of the year he reigns supreme. No victory is ever complete, nor ever enough to last the whole year. Neither Apollo nor Dionysus can reign forever, neither can do without the other, neither can be there all the time. When Apollo reappears and squeezes Dionysus's arm, we hear the last notes of the dithyrambs, and immediately afterward the first of the paeans. The only continuity is sound.

In the Pythia's *ádyton*, Apollo has a golden statue, Dionysus only the base of his tomb. Yet everything seems to proceed smoothly enough. As interlocking and alternating powers, Apollo and Dionysus are loath to let anything of their past emerge in this place. Few recall that, beneath the bronze lid of the tripod where the Pythia now sits, the dismembered limbs of Dionysus Zagreus once boiled. Or even that Dionysus, as some claim, was the first to prophesy from the tripod. Or even that a snake once coiled around the feet of that tripod. All this would have made it all too easy to confuse the stories of Dionysus with those of the Enemy: Python, a snake, and thus close to Dionysus, the god generated by Zeus when in the form of a snake and escorted by virgins who tied snakes around their foreheads like ribbons; Python forerunner of Apollo as prophet; Python who was himself (or herself) buried in the *ádyton*, beneath the *omphalós*. Had all this been remembered, Dionysus, who reigned in Apollo's stead during his winter absence, would have been revealed in his occult role as the Enemy, an emanation of Python, of the power Apollo had killed and left to rot in the sun.

In its heyday, and likewise in its decadence, Delphi was the opposite of what the Hellenophiles of the last century imagined as the classical spirit. It was a market, a hoard of trophies, a burial ground. Its guiding principle demanded accumulation. Shields and figureheads, the gifts of victorious soldiers. Lyres, tripods, chariots, bronze tables, basins, paterae, caldrons, wine bowls, spits: such was the vision that greeted the eye in the *mégaron* of Apollo's temple. Leading through to the Pythia's chamber, this hall was cluttered with objects leaning against the walls and columns, and hanging from the ceiling. Each of these objects was an event, summed up a life, sometimes many lives and many deaths. Up in the air, moving ever so slightly when a draft slipped in from outside, hung light chariot wheels. And the sashes and bands of athletes drifted back and forth like gossamer fans.

On entering Apollo's temple in Delphi, bewildered by the throng of metallic objects leaning from the walls and sparkling in the shadows, you could sometimes make out, in the background, the bust of a woman (and for many years it would have been a young woman) who seemed to grow right out of the floor: she wore the simple tunic local girls wore; she was the Pythia. Squatting on her tripod, as though on a stool in a bar, she watched the new arrivals as they came into the *mégaron.* The Pythia's chamber, the *ádyton,* was smaller than the main hall of the temple, and a little over a yard lower. Beside it was a small booth with a bench where those who came to consult the oracle would sit, unable to see the Pythia as she prophesied among her sacred objects: the tall tripod anchored to the floor above a crevice in the ground, the umbilical stone wrapped in the cords of a double net, the base of the tomb of Dionysus, a golden statue of Apollo, a laurel tree that got a little light from above, a trickle of water that ran behind her.

There is an object that represents one of the highest peaks of civilization, with respect to which all others we are familiar with are but watered down derivatives: the bronze caldron. In the China of the Shang dynasty it became the cult object around which people's lives revolved. Even today we can only reconstruct that world through those bronze caldrons. It was then that the sacred vessel was given a certain number of canonical forms (how many is still a matter of debate), which were to survive for more than two thousand years, the materials changing, the caldrons themselves becoming ever more fragile and secular. In Doric Greece, the caldron was made in just the one dominant form: the tripod.

During the geometric age, the formal thrust of the Greek mind seemed to concentrate on these objects. They become the sacred objects par excellence. That which has an indispensable, humble function—to cook food—is imperiously subtracted from any function other than that of making offerings to the gods. *Iaròn Diós*, "sacred to Zeus," we read on the rim of a three-legged basin in the Olympia Museum. And in both China and Greece we find bronze caldrons being decorated with animal figures: in China the most common is the *tao-t'ieh*, a monster made up of other animals and ideograms, from the owl to the cicada, the leopard to the snake; in Greece it is usually the griffin, its powerful beak open and tongue darting out, but there are also bronze caldrons decorated with lions and bulls.

The choice of those canonical forms, established as early as the Shang dynasty, was to put a stamp on the whole of Chinese civilization, right down to the present day. The time would come when the bronzes with their green patina would be lost, buried in the loess or in museum collections. But Chinese design would be a genetic continuation of the canon of these bronzes. Decorative devices and features of architectural style would always hark back, some more directly, some less, to that beginning. In Greece too the tripod design has the splendor of an important beginning, but then it disappears forever, replaced by another form: the human figure. From that moment on, in both Delphi and Olympia, we find fewer and fewer bronze tripods being dedicated to the gods, and more and more statues. Often they were statues of gods, but sometimes they represented the winners of some war or race who wanted to dedicate themselves. It was the opposite of what happens today: instead of the winner receiving a laughable little statuette as a prize, his prize was the permission to raise a statue of himself, sometimes a huge statue, and dedicate it to a god. Human figures appeared on tall columns, figures with names and dedications. And yet these figures, at the opposite extreme from the complete anonymity of the tripod, for a while inherited its sacred quality. What disappeared entirely was the food or drink that had bubbled in the caldron for the god. That energy migrated into the drapes of a marble tunic, into a horse's harness, the wings of a Sphinx. The offering was no longer something that could be eaten: now, for the first time, you could only look.

The first human beings the Olympians saw from their ether were the mountain Nymphs. These extremely long-lived though ultimately mortal women would appear and disappear among woods and undergrowth, often in pursuit of wild beasts. It was they who kindled the first fires of desire in the Olympians, served as their initiation almost into the creatures of the earth. Apollo was not always happy in his loves, male or female. At a certain point, something would go wrong—a fatal frenzy, as happened with Hyacinthus, and with Coronis. But at least with Cyrene it would seem that all went well.

He watched Cyrene for a long time, from on high, while she hunted on Mount Pelion. He was impressed and pleased by her scorn for things domestic. The loom was not for her. She went out day and night to chase the wildest of beasts. This reminded Apollo of his sister, Artemis. And what reminded him even more strongly of his sister was that Cyrene "liked being a virgin and keeping an unstained bed." Playing innocent, Apollo called on Chiron, Cyrene's father, and asked him who this girl fighting the lion might be. Chiron smiled at the god's ingenuousness in pretending he didn't know. In the meantime, Cyrene had beaten the lion yet again. To have her surrender her virginity without regrets, Apollo chose one of his most secret forms: the wolf. It was the form that would give most pleasure both to her and to himself. Afterward there were the usual nuptial honors: Apollo took Cyrene to Libya in a golden chariot, and Aphrodite led them to a golden palace deep in a luxuriant garden. But as far as sex was concerned, they were never to improve on that first time. Apollo gave Cyrene this part of Africa for her to hunt her wild beasts in, and he brought along other

Nymphs to serve her. Then their child, Aristaeus, was born. Like another child of Apollo, Asclepius, he possessed the gift of healing. The Muses brought him up on prophesy and honey.

The power of the abstract begins as a rejection of that epic encyclopedism where every element, whether it be a comment on the power of the gods or instructions on how to fix the axles to a cart, has the same importance, the same impact on the mosaic surface of the narrative. Anaximander and Heraclitus aimed for the opposite: sentences that subsumed whole cycles of reality and almost eclipsed them, dazzling the reader with their own light. The *lógos*, when it appears, annihilates the particular, the accumulation of detritus typical of every experience, that obligation to repeat every detail. Like the cipher, like the arrow of Abaris, the *lógos* transfixes in the merest atom of time what the rhapsodies had strung together and repeated over and over for night after smoky night.

The resulting thrill was without precedent. People had heard stories from the East, stories more occult than their own. But it was no longer a question of stories. In comparison with what had gone before, these were bare propositions that stamped things with "the seal of 'that which is.'" And the seal would live on, closed away inside itself, proud, immobile, like the epsilon engraved on the temple at Delphi. There, for the first time, the priests realized that the knowledge that is power derives not only from the secret stories of the gods but from the hypothetical syllogism.

Every day, at dawn, Ion would begin to sweep the area in front of Apollo's temple in Delphi. He picked up the leftovers from the sacrifices, watched the hawks circling down from Parnassus, and threatened them with his bow before they could peck at the golden rooftops. Carefully, he laid out fresh olive garlands and poured buckets of cold water on the temple floor. It was a chore he liked, a humble, solemn duty. Everything had to look clean and whole for when the crowd of visitors and those who came to consult the oracle would swarm up the twisting path to the sanctuary. This temple of prophecy perched high up on the rocks was all Ion had ever seen of the world. And he imagined he would always live here, as though in an eternal orphanage. In the end he was only alive at all because one day, at this same time, in the early morning, the Pythia had found a basket in the temple gardens and, with strange benevolence, picked it up. With similarly strange benevolence, the god let the little boy grow up, playing among the altars. Then they made him guardian of Apollo's treasures. He knew nothing of his father or mother, he was less than a slave, a nobody, and nobody's child; yet he thought of Apollo as his father and of the Pythia as his mother. He owed his life, he felt, to them alone. Nothing else mattered, or even existed for him really. Young, pure, devout, cheerful, Ion welcomed the visitors, showed them the various rooms, the various ceremonies. But the best time of the day was this silent hour at dawn, when he swept and cleaned and all the while looked about him.

One was never alone at Delphi: hundreds of sculpted and painted figures greeted you wherever you went. By now he knew them one by one and could recount all their adventures. Heracles, the Giants, Athena, the thyrsus, the Gorgons . . . He would think about their struggles and flights, about those monsters, those weapons, those embraces, those ambushes. He would think about the gods, and he talked to no one. Visitors would tell him the most awful things that were happening in the world outside, the world he had never seen. But as he listened, Ion would have a faint smile on his face, and he thought how he had heard it all before. For the tales they told him were all repetitions of the silent stories sculpted and painted round about him, dull repetitions when set against the temple's pediments flooded with the day's first light. And perhaps somewhat less malign too. A swan was waddling up to the altar, on the lookout, like the

hawks, for sacrificial crumbs. Cheerful as ever, Ion chased
the creature away, told him to fly off to Delos. Everything
in Delphi must be fragrant, completely free from the wear
and tear that man brings with him, not so much as a footprint on the ground, inviolate, like Parnassus at dawn.

Then he set to thinking again: the gods were the example
and model of every evil, and it wasn't fair to blame men for
imitating actions the gods had committed before them. His
favorite mental game was to try to recall, as exhaustively as
possible, all the rapes attributed to Zeus and Poseidon. But
there was always one that got away. And Ion chuckled to
himself. He didn't realize that he himself was part of those
stories, didn't realize that he was the fruit of one of those
rapes, but one by Apollo, the god Ion thought of as his real
father. And he was.

The chain of Erichthonius, majestic heirloom of the ruling
house of Athens, was passed down from generation to generation. When Erechtheus gave it to Creusa, the girl wore it
on her wrist like a bracelet. And on her white wrists, one
day as she was gathering crocuses on her own, lost in
thought on the northern slopes of the Acropolis, Creusa felt
the iron grip of Apollo. All she saw of the god was a glimpse
of flashing light from his hair. Something of that light was
picked up in the saffron flowers she had gathered in the fold
of her tunic, over her lap. Creusa screamed: "Oh, Mother!"
and that scream was the only sound to be heard as Apollo
dragged her to Pan's cave a little farther up the slope. The
god never let go his grip on the girl's wrists. Creusa felt the
links of the bracelet being forced into her flesh. Apollo
stretched her on the ground in the dark, opening her arms
wide. It was the fastest and most violent of all his loves. Not
a word said, not a moan.

When Apollo had gone, Creusa lay motionless in the dark,
hurt, and determined to hurt the god in return. She swore
no one would know. Months later she gave birth in the cave,
in the exact place where the god had held her with her arms

outspread. Then she wrapped the tiny Ion in swaddling clothes and laid him in a round basket on a piece of embroidery she had sewn as a child: it showed the head of Medusa, the features vague and clumsy. The baby's screams as the hawks and wild beasts came to devour him were the only voice that might get through to the hateful, impassive god, busy strumming his lyre; it was the only outrage Creusa could commit to reproduce the outrage of her "bitter nuptials."

Apollo the Oblique tangled up the threads that were Creusa's and Ion's lives. Indeed he so arranged matters that mother and son were only to recognize each other after the mother had tried to kill her son, and the son his mother. To kill Ion, Creusa used the lethal drop of Medusa's blood still sealed in her bracelet. But the drop fell to the ground, and only a greedy dove was killed. To kill Creusa, Ion was about to violate the sacred law that protected suppliants in the temple. But his devotion made him hesitate. Pinned against the altar of Apollo, Creusa awaited her death at the hands of her son, whom she still imagined to be some nameless guardian of Delphi. Then the Pythia came in. She was holding a basket. She opened it and from among the swaddling clothes and wickerwork, still undamaged by mold, took out a clumsy piece of childish embroidery showing Medusa's head in the middle of a piece of cloth fringed with snakes, as in the aegis.

At which the mother recognized her son. Now Ion could become king of Athens. For he, like Erichthonius, had lain beside Medusa's head. He too had been wrapped in the aegis. Of course, this was not, as in Erichthonius's case, the aegis Athena had warmed at her breast but a common piece of cloth embroidered by a little girl. But that was in line with the way the world was going. A unique blazon of unbearable intensity gradually rippled outward in a thousand copies sculpted on the pediments of temples or embroidered on shawls. And, as the copies multiplied, the original power was diluted. Even the gifts of the gods were subject to the passing of time, lost their brilliance: Creusa had wasted the lethal drop sealed in her bracelet, and the other drop, the healing drop that contained "the nutrients of life," she forgot about. Nobody ever bothered to use it. Ion and Creusa had other things on their minds now: they thought of things divine, of how one way or another they always come too late, "yet are not powerless in their conclusion [*télos*]."

The hawks that flew over Delphi would drop turtles on the rocks to break their hard shells. Croesus reigned far away from Delphi, on the other side of a wide sea, and felt, like many others, spied upon from that nest of priests perched way up on the mountain. It occurred to him to put the Pythia and those elusive figures around her people called "the saintly ones" to the test. He challenged the Delphic oracle, together with six of the other most famous oracles in the world, to divine what he, Croesus, would be doing the hundredth day after the departure of his messengers.

The messengers came back with their sealed answers. All wrong. But the Pythia had answered in hexameters even before she'd heard the question: "I can count the grains of sand and the waves. / I hear the dumb. I understand the silent. / I smell a smell of giant turtle. / It boils in bronze with lamb's flesh. / There's bronze beneath it, and bronze above covering it." Now, on the day in question, Croesus had in fact cut up "a turtle and a lamb, and with his own hands put them to boil in a bronze cooking pot with a bronze lid." He claimed to have thought up this charade because he felt it would be the most unlikely of all. A pathetic lie. The scene was a mute message, in which Croesus mimed exactly what had been going on back in the sanctuary since time immemorial: sitting on the lid of a bronze tripod, swathed in smoke, the Pythia gave her answers to whoever came to consult her. But did that smoke rise only from the crevice in the ground beneath the tripod, or from the tripod itself as well? Right from the beginning, lamb's meat had been mixed with turtle meat beneath that lid. The lamb was the lamb the Thyiads, followers of Dionysus, had torn apart only a little farther up the slopes of Mount Parnassus. The turtle meat had been separated from the shell that Apollo used, as Hermes had taught him, to make his lyre and play, again on the slopes of Parnassus, to his Thriai. Apollo and Dionysus boiled together in the caldron: that was the mixture, the sharp, sharp smell of Delphi.

Far more than the strangled voice of the Pythia or the crevice in the ground archaeologists have searched for in vain, the source of Delphic power was a three-legged bronze caldron protected by animal masks, where something was simmering away. Something offered, sacrificed. From the sacrifice came the voice, the meaning. That was the primordial talisman, the object Apollo's enemies would want to steal, to rob him of his voice. Pythias or priests were two a penny, but power resided in a bronze caldron protected by griffins and caked with meat. The Pythia sat on the lid to demonstrate her possession. And the oracle would fall into decline the day Delphi was stripped of all the innumerable tripods that had been consecrated there. Nor were they taken just for the metal. The plunderers were absolutely determined to strip of all its talismans the place that for so long had radiated their power.

Thus in challenging the oracle from his kingdom far away, Croesus had wanted to show that not only was he able to fill it, as he had done, with gifts of images of lions and of girls bringing bread, all in solid gold, but also that he knew where its power base lay. Most likely the oracle was not impressed, since every oracle wants to know but not to be known. When Croesus consulted Delphi before taking the most momentous step in his long reign—the war against Cyrus of Persia—the Pythia's answer was perfect in its ambiguity: "You will destroy a great empire." Croesus thought the great empire was Cyrus's, whereas in fact the oracle was referring to his own. Old and beaten, enslaved by Cyrus,

Croesus chose to send to Delphi a last gift, his chains. No king had ever had, nor would have, such a long and intimate relationship with the oracle.

When accused of ingratitude, Delphi's answer to Croesus showed a level of pathos and sense of compassion quite unusual for the oracle. As though to justify himself, Apollo told this extremely rich king that he had done everything he could to wring out of destiny what little destiny would concede. He had managed, for example, to delay the fall of Sardis for three years. It was one of those rare occasions when the god was sincere. With a gesture of humility almost, he revealed that he reigned only over what was surplus, over the excess that destiny left to his control. And this he had indeed given to Croesus, just as Croesus had given Apollo another kind of surplus, the thousands of slaughtered animals and thousands of pounds of gold he had sent up to Delphi.

But isn't the surplus life itself? Isn't life always a fragment of life, an unhoped for delay in the death sentence, like the three years Croesus was granted, like the extraordinary moment when, with a sudden rainstorm, Apollo put out the flames of Croesus's pyre? But one can go so far and no further. As a last gift the king bequeathed his chains. And those were not a surplus. Faced with those, even the god was helpless.

In his dialogue between Croesus and Solon, Herodotus sets up the first verbal duel between Asia and Europe. Of all potentates, Croesus is the one who possesses the most gold. Solon is chief legislator in Athens, and since the Athenians have committed themselves to maintaining the law unchanged for ten years, he sets out on a ten-year journey. Then Solon doesn't trust the Athenians. "That is the real reason why he went away, even if he claimed he wanted to see the world." One of the curiosities the world has to offer is Croesus's palace, where Solon duly arrives.

Croesus is eager for Solon to recognize him as not only

the most powerful but also the happiest of men. Solon responds by citing, as an example of a happy man, an unknown Athenian who died, old, in battle. Solon doesn't mean to contrast the common man with the king. That would be banal. He is explaining the Greek paradox as far as happiness is concerned: that one arrives at it only in death. Happiness is an element of life which, before it can come into being, demands that life disappear. If happiness is a quality that sums up the whole man, then it must wait until a man's life is complete in death.

This paradox doesn't exist in isolation. On the contrary, it is only one of the many paradoxes of wholeness to which the Greeks were so sensitive. Their basis can be found in the language itself: *telos*, the Greek word par excellence, means at once "perfection," "completion," "death." What we hear in Solon's voice is the Greek diffidence toward the happy man's obtuseness, and the national passion for logic. But it is the elegance with which he puts his case that strikes us most. Never has such an effective circumlocution been found for telling a truth that, if told straight, would be too brutal, and perhaps not even true anymore: that happiness does not exist.

By the time the Hellenistic age was ushered in, the open space in front of Apollo's temple in Delphi had grown crowded indeed. On the left, the bronze wolf donated by the people of Delphi kept guard. On the right, Praxiteles' golden Phryne shone out among numerous Apollos (commissioned by the Epidaurians or Megarians after some victory), as though the hetaera were still conversing with her admirers; a conversation made possible by her lover, Praxiteles, who had sculpted her body. One of those Apollos was enormous: the Apollo Sitalkas rose above a column to a height of seventy feet, more than double that of the temple columns. Then there was a bronze palm tree with, next to it, a gilded Athena from which a flock of crows had pecked away part of the gilding when the Athenians set out on their Sicilian

expedition. Or at least so Clytodemos would have us believe.
There were also numerous statues of generals from various
places, as well as the bronze donkey of the Ambracians and
the sacrificial procession, again in bronze, of the Sicyonians:
this was their way of fulfilling a vow that would otherwise
have obliged them to sacrifice an enormous number of animals to Apollo every year, so many they would have been
ruined. In bronze, their sacrifice became eternal. Beyond
Phryne stood another solid gold statue whose model owed
nothing to matters military: this was Gorgias of Leontini,
the defender of Helen, and the man who had preached the
supreme power of the word.

In 279 B.C. the Gauls, under Brennus, reached Thermopylae,
the "hot gates" of Greece, with just one thought in mind:
to sack Delphi. They weren't interested in anything else.
They didn't care about Athens, or Thebes, or Sparta, just
the treasures of Delphi. Even Brennus, in the remote North,
had heard tell of the "cave of the god that spewed up gold."
To the Greeks it seemed that history was repeating itself,
though stripped of its glory this time. Instead of the great
Xerxes' Persians with their pointed helmets and colorful
Oriental pomp, these new invaders were bands of blond
"beasts, full of dash and fury, but brainless," advancing out
of sheer impetuosity, even when shot through with arrows
and javelins, so long as their madness, their *berserk*, was
upon them. To oppose them, instead of the Spartans of
Leonidas, were a rabble of desperate provincials, Aetolians,
Boeotians, and Phocians. The defenders were aware that the
war could end in only two ways: either they won or they
would be exterminated. It wasn't a war for liberty, as it had
been against the Persians, but for survival.

In the first battle at Thermopylae, the Greeks once again
managed to hold out, while many of the Celts were swallowed up by the marshes: how many we shall never know.
At this Brennus decided to attack the Greek flank to draw
forces away from the center. Forty thousand infantry and

a few hundred cavalry stormed into Aetolia. They mas-
sacred all the males they could find, including newborn
babies. "They raped the dying and the dead." But less
than half of the Gauls who had set off on the expedition returned to the main camp at Thermopylae. Brennus was
undeterred: this time he went around the Greeks under
cover of fog. Just before they could be completely encircled,
the Greeks withdrew toward their hometowns. Brennus
didn't even wait for his own men to regroup before ordering
the march on Delphi. Perhaps that was the last time the god
of the tripod made his power known. In reply to the terror-
ized people of Delphi, the oracle told them it would look
after itself.

Brennus's men arrived to find Delphi protected only by
the Phocians and a few Aetolians, the rest being busy in their
own lands. Also waiting for them, however, was a divine and
invisible coalition. Apollo had gone for help to Poseidon and
Pan, the earlier divinities of the place, whom he himself had
eclipsed. The ground the Gauls advanced across quaked
every day, shaken deep below by Poseidon. And, fighting
beside the Greeks, their enemies would see the shades of the
Hyperborean heroes, Hyperocus and Laodocus, together
with the White Virgins. Thus the mythical North of Apollo
took on the historical North of biology. Even Neoptolemus,
Achilles' son, who Apollo had killed in his temple in Delphi,
as years before in another temple he had killed Achilles,
fought among the lightning bolts that consumed the wicker
shields of the Gauls.

Delphi's entire past, a long saga of murders and treachery, an arcane and seething history, rallied around that day
to offer an impregnable front of gods, ghosts, and soldiers.
And if the day brought horror to the Gauls, that horror only
grew when night fell. Pan came down from the Corycian
Cave and sowed terror among the barbarian troops, for
"they say that terror without reason is the work of Pan."
No sooner had twilight faded than the Gauls heard a drumming of hooves. They split into two ranks and faced each
other. "So delirious with panic were they, that each of the

ranks imagined they were facing Greeks, wearing Greek armor and speaking Greek, and this madness brought upon them by the god led to a huge massacre of Gauls." More of Brennus's soldiers were slain by one another that night than had died during the battle. Brennus himself was wounded, without hope, and chose to die, drinking wine unmixed with water.

There was a drought that year in Delphi. Followed by famine. The people knew they couldn't survive with the food they had left, so they decided to go, all of them, with their women and children, to the gates of the king's palace to beg for food. The king appeared and looked at them. Next to him his servants had a few meager baskets. The king scooped out barley and vegetables and handed them out to the people. He began with the local worthies. As he drew closer to the poorer people, his servants dug deeper and deeper into the baskets, pulling out smaller and smaller portions. Finally the baskets were empty, and there were still many poor people waiting. One of them, an orphan girl, Charila, who was there on her own with no one to look after her, stepped forward to ask the king for food. Grim faced, the king took off a sandal and flung it in Charila's face. The orphan went back to stand in line with the poor. Then everybody went home, hungry.

Charila left Delphi. Walking across the slopes of the Phaedriades, she found a place that fell away into the dark green of a ravine. Beside a tall tree, Charila undid her virgin's girdle and tied it in a noose around her neck. Then she hung herself from a branch. In Delphi the famine showed no sign of abating. Epidemics were raging now too, making an easy prey of wasted bodies. The king went to consult the Pythia. "Appease Charila, the virgin suicide" came the response. But the king didn't know who Charila was. He went down to Delphi and called an assembly of the people. Who was Charila? No one knew. Could she be some mythical figure everybody had forgotten about? Or was this "virgin suicide" a riddle, hardly a novelty for the oracle? Everybody in Delphi was obsessed by the name Charila until one of the Thyiads, the priestesses of Dionysus, remembered the king's angry gesture, the thrown sandal, and connected it with the fact that the girl hadn't been seen since. The priestess knew Charila because she was soon to have become one of them. She would have followed them up Parnassus, in the December frosts, and perhaps one day the people of Delphi would have found her in the thick of the blizzard, her cloak "stiff as a board, so that it broke when you opened it." But wrapped in that cloak would be the body of a Thyiad, resisting the icy cold with her torrid excitement. The priestess left Delphi with other Thyiads. In an inaccessible place, amid the dark green foliage, she saw Charila's body, still hanging from a branch, swinging in the wind. The name Thyiads means "the rustling ones." Some call them the Brides of the Wind. With loving care, they took the girl's body down from the tree. Then they laid it on the ground and buried it. Back in Delphi, the Thyiads explained how they had found Charila. Now she would have to be appeased, through expiation. But how?

The highest ranking Delphic theologians, the five Hosioi, the college of the Thyiads, the king: all mulled the problem over. They must find the right formula to respond to the Pythia's command. In the end, they decided to combine a sacrifice with an act of purification. But how could they make a sacrifice in a time of famine? The Delphic theologians knew that a sacrifice was a sign of imbalance in life with respect to the necessary: imbalance in terms of surplus but also in terms of deficiency. In both cases, whether it be dissipation or renunciation, there was a part of life that had to be expelled before one could achieve a balanced distribution, that state, as the Apollonian precept put it, of "nothing too much." By leaving out the poor when he distributed the food, the king had expelled them from life. Striking Charila, he had made a sacrifice without ceremony. Charila had raised that gesture to consciousness by hanging herself. But still her sacrifice had passed unnoticed. Decimated by starvation and epidemics, the people of Delphi didn't register her disappearance, hadn't realized that Charila was not just another victim of the famine but a sacrifice. They had forgotten her because she was too perfect a victim: a virgin, an orphan, overlooked by everyone, insulted by the king. And victims who are too perfect scare people, because they illuminate an unbearable truth. The Delphic theologians were profound inquirers into the art of dialectics and hypothetical syllogisms, if only because they were faithful to the god "who loves the truth above all things." The ultimate goal for them was not mindless devotion but knowledge. To expiate a crime didn't mean to do something that was the opposite of that crime but to repeat the same crime with slight variations in order to immerse oneself in guilt and bring it to consciousness. The crime lay not so much in having done certain things but in having done them without realizing what one was doing. The crime lay in not having realized that Charila had disappeared.

So the people of Delphi organized their ceremony. The citizens came to the king to ask for food, as they had done the day Charila was with them. The king distributed the food, but this time gave a portion to everybody, even the foreigners. Then an effigy of Charila was brought out from the crowd. The king took off his sandal and flung it in the effigy's face. The head priestess of the Thyiads then took the effigy, tied a rope around its neck, and carried it to where Charila had been found. She hung the effigy from the branches of the tree, letting it swing in the wind. Then the effigy was buried next to Charila's body. That ceremony marked the end of the famine. From then on the ritual would be repeated every eight years. But, just as the people of Delphi hadn't realized that Charila was gone until the lone voice of the Pythia reminded them, history would soon forget Charila and the ceremonies that were held for centuries in her name, until another lone voice, that of Plutarch, priest of Delphi, mentioned her again.

By now she had become one of the many "Greek Questions," one of the hundreds of fragments of the past whose meaning and origin no one could remember. Patient and erudite, Plutarch answered the question that he himself had put: "Who was Charila in Delphi?" His answer is the only trace of the little orphan's life that now remains to us.

VI

SINCE OLYMPIA IS THE IMAGE OF HAPPI-ness, it could only have appeared in the Golden Age. The men who lived at that time built a temple to Kronos in Olympia. Zeus hadn't even been born. In fact the first to run races in Olympia were the guardians Rhea gave the baby Zeus to when she wanted to hide him. The five Curetes, Heracles among them, came to Olympia from Crete, and Heracles was the first to crown a winning athlete with a chaplet of wild olive. He had brought the plant from the extreme North, beyond the source of the Danube, brought it back for the sole purpose of providing shade for the winning post in Olympia. The shade and the winning post, that was Olympia forever: the supreme exposure and the most profound withdrawal, the perfect pendulum. But the generations passed, and between the reigns of Oxylus and Iphitus the Olympic games were abandoned, forgotten. "When Iphitus restored the games, people still couldn't remember how they had been in ancient times; gradually they did remember, and each time they remembered something, they added it." It is the very image of the Platonic process of learning: nothing is new, remembering is all. What is new is the most ancient thing we have. With admirable candor, Pausanias adds: "This can be demonstrated." And he tells us when each memory surfaced: "At the eighteenth Olympiad, they remembered the pentathlon and wrestling."

Climbing the spiral staircase inside the temple took you to the upper galleries, where you could get a closer view of Phidias's Zeus. To Quintilianus's mind, this statue had "added something to the religion of men." Its gold and ivory surfaces were broken only by gems, except on the throne, which also had some ebony. The drapery was strewn with animals and lilies. Zeus wore a crown of olive twigs and in his right hand held a Nike, goddess of victory, with a ribbon and a crown. Beneath each of the throne's four feet were other small Nikes, like dancing elves. But something else was going on among those feet: winged Sphinxes carried off Theban youths in their claws, and Apollo and Artemis loosed their arrows at Niobe's children again. And as it grew accustomed to the teeming dark, the eye would make out one new scene after another, sculpted on the cross-struts of the throne. The farther down you looked, the more figures you saw. Twenty-nine in all on the cross-struts: the Amazons, Heracles with his escort, Theseus. A boy is adjusting a ribbon on his forehead: is it Pantarckes, Phidias's young lover? You can't go right up to the throne, because of the painted barriers, which again show Theseus and Heracles, and then Peirithous, Ajax, Cassandra, Hippodamia, Sterope, Prometheus, Penthesilea, Achilles, two Hesperides. Other beings sprout from the top of the throne: three Charites and three Hours. Then the eye moves back down to Zeus's footstool and finds still more figures: Theseus yet again, and again the Amazons and golden lions. As one looks down even farther, at the base that supports the huge Zeus and his parasites, other scenes become apparent: Helios climbs onto his chariot, Hermes advances as Hestia follows, Eros greets Aphrodite as she rises from the waves and Peitho crowns her. Nor has the sculptor forgotten Apollo and Artemis, Athena and Heracles, Amphitryon and Poseidon, and Selene on a horse. A seated giant encrusted with creatures, Zeus was reflected in a floor of shiny black stone where oil flowed in abundance to preserve the ivory.

No other statue was so admired by the Greeks, nor even by Zeus himself, who hurled an approving thunderbolt down on the black paving when Phidias finished the job and asked the god for a sign. Olympia's chryselephantine Zeus was destroyed in a palace fire in Byzantium in the fifth century. All that remains are some Elean coins showing the statue, and the words of those who, like Callimachus and Pausanias, saw it and were impressed. Paulus Aemilius claimed that Phidias had given form to Homer's Zeus.

The moderns have been cowed and confused by these descriptions. Too many colors, too much Oriental pomp, the suspicion of a lapse of taste. Could Phidias, they wonder, in this, his most ambitious project, have tossed aside all the qualities so admired in the Parthenon friezes? The mistake of the moderns is to think of Phidias's Zeus as a statue, in the sense in which Praxiteles' Hermes is a statue. For it was something else. Shut away and sparkling in its temple cell, Phidias's Zeus was closer to a dolmen, a bethel, a stone fallen from heaven, to which other gods and heroes clung in order to live. The gold and ivory seethed like an ants' nest. Zeus didn't exist except as a support for animals and lilies, arches and drapes, old scenes forever repeated. But Zeus was more than just the motionless guardian seated on his throne: Zeus was all those scenes, those deeds, muddled and shuffled about, rippling his body and throne in tiny shivers. Without meaning to, Phidias had illustrated that Zeus cannot live alone: without meaning to, he had represented the essence of polytheism.

Olympia was happiness itself for the Greeks, who were experts in unhappiness. The dense green in the Peloponnese has a hallucinatory glow to it, a glow the more intense for being so rare, with something final about it. All the different species of green gather around Olympia, as once the athletes of every Greek-speaking settlement would come here to compete. The acid phosphorescence of the Aleppo pines, the darkly etched cypresses, the glassy streaked leaves of the lemon trees, the primordial bamboo—see them all against a background of gently contoured hills modeled by Poseidon's thumb, the earthquake. The place was the gift of a man who became a river, Alpheus. Having forced a path between the bare, scorching peaks of Arcadia, having washed the slopes of Lykaion—mountain of wolves and cannibals on whose summit the sun casts never a shadow—the Alpheus finally astonishes when, emerging from the gorges of Cerynite, it broadens into the rolling slopes of a valley as dear to Zeus as the archaic Lykaion had once been hateful. The Greeks were not in the habit of mentioning nature to no end, but Pausanias extols the Alpheus on three separate occasions: "the greatest of rivers for the volume of water passing through it, and the most pleasing to the eye"; a river "legendary to lovers," thanks to its origin; and finally, to Zeus's mind, "the most exquisite of all rivers."

But who was Alpheus? A hunter. He saw the goddess-huntress Artemis, fell in love with her, and with vain mortal brashness began to follow her. All over Greece, the goddess heard those footsteps behind her and laughed. One night, in Letrinoi, not far from Olympia, she decided to celebrate a feast with her Nymphs. Before Alpheus caught up with them, goddess and Nymphs smeared their faces with clay. Alpheus saw whitish faces looming in the dark. Which was the goddess? He couldn't say. So the hunter who had "mustered up the courage to attempt to rape" the goddess was forced to give up and "went away without having achieved his goal," his ears smarting with the sound of shrill, mocking laughter. Yet never had Artemis, that most cruel of goddesses, been so kind to an admirer, nor would she be again. Instead of having him torn to pieces by his dogs, like Actaeon, who hadn't even come near her, she let Alpheus walk off unharmed, and initiated. In Greek stories, smearing one's face foreshadows a momentous and terrible event. The Titans smeared chalk on their faces before tearing Zagreus to pieces. But here, instead of being the prelude to carnage, the smearing serves to stave off the dire event. The virgin goddess avoids being abused precisely by making herself similar to her Nymphs. She does the opposite of what her initiates do: dress up and wear masks to look like the goddess. Artemis's gesture dissolves an impending horror in laughter.

Alpheus encounters the goddess and her Nymphs as a group of people wearing masks, or dead. And it is difficult to get your bearings among the masked and the dead; even goddesses can no longer be recognized with confidence, because here one has crossed the threshold of another world. The laughter that rang in the retreating Alpheus's ears was, for the goddess, the greatest possible token of affection, an act of kindness. After all, she had demonstrated to this rash and ignorant man the elusive and insurmountable distance between woman and goddess: and all it had taken was a bit of clay. The huntress-goddess escapes all the more irretrievably when disguised as a woman.

But Artemis wanted to protect the hunter. She couldn't give him her body, so she chose a Nymph, Arethusa, as her substitute. And Alpheus began a second passionate chase. In the fury of flight, Arethusa crossed the sea and transformed herself into a freshwater spring near Syracuse. This time Alpheus could not renounce his love. The hunter became the river Alpheus, flowed out into the sea just before Pyrgos, and traveled, for hundreds of miles, right across the Ionian Sea as an underwater current. When he surfaced again with his frothy crown, he was in Sicily, near Arethusa. Where he mingled his own waters with the Nymph's.

Hence Olympia came into being thanks to Alpheus. Hence the Master of Olympia placed a slim, muscular young man with prominent rib cage in a corner of the eastern pediment of the temple to Zeus, making Alpheus the first river to appear in a Greek temple. Hence in Olympia people sacrificed to Artemis and Alpheus on the same altar. Hence in the Middle Ages the waters of Alpheus shifted their course so as to submerge the stones and offerings of Olympia and protect it in their silt.

Alpheus was not a part of nature eager to become an affable allegorical figure, an old actor to be recycled one day in the lunettes of some Renaissance villa. No, Alpheus was that young man with the short hair and nervous spine depicted by the Master of Olympia, a man who would one day "transform himself into a river for love." He was a hunter who one day decided to become nature. He was the only lover who, when his beloved turned to water, agreed to become water himself, without wanting to be held back by the boundaries of an identity. Thus he achieved a union no other man or woman had ever achieved, the union of two freshwater streams soon to plunge together into the sea. One eminent guarantor for the truth of the story of Alpheus was the oracle of Delphi, who celebrated the metamorphosis in some of her finest lines: "Somewhere, in the fog-bound plain of the sea, / Where Ortygia is, near Thrinakia, / Alpheus's foaming mouth mingles / with the gushing spring of Arethusa."

Alpheus and Arethusa: water with water, the spring that gushes from the earth, the current that rises from the depths of the sea, the meeting of two lymphs that have traveled far, the ultimate erotic convergence, perennial happiness, no bastions against the world, gurgling speech. Between the waves of the Ionian and those of the Alpheus, the difference lies in the taste, and perhaps a slight variation of color. Between the water of Arethusa and the water of Alpheus, the only difference is in the foam on Alpheus's crest as he rises from the sea. But the taste is much the same: both come from Olympia.

The Greek activity par excellence was the shaping of molds. That's why Plato was so intrigued by the modest craftsmen (*dēmiourgoí*) who plied this trade in Athens; that's why he gave the name of their guild to the artificer of the whole world. In whatever walk of life, the Greeks were chiefly interested in shaping molds. They knew that, once made, those molds could be applied to an extremely wide range of materials. We think of the bourgeoisie as of something peculiarly modern, but when we describe it we are applying the mold of the *mesótēs*, which Aristotle developed in his *Politics*. When a company tries to impose a brand name, they are responding to a perception of the hierarchical supremacy of the *týpos*, the mold, over every other power.

The image that comes closest to the ideas of Plato is to be seen in the molds for fragments of the drapery of Phidias's Zeus found in the sculptor's studio in Olympia: the material is neutral and the same throughout, only the curves of the folds vary. In the end it is what is cast that survives. We live in a warehouse of casts that have lost their molds. In the beginning was the mold.

Mythical stories always lie at the foundation of something. But what they found can be either order or disorder. Greece split those stories up geographically with a sharp dividing line along the Gulf of Corinth. To the north, if we go back to the beginning, we find the slayers of monsters. Apollo for Delphi, Cadmus for Thebes, Theseus for Athens. And just as Apollo, model for all monster slayers, was also a musician and leader of the Muses, so Cadmus introduced the Phoenician alphabet into Greece, and Theseus brought together a few modest villages into a new entity, which from then on would be known as Athens. Common to all of them is the civilizing seal that stamps itself on an animal material.

South of the Gulf of Corinth that seal is nowhere to be found. The area was known as the Peloponnese, "the Isle of Pelops," because many of its kingdoms dated back to a single man, Pelops. Some of those kingdoms, such as Mycenae, Argos, and Tiryns, could boast an ancient past and considerable power. Yet the story of Pelops and the Pelopides has nothing civilizing about it at all, except perhaps by accident. On the contrary, it lays the basis for an incurable disorder, a sequence of family vendettas, of curses that echo for generations, of actions that are repeated compulsively, of murderous treachery. It is the very *karman* between men and gods that surfaces here in all its tangled complexity. And it all began when a mortal invited the Olympians to dine at his table.

Pelops was son to a king of the immensely rich country of Lydia. The king's name was Tantalus, and he often visited the gods. Tantalus talked a great deal, too much in fact. In his palace he would tell people about the nectar and ambrosia he had tasted on Olympus. Sometimes it seems he would steal a small amount and offer it around. He would also talk about the divine secrets he'd learned. When he was up in the heavens, he would say the wildest things, things that didn't always please the Olympians. But Zeus went on being kind to him and inviting him. Some believe that Tantalus was his son.

One day Tantalus decided that he would like to invite the Olympians to his place. Pelops was scarcely more than a boy then. He watched a big bronze pot being prepared and put on the fire. Then he remembered hands tearing him limb from limb, but he didn't lose consciousness. Now the gods were sitting around the bronze pot where the dismembered little Pelops was simmering away. Tantalus offered the gods the delicious food he had prepared for them. They all fell silent; the meat stayed where it was on their plates. Only Demeter, wrapped in thought, dazed and distracted as she had been ever since her daughter Kore disappeared, picked up a piece of meat and ate it. It was Pelops's shoulder blade. Immediately afterward, Zeus unleashes his fury. All the kindnesses he had hitherto heaped on Tantalus were transformed into atrocious punishments. The other gods still sat silently in front of their plates. Zeus ordered Hermes to collect all the pieces of Pelops's body. He must put them in the pot and bring them to the boil again. Then Clotho, one of the Moirai, the Fates, took them out one by one and began to sew them together as if she were mending a doll. But there was still the big hole in his back. So Demeter fashioned a shoulder blade of ivory. Rhea breathed life into Pelops. Now the boy was alive, whole and radiant. Pan was so happy he danced around him. Poseidon was dazzled by Pelops's beauty and promptly decided to abduct him. On a chariot drawn by golden horses, he fled to Olympus with the boy. He wanted Pelops to be his lover and his cupbearer.

Having lived—we don't know how long—with Poseidon, Pelops found himself king of his father's lands. Soon the neighboring peoples were harassing him with their attacks. Pelops decided to cross the sea with his men and his treasure in search of a woman. He would go and present himself to a distant princess, in the part of Greece that looked westward: the girl was Hippodameia, daughter of Oenomaus.

Around the gateway to Oenomaus's palace on Kronos hill in Olympia, thirteen human heads had been nailed. Pelops crossed the threshold as a foreigner and the fourteenth suitor to Hippodameia. He was told that Oenomaus planned to collect a few more heads before bringing them all together in a temple dedicated to his father, Ares. The king of Olympia was obsessed by two violent passions: his horses and his daughter, Hippodameia. Both were protected by a law. No mules must be born in Elis. Whoever mated an ass with a mare would be put to death. Hippodameia's suitors had to try to beat the magic horses of Oenomaus, a gift from Ares. Oenomaus thought of these foreign kings as inferior beasts who wanted to defile his magnificent mare Hippodameia by generating a bastard child on her. His horses and his daughter, "subduer of horses," formed a ring. One half circle was continued in the other. In bed sometimes, he would see a white mare's head pop up from under the covers, and it was his daughter.

Pelops looked about him and decided to defeat trickery with trickery. Oenomaus's horses were a gift from Ares, but who had the best horses in the world, if not Poseidon? And hadn't Poseidon been his first lover? Alone on the beach, Pelops called on the god, reminding him of their past love. Did Poseidon want to see him run through by the lance of a cruel king? Did he want his head to wind up next to the others like a hunting trophy? Long ago the god had snatched him away in his flying chariot: those same horses were now needed to snatch him from death. Poseidon agreed. Pelops looked at the wonderful horses and thought that Ares was, yes, a powerful god, but not on a par with Poseidon, who split open rocks to clear a path for his horses and had them gallop up from the foam of the waves. But even that wasn't enough. Pelops felt that three tricks were safer than just the one. And he decided to win over Hippodameia before the race had even started. Hippodameia had long been used to going to bed with her father. She even helped and defended him. She had seen thirteen foreigners arrive; she had climbed on their chariots and disturbed or distracted them during the race just as her father had asked. Knowing full well where their corpses would end up. But this time she was dazzled by the new stranger with the ivory sparkling on his back. For the first time she felt she wanted to share a different bed. And she decided to destroy her father. Oenomaus's charioteer was a boy called Myrtilus, who was crazy about Hippodameia. The evening before the race, Hippodameia promised him her body if he would put wax instead of iron linchpins in the wheels of her father's chariot. Myrtilus was obsessed by Hippodameia's body and accepted. Pelops and Hippodameia agreed that they would eliminate Myrtilus as soon as possible after winning the race.

The morning of the race there was a moment of frightening stillness. Everybody was there and almost ready. In their midst, taller and invisible, stood Zeus. He held the lightning in his left hand while his right fell empty on his hip but radiated tension. His chest was a wall. Everybody seemed to be concentrating on his or her own fate, not realizing that the fate of the whole land, and of many others hidden beyond the green rim of the horizon, was about to be decided. The bloody scenario Oenomaus had planned, and around which his life had revolved for years now, was as follows: first the suitor would carry off Hippodameia on his chariot; as a head start Oenomaus would then give him the time it took to sacrifice a black ram. After which he would climb on his own chariot, alongside Myrtilus and set off after the fugitives.

A slave girl was tying Hippodameia's sandals. This was the moment when, thirteen times before, father and daughter had exchanged glances of complicity. Hippodameia looked at her father. Oenomaus's body had the assurance of age, and of the many dead impaled on his lance. Naked but for a drape over his shoulders, he pulled his helmet right down over his forehead, so that between beard and helmet only his eyes stood out, his steady eyes. Tonight we sleep together again, those eyes were saying. Hippodameia was wearing the complicated Doric tunic, hardly suitable for a race. Her curly hair fell on her forehead in perfect little ringlets, and her heart was suddenly cold, as though it were all over even before it had started, as though father, palace, and heaped corpses had already gone up in smoke. Pelops was completely naked, leaning on his lance. The ivory on his shoulder blade gleamed. Shaking with excitement, Myrtilus crouched, awaiting orders, a lean, skillful hand fidgeting with his big toe. Sterope, Oenomaus's wife, looked on, motionless and expressionless. Born from the love of a god for a star, she had long been treated as no more than a servant of Oenomaus's passion for Hippodameia, a gravedigger for her daughter's suitors. She had learned to live without hope: whatever the outcome of the race, for her it would be just one more horror. But duty required her, as a queen, to look on. Only an old priest, standing away to one side, dug his fingers into his beard and noticed something. He was one of the Iamids, a race brought up on violets and fed honey by snakes. Apollo had granted him the gift of understanding nature's voices and likewise of realizing when speech was pointless.

What followed, the race, was over in a flash. The spectators glimpsed the wheels of Oenomaus's chariot shooting out into the sunlight, saw the horses tear the king's body apart, heard his voice cursing Myrtilus. But that was only the beginning of it: for four generations the race, the dust, the blood, the splintering wheels would never stop. Until there were few who remembered how it had all started at that moment when Oenomaus lifted his knife over the black ram and Poseidon's horses shot off, spiriting away Pelops and Hippodameia in a cloud, where the two conspirators in crime and victory exchanged their looks of complicity.

Pelops is not unique, the way Theseus is, or Cadmus. Nor is he a great warrior, or a hero, or an inventor. He is merely the bearer of a talisman. The uniqueness he does not have by birth has been inserted in his body. His ivory shoulder blade forms an artificial connection with the divine, covering for what man lacks. The artifact that fills this empty space and meshes with Pelops's body possesses an immense and concentrated power, a power that goes far beyond that of its bearer, a power that will be transmitted as a surplus from one generation to another, gradually losing its influence in the process.

The talisman set in Pelops's flesh becomes the golden fleece of the lamb that Pelops's sons, Atreus and Thyestes, fight over, and that Atreus keeps locked away in a chest as if it were a bag of coins. Before being individuals with individual destinies, Pelops and the Pelopids, right down to Orestes and beyond, and as late even as Penthilus, are ripples in the history of a noble house, and of the talisman that destroys it. Generation after generation, the lineage runs through the Peloponnese like the gray nerve of an ancient fortification along a mountain ridge.

The evening after the race was a sad one because everything happened as foreseen and agreed. In the heat of the chase, Poseidon's horses opened their wings and carried off the victorious three as far as the island of Euboea. "I'm thirsty," Hippodameia announced, and Pelops went off to get some water in his helmet. The young Myrtilus looked at Hippodameia and tried to put his arms around her. Hippodameia quickly wriggled free. "Later," she said. When Pelops got back with the water, her nod was so slight it was almost imperceptible. The two lovers were aware of the first law of criminal life: as soon as you've seen off the enemy, kill the traitor who made it possible. After a while they reined in their horses on the southernmost tip of Euboea, where the cliffs fall sheer to the sea. Myrtilus looked down at the rocks. Pelops pushed him from behind. Distant, but distinct, the lovers heard the curse that the dying Myrtilus cast on the house of Pelops.

Pelops was a powerful king, but nothing more than that. He conquered lands north, south, east, and west, and he called his kingdom the Peloponnese. His deeds are not remembered for their courage, although one was memorable for its baseness and treachery. Unable to beat him on the battlefield, Pelops invited Stymphalus, king of Arcadia, to take part in friendly discussions. When the king arrived, unarmed, Pelops had him cut to pieces, just as, long ago, his father had had Pelops cut to pieces. Then he ordered the king's bloody limbs to be scattered across the countryside. A famine followed throughout Greece.

Pelops had twenty-two children by Hippodameia. They became kings, heralds, bandits. But Pelops's favorite child was his twenty-third, the bastard, Chrysippus, whom he had by Axioche, a Nymph. Chrysippus was extremely handsome, and Pelops was not at all surprised when a guest of his, the noble Laius of Thebes, who had a weakness for young boys, abducted him. After all, Pelops's own life had begun the same way, and his abduction had brought him luck. No, the person nursing a silent hatred was Hippodameia. She had given birth to twenty-two children on Pelops's bed, and now she was obsessed by the awful suspicion that the twenty-third, the bastard, had been chosen as the heir. She felt the blood of her father, Oenomaus, rising in her, his loathing for every bastard breed. She began to pester her favorite sons, Atreus and Thyestes, nagging them to

kill Chrysippus. But in the end it was she herself who buried
Laius's sword in the boy's soft body as he lay sleeping beside
his lover. Pelops cursed Hippodameia, Atreus, and Thyestes,
and threw them out of his palace. Hippodameia killed herself in exile. Atreus and Thyestes went to Mycenae because
the town's throne was vacant and the oracle had prophesied
that one day it would belong to one of Pelops's sons. There
was one throne available in Mycenae, and two sons turned
up to claim it.

The glory of Pelops was Olympia. In the history of the gods,
the games were founded in the Golden Age, when the Curetes ran. In human history, the games began their glorious
period under Pelops. The most rigged and bloody of races
had thus breathed new life into that place that enshrined
the notion of Hellenic peace, a place where those who
cheated were punished. Between the temples of Zeus and
Hera, a sacred burial mound with polygonal perimeter, trees
and statues was given over to Pelops. "In Olympia, the
Eleans venerate Pelops above all other heroes, just as they
venerate Zeus above all other gods." In the area dedicated
to Pelops, the Eleans sacrificed a black ram every year, making the same gesture Oenomaus had made before his last
race. Nobody who wanted to enter the temple of Zeus could
taste the meat of that sacrifice.

When Hippodameia's bones were brought back to Olympia, she found herself beside Pelops once again, bones beside
bones. By now they had become the guardians of the place.
And, although the women's games were no less old than the
men's, it had been Hippodameia who first got together sixteen virgins and had them race with their hair loose, their
tunics over their knees, right shoulders and breasts uncovered. This had been her way of thanking Hera for her marriage to Pelops. Later she was responsible for a gift to the
temple of Hera: a small ivory bed. It was still there when
Pausanias visited Olympia and commented: "They say it
was Hippodameia's toy."

There are two strands to the story of the Pelopids: the tale of a king's descendants, a succession of atrocities, each worse than the one before; and the tale of a series of talismans, each taking over from another in silence, each deciding the fate of men. In the beginning we have Pelops's ivory shoulder, but later there is his scepter too, the scepter he intended for his son Atreus; then we have the golden lamb that Atreus and Thyestes fought over; then Pelops's lance, which his great-granddaughter Iphigenia would keep in her bedroom; then the ancient wooden statue of Artemis that Orestes brings to Greece from the land of the Tauri.

Pelops was long dead and the Trojan War dragging on interminably when the sages prophesied that the city could only be taken with the help of Heracles' bow and Pelops's shoulder blade. So Pelops's bones were sent off to Troy. On the return trip, the ship carrying the bones sank off the island of Euboea, not far from the place where Myrtilus had long lain at the bottom of the sea. "And many years after the sacking of Troy, an Eretrian fisherman called Damarmenus cast his nets into the sea and pulled up the shoulder blade. He was amazed how big it was and kept it hidden in the sand, but in the end he went to Delphi to ask the oracle whose bone it was and what he should do with it. Thanks to some stroke of divine providence, a delegation of Eleans had come to Delphi at exactly the same time to ask advice about how to cure the plague, so the Pythia told them they must recover Pelops's bones, and told Damarmenus to give the Eleans what he had found. He did as the Pythia said and, among other acts of gratitude, the Eleans named him and his descendants guardians of the bone. When I visited, the shoulder blade of Pelops was no longer there, I suppose because it had been on the seabed for so long and the salt water together with the passage of time had reduced it to dust." So writes Pausanias. The talisman had outlived Pelops's descendants, but in the end it too succumbed. Only the guardians of the bone remained.

The tension we find in Pelops, dismembered and dismembering, splits apart into two poles, two sons: Atreus and Thyestes. They are brothers and enemies, like so many one comes across in myths, in history, in the street. But in comparison with those of all other analogous pairs, their quarrel is a little more cruel, more comic, more abstract, if by comedy and abstraction we mean an algebraic elevation of horror to a far higher power. Every story of two is always a story of three: two pairs of hands grab the same thing at the same time and tug in opposite directions. In this case the third thing is the golden lamb, the talisman of sovereignty. Times have changed: Pelops's shoulder blade is no longer something given by a god and thrust inside a body but an external body that hands must grasp and offer to a god, in this case, Artemis. Atreus tightens his grip on the lamb to strangle it, then hides it away in his house, attempting to transform the talisman into a treasure. Until Thyestes manages to steal it from him, with the help of Atreus's wife, the Cretan Aërope, whom he has been busy seducing.

This should be the first link in the chain of wrongs. But we immediately realize that it isn't: before Thyestes proved treacherous to Atreus, Atreus had already deceived Artemis, by refusing her the beast promised as a sacrifice. Up to this point, the brothers were exactly equal in terms of their crimes. Both had helped their mother murder their bastard brother, Chrysippus. And both had been afflicted by the curse of their father, Pelops, which echoed and renewed the curses of Myrtilus on Pelops, of Oenomaus on Myrtilus, and, at the beginning of it all, of Zeus on Tantalus, ancestral founder of the family. Henceforth, the struggle between the two brothers will be admirably balanced, in the sense that it would be quite hopeless to attempt to establish which of the two is more unjust. Both strive for the worst. Any difference lies in style and in divine whim, which initially favors Atreus. In fact, in order to trick Thyestes, as Thyestes tricked Atreus, and so have Atreus win the struggle for sovereignty over Mycenae, Zeus goes so far as to invert the courses of the sun and stars. This intervention is equivalent to his gesture of turning over the table in anger at Lycaon's cannibalism: it is an allusion to the tilting of the earth's axis, to the new world that comes into being with the obliquity of the ecliptic. But Zeus's intervention is only one small episode in the thrilling struggle between two brothers who have now discovered that man is autonomous and proceed to try out the mechanics of that autonomy to the full.

Having recovered the talisman, and with it his power, and having thrown Thyestes out of Mycenae, Atreus, one would imagine, would be satisfied, that the struggle had run its course, or at most would flare up again with Thyestes seeking revenge. Instead the conflict is raised to a higher power: it is the winner who wants to revenge himself on the loser, and what's more wants his revenge to outdo all others. Giving the impression that he is eager to make up with his brother, Atreus invites him back to Mycenae. Thyestes returns and is welcomed with a sumptuous banquet. In a big bronze pot lashings of white meat are bubbling away in little chunks. Atreus chooses a few and offers them to his brother. So memorable is the stony stare on his face as he does so that ever afterward people will speak of making "Atreus eyes." At the end of the banquet, Atreus has a servant come in. The servant carries a plate crammed with human hands and feet. Thyestes realizes he has been eating the flesh of his children. With a kick he turns over the table. And curses the house of Atreus.

From this point on the vendetta between the two brothers loses all touch with psychology, becomes pure virtuosity, traces out arabesques. Thyestes disappears again, a horrified fugitive. There's just one thing on his mind: how to invent a revenge that will outdo his brother's, who in turn had thought up his with the intention of making it unbeatable. Thyestes looks to future generations now. It would be too simple to kill Atreus. He will have to get his son too, and his son's son. At this point the gods come to his aid. On a pilgrimage to Delphi, Thyestes asks for Apollo's advice. With perfect sobriety, the god replies: "Rape your daughter." The avenger would be born from that rape. Pelopia, Thyestes' daughter, had taken refuge at the house of King Thesprotus in Sicyon. She was a priestess of Athena. One night she was sacrificing to the goddess along with some other girls. Thyestes watched from behind a hedge. The priestesses were dancing around a sheep that had had its throat cut when Pelopia slipped in a pool of blood, staining her tunic. Thyestes saw her leave the others to go to a stream. She slid off the bloodstained tunic. It was the first time the father had seen how beautiful his daughter was naked. He leaped on that white body, covering his head with his cloak (or did he have a mask?). Pelopia fought furiously. The two rolled over on the ground. Thyestes managed to penetrate and empty his sperm into her. When it was over, Pelopia found herself alone again, holding the sword she had grabbed from her unknown assailant. That night Aegisthus was conceived, the man Homer would call "the blameless one."

Meanwhile, after Atreus had slaughtered Thyestes' children, Mycenae had been afflicted by a terrible drought. An oracle claimed that the drought would only end when the fugitive Thyestes had returned. Atreus knew that Thyestes was staying with King Thesprotus. He went to Sicyon, but Thyestes had fled again after raping his daughter. At the court of Thesprotus, Atreus met a priestess of Athena and immediately fell in love with her. He asked the king for her hand, imagining that Pelopia was his daughter. Thesprotus chose not to enlighten him and granted him Pelopia's hand. Atreus went back to Mycenae without his brother but with a new wife, who was carrying in her bags a sword that belonged to she knew not whom. Having been betrayed and made a fool of by Aërope, Atreus wanted a new family, a family without sin. Nine months later, Pelopia gave birth to Aegisthus. She gave him to some shepherds to have him grow up in the mountains, fed on goat's milk. Atreus imagined that Pelopia must be suffering from a momentary and forgivable attack of insanity. He sent his men off to the mountains in search of the child. They brought him back.

Of all his children, Atreus thought, this one alone had not been contaminated: so this one would be his heir.

In Mycenae nature was still refusing to budge, refusing to bear fruit until Thyestes came back. Eventually he was captured and thrown into prison. Atreus called Aegisthus and gave him his first man's job: he must take the sword his mother always kept beside her and use it to run through their prisoner in his sleep. In the prison, Thyestes managed to elude his son and grab the sword from his hand. He looked at it. Then recognized it: it was the one he'd lost that night in Sicyon. He told Aegisthus to call his mother. On seeing the sword and Thyestes, Pelopia realized what had happened. She took hold of the sword and buried it in her body. Thyestes drew it out from Pelopia's flesh and gave it, still dripping with his mother's blood, to the little Aegisthus. He told the boy to go back to Atreus and show the sword to him as proof that his orders had been carried out. Euphoric to find himself at last rid of his brother, and hence of his obsession, Atreus decided that the first thing he must do was show his gratitude to the gods. A solemn sacrifice was prepared on the seashore. While it was being celebrated, the little Aegisthus approached and plunged Thyestes' sword into Atreus's body. Thyestes became king of Mycenae. A new golden lamb appeared in his flock.

Thus, for the moment, the conflict between the two brothers came to an end. At least in the sense that one was dead and the other wasn't. But the grindstone that had accelerated during their feud would go on crushing bones for one, two, three generations to come. The clash between the two hostile brothers had become a war between forms, a duel between two fanatics of form. If Thyestes achieved a momentary victory, it was because his formal inventiveness had gone far beyond his brother, who, in the end, had stopped at the cannibal's banquet. Thyestes is the true modern: he sets up a dizzying equivocation and uses it to satisfy his ends. Thyestes' triumph is alluded to in Euripides' *Cretans* (and confirmed in Seneca's *Thyestes*). Here, the Cretan woman Aërope, the traitor, who in most versions betrays

Atreus with Thyestes in Mycenae, turns out to have already met Thyestes earlier on in Crete. He was on the run, a vagabond exiled by his brother. But he scored an immediate success with the princess, just the way Theseus did with Ariadne. King Catreus surprised the two of them in bed, upon which he took Aërope and her sister Clymene and handed them over to another king, Nauplius, to have them drowned or sold off as slaves. But Nauplius decided to marry Clymene himself and took her to Argos. There, Plisthenes, Atreus's son, born a weakling as part of Artemis's vendetta against his father, chose Aërope as his bride. Aërope, however, had already conceived Agamemnon and Menelaus by Thyestes.

So when, on his return from Troy, snared in a net, one foot still in the water of his bath, Agamemnon is slain by the avenger Aegisthus and by his wife, Clytemnestra, the blood flows from Thyestes at the hand of Thyestes, from a son of Thyestes at the hand of another son of Thyestes and of his own stepsister. In the house of Atreus, that is, there's not a trace of Atreus left. There is only Thyestes' curse, which Cassandra senses in the air, a curse that now circles back on itself, cut off from everything else, pure form, autistic glory.

While Agamemnon, Atreus's son, was off fighting beneath the walls of Troy, everybody expected Aegisthus, Thyestes' son, to take his place in Clytemnestra's bed and hence on the throne of Mycenae. Yet the players were slow to make their moves. They wanted to savor the inevitable. Like a sales rep, King Nauplius was cruising up and down the coast of Attica and the Peloponnese. He tied up in the larger ports, visiting all the palaces where there was an empty throne. In the evenings he would talk about Troy, about how tough the war was, about there being no end in sight. He talked on into the small hours with lonely queens. And then proposed adultery. Not with himself, no no no, but with some ambitious fellow from a good family in the vicinity. It was his way of reminding those empty thrones how treacherously they had murdered his son Palamedes, beyond the sea, beneath the walls of Troy.

When, in Mycenae, he tried his spiel on Clytemnestra, he noticed that the queen couldn't suppress a sardonic, distracted smile. Did she really need someone to come and suggest what she had long known she was going to do? And Agamemnon was wise to it too. He had left a tiresome court bard breathing down her neck with instructions to keep a close eye on her and write with any news. That man was the first State intellectual. But one day Aegisthus grabbed him by the scruff of the neck and had him bundled onto a boat. They dumped him on an island where only thistles grew. So the vultures could gorge themselves on his old flesh.

Thus Aegisthus at last entered the palace of Mycenae, wore Agamemnon's sandals, soiled the king's bed with his sweat, sat on his throne, possessed Clytemnestra, more in rage than pleasure. But that was exactly what Clytemnestra liked. There was a profound complicity between them, and they began to look like each other, the way some old couples will. Sometimes, in the evening, in front of the fire, they would talk about how they would kill Agamemnon, ironing out the details, weighing alternatives, relishing their anticipation. And even afterward, when from the summits of Athos and Arachne the beacons had announced the king's return, when Agamemnon had trodden the purple with terror, when Aegisthus had stabbed him twice and Clytemnestra had beheaded him with her ax, even then, in the evenings, the two would pass the time together, thinking of Orestes now, of how they would kill him, how he would try to kill them. Finally the moment was upon them; Orestes tricked them into letting him into the palace and slew his mother and her lover: it was an easy murder, like a scene rehearsed over and over, year in, year out, with actors who are in a hurry to have done and get on home.

The grim mechanics of the Pelopids seems to break down with the noble debate on Orestes at the Areopagus, the Athenian Council. And when Athena's vote absolves him, they all lift up their faces, as if waking from a nightmare. But Orestes' trial did more good for the Athenians than for Orestes. It gave them the pride of placing themselves beyond crime, of understanding crime, and this was something that nobody hitherto had dared. As for Orestes, he was as wretched afterward as he had been before. The day he appeared in Athens and everybody shunned him, willing, yes, to give him something to drink, but only so long as he drank it alone, upon which they all, even the children, began to drink on their own from little jugs—that day Orestes realized that he was doomed to drinking at that table, alone, for the rest of his life, even if he was absolved, even if he was king, even if there were women beside him.

And who might these women be? His sisters, Electra and Iphigenia, who he felt condemned to look for, to find again. And sisters meant family. Orestes' greatest torment was this: that wherever he went, all his affairs were family affairs. Even Pylades, to whom he had given his friendship, was a relative in the end. And he'd had him marry one of his sisters. Outside his family, the world might as well not have existed. What other women then? Orestes sought out Hermione, another relative, cousin twice over. But then realized that his reason for seeking her out made matters even worse; it paralyzed him. Hermione had been betrothed to Neoptolemus, Achilles' son. When Neoptolemus was killed by Apollo in the god's temple in Delphi, just as his father had been killed by Apollo, Orestes took the murdered man's place next to Hermione. He was perfectly aware that he was not, as he did so, himself, Orestes; he was Agamemnon once again depriving Achilles of the beloved Briseis.

Orestes never was Orestes, except in the periods when the Erinyes goaded him to insanity. Or the brief moments of respite from madness, as when he rested his head on a stone on a small island off Gythion. Then he started: someone was telling him that Helen and Paris had spent their first night of love together right on this spot. And he immediately decided to set sail again. Or in that suffocating place in Arcadia where he realized that he could no longer bear the Erinyes, or rather not so much them, for he had lost all hope of being rid of them, but their color, that impenetrable black in the noonday brilliance, and in exasperation he bit off a finger of his left hand. Upon which the Erinyes turned white.

But this reprieve didn't last long. Even when they were white they terrified him, more than before maybe, and they never stopped following him, despite falling asleep sometimes, despite taking wrong turns, slovenly but stubborn. He would see them plunging toward him, like bits of statues falling from the sky. And sometimes, as once along the gloomy bank of the Taurides, the terror was too much for him and he began to howl like a dog: a herd of white calves came toward him and Orestes thought they were all Erinyes, closing in around him.

But it was when he met Erigone that Orestes got the ultimate proof that his actions were not his own but part of something else, as alien to him as a stone set in his flesh. Erigone was the daughter of Aegisthus and Clytemnestra, his mirror image on Thyestes' side of the family, and hence his number one enemy. She arrived in Athens with Clytemnestra's father, Tyndareos, king of Sparta, to accuse him, Orestes, before the Areopagus. She had the wild pride of Artemis, whose favor the Atridae had never regained after Atreus had kept back the golden lamb he should have sacrificed to her. Orestes looked at Erigone and saw himself as a woman, and at the same time he saw the creature most alien to him in the whole world, and most invincible. She, he at last understood, was the only creature he could desire: to kill or to throw down on a bed.

During the trial, Orestes looked like a carcass animated by Delphic prompters. Some say that when he was absolved Erigone hung herself in rage. But Orestes' life didn't change much after his absolution. He still wandered about endlessly. Finally he came back from the land of the Tauri clutching a small wooden image of Artemis, the only remedy he had found against his madness. And now he gave Erigone yet another reason for hating him. Aletes, her brother, had usurped the throne of Mycenae. Orestes killed him. But Aletis, "wanderer" or "beggar," was also one of Erigone's names in her other existence as daughter of Icarius. After killing Aletes, Orestes in his fury tried to kill Erigone too. And it was like wanting to kill her twice over. But Artemis rescued her. So many were the corpses heaped up between Orestes and Erigone that the two couldn't even see each other. One day Orestes realized that she was the only woman who attracted him. He managed to find her again and they had a son together: Penthilus. This illegitimate child reunited the descendants of Atreus and Thyestes, who had fought so long for the legitimacy, fought above all to deny the other that legitimacy. In his blood, the two houses were condemned to be mixed together forever. Unless we accept Euripides' insinuation, that the blood of Penthilus was made up only of the purest blood of Thyestes and his children, in which case Orestes and Erigone were really brother and sister, and the house of Atreus only a phantom that had never existed in the flesh.

Whether by inheritance or conquest, Orestes was now ruler over a large kingdom stretching from Laconia to Arcadia. Yet he had a feeling that the whole thing must end with him—or would have to begin again far away as a totally different story. An oracle said he should set up a colony on Lesbos. Lesbos? The name meant nothing to him; it was one of the few places he had never set foot. Only one small detail linked him to Lesbos: it was said that the cruel king Oenomaus, who in the end was his great-grandfather, had lived there before coming to Olympia. Perhaps Lesbos meant a return, a buckle closing, beneath the water. But it was not to be Orestes who colonized Lesbos. Penthilus went there, taking the blood of the Pelopids over the sea, locked away in his body as though in a casket. What came next were years of provincial goings-on, of which little would be known. And finally silence. For the first time Orestes felt easier in his mind. He was nearly seventy now, and something prompted him to go back to the places where he had been most afflicted by his madness. He withdrew to Arcadia. For all his large kingdom, he wasn't cut out to be a powerful sovereign. He would always be the one who drinks alone.

One day, not far from the place where he had bitten off
a finger to make the Erinyes turn white, Orestes was bitten
on the heel by a snake and died of poison, just as it was by
poison, his only companion apart from Pylades, that he had
always lived. And years later people came to look for his
bones, for much the same reasons that had prompted other
people to look for the bones of his grandfather Pelops. They
were supposed to help bring down a city. Nothing as grandiose as Troy this time, but an important town all the same:
Tegea. The Spartans had been trying and failing to take it
for generations. The oracle said that Orestes' bones would
be found "there where blow follows blow, wrong lies over
wrong." Blow on blow, wrong on wrong: buried in a black-
smith's shop, Orestes' bones were still trembling at the
blows of iron beating on iron.

VII

A NECESSARY PREMISE OF THE GREEK mysteries was the following scene, which took place between the two divine brothers Zeus and Hades. One day Zeus saw his powerful brother coming to meet him on Olympus. There was only one reason for Hades' coming here: to ask for something. And Zeus knew perfectly well what. So the time when Zeus would see men and women appear and disappear down on earth without asking themselves why, hard and bright, but still close to the realm of metamorphosis, ready to live a brief span as bodies and a far longer time as exhausted shades in Hades—that time was coming to an end. The division between life and death had been a clean cut, sharp as the bronze blade that cut the throats of the sacrificial animals. And nothing could have pleased Zeus more. Zeus liked everything that existed without justification. But now Hades was coming to ask for a hostage. He wanted a woman in the palace of death. And the only woman who would do was a daughter of Zeus, a niece whom Uncle Hades had had his eye on for some long time: Persephone, or Persephatta, obscure names, in whose letters we find echoes of murder (*phónos*) and pillage (*pérsis*), superimposed on a beauty whose only name is Girl: Kore.

Zeus nodded. These two hardly needed to speak to each other. When the three brothers—Zeus, Hades, and Poseidon—had first divided the spoils, Zeus had been lucky: he had drawn the lot of life within the light. Poseidon had retreated beneath the waves, Hades underground. But how

long could such a sharp division last? Just as Zeus sometimes meddled among the dead and Poseidon sometimes
forayed forth on earth, so one day—it was inevitable—
Hades would come up to Olympus to ask Zeus for a living
creature. Hades reminded Zeus that they were closely related, even if they never saw each other, and now the bond
between them would be closer still. He wanted to carry off
a woman too, the way he so often saw his brothers doing
when he looked up from his home beneath the earth. Hadn't
they decided, before drawing lots for the world, that they
should think of themselves as equals? Well, for the moment
it was mostly Zeus and Poseidon rampaging over their playground, the earth. Hades never appeared: he just welcomed
the shades of the dead into his immense and gloomy inn.
Yet he did have the most impetuous horses in the world.
What were they waiting for, drumming their hooves behind
the palace gates, if not abduction? As far as earth was concerned, the brothers should have equal rights in at least one
thing: this business of carrying off women. And, whereas
Zeus and Poseidon always thought of women in the plural,
Hades would be satisfied with a single abduction. For him,
he added with that irony no one would ever equal, a single
woman was quite enough. He paused. Then he explained:
the girl he wanted must be *the* Girl: Kore. He wanted her to
sit on the throne of the dead, forever.

Hades disappeared, leaving Zeus alone on Olympus. And
now Zeus began to think of the past, of that part of the past
that only he among the Twelve knew about, that part that
always echoed in his mind whenever some event occurred
that was pregnant with the future. Hades' visit had been one
of those events, perhaps the most momentous, although no
one knew that as yet, and few would realize it for thousands
of years.

Zeus had been born into a world already old, dangerous,
and full of divine beings. In his life he had performed only
one exploit truly worthy of the name of Living Being for

every living being. He was still hidden in Night's cave. Night was the wet nurse of the gods; her very substance was ambrosia. She advised Zeus to swallow up Phanes, the Protogonos, firstborn of the sovereigns of the world, and then to swallow the other gods and goddesses born from him, and the universe too. Thus gods, goddesses, earth and starry splendor, Ocean, rivers, and the deep cavern of the underworld all wound up in Zeus's sacred belly, which now contained everything that had been and ever would be.

Everything grew together inside him, clutching his innards as a bat clutches to a tree or a bloodsucker to flesh. Then Zeus, who had been just another of the Titans' children, became, alone, the beginning, the middle, and the end. He was male, but he was also an immortal Nymph. Then, in his overflowing solitude, he saw the life that had come before his birth as a child of Kronos, the father who had immediately threatened him and wanted to swallow him up. And he understood why his father had been so fierce. In the end, Kronos had only tried to do what Zeus alone had now succeeded in doing. But everything seemed luminous and clear to him now, because everything was in him. With amazement he realized he had become the only one. He lived in a state of perfect wakefulness. He went back to the times preceding his father, Kronos, further and further back, until he reached a point that was furthest, because it had been the first.

Space no longer existed. In its place was a convex surface clad with thousands upon thousands of scales. It extended beyond anything the eye could see. Looking downward along the scales, he realized that they were attached to other scales, the same color, interwoven with them in knot after knot, each one tighter than the one before. The eye became confused, could no longer tell which of the two coiling bodies the scales belonged to. As he looked up again, toward the heads of the two knotted snakes, the body of the first snake rose, and its scales merged into something that no longer partook of the nature of a snake: it was the face of a god, the first face to reveal what a god's face was, and on either side of it were two other huge heads, one a lion and one a bull, while from the shoulders opened immense, airy wings. The white arm of a woman was twined to the arm of the god, just as below the tails of the two snakes were knotted together. The woman's face gazed steadily at the god's, while with her other arm, behind which trembled an immense wing, she stretched out toward the farthest extremity of everything: and where the tips of her fingernails reached, there Everything ended. They were a royal and motionless couple: they were Time-Without-Age and Ananke.

From the coitus hidden in the knot of their interwoven bodies, Ether, Chaos, and Night were born. A shadowy vapor lay over the two winged snakes. Time-Without-Age hardened this gloomy fog into a shell that gradually took on an oblong shape. And, as it did so, a light spread from the shell, fluttering in the void like a white tunic or a shred of mist. Then, breaking away from Ananke, the snake wrapped himself around this luminous egg. Did he mean to crush it?

Finally the shape split open. Out poured a radiant light. Appearance itself appeared. You couldn't help but be invaded by light, but you couldn't make out the figure it came from. Only Night saw him: four eyes and four horns, golden wings, the heads of a ram, a bull, and a lion, and a snake spread across a young and human body, a phallus and a vagina, hooves. Having broken the shell, the father snake wound himself around his son's body. Above, the father's head looked down on his son; beneath, a boy's fine face looked into the light emanating from his own body. It was Phanes, the Protogonos, firstborn of the world of appearance, the "key to the mind."

Phanes' life was like no other life since. Alone in the light, "he grazed in his breast." He didn't need to look at anything but the light, because everything was in him. Copulating with himself, he impregnated his own sacred belly. He gave

birth to another snake, Echidna, with a splendid woman's
face framed by a vast head of hair. From her sweet-smelling
cheeks, from the incessant flashing of her eyes, she emanated violence. Speckled scales, like the waves of a swollen
sea, stretched right up to her soft, white breasts. Then
Phanes begot Night, who had already existed before him.
But Phanes had to beget her just the same, because he was
everything. He made Night his concubine. He was a guest
in her cave. Other children were born: Uranus and Ge.
Little by little, with the light constantly pouring from
the top of his head, Phanes made the places where gods
and men would live. Things were ushered into the world of
appearance.

Time passed, and Phanes stayed in the cave, scepter in
hand. The world's first king, he didn't want to reign. He
handed the scepter to Night. Then went off alone. Now that
the cosmos existed, Phanes rode his coach and horses up
onto the back of the sky. And there he stayed for a long time,
alone. Occasionally he would ride across the crest of the
world. But no one could see him. Inside the heavens, the
beings multiplied.

Ever since Phanes had withdrawn to the place farthest from
life on earth—Zeus reflected—events had begun to resemble one another. Time and again there would be a king,
children, enemies, women who helped and betrayed. He remembered the never-ending coitus of Uranus and Ge, their
children chased back into their mother's womb. And Ge,
who, deep inside herself, felt she was suffocating and
brooded on her bitterness. He remembered the serrated
sickle, made of a white, unyielding metal, in the hands of
their son Kronos, who would later become his father, and
Uranus's testicles sinking into the sea. Circles formed on the
surface of the water, and one of them was edged with white
foam. From the middle rose Aphrodite, together with her
first serving maids, Apate and Zelos, Deceit and Rivalry.
Uranus had been a cruel father, and Kronos, who took his

place, was likewise cruel. But his mind was supple and powerful. Kronos possessed the measures of the cosmos.

By this time many beings had spread out across space, both on high and below: the Titans, the Cyclopes, the Hecatoncheires. And Kronos went on generating children, coupling with Rhea. So Zeus was born, just one of many. And, like the others, he ought to have been swallowed up by his father. But Rhea hid him in a cave—and it was then that she took on the second name of Demeter. Of his early infancy, what Zeus remembered most clearly was a din of cymbals coming from the dazzling light at the entrance to the cave, the outline of a woman waving those cymbals about, and the shadows of young warriors dancing and shouting. Then Night, whose cave it was, explained to baby Zeus that he was to become the fifth sovereign of the gods. But Zeus didn't know who the other four had been. All he knew was that his father was waiting within the light to devour him.

Just as Ge had given the white sickle to her son Kronos so that he could cut off Uranus's testicles, so it was Night who thought up the trick that allowed Zeus to see off Kronos. It was the male, then, who acted. But only the female had the *mêtis*, the intelligence that preordains action in the silence of the mind. Night prepared a big feast for Kronos. Numerous serving men and women went back and forth, laden with ambrosia, nectar, and honey. Gratified and solitary, Kronos went on eating his honey, reveling in sensual pleasure. Then he got up, intoxicated, and went to lie down under an oak tree. His face still wore the rapture of a pleasure that knows no end. Zeus, meanwhile, had climbed up into the sky on the back of a goat. Now he approached his father, treading silently. He looked at him and wound a chain around his body. But that was only the beginning of Night's plan. Zeus must now grab hold of everything wandering about in the world, bind it with a chain of gold, and swallow it. When the skies, the seas, the earth, and the divine beings had disappeared in his belly, it occurred to Zeus that one last exploit remained to be accomplished: he must swallow Phanes. So he climbed onto the world's back, where Phanes lived alone with his horses. There was no need to hatch a trick this time, because Phanes was absorbed in self-contemplation, and unarmed.

Then, little by little, Zeus vomited everything that had settled in his belly out into the light. Back came the trees and the rivers, the stars and the subterranean fire, the divine beings and the beasts. Everything looked the same as before, yet everything was different. From the grain of dust right up to the immense bodies revolving in the heavens, everything was linked by an invisible chain. Everything appeared to be coated in light, as if born for the first time. But Zeus knew this wasn't so: through him, on the contrary, everything had been born for the last time.

The sovereign gods suffer from a nostalgia for the state of their forerunner, Phanes. And they try to return to it. Zeus's nostalgia for Phanes takes the form of the snake. Only Zeus could remember the image of the two intertwined snakes, before the world existed. And Phanes had appeared from among the coils of a snake. After Zeus had expelled the world from within him, he felt the desire to couple with his mother. That desire was prompted by a distant memory. His mother fled, and Zeus chased her tirelessly. In the end, Rhea Demeter turned herself into a snake. So then Zeus became a snake too. He closed on his mother and wrapped his scales around hers in a Heracleotic knot, the same knot two snakes would one day make on Hermes' staff. It was a violent thing to do, so much so that one ancient commentator tried to demonstrate that the name Rhea Demeter (Deó) came from *dēioûn*, "to devastate." But why did the god decide to make that particular knot to rape his mother? Zeus was remembering something and wanted to repeat it. Just as men would one day recall a divine precedent in everything they did, so Zeus recalled those gods before the gods whom he had been able to contemplate when he swallowed Phanes and all his powers.

Zeus repeated the most majestic image he knew, the oldest his memory went back to: the image of Time-Without-Age and Ananke intertwined in the Heracleotic knot before the world was born. So the rape of Rhea Demeter, the model for so many of Zeus's later adventures, was not a prototype of his own invention but rather a gesture back toward a preexisting past that only Zeus could have known about. To repeat it was a pledge of fidelity. From snake to snake the world went on propagating itself in era after era. Every time Zeus transformed himself into a snake, time's arrow flew backward, to bury itself in the origin of things. At which the world seemed to hold its breath, listening for that backward movement that marks the passage from one era to another. And so it was when, from the union of Zeus and Rhea Demeter in the form of snakes, Persephone was born, "the girl whose name cannot be uttered," the unique girl to whom Zeus would transmit the secret of the snake.

At birth, Persephone would have been horrible to anybody, but not to her father, who was the only one able to look at her in her first form. She had two faces, four eyes, and horns that sprouted from her forehead. Neither men nor gods could have understood the glory of Persephone. But Zeus understood it. For, seeing her, he remembered how Phanes had risen to the light. And just as a snake had once wound itself around Phanes' radiant flesh, so one day Zeus went to his daughter and wrapped her in his coils, once again assuming the form of a snake. It happened in Crete. Rhea Demeter had hidden her daughter in a cave, and there Persephone wove a garment strewn with flowers, working on a loom of stone. The entrance to the cave was guarded by snakes. But another snake, Zeus, put them to sleep by staring into their eyes as he slithered into the cave. And, before Persephone could defend herself, her white skin was tight against the scales of a snake, who licked and dribbled amorously. In the darkness of the cave, Persephone's horrible body radiated light, just as Phanes' once had. From that violent coupling Zagreus was born, the first Dionysus.

The Christian Fathers did not believe in the copulation of snake Zeus with Demeter. Their version of events was even more vicious. Clement is brusque and elliptic in his account. But the African Arnobius couldn't resist the story. He bubbles over with the eloquence of a baroque preacher abandoning himself to *delectatio morosa*. In his version, Zeus copulates with Demeter not as a snake at all but as a bull. "*Fit ex deo taurus.*" From the moment Zeus becomes a bull, Arnobius's prose takes off: "*Cum in Cererem suam matrem libidinibus improbis atque inconcussis aestuaret . . .*" *Aestuare:* a flood spreading out, a fire raging: such is the lust of Zeus. He is a god who tricks his mother by transforming himself into a bull so he can rape her. And that's when Demeter's anger flares; that, and not when another son of Kronos carries off her daughter, is when the goddess gets the name Brimo.

So it was after that rape that Demeter first paralyzed both the gods and the world: "*adlegatur deorum universus ordo.*" And it was then that Zeus, to placate her, resorted to a cheap trick, not unlike the one men would later use to placate the gods. He chose a ram with big testicles and cut them off. Then he went back to his mother with a sad, repentant look. Pretending they were his own, he tossed the ram's testicles onto his mother's lap. The sacrificial substitution, that powerful weapon men would one day use to defend themselves from the gods, was thus invented by Zeus. And Demeter was placated.

Persephone was born in the tenth month. Zeus watched her grow. When she was strong, flourishing, and "swollen with lymph," he felt an overwhelming desire to do the same thing over again: "*redit ad priores actus.*" This time he transforms himself into a snake, wraps his daughter in immense coils, and, gripping her in a ferocious lock, plays with her tenderly and whispers his adoration through their coitus, "*mollissimis ludit atque adulatur amplexibus.*" Impregnated with the seed of a bull, Demeter had given birth to a girl. Filled with the seed of Zeus as snake, Persephone gave birth to a bull.

The cosmos pulses back and forth between snake and bull. An enormously long time would pass before the snake, Time-Without-Age, was followed by the drumming of the bull, who was Zeus. Then a much shorter time before the bull Zeus coupled with Demeter to generate a woman in whom the nature of the snake pulsed once again, Persephone. And hardly any time at all, the time it takes for desire to flare, before Zeus, realizing that the baby Persephone had become a girl, transformed himself into a snake, coupled with his daughter, and generated Zagreus, the bull, the first Dionysus.

The story of the world was all contained in this becoming a bull, then a snake once again, to generate another bull. Told by Zeus, it was a story that began with a bull and ended with a bull. Told by Time-Without-Age, it was a story that began with a snake and waited to coil itself up in a snake once more. Time-Without-Age has been waiting ever since for:

. . . bull
father of snake and father of snake bull,
in the mountain the hidden one, oh herdsman, the goad.

Theós, the indeterminate divine, was an invasion, of body and mind. It was our becoming intimate with what is most alien. And nothing is more alien than the snake. A hand lifted the snake toward the neck. The hand slipped the snake under the tunic of the initiate. From the throat, down the cleavage between the breasts, if it was a girl, or across the taut chest, if it was a boy, the snake slithered into darkness, hidden beneath the cloth, toward the belly. Did it linger there? Did it wrap itself around the youth's waist? It slid over the thighs and poked out down below, between the legs. "*Theòs dià kólpou*": "god across the belly."

. . .

The sea is the continuum, the perfection of the undifferentiated. Its emissary on earth is the snake. Where the snake is, there gushes water. Its eye is liquid. Beneath its coils flows the water of the underworld. Forever. Being sinuous, it has no need of joints. The same pattern covers its whole skin; its scales are uniform, its motion undulating and constantly self-renewing, like waves. The snake is to the bull as the sea to the land. The earth emerges from the sea, as the bull from the snake. To carry off Europa, the bull Zeus emerged from the sea and then plunged back into it again. Fending off the waves, Europa had one foot immersed in the sea, one hand gripping the animal's back.

Where force reigns, the spirit is alien, detached from both earth and water. But Apollo and Athena were envious of force, that force which, by the time they were born, had already been pushed back to the ends of the earth. There, near the snaking coil of Oceanus, sleepless or lethargic creatures could still be found, lurking in caves or on mountains, creatures that still possessed an unextinguished force. Apollo and Athena knew they would have to flush out those creatures, kill them, and make that force their own.

Bearers of an opposite perfection, new and unimagined, Apollo and Athena were jealous of the perfection of the undifferentiated. But, in line with the division of the spoils between the sons of Kronos, they couldn't intervene in the watery realm of Poseidon, nor in the subterranean kingdom of Hades. That left the earth as their playground. And meant they would have to play out their game with the snake. Athena killed Gorgon, who was crowned with snakes. Apollo killed Python, coiled around the spring of Castalia. Gorgon's snakes stirred in the wind on Athena's breast. They had become the fringe of the aegis. Python's teeth and bones were kept in the bronze pot of the tripod, from which the Pythia chanted Apollo's prophecies. Python's scales were wrapped around the *omphalós*, the navel stone. The navel is the point, the only and indispensable point, where the perfect links up with the perfection of the undifferentiated. It is Europa's foot dipped in the sea.

Two sovereign lines descend from Zeus: that of Dionysus and that of Apollo. Dionysus's line is more obscure than Apollo's; only rarely does it emerge from the shadow. Since he is both snake and bull, all history before Zeus is recalled in him and begins again with him. Apollo's line is the more visible, yet even more secret than Dionysus's when it comes to Apollo's transgression against his father. Apollo is neither snake nor bull, but he who kills snake and bull, either loosing off the arrows himself, as with Python at Delphi, or sending his emissary, Theseus, to bury his sword in the Minotaur in Crete or capture the bull in Marathon.

Dionysus and Apollo: one is the weapon, the other uses the weapon. Ever since they appeared, Psyche has been running back and forth into the arms of first one, then the other.

When Hades asked to carry off Kore, Zeus sensed the time had come for a new ring to be added to the knot of the snakes. But this time it wasn't up to him to act. He would be a consenting witness. The invisible would now reassert its rights over the body of the visible more strictly than before: their dealings with each other, long diluted and mingled together in life on earth, would find a new center of gravity.

Hades was claiming the supremacy of a world that was *other*: isolated, separate, and silent. But this other world culminated in the flower of the visible, and that flower was Persephone. With her, the secret of the snake, a secret passed on from snake to snake right up to snake Zeus, would now go over to the invisible world, and Zeus himself would have to surrender it if it was to go on functioning. Hades' visit was prelude to a moment of enormous imbalance, both on Olympus and on earth.

It was a place where dogs would lose their quarry's trail, so violent was the scent of the flowers. A stream cut deep through the grass of a meadow that rose at the edge to fall sheer in a rocky ravine into the very navel of Sicily. And here, near Henna. Kore was carried off. When the earth split open and Hades' chariot appeared, drawn by four horses abreast, Kore was looking at a narcissus. She was looking at the act of looking. She was about to pick it. And, at that very moment, she was herself plucked away by the invisible toward the invisible. Kore doesn't just mean "girl," but "pupil" too. And the pupil, as Socrates says to Alcibiades, "is the finest part of the eye," not just because it is "the part which sees" but because it is the place where another person looking will find "the image of himself looking." And if, as Socrates claims, the Delphic maxim "Know thyself" can be understood only if translated as "Look at thyself," then the pupil becomes the sole means of self-knowledge. Kore looked at the yellow "prodigy" of the narcissus. But what is it that makes this yellow flower, used at once for the garlands of Eros and of the dead, so marvelous? What sets it apart from the violets, the crocuses, and the hyacinths that made the meadow near Henna so colorful? Narcissus is also the name of a young man who lost himself looking at himself.

Kore, the pupil, was thus on a threshold. She was on the brink of meeting a gaze in which she would have seen herself. She was stretching out her hand to pluck that gaze. But Hades burst upon the scene. And Kore was plucked away by Hades. For a moment, Kore's eye had to turn away from the narcissus and meet Hades' eye. The pupil of the Pupil was met by another pupil, in which it saw itself. And that pupil belonged to the world of the invisible.

Somebody heard a cry. But what did that cry mean? Was it just the terror of a young girl being carried off by a stranger? Or was it the cry of an irreversible recognition? Some early poets suggest that Persephone felt a "fatal desire" to be carried off, that she formed a "love pact" with the king of the night, that she shamelessly and willingly exposed herself to the contagion of Hades. Kore saw herself in Hades' pupil. She recognized, in the eye observing itself, the eye of an invisible other. She recognized that she belonged to that other. At that moment she crossed the threshold she had been about to cross while looking at the narcissus. It was the threshold of Eleusis.

If the pupil is *kórè*, it follows that the eye par excellence is Hades'. For it was in that eye, as he carried her off, that Kore saw herself reflected. It was then that this girl within the eye became the pupil for us all. As if the eye had only now stormed out on a raid from the kingdom of the dead. Vision was a prey. And the eye pounced from the shadows to capture a girl and shut her away in the underworld palace of the mind.

The meaning of Kore in Hades' eye is twofold: on the one hand, insofar as Kore sees herself in her abductor's eye, she discovers reflection, duplication, the moment in which consciousness observes itself: and paradoxically that duplicated gaze is also the ultimate of visions; it can't be divided up anymore, for every further division would merely be a confirmation of the first. On the other hand, in meeting the pupil, the cavity of vision for the first time welcomes and draws into itself its great desire: the image. For a split second the extremes of the mind are copresent in the eye of an abductor.

What happened in Eleusis was the separation and reunion of the dual goddess Demeter-Kore (Deó), she who sometimes appears as two barely differentiated figures, cloaked in the same mantle. It was the drama of the reflection that detaches itself from the body, from every object, from the earth even—to then be reunited with its origin. But only in certain recurrent moments. Like the eclipses.

With the arrival of Kore, the marvelous passes from the object to the act of looking. At the beginning of her adventure, Kore looks at the narcissus, "that wondrous, radiant flower, awesome to the sight of gods and mortals alike." At the end, when she returns from the underworld, Kore herself is "a great wonder for gods and mortals alike." By repeating the same formula, the anonymous author of the Homeric *Hymns* intended to underline the completion of an irreversible process: the passage to the soul. And the formula alerts us to the fact that the event was a source of amazement not just in the history of men but in the history of the gods too.

When Hades asked his brother Zeus for a living woman, he upset the simple world order that had pertained hitherto: life abounded, was marked and scarred by raiding gods, then consigned to an empty, inert, incorporeal afterlife. Zeus wouldn't have his mortal mistresses vanish. He would possess them, then abandon them. But Hades wanted Kore as his bride, wanted to have a living person sitting on the throne beside him. We could say that with this demand death aimed to inflict a further outrage on the earth above. But it is precisely now, in its insolence, that death deceives itself. With the abduction of Persephone, death acquires a body, acquires body: in the kingdom of the shades, there is now at least one body, and the body of a flourishing young girl at that.

In the past, few had had the privilege of being led by a god to the Elysian Fields with their bodies still intact. And Hades was defined as that place where there is no body. But now, along with Kore's body, Eros penetrated the kingdom of the dead. The slender-ankled Persephone was the supple arrow Aphrodite ordered Eros to let fly at Hades when the goddess summoned her son to the black rock of Eryx. The world had reached a point at which the economy of metamorphosis that had sustained it for so long through the period of Zeus's adventures was no longer enough. Things had lost their primordial fluidity, had hardened into profile, and the game that had once been played out between one shape and another was now reduced to the mere alternation of appearance and disappearance. From now on, it was a question not only of accepting life in a single immutable form but of accepting the certainty that that form would one day disappear without trace. Demeter's anger is the revolt against this new regime of life. But the goddess didn't know that at the same moment a new regime of death had also been inaugurated.

When Persephone took her place on Hades' throne and her scented face peeped out from behind the spiky beard of her partner, when Persephone bit into the pomegranate that grew in the shadow gardens, death underwent a transformation every bit as radical as that which life had undergone when it had been deprived of the girl. The two kingdoms were thrown off balance, each opening up to the other. Hades imposed an absence on earth, imposed a situation where every presence was now enveloped in a far greater cloak of absence. Persephone imposed blood on the dead: not, as in the past, the dark blood of sacrifice, not the blood the dead used to drink so thirstily, but the invisible blood that went on pulsing in her white arms, the blood of someone who is still entirely alive, even in the palace of death.

Dionysus wandered about Greece looking for an entrance to Hades. He wanted to go down to the underworld to bring back his mother, Semele. One day he found himself on the shores of a lake whose water was uncannily still. This was near Lerna, and the lake was called Lake Alcyonius. The water was still as metal. In the silence all around, reeds and marshgrass bowed in the wind. Dionysus saw Prosymnus (or was he called Polymnus?) coming toward him. He asked him the way to Hades. Prosymnus said he would show him, on condition that Dionysus let himself be made love to like a woman. Dionysus promised he would, but only after he had returned from Hades. Together they approached the

water. Nothing could have been calmer than that dense surface. But the small lake was bottomless. Try to swim in it
and it would suck you down, endlessly. Prosymnus told Dionysus he must dive into that water if he was to get to Hades.

To a man, the ancients kept quiet about what happened
at the end of Dionysus's journey to the underworld. But one
of the Fathers of the Church spoke out. With the brutal directness of those early Christians who had previously been
initiated in the mysteries, Clement of Alexandria tells how
Dionysus sodomized himself. "Dionysus yearned to go down
into Hades but did not know the way. A certain Prosymnus
promised to show him, but not without a reward [*misthós*]
and the reward he wanted was not a good thing, though
good enough for Dionysus; this favor, this reward Prosymnus asked of Dionysus, had to do with the pleasures of
Aphrodite. The god agreed to the reward and promised to
grant it, if he succeeded in returning from his journey, and
he backed up his promise with an oath. Having been told
the way, he set out. But when he returned he couldn't find
Prosymnus (who had died while he was away); determined
to keep his promise to his lover, Dionysus went to his grave
full of amorous desire. He cut a branch from a fig tree that
happened to be there and, having fashioned it in the shape
of the virile member, pushed it into himself, thus maintaining his promise to the dead man."

Dionysus wasn't the only god who'd had to ask a man the
way to Hades. When Demeter was searching for Kore, she
asked Celeus, king of Eleusis, where she might find her
daughter. Celeus pointed her to Hades. As a "reward" (*misthós*], Demeter gave him the secret of bread, but she also
allowed him to possess her body, "illicitly." It's not a Father
of the Church who gives us the details this time but an obscure scholiast. Gregory of Nazianzus "is ashamed" even to
mention "those certain things that Demeter does and submits to." Gregory had good reason to be scandalized: Demeter is the goddess of the *thesmoí*, the strictest of laws, and
here she is agreeing to give herself *athésmōs*, "lawlessly,"
to a mortal. Then from that union a child would be born,

"out of mortal necessity," as the Orphic hymn later puts it. At this point order has been turned completely on its head. How can Ananke, Necessity, who is more divine than the gods, because she precedes them, become "mortal," and as such subdue a goddess to herself? The goddess's humiliation took place in Eleusis—and marked an irreversible turning point in the history of the Olympians. But what had pushed Dionysus and Demeter to that point?

The Eleusinian crisis came about when the Olympians developed a new fascination for death. Zeus gave his daughter Kore to Hades, Demeter gave herself to a mortal. To find out more about death, the gods had to turn to men, death being the one thing men knew rather more about than they did. And, to get help from men, both Dionysus and Demeter had to prostitute themselves. A god surrendering himself to a mortal is like a man surrendering himself to death: every dead man has to bring a coin with him, to pay his way to Hades. Gods don't use money, so they give their bodies. After all, from the Olympians' point of view, men are already dead, because death lurks within them.

Just as Persephone let herself be carried off by the king of the dead, so Dionysus ties a fig branch to a gravestone and lets it penetrate him, and Demeter gives herself to the mortal Celeus. The memory of this divine prostitution was buried deep in the mysteries. We would know nothing of it at all were it not for the vindictive zeal of a Father of the Church and the loquacity of a scholiast. But no sooner have those events been disinterred from the silence than all kinds of other authors come running to confirm a complicity between Dionysus and Demeter vis-à-vis their love affairs on the road to Hades.

In Lerna, near the lake where Dionysus was sucked down into the underworld, people worshiped Demeter Prosymna. And Polyhymnia, partner of Polymnus, the other form of the name Prosymnus, was mother to Phylammon, founder of the mysteries of Lerna. Another Polyhymnia is mentioned as being the mother of the young Triptolemus, who scattered Demeter's corn seeds across the world from his winged

chariot. And his father was supposed to be Celeus: meaning
that Polyhymnia has taken Demeter's place as Celeus's mistress. One of the Nymphs who suckled Dionysus was called
Polymnos. And *polýymnos* was an epithet for Dionysus before coming to mean simply "whore." Plato throws some
light on this last development. First and foremost Polyhymnia is one of the Muses, patron of intimate lyric song. But
in the *Symposium* Plato tells us that Polyhymnia is a fearful
Muse, not devoted to "fine love," at all, "which is of the
heavens, and the realm of the Muse Urania," but to eros
pándēmos, the love that grants itself to all and sundry. Divine prostitution and lyric song are linked together in the
shadows. One of the many who offered hospitality to Demeter during her wanderings was Phytalus, king of the land
of the Cephisus, on the road to Eleusis. The procession that
went from Athens to Eleusis always stopped to rest here, in
a place known as the "Holy Fig," where a tree Demeter
had given to Phytalus still grew under a tiled roof that the
Eleusinian priests took care to keep in good repair. The inscription on Phytalus's tomb read: "Hero and king, here
Phytalus received the majestic Demeter, when first she
brought forth the first fruit of autumn, which mortal men
called the sacred fig."

Having gone down to the underworld to ransom his mother,
Dionysus found himself face to face with Hades, as though
looking in a mirror. The eyes staring at him were his own.
Hades told him he would let Semele go, but only on condition that Dionysus gave up something very dear to him.
Dionysus thought. Then he offered a twig of myrtle to the
lord of the invisible. Hades accepted. How was it that that
humble plant could settle such a portentous deal? Myrtle
was the plant young spouses were crowned with on earth.
And Hades couldn't get enough of spouses and their nuptials. He wanted the kingdom of the dead to be mingled with
the realm of eros. Not so as to conquer it or subdue it: in
fact Hades agreed to let Zeus's lover, the mortal Semele,

ascend to the heavens, "having been granted permission by
the Parcae." No, what he really wanted was to mix the two
kingdoms together. The myrtle was Aphrodite's plant before
it was Dionysus's, and until this visit to the underworld it
had been just the casual, fleeting fragrance of lovemaking.
But from now on it would spread the fragrance of another
world as well, the unknown. Thus the myrtle became the
plant of both eros and mourning.

Leading his mother by the hand, Dionysus returned to
earth at a place that would later be the site of the town of
Troezen. Years passed, and now a stadium had been built
close to the spot where Dionysus and Semele had climbed
up from the underworld. Every day Prince Hippolytus
would train there. He was a disciple of Orphism and hence
a vegetarian and a virgin. All he knew about sex was what
he saw in plays or statues. The son of an Amazon, he didn't
care about becoming an important person in the town. He
expressed amazement when people talked about the "sweetness of power." He worshiped his books, and the intoxicating fumes of "majestic words." He exercised, he improved
himself, and that was all he cared about. His detractors said
he practiced a "cult of self." But in fact, sealed away in its
integrity, his "virgin soul" adored only one being, at once
outside himself and intimate: the virgin huntress, Artemis.
He hunted for her in the forest, served her as a slave, protected her images.

Hippolytus assumed he was alone as he exercised naked
in the stadium at dawn. His body was glistening, untouchable. But a woman's eyes were following his every move.
Hidden away in her observation post above the stadium, in
the temple of Aphrodite Kataskopia, Aphrodite "who spies
from above," his stepmother, Phaedra, was familiar with
every tensing of the young man's muscles. Alone as Hippolytus was alone, she watched him and burned with desire.
Her sweaty hands fidgeted with tender myrtle leaves. Then,
when desire became unbearable, she took a brooch from her
hair and, eyes following Hippolytus's every move, pricked
holes in the myrtle leaves with the pin of the brooch. As well
as "myrtle berry," *mýrton* means "clitoris."

Detached though he was from the world, Hippolytus was not as yet beyond the world's sorcery. He would meet his death when his young fillies fled terrified before Poseidon's monstrous bull, risen from the waters of the Saronicus. Hippolytus tried desperately to control them and was flung to the ground, tangled in the reins. As the horses dragged his dusty, blood-bespattered body over the sharp rocks that tore it apart, as he felt "the approaching dissolution in his brain," Hippolytus was also aware of being that same myrtle leaf, torn apart by the precious brooch of a lover who had known his body only through her eyes and had hung herself for him: Phaedra.

Hippolytus exuded the fragrance of death, which mingled in the air with another, purer fragrance, announcing the presence of Artemis. Dying, he spoke to her, and she to him, but toward the end the goddess deserted him, even though she did call Hippolytus "the dearest of mortals." She deserted him because Artemis cannot "corrupt her eyes with a mortal's death throes."

When her abductor led her into the palace of the dead, Persephone noticed a young girl, "lying on Aidoneus's bed." It was Minthe, they told her, Nymph of the river Cocytus. So even in these still and silent woods, even in this freezing, marshy, corrosive river where the dead sailed toward their torments, there were Nymphs! And where there were Nymphs there was seduction, the invincible impulse. Just as Zeus, her father and celestial lover, came down to pluck them from the hills, so Hades, her partner, chary of word and gesture, coupled with them in his bed. Betrayal spanned the cosmos from end to end.

Persephone grabbed hold of Minthe and dragged her out into the light, on the sands of Pylos, gateway to the West. There she hurled herself on the Nymph and stamped on her with that fury she had inherited from her mother. She wanted to trample her to death, to tear her apart like a mortal woman. And as Minthe's soft body was reduced to a pulp of flesh and blood, her lifeless limbs released an intense, balmy fragrance. It was the wild mint that would grow ever afterward on the slopes of Samikon, looking out to sea.

Not far away, her divine lover, Hades, had himself once been wounded by Heracles while fighting to defend Pylos. He was surrounded by corpses, so much so that he no longer knew whether they were his own subjects or the bodies of warriors freshly dead. And one of the hero's arrows pierced his shoulder. When one remembers that on that very day Heracles also struck the white right breast of Hera, it is clear this was a moment of great confusion between heaven, earth, and underworld. In pain, "the monstrous Hades" took the unusual step of climbing up to Olympus to have his wound dressed. On that long Elean beach, death had exposed itself to the risks of life. And it was there that Persephone squeezed a sweet and sterile perfume from Minthe's body.

Demeter sat in the temple of Eleusis, wrapped in her deep blue tunic: she was waiting for mankind to die of hunger; she was waiting for the moment when the gods would know for the first time what it meant to smell the smoke of sacrifice no more. She wanted to break the life cycle, now that the "unbearable deeds of the blessed gods" had taken her Persephone away from her. Demeter herself had ordered the Eleusinians to build this temple; she had taught them the ceremonies to hold for Demophon, the child who lost his immortality thanks to his stupidly devoted mother, Metanira, "*stulte pia.*"

But the temple and its ceremonies couldn't survive much longer now: all around, the Eleusinian plain was a skinned and dried up corpse. Seeds, flowers, and fruit had withdrawn into the earth as though into an inviolable shell. The plows bumped across clods that were lumps of dust.

Hermes came to see Hades and Persephone sitting on their throne and spoke the words he had himself heard time after time; Demeter wanted to see Persephone again, "with her eyes." But how else could she have seen her? Demeter's insistence on this plainly pleonastic formula contained a hidden message for Hades, as if Hades knew of another way of seeing and was planning to play that card, as if he wanted to cheat men out of seeing "with their eyes," counting on another vision, which needed neither light nor eyes, because it was in itself both light and eye. Thus Hermes, perfect among messengers, faithfully repeated the words Demeter had first delivered to Olympus, and which now echoed in the darkness.

Hades' eyebrows arched in a hint of a smile: we know of no smile more mysterious than the one that wrinkled the forehead of the lord of death that day. It wasn't the serving maid Iambe's lighthearted, intemperate, feckless laughter that had irresistibly infected Demeter and shaken her from her stony immobility. It was the smile of one who knows, and registers with that faint allusion his distance from everything that is going on. Beside him, Hades senses the warmth of the queen he has carried off and set on his throne. No one, not even Zeus, could take her away, except perhaps for a time: and time is one thing death always has. Now that the Olympians needed him, and had even sent the most intelligent of their number to persuade him—a sign that they were losing their nerve—Hades thought he might pretend just this once to play along with their comedy, a comedy they usually kept him out of. With a gesture of kindness, he turned to Persephone. His hand touched her arm, and that arm communicated a mute disquiet. He told her, in the presence of the Olympian messenger, that of course she could go back to her mother, but she would have to preserve her serenity. Again his words sounded mysterious and ironic, because until now Persephone had never been serene with him. Then he urged her not to be ashamed of her husband: in the end he was a great king and he had made her a queen.

Persephone, who had been sitting motionless on her throne for days, leaped to her feet like a little girl, her face lit up with joy. She wanted to leave now. Hades ordered his dark horses to be harnessed to the golden coach. Then he arranged to be alone with Persephone in the well-kept gardens of the underworld. While they were walking along the paths, he picked a pomegranate from a tree and offered three seeds to his spouse. Persephone's mind was elsewhere and she refused. But Hades insisted, in his subtle way. Persephone lifted the seeds to her mouth. She was distracted, her heart in a flurry at the thought of leaving. They imagined they were alone, but from the shadows they were being watched by a gardener: Ascalaphus, son of the love between Acheron and a Nymph. One day he would say what he had seen, which is how we know what happened in that garden. That tiny gesture of Persephone was perhaps the most important event ever, the most pregnant of consequence since Zeus swallowed Phanes and took up residence on Olympus.

The chariot was ready at last. Hermes grasped the bridle and whip. The horses came slowly out of the palace, then took off and flew away. From high above, Persephone once again saw the sea, and branching rivers and grassy valleys, like the one that had been her last vision on earth. Sitting on her throne in the underworld, she had often thought she would never see them again. Whereas now they appeared and disappeared, as though in a game, as the chariot came out of the fat, fleecy clouds. Finally they reached a place Persephone didn't recognize. The chariot stopped before a newly built temple emanating a strong smell of incense. Demeter appeared between the columns. And ran like a Maenad on the mountains toward her daughter.

Persephone jumped down from the chariot, and the two embraced without a word. Then Persephone felt her mother restraining her; she had pulled her face away and wanted to say something. "Did you eat anything at all, when you were down there?" Persephone remembered the pomegranate seeds, a sweet, sharp taste, still there, like a distant memory, in her saliva. That taste of the invisible would never leave her. Sitting outside the temple, they spent hours and hours telling each other their adventures. They touched each other's arms and hugged. From time to time, Demeter would walk away from her daughter and turn to stare at her. The pain flowed away with the words, and they rediscovered joy. Demeter explained the consequences of the three pomegranate seeds: every year Persephone would have to go back and be Hades' bride for half the year. They didn't actually say it, but both now accepted this decree from Zeus. The rigidity of stone was dissolved forever.

That day the only people to come to talk to them were two women. The first was Hecate, crow black and with a shining crown. She had helped Demeter when the goddess mother had been wandering about in desperation; now she would be a precious guide for her daughter. No woman knew the paths that linked earth and underworld better than she. Then Rhea came to bring a message from Olympus. Shaking her thick hair, she repeated Zeus's promises and sealed the peace between them. Demeter stood up to go back to Olympus. As the goddess set off in her long blue tunic, the white barley that had remained spitefully hidden in the ground poked out into the light. The arid furrows became damp clods of rich earth, while leaves and flowers opened once again to the sun, as if nothing had happened and nature were lazily reawakening from a long sleep.

VIII

ZEUS WAS SITTING ON A STOOL. HE stared into the distance. A breeze twitched his beard, which was streaked with gray. Something was going on inside his head, bringing on a drunken weariness. When Zeus had swallowed his wife Metis, on the advice of Ge and Uranus, who told him she would one day give birth to a god even stronger than himself and capable of usurping his power, Metis was already pregnant with Athena. The baby girl had flowed into Zeus's body, and there, in that recess hidden even from the gods, Zeus had passed on to her his weapon of old, the aegis, the flayed skin of Aegis, the monster with fiery breath. Now Zeus felt the crown of his skull being scraped by Athena's sharp javelin. Everything about that little girl was sharp: her eyes, her mind—now living in the mind of her father—the point of her helmet. Every female concavity was hidden away, like the reverse side of her shield.

Zeus saw two women coming toward him: the Ilithyias, experts in midwifery. Without a word, their hands reached toward his head, gingerly, not daring to touch. Then Hephaestus arrived with a bronze ax. Before Zeus could utter a word, Hephaestus brought the ax down on his head and ran off, followed by the Ilithyias. Why did he run? Zeus still hadn't said a word. He heard a desperately shrill scream inside his head, like the sound of a Tyrrhenian trumpet.

And all at once he realized he wasn't alone: with silent steps the other gods had converged on him from all directions. He saw Hera and Hebe, Demeter and Persephone sitting on their baskets, Dionysus lying on a panther skin, thyrsus in hand. And to his other side, Poseidon, Aphrodite, Eros, Apollo, Artemis, Hermes, and the three Moirai, the last apparently confabulating together. All of them were looking at him, but not so as to meet his eyes. They were looking at a point slightly above. Athena had appeared in the crack in his skull, her weapons sparkling, while Nike fluttered around her with a crown in her hand.

Now he could see her too: she had climbed down to the ground and was walking away from her father. Turning her head in silent greeting, she was the only one who looked him in the eyes. Was it his daughter he saw, or his own image gazing back at him? Then Zeus turned to look at the other gods. From the solemn expressions on their faces, it was clear that a new era had begun on Olympus.

Athena was the only being who, at birth, did not grab at something but took something off. Helios's chariot had stopped in the sky when the goddess emerged from Zeus's head. The air on Olympus was tense, breathless, as Athena slowly began to strip off her weapons. She put down her shield, her helmet, her javelin; she undid the aegis, and then, just before she slipped off the tunic that hung down to her ankles, a group of Libyan Heroines, clad in red-dyed goatskins thickly decorated with fringes, crowded around to hide her.

Unseen among them, she set off toward Lake Tritonis, in Libya. There she immersed herself in the water, as if to renew a virginity she would never lose. But she had a far deeper intimacy to break away from: the fact that she had been mingled with the body of her father. Athena came out of the water into the dry African air, her body glistening and strong. The Heroines handed her her clothes and weapons one by one. Now Athena could begin her life.

. . .

During her African childhood, Athena played at war with
Pallas. The two little girls looked almost exactly the same,
Pallas's complexion being just a shade darker. Athena was
a guest who had come down from the heavens. Zeus had
entrusted her to Triton to bring up. And Triton left her with
his daughter Pallas all day. Shut away in their playground,
they saw no one else. Violent and brazen, they often came
to blows. And they already had their own weapons, child-
sized but lethal.

One day they found themselves face to face, spears quiv-
ering in their hands. It would have been hard to say who
was the mirror of whom. Zeus saw the danger: he threw down
his aegis from the sky to form a screen between them. Pallas
was dazzled, spear in hand. And a moment later Athena's
spear plunged into her. It was Athena's first and perhaps her
greatest bereavement. Back in Olympus, she decided to fashion a wooden statuette of her dead friend and set it beside
Zeus. The image was four cubits high, about the same height
as Pallas, with its feet together. When it was finished, Athena
covered its breast with the aegis, as though dressing a doll.
Then she looked at the statue and recognized herself.

Athena was to slay many a man and monster after this
episode, but always knowing exactly what she was doing.
One of these victims was a giant who was also called Pallas
and who, like other giants, was partly covered by scales and
feathers. He claimed to be Athena's father. He attempted to
rape her. So Athena killed him and, with the skill of a
woodsman, skinned him from top to toe. She was always on
the lookout for scales and feathers: they would go to improve her aegis. But the little girl Pallas, her warrior friend,
had prompted the one involuntary action of her life: the action with which she had done to death her own image. What
happened that day in Africa was to be Athena's secret. Few
would get to know this story of her childhood.

The Palladium, celestial model for all the statues of antiquity, was conceived as an evocation of a girl who was

dead and as the double of a being who was immortal. It
carried the mark of uniqueness, partly because it wasn't
fashioned by human hand and partly because Zeus decided
to make it the unique guardian of the unique city of Troy.
Yet it partook of duplicity from its very conception, and that
duplicity would soon begin to work. The primordial image
of Athena did not represent Athena, but two other women:
Pallas with her spear, and Medusa at the center of the aegis—the friend and the enemy. In each case she was the
other, the unique other, separated from Athena thanks only
to the screen of the aegis.

For the aegis had been important in Medusa's story too.
On the floor of one of Athena's temples, Poseidon was licking Medusa's pearly body, white in the shadows, with his
marine saliva. Athena stood before them, a statue in her cell,
obliged to watch those two writhing bodies twining together
in the silence of her temple. She felt horror at this outrage,
and at the same time a deep disquiet, because she knew that
Medusa looked very much like herself. So she raised the aegis to annihilate them, to detach herself from them. It was
a gesture that rose from Athena's deepest self, like Artemis's
gesture of drawing her bow. And as, once again, Athena separated herself from everything else behind this screen of
scaly skin, the soft filaments of Medusa's hair, spread out
on the floor, began to swell, and already you could see that
the tips were turning into so many snakes' heads.

Ever since the young Ate crashed into the ground there,
hurled down by Zeus's whirling hand, Troy had been the
hill of infatuation. But the wooden statuette of Pallas,
henceforth to be known as the Palladium, also crash-landed
there. Zeus tossed it down in front of Ilus's tent, so that he
would found his city on the hill. Infatuation and the image
now lived together in the same place: a city prone to phantoms. And it was to Troy that Helen would come: body or
phantom image? That doubt would be drawn out for ten
years, then to echo on and on for centuries. Yet the doubt

emanated from the statue hidden in Athena's temple, from the Palladium itself. All the complicated adventures of the Palladium are bound up with the question of the original and the copy.

Long before Plato, there were two disturbing things about the statue: that it might not have been fashioned by human hand, and that it might be only a copy. These two extremes came together in the Palladium. When the Achaeans began their siege of Troy, the Trojans immediately decided to make an identical copy of the Palladium. Thus, if the Greeks managed to steal it, Troy would not fall. Odysseus and Diomedes did break into Athena's temple and ran off with the Palladium. But, as with every audacious exploit, there are a host of different versions. Was it the real Palladium? Or did they steal two, one real and one false? Or were there, as some suggested, any number of Palladiums, the real one being the smallest? Or were the two Palladiums the two heroes stole both false, the only real one being the one Cassandra clutched in her hand the night Troy was sacked and Ajax dragged her across the floor of Athena's temple like an old sack? The Athenian version was that, after it had been fought over by all and sundry, it was Theseus's son, Demophon, who managed to get hold of the statue by pretending to defend a false Palladium from Agamemnon and finally letting him have it, whereas in fact he had already given the real one to Buzyge so that it could be protected in Eleusis.

Once you have a double on the scene, it's like entering a hall of mirrors; everything is elusive, stretching away into a perspective where nothing is ever final. There was a place in Athens known as the Palladium: it was the courthouse where involuntary homicides were judged. The first defendant was Demophon himself, but behind him, and in the same guilty role, homage was being paid to Athena, who had killed Pallas without meaning to. That was the beginning, the first crack in the double, the danger that is Athena, the fact that her consciousness is hostile to the shadow—it brings forth the double but then ends up by wounding it.

And the double takes its revenge by reproducing itself as an image, first in the one true Palladium, whose eyes would glow and wooden body exude a salty sweat whenever the goddess descended into it, but likewise in the endless other Palladiums to be found all over the world, all false.

The capacity for control (*sophrosýnē*), the ability to dominate oneself, to govern things, the sharpness of the eye, the sober choice of the means to achieve an end—all these things detach the mind from those powers that came before Athena, give us the impression of using them without being used by them. It is an effective illusion, and one that frequently finds confirmation. The eye becomes cold and clearsighted toward all it sees, ready to take advantage of any opportunity that presents itself. But for all this 360-degree field of vision, there remains a black speck, a point that the eye cannot see: itself. The eye cannot see the eye. It does not appreciate that it is itself a power, like the powers it claims to dominate. The cold eye looking out on the world modifies that world no less than the fiery breath of Aegis, which shriveled up a vast expanse of earth from Phrygia to Libya.

Athena is the power that helps the eye to see itself. So intimate is she with those she protects that she installs herself in their minds and communicates with the very mind of the mind. Which is why Ajax's father says to his son: "In battle, fight to win, but to win together with a god." To which Ajax replies: "Father, with a god on his side, even a nobody can win; but I am sure I can achieve glory even without them." So Athena intervenes and destroys the hero's mind, like one of those cities she loves to sack. She is ruthless with those who use her tokens—the sharp eye, the quick mind, deftness of hand, the intelligence that snatches victory—only to forget where they came from. It is here that the difference between Odysseus and an ingenuous, insolent hero like Ajax becomes gapingly obvious. For Odysseus, Athena's presence is that of a secret and incessant dialogue: he finds her in the cry of a heron, the bronzed timbre of a voice, the wings of a swallow perched on a beam, and any number of other manifestations, because, as he says to the goddess on one occasion, "you mimic all manner of people." So the hero knows he can see her everywhere. He knows he need not always be waiting for the dazzling splendor of epiphany. Athena may be a beggar or an old friend. She is the protecting presence.

The relationship between Athena and "the male," which the goddess loves "with all her heart," is conditioned by an age-old misunderstanding. Athena gives men the weapons they need to escape the oppression of all kinds of sovereigns, and above all of the sky and earth, who had trembled that day they heard the shrill, high-pitched cry with which the goddess emerged from Zeus's head—and trembled because they recognized that this young girl was their new enemy. But Athena does not give men the weapon they need to escape herself. Whenever man celebrates his autonomy with preposterous claims and fatal deeds, Athena is insulted. Her punishment is never long in coming, and it is extreme. Today, those who do not recognize her are not insolent heroes such as Ajax but the many numerous "nobodies" Ajax despised. It is they who advance, haughty and blind, polluting the earth they tread. While the heirs of Odysseus continue their silent dialogue with Athena.

The Olympians visited one another in their huge palaces. They'd get together for banquets of an evening. Or they might assemble like a group of curious onlookers to watch some unusual event: Athena emerging from Zeus's head; Aphrodite and Ares caught in Hephaestus's golden web.

But even Olympus had its forbidden room, its sealed, inviolable place where no one could go. The gods would pass by, knowing they could never cross the threshold. It was a square, empty, windowless room. On the floor, the darkness was pierced by a bar that was as if fringed with light, a light that simmered in the stillness: Zeus's lightning bolt. For anyone daring to approach, the luminous fringes would take on the soft shape of lotus petals. In the lightning blossomed "the flower of fire."

Zeus once asked Athena to lend him a powerful weapon she often flaunted: the flayed skin of a monster, the aegis. In return, and because he was irresistibly partial to his daughter, he offered her occasional access to his lightning. It was the privilege Athena was most proud of. Even in the presence of the Athenians, when called on to decide the fate of Orestes, Athena reminded the accused that "I alone among the gods have the keys to the room where the lightning is sealed."

The Athenians claimed to have two main reasons for feeling proud of themselves: first, they were autochthonous, actually born, that is, of the earth of Attica, rather than immigrants from other lands; and, second, Athena was their protectress. But, even to be born of the earth, one needed a seed, and a womb—yet the Athenians always avoided mentioning this. Why?

Of all the styles of virginity on Olympus, none was so enigmatic and provocative as Athena's. No woman was ever so profoundly intimate with men as she. None of Odysseus's women ever felt the hero's voice as close to them as she did. Yet Athena denied her body to gods and men, even to those men she helped with such impassioned intelligence. Though in punishing them, she wasn't as ferocious as Artemis. When Tiresias spied her bathing, Athena blinded him, out of divine duty, but then chose to grant him the gift of clairvoyance.

One day Athena approached Hephaestus, the ugliest of the Olympians but also the one who would find Aphrodite in his bed every night. She asked him to make a piece of armor for her. And in her solemn way she added that she didn't really know how to pay him for it. "I'll do it for love," Hephaestus said. Athena nodded. Athena was the only woman who could make Hephaestus forget Aphrodite. During her visit, she hadn't noticed the glint in his eye, because that wasn't the kind of thing she was in the habit of noticing.

Time passed. When Athena came back to Hephaestus's
forge to pick up her armor, the divine craftsman began hob-
bling around her in the dark. The goddess felt long, sinewy
fingers squeezing her and thin, muscled legs forcing her
back against the wall. As the goddess was wriggling free
from his clutches, Hephaestus's sperm squirted out against
her thigh, just above the knee. None of this prompted the
slightest comment from the goddess. Athena was merely
concerned to grab the first rag that came to hand in the
forge. She cleaned her thigh and, never wanting to see it
again, tossed away the wet cloth from on high. The rag fell
on Attica. As it happened, Ge, mother earth, a figure not
unused to acts of primordial generation, was passing by.
Sodden with Hephaestus's sperm, the cloth fell into her
womb, and she conceived. When Ge gave birth and didn't
know what to do with the newborn child, Athena decided to adopt this creature nobody wanted, decided with
the same swiftness and confidence with which she had
wiped away Hephaestus's sperm. She picked up this little
child who ended in a coiled snake's tail and called him
Erichthonius.

Even though they tend to avoid speaking of his birth, the
Athenians are devoted to Erichthonius. They see themselves
in him, fruit of a craftsman's not-to-be-satisfied desire for
a goddess. Neither peasants, warriors, or priests, they know
they spring from the seed of a craftsman, whether it be the
talkative artisan with his workshop in the agora or the solitary cosmic artificer. Their desire for Athena is greater than
that of any other people. And this brings them closer than
others to the unnatural gods of Olympus, the gods of detachment, the gods who cannot be satisfied with nature and
its cycles but seek a form hard as crystal, as crystal closed
in on itself, autonomous, autochthonous of the spirit.

Callimachus, who never spoke an unsound word, described
the sperm Hephaestus spilt in his vain desire for Athena as

"dew." On penetrating the earth, Ge's womb, that dew generated the snake-child. Athena lifted him up from the earth
in her virgin arms. But she couldn't embrace him as any
other mother would. Athena was more than a mother. Her
first gesture on the child's behalf was to hang a golden chain
around his neck with a locket containing two drops of Medusa's blood: one was lethal, the other healing. Then she
put Erichthonius in a wicker basket and tied the lid closed.
She gave the basket to the three daughters of Cecrops, king
of Athens, telling them not to open it for any reason what-
soever. The three girls didn't know that Athena, in her love
for Attica, wanted to make Erichthonius immortal without
the other gods finding out.

But whenever a god, or someone who partakes of the divine, wants to make a child immortal, something always
goes wrong. As when Thetis tried with Achilles, Demeter
with Demophon, Medea with her children. There is always
someone who turns up, disturbs the delicate process, and
ruins everything. Whether because distracted or curious.
Distraction and curiosity are the two ultimate sins, outward
signs of that impatience which has always prevented man
from rediscovering the gate of Paradise. Cecrops's three
daughters all had dewy names: Aglauros means "sparkling"; Pandrosos, "all dew"; and Herse, "dew." With
the same impatience with which Hephaestus had grabbed
Athena, squirting his sperm over the goddess's thigh, two
of Cecrops's daughters opened the basket and saw the
snake-child come out, protected by two other snakes, his
"bodyguards." There was nothing shocking about this for
Cecrops's daughters. Indeed, they might well have seen
Erichthonius as a baby brother: after all, their own father's
body also ended in a coiled snake's tail. Yet they sensed an
incipient terror, because they knew they had committed
what for the Greeks was the worst of all crimes: they had
opened the secret basket at the wrong moment.

Athena was on her way back from Pallene at the time.
She had been there to look for a bulwark for her city and
was walking along with an enormous rock in her arms. Her

plan was to place it on the Acropolis, thus making Athens impregnable. A crow, bearer of ill tidings, came flying toward her and told her what had happened. In her rage Athena dropped the huge rock, which buried itself in the ground opposite the Acropolis, never to be moved again. It was the Lycabettus, and it still dominates Athens today, but without defending it. Then Athena appeared to the daughters of Cecrops, who fled terrified. They guessed a tough punishment was in store for them, and, even as the thought formulated in their minds, they were seized by a mad frenzy. They rushed to the steepest rocks of the Acropolis, stared into the void, and jumped. As they were dashed to pieces, their blood squirted out over the rocks.

Athena recovered the snake-child. Once again what she did was destined to remain shut away in herself. She bent the skin of the aegis to form a sort of marsupial pocket and slipped Erichthonius inside. Now the snake-child looked down on the world from on high, intrigued, his head peeping out from Athena's breast beside Medusa's face, which, with the passing years, had taken on an austere beauty, not unlike that of the goddess herself. You could see why she had wanted to vie with her in beauty. Erichthonius propped himself up on the abundance of Athena's magnificent breasts. He looked down into their cleavage to see Medusa with her hair of snakes, and he felt the fringes of the aegis, which again were snakes, stirring round about him. The child immediately took a liking to Medusa. He didn't realize as yet that she was his sister, born, like him, from Ge's womb. Erichthonius felt happy, at home, a snake among snakes. Through the dried pelt of the aegis, he sensed the hidden warmth of his adoptive mother.

The more he looked at the world, the more he was convinced that the only person he bore any resemblance to was Athena, this strong, radiant woman, seething with snakes. She hadn't born him in her womb, she had spurned the seed from which he was born, yet they were closer than any mother and son. No one else would ever lie on those perfect white breasts, no one else would ever see them, except perhaps in the heat of action, when a breast might sometimes slither out of the aegis. And wasn't the aegis, Erichthonius's home, almost part of Athena's body? More than a weapon, it was a second skin. Erichthonius spent his youth dreading the moment when he would be separated from the body of his adoptive mother, separated from that little pouch inside the aegis, that warrior pregnancy, exposed to sun and wind. But one day Athena did set him down on the ground, inside the Acropolis compound. And there she raised him. The place was to become sacred. Then, sadly, they separated. For Erichthonius it marked the end of the divine period of his life. He became a king, one of the many kings of Athens. He married a Naiad, inaugurated the Panathenaea, invented the quadriga and money. At his death he wanted to return to his adoptive mother. He was buried in the compound where Athena had raised him, which was now the home of a snake.

The Athenians were aware of their original sin, what the daughters of Cecrops did. They worshiped Athena, despite knowing that the goddess had chosen not to make them invincible. The spirit of the city was a nameless snake, living in the Erechtheum. Every month they offered it a cake with honey, which the Greeks thought of as a type of dew. One day, when the Persians were marching on Athens, the snake for the first time left its cake untouched. Upon which the Athenians decided to flee the city, because the goddess had abandoned the Acropolis.

Seven centuries later, when Athens was no longer under threat, having already lost everything except its statues, the traveler Pausanias was amazed to come across a ceremony not many people knew much about. Every year two girls from seven to eleven years old were chosen by the king-archon from among the most ancient families of Athens and made to live for a certain period of time near the sanctuaries of Athena Polias and Pandrosos. Pandrosos was the only one of Cecrops's daughters who had obeyed the goddess. The girls were given a small enclosure where they could play hall, and in the middle of the enclosure was a statue of a boy on a horse. They were called the Arrhephoroi or the Hersephoroi, the name being taken to mean "bearers of the unspeakable" (*árrēta*) or "bearers of the dew" (*hérsē*). In fact they were both. One night, the priestess of Athena comes to the girls: "They carry on their heads what the priestess of Athena gives them to carry; she who gives knows not what she gives, nor do those who carry know what they carry." The two girls then walk along an underground tunnel that skirts the sanctuary of Aphrodite in the Gardens, going down the steep northern slope of the Acropolis. At the bottom of the passage, "they lay down what they have carried and pick up another thing, all wrapped up, which they bring back to where they began."

A swapping of bundles, an underground walk in the night, two little girls on their own: it was the enacting of a religious mystery. Thus the Athenians demonstrated under Athena's glaucous gaze that they had not forgotten their sin. No one ever revealed what it was the Arrhephoroi carried and brought back on their heads. But more important than what was in the bundles was the fact that they should remain unopened, and that the two girls should move them in darkness.

After the ceremony, the girls were sent home. The following year two others would take their place. And one day they would all feel moved when they remembered the "splendid education" Athens had given them. The companions of Lysistrata recalled their girlhood thus: "At seven I was an Arrhephoros; at ten I was an *aletrís*, I ground the holy cakes in the service of our protectress; then I put on the saffron tunic and danced the bear dance at the Brauronia; and when I'd grown up to be a fine girl I was a basket bearer and wore a necklace of dried figs." These girls had been through mystery the way other children cross a playground, and now, barricaded up on the Acropolis, they refused to let their coarse, lustful husbands so much as touch them.

.   .   .

Whatever happens in Athens, "splendor," *lamprótēs*, always has a part to play. It was not because the tyranny of the sons of Pisistratus was unbearable that Harmodius and Aristogiton rebelled and thus became the model for all later reflections on conspiracies and tyrannicides. No, it was because Harmodius's body was "in the splendor of youth," and Hippias, Pisistratus's son, desired him. But Aristogiton, an average citizen and Harmodius's lover, also desired the boy. Their assassination attempt was motivated by "the pangs of love."

And when the Athenians began flocking down to Piraeus at dawn on what they didn't realize would be their last day of shared exhilaration albeit mixed with fear, when, that is, Alcibiades' fleet set sail for Sicily—even on this occasion, in a scene colored by boldness, conquest, and death, the eye came to rest on "the splendor of the view" of those ships laden with ornaments, until the herald blew on his trumpet, silence fell, and the soldiers and commanders lifted their gold and silver cups to make a libation. So recounts Thucydides, most sober among Athenians.

Phye was a beautiful country girl, four cubits tall. She lived in the district of Paeania. When Pisistratus decided to return from exile and reestablish his tyranny, they went to find her. They dressed her in lavish armor and showed her how to stand and move so as to seem even more impressive. Then they got her to climb on a chariot and set off to Athens, preceded by a number of heralds. The heralds announced around the town that Pisistratus was returning and that the goddess Athena, who had always favored him, was leading him back to the Acropolis. "And convinced she was the goddess in person, the citizens worshiped a human creature and welcomed Pisistratus back."

Herodotus claims that this piece of deception was "by far the most naive since the Hellenic race split off from the barbarians in ancient times, being shrewder and less prone to childish naïveté than they." But, as always, it is the decep-

tion that reveals a truth which might otherwise escape us.
This second return of Pisistratus happened in 541 B.C., just
a few decades before Heraclitus began to write. And for all
the extraordinary shrewdness they showed in their political
struggles, the people of Athens were still willing to accept
the possibility that one day the goddess Athena might ride
into their city on a chariot.

It is easy to imagine the fate historians have reserved for
what Gaetano De Sanctis refers to as "the absurd story of
the shapely woman who, dressed up as Pallas, is supposed
to have escorted Pisistratus into the city." As we know,
scholars have long been in the habit of pointing out the
"childish naïveté" of Herodotus, just as he had pointed out
the "childish naïveté" of the barbarians.

The fact remains, however, that Aristotle, who was to become the model of rational thought for every scholar of the
classical world, tells the story of Pisistratus's second return
in exactly the same terms as Herodotus. Indeed, he even
adds a few extra details about Phye, thus irritating Gaetano
De Sanctis even more with this "worthless claptrap that
demonstrates nothing but the poor historical sense of the
author who collected it." Aristotle writes: "Eleven years
later, having been put in a difficult position by his own fac-
tion, Megacles opened negotiations with Pisistratus and, on
the understanding that the latter would marry his daughter,
had him return in a manner at once worthy of ancient times
and extremely simple. He spread a rumor that Athena was
leading Pisistratus back and, having found a tall and beautiful woman from the district of Paeania, as Herodotus says,
or from the district of Collytus, as others claim, a flower
seller of Thracian origin who went by the name of Phye, and
having dressed her up to look like the goddess, he had her
ride into the city at the tyrant's side—thus Pisistratus entered the city on a chariot with the woman beside him, and
the citizens bowed down in amazement and welcomed
him."

The most interesting thing about Aristotle's account is his own comment on Pisistratus's return, that it was "worthy of ancient times and extremely simple." A century before him, Herodotus was still having to make an effort to exercise that marvelous new Greek quality, that shrewdness "alien to childish naïveté." Hence he was obliged to present Pisistratus's return as an almost unbelievable event.

The more sober Aristotle, by contrast, already had an entirely modern vision of events. Which is precisely why he was not in the least surprised by what happened, recognizing in this return led by the flower girl–goddess a last apparition of a lost world in which the line separating gods and men was constantly shifting, and thus hazardous. Pisistratus's return could thus truly be considered "worthy of ancient times," of the times when the power of metamorphosis was still such that a flower seller could be mistaken for a goddess in the streets of Athens.

Right from the beginning, Greek elegance is opposed to Asiatic sumptuousness with its prodigal mix of solemnity and abundance. As the Greeks see it, elegance arises from excavation, from the cavity. *Glaphyrós*, "concave," the word Homer used to describe ships and caves, gradually came to refer to that polish and brightness typical of a carved and honed surface. The spare incision of a sign, or the compact, vibrant surface: these were the desirable goals, and each must be achieved by planing away and streamlining one's material.

The epidermis of the Greek statue is so sharply separated from all that surrounds it because it is carved out of the air, whereas Mesopotamian or Egyptian statues seem to have grown up from the ground. The intensity that resides in a line of Homer is such above all because the word stands out against the emptiness of all the many details the poet denies us, the splinters hacked away from the word. Later, turning aside from the realm of palpable surfaces, the *glaphyría* opens up a passage toward the interior, toward the sharpness of the mind. Until finally it installs itself in a surface bereft of any foothold when Iamblicus uses the word *glaphyría* to define the elegance of mathematical demonstrations.

On the one hand, long, pleated skirts with long, thin feet poking out beneath, corsets squeezing the ample breasts of Minoan women; on the other, seamless tunics held by a buckle at the shoulder to create an alternation of soft, ruffled drapery, through which the body could be sensed, and smooth, bright surfaces which prevented it from actually being seen, so that "what must be kept hidden is kept hidden, while much blows in the wind." There could be no greater incompatibility than that revealed by this change in the way women dressed. Between the one style and the other lies the forever obscure process that was the evolution of Greek uniqueness. What happened in that interval? The Dorians, always a riddle for archaeologists, left nothing that could be attributed to them with any certainty, except perhaps a simple form of clothing, a rectangular drape pinned at the shoulder.

The first enemy of the aesthetic was meaning. The symbol appears as an image that is also something else. The aesthetic appears in a figure that is *like* many others. The god is a boy; he appears on the scene like any Athenian boy, naked as they are, face creased in a light smile. Often he has no attributes that might allow us to recognize him. He relies entirely on presence. Scholars are still puzzled by the *kórai*: are they dead girls? or the goddess's maids? or the goddess herself? or the figurative representation of thoughts on the tomb of a boy or man, with whom these women had nothing at all to do? Here meaning seems to melt away, doesn't impose itself. What does impose itself is a presence, as if of someone we don't know. And one doesn't think immediately of any meaning, but of what appears to the eye.

In contrast, the smallest Mesopotamian seal challenges us to decipher it: it is a memory condensed into a few stiff notches. It presupposes a scene, an order of events and figures. The statue defies such interpretation. At most it will hold a piece of fruit in one hand. But we sense that, before conveying any meaning, it wishes only to attract our eye—and install itself there.

The Greek god imposes no commandments. How could he forbid anything, when he has already done it all himself, good deeds and bad? The Greeks did have maxims that aspired to the same universality as commandments. But they were not rules descended from heaven. If we look closely at these maxims, at their insistence on *sōphroneîn*, on control, on the dangers of any kind of excess, we discover that they are of an entirely different nature: they are maxims elaborated by man to defend himself from the gods. The Greeks had no inclination for temperance. They knew that excess is divine, and that the divine overwhelms life. But the more they found themselves immersed in the divine, the more they wished to keep it at arm's length, like slaves running their fingers over their scars. Western sobriety, which two thousand years later would become everyman's common sense, was at first no more than a mirage glimpsed through the tempest of the elements.

So what did these Greek gods want of men? What they certainly did not require was that we behave one way rather than another. They were as ready to defend the unjust actions of a favorite as to condemn the just actions of someone they disliked. So what did they want? To be recognized. Every recognition is an awareness of form. Hence in our enfeebled modern vocabulary we might say that the way they imposed themselves was first and foremost aesthetic. But in a sense of the word which, with time, has been lost: the aesthetic of a mesh of powers concentrated in a figure, a body, a voice.

If, driven by an old compulsion, we were to define what the gods were to the Greeks, we might say, using the principle of Occam's razor, everything that takes us away from the ordinary sensations of life. "With a god, you are always crying and laughing," we read in Sophocles' *Ajax*. Life as mere vegetative protraction, glazed eyes looking out on the world, the certainty of being oneself, without knowing what one is: such a life has no need of a god. It is the realm of the spontaneous atheism of the *homme naturel.*

But when something undefined and powerful shakes mind and fiber and trembles the cage of our bones, when the person who only a moment before was dull and agnostic is suddenly rocked by laughter and homicidal frenzy, or by the pangs of love, or by the hallucination of form, or finds his face streaming with tears, then the Greek realizes that he is not alone. Somebody else stands beside him, and that somebody is a god. He no longer has the calm clarity of perception he had in his mediocre state of existence. Instead, that clarity has migrated into his divine companion. A sharp profile against the sky, the god is resplendent, while the person who evoked him is left confused and overwhelmed.

Looking at Athena, her breast fringed with snakes, her clear-cut monochrome face, we get a sense of what the classical is: a hybrid between the barbaric and the neoclassical.

At a certain point in their history, when the palaces had been burned down, writing lost, gold become unobtainable—at a certain point in their history, about which we know very little, since it left us neither words nor monuments, the Greeks chose perfection as opposed to power. Power dreams of indefinite expansion, perfection cannot. The perfect is only one of the innumerable points in the process that is ceaselessly transforming existence. But this point has a hidden flaw, which terrifies the Greeks: the point of perfection is the moment that closes the circle, that brings death. Only in the experience of Eleusis did this huge obstacle appear to melt away. That was why the Greeks respected Eleusis more than anything else.

What was celebrated at Eleusis was not just one of the everyday and extremely tedious agrarian rituals. It was the simultaneous presence of perfection and death. Eleusis was not for peasants worried about their crops. Eleusis was for those languishing for perfection, and it was meant to heal their sickness. There, and only there, could one find a perfection that did not die. People coming back from Eleusis would laugh and cry like everybody else. But only they could claim to be really laughing and crying. Because their laughter and tears came *after* perfection, and not as its feeble precursors.

"Pure light of midsummer." Such, according to Pindar, is Dionysus. He is the *opóra*: the fifty days that follow the rising of Sirius, after the first half of July. When the *opóra* was over, the Eleusinian procession set off from Athens. The festival began with an extremely high-pitched cry and ended with the appearance of a "sacred youth." For the Athenians he was a "beautiful god," the god of that moment. The cry and the youth had the same name: Iacchus. The cry was the youth.

At the beginning of the procession, when on a September afternoon, the day of the battle of Salamis, the people left the Dipylon and headed off down the Sacred Way, the presence of Iacchus, in the role of "traveling companion," roused the young dancers for a dance that was to last twelve and a half miles and would take them as far as Eleusis. The crowd of boys, women, and old men would let themselves be ruled by this "tireless god." Iacchus was a sound and a torch, one amid the many flickering on the flowery plain, even though it was September and the fields scorched by the summer heat.

What are the mysteries? "The saying of many ridiculous things and many serious things" is the definition Aristophanes offers, and no one has ever bettered it. In the midst of "the laughter and the jokes," as the procession proceeds, the sidelong glance of a dancer comes to rest "on a very attractive young girl, an old playmate, one small breast poking through a tear in her tunic." The air is full of the smell of resin and roast pig. The dust is strewn with sandals and torn clothes, which would be even more torn before the dance was through, because "he who celebrated the mysteries would not take off the tunic he wore at the festival until it was reduced to rags."

They were a group of small states, enemies for the most part, or halfhearted friends. But they felt they had something in common to defend: *tò Hellēnikón*, the "Greek thing." They didn't bother to define it, because they knew perfectly well what it was. Not high-ceilinged palaces, or guards lined up in ranks, or deferent ministers, or gold. But a certain spareness of expression, as though among athletes who compete in physical speed and beauty, and in nothing else. Perhaps this partly explains why, unlike the barbarians, even the imperial barbarians, the Greeks would go around naked. And there was something else the Greeks, and only the Greeks, were interested in: an empty space, sun-drenched and dusty, where they could exchange goods and words. A market, a square.

When Cyrus the Great, first ideological opponent of the Greeks, received a threatening Spartan herald, he sat up on his throne for a moment to ask what on earth this unknown city called Sparta might be, and how many men they could muster. One of his Greek advisers explained. At which Cyrus answered with an expression that would clear up once and for all the question of why Asian power could not tolerate the "Greek thing": "I've never been afraid of men who have a special place to meet in the middle of their city, where they swear to this and that and cheat one another."

Among the most significant of epithets applied to Zeus is *Phanaîos*, "he who appears." The same name is also used for Apollo, "because through him the things that are [*tà ónta*] are made manifest, and the cosmos is illuminated." The supremacy of appearance begins with Zeus, and from it derive the tensions that galvanize Greek culture. The fact that Plato launched a devastating attack on appearance shows that appearance was still dominant and oppressive to him. The messenger of the realm of appearance is the statue. No other ancient language had such a rich vocabulary for referring to different kinds of images as Greek. And this markedly visual vocabulary contrasted sharply with that of the Greeks' enemies par excellence: the Persians. Behind the long historic rivalry, one glimpses an insuperable metaphysical divide, which Herodotus describes thus: "[The Persians] do not raise statues, or build temples and altars. On the contrary, they reproach those who do so for their folly, I think because they don't believe as the Greeks do that the gods have a human form. Their practice is to make sacrifices to Zeus from the top of the highest mountains, and they think of Zeus as the whole blue sky."

Unlike the Greeks, who adored stones and pieces of wood, and the Egyptians too, who prostrated themselves before ibis and ichneumons, the first Persians would bow down only before "fire and water, like philosophers." Breaking away in very early times from those philosopher-priests, the Magi, the Greeks generated a new race of philosophers, who were not priests and did not always dispense with images to then climb up on the highest mountains and worship the sky. Some would dispense with images and find nothing at all to worship. But, before that could happen, appearance had to impose itself as a hitherto unknown force, a challenge.

Nowhere so much as in Athens was sovereignty in both its guises, regal and priestly, so scornfully written off. *Basileús,* "king," became the name of a kind of priest who was en trusted with limited duties only at certain of the annual festivals, such as the Anthesteria. For the rest of the year the *basileús* was an Athenian like any other. And priests in general were respectable, physically whole members of the community, but they were not granted any power beyond the roles they played in their cults. They were priests without books, without an all-embracing secret doctrine.

There could be nothing more Greek than Herodotus's amazement on discovering that in Persia no one could make a sacrifice unless a Magus was there to oversee the ceremony. In Greece, anyone could offer a sacrifice. And no one checked up on him. But the image of the Magus, of that cold eye watching, checking, keeping guard, would make itself felt through occult paths, building up the image of an unassailable power that exercised total control over reality. The Guardians were the peculiar image of such a power that was to develop in Greece. In two forms: practical and authoritarian in Sparta's ephors; theoretical, always ruthless, but linked to the heaven of ideas, in Plato.

Greece cherished two secrets: that of Eleusis and that of Sparta. Jacob Burckhardt came close to the secret of Sparta. With typical sobriety he comments: "Power can have a great mission on earth; for perhaps it is only on power, on a world protected by power, that superior civilizations can develop. But the power of Sparta seems to have come into being almost entirely for itself and for its own self-assertion, and its constant pathos was the enslavement of subject peoples and the extension of its own dominion as an end unto itself."

As an end unto itself: how often we hear that expression, and always with a shiver, as when drawn to something dangerous: hoarding of money, dandyism, experimental research. But the first *end unto itself* was laconic, Spartan: the grim reticence of a power that devoured all, that saw nothing else, needed nothing else. The first self-sufficiency, first indifference toward everything that was not part of its own mechanism, the divine machine designed by a craftsman who has a name but no face: Lycurgus. The Spartan state subjected every form to itself, subordinated every usage to its own existence. This was the ancient and thoroughly modern philosophy that the Spartans tried so determinedly to hide by passing themselves off as ignorant warmongers. Otherwise their enemies might also have been seduced by this power-enhancing mechanism, which the Equals felt was invincible. And a sad contradiction that would be . . . The philosophy turned out to be the most effective weapon of war and self-preservation. And it was not discovered by the Athenians, as always too garrulous, vain, and distracted for that kind of thing. No, this philosophy was *the* Spartan discovery, one that rendered any other discovery, and above all any other philosophy, superfluous.

This explains the yawning depths of Socrates' irony as he puts together an argument to counter Protagoras: "The greatest and most ancient of Greek philosophies is that of Crete and Sparta, and it is there that most of the earth's sophists reside: but they deny it and pretend to be ignorant, so as not to stand out among the Greeks for their wisdom, but to appear to excel only in battle and courage, fearing that the others, were they to know what they are really good at, might set themselves the same goal: knowledge. Their sham takes in the admirers of Sparta in other cities, who thus butcher their ears to imitate them, put leather bands around their legs, go to gymnasiums and wear short tunics, imagining that these are the keys to Sparta's supremacy among the Greeks. For their part, the Spartans, when they want to talk freely with their sophists and are tired of concealing their true selves, expel all the Spartophiles and other foreigners in the land, so as to be able to spend time with their sophists without any foreigners knowing; what's more, they, like the Cretans, don't let any of their young men travel to other cities, so that the teaching they have received cannot be spoiled."

The old Plato of the *Laws* was still thinking of Sparta with obscure regret: "When I saw the organization we were discussing, I found it most beautiful. If the Greeks had had it, it would, as I said, have been a marvelous possession, if someone had been able to use it in an attractive way." What comes through these words is the dawning fallacy of the technical, the illusion that one might set up a perfect mechanism and deploy it for the Good. The point is that the Spartan mechanism was based on the exclusion of every Good that was not part of its own operations.

Everything repeats itself, everything comes back again, but always with some slight twist in its meaning: in the modern age the group of initiates becomes the police force. And there is always some tiny territory untouched by the anthropologists' fine-tooth comb that survives, like an archaic island, in the modern world: thus it is that in antiquity we come across the emissaries of a reality that was to unfold more than two thousand years later.

Part of a Spartan's training was the exercise known as the *krypteía:* "It was organized as follows. The commanders of the young men would from time to time send off into the country, some in one direction, some in another, those young men who seemed smartest. They would be armed with daggers and supplied with basic rations, but nothing else. During the day they would fan out into uncharted territory, find a place to hide and rest there; at night they came down onto the roads and, if they found a helot, would cut his throat. Often they would organize forays into the fields and kill the biggest and strongest helots."

The usefulness of history and historians lies in the presentation and narration of events that can then reveal their meaning hundreds, even thousands of years after they happened. Burckhardt writes: "In Thucydides there may be facts of primary importance that will only be understood in a hundred years' time." He doesn't offer any examples. But we can find one ourselves that Burckhardt couldn't have found, because history hadn't as yet revealed it, for Burckhardt hadn't lived through the age of Stalin: "Likewise concerned about the ill-feeling among the helots and by their huge numbers [the Spartans' relationship with the helots having always been based on the need to defend themselves], they went so far as to do as follows: they announced that if any of the helots considered that during past wars they had given the best possible service to Sparta, they should come forward with their evidence. Once this had been examined it could lead to their being set free. But really this was a test, for those who, out of pride, considered themselves most deserving, were also those who would be most likely to rebel. About two thousand were selected. Crowned with garlands they went around from temple to temple under the impression they had been freed. Not long afterward the Spartans did away with them and no one ever knew how they were all killed."

"When the Spartans kill, they do so at night. They never kill anybody in daylight." Thus writes Herodotus, dwelling on the fact for no apparent reason.

Initiation involves a physiological metamorphosis: the circulating blood and thought patterns of the mind absorb a new substance, the flavor of a secret wisdom. That flavor is the flavor of totality: but, in the Spartan version, it is the flavor of the society as totality. Thus we pass from the old to the new regime.

Equality only comes into being through initiation. It does not exist in nature, and society wouldn't be able to conceive of the idea if it weren't structured and articulated by initiation. Later, there comes a moment when equality is geared into history and thence marches on and on until the unsuspecting theorists of democracy imagine they have discovered it—and set it against initiation, *as though it were its opposite.*

That moment is Sparta. The Spartans were above all *hómoioi,* "equals," insofar as they had all been initiated into the same group. But that group was the entire society. Sparta: the only place in Greece, and in all European history since, where the whole citizenry constituted an initiatory sect.

Having drunk deep the liquor of power, though more the idea than the reality, they soon ignored and scorned all immortality's other drinks: they had no time for the sciences of the heavens ("they can't bear talk about the stars or the celestial motions," observed the irritated Hippias) and cared nothing for poetry. Indeed, despite the fact that in years past Alcman had produced enchanting lyrics to sing the beauty of the Leucippides running like colts along the banks of the Eurotas, "the Spartans are, of all men, those who admire poetry and poetic glory least." Their attitude to every form, every art, every desire can be summed up in their approach to music: they wished to make it "first innocuous, then useful."

They were the first to train naked and grease their bodies, men and women alike. Their clothes became ever more simple and practical. They were the grim forebears of every utilitarianism. They kept their helots in a state of terror— yet were compelled to live in terror of their helots. They carried their spears with them everywhere, for death might be lurking at every turn. Not at the hands of their "equals" but at those of the endless mutes who served them, before being mocked and decimated.

Sparta is surrounded by the erotic aura of the boarding school, the garrison, the gymnasium, the jail. Everywhere there are *Mädchen in Uniform,* even if that uniform is a taut and glistening skin.

Sparta understood, with a clarity that set it apart from every other society of the ancient world, that the real enemy was the excess that is part of life. Lycurgus's two ominous rules that forestall and frustrate any possible law merely dictate that no laws be written down and no luxury permitted. It is perhaps the most glaring demonstration of laconism the Spartans offer, always assuming we leave aside the grim moral precepts tradition has handed down to us. One can almost smell the malignant breath of the oracle in those dictates: forbidding writing and luxury was in itself enough to do away with *everything* that escaped the state's control.

"When it came to reading and writing they learned only the bare minimum." In every corner of their lives, like an ever-wakeful jailer, Lycurgus had hunted down the superfluous and strangled it before it could grow. There was only one moment when the Spartans had a sense of the overflowing abundance of life: when the flautists played Castor's march, the paean sounded in reply, and the compact ranks advanced, their long hair hanging down.

"A majestic and terrifying sight," war. That was the moment when god resided in both State and individual, the one moment when the rules allowed the young men "to comb out their hair and dress up in cloaks and weaponry" until they looked like "horses treading proudly and neighing to be in the race." When the march stopped, the Spartan "stands with his legs apart, feet firmly planted on the ground, and bites his lip."

"Just as Plato says that god rejoiced that the universe was born and had begun to move, so Lycurgus, pleased and contented with the beauty and loftiness of his now complete and already implemented legislation, wanted to make it immortal and immutable for the future, or at least so far as human foresight was capable." The divine craftsman of Plato's *Timaeus* composed the world and brought it into harmony; Lycurgus was the first to compose a world that excluded the world: Spartan society. He was the first person to conduct experiments on the body social, the true forefather all modern rulers, even if they don't have the impact of a Lenin or a Hitler, try to imitate.

The Athenians knew there was a surplus of beauty in relation to power in their city. They could already see the ruins of Athens, whereas, to Thucydides' eyes, "if the Spartans were to abandon their city, so that only the foundations of the buildings survived, with the passing of time posterity simply would not believe the town had ever been so powerful as it was said to be."

What distinguishes Sparta from Athens is their different responses to the practice of exchange. In Sparta it provokes terror, in Athens it arouses fascination. Thus the wholeness of the sacred is split into two chemically pure halves. Gold is taken into Sparta but never comes out: "for generation after generation gold has been flowing into Sparta from every people in Greece, and often from barbarian countries too, and it never flows out." Coins are so heavy and burdensome they can't even be moved. In Athens, "friendly to speech," words run spontaneously from the lips in a stream that sluices every culvert of the city. In Sparta the word is always kept tightly in rein.

Spartans' morality was not based on the weighty precepts that made up the wisdom of the people but on the decision to treat the word as an enemy, foremost exponent of the superfluous. Sparta was an invention for freezing exchange and stabilizing power as far as is humanly possible, which explains the attraction Plato always felt toward Sparta, right up to the late *Laws:* that order of theirs seemed capable of putting a stop to the proliferation of images.

But here is Sparta in a nutshell, courtesy of a Plato at once laconic and vicious: "These men . . . will be greedy for wealth, fiercely devoted behind the scenes to gold and silver; they will possess storehouses and domestic treasuries where they can hide that wealth, and well-fenced villas, veritable nests of privacy, where they can spend money on women and whomever else they want and enjoy being thoroughly dissolute. . . . And they will be miserly with their wealth too, earning and honoring it in secret, prodigal only with other people's, which they covet, and they will take their pleasures behind closed doors, snubbing the law the way a child snubs his father, and they will not respond to persuasion, but only to violence, because they will have ignored the real Muse of reasoning and philosophy and esteemed physical exercise more praiseworthy than music." One can never be too sure where Plato's sentiments lie.

It was to the Spartans' credit that they were the first to appreciate the extent to which the social order is based on hatred—and can survive only so long as that base is maintained. They accepted the consequences of this discovery: equal and interchangeable among themselves, they formed a rock-solid front against the outside world. And in the outside world were the masses (tò plêthos), whom, unlike the Athenians, the Spartans had no illusions about winning over and manipulating. "The best Spartan thinkers do not believe it would be safe to live together with those they have so seriously wronged. Their way of doing things is quite different: among themselves they have established equality and that democracy necessary to guarantee a constant unity of intent. The common people, on the other hand, they keep out in the surrounding countryside, thus enslaving their own spirits no less than those of their slaves."

The Spartans were perfectly aware of the atrocious suffering they were inflicting and never imagined their victims could forget it. The solution was to establish terror as a normal condition of life—and that was Sparta's great invention: to create a situation in which terror was seen as something normal. The pure Athenian Isocrates was outraged: "But what would be the point of describing all the sufferings inflicted on the masses? If I just mention the worst enormity, leaving aside all the others, it will be quite enough. From among those who have constantly been subjected to horrible wrongs, and who are nevertheless still useful in present circumstances, the ephors are free to choose whomsoever they want and have them put to death without trial; while for all the other Greeks, even the killing of the most reprobate slave is a crime that must be paid for." The ephors were powerful bureaucrats; they were not remarkable for their "bold thinking" (*méga phroneîn*), as were the eminent and feared men of Athens. To make up for that, they could at any moment, and without a word of justification, kill anybody they wanted to from the nameless mass of the helots.

Athens never achieved the full horror of Sparta, but then it was never far behind. The city had barely discovered liberty, that experience no one in Persia or Egypt had ever dreamed of, before it was also discovering new methods of persecution, methods more subtle than those practiced by the great kings and the pharaohs. An army of informers invaded city square and market. They were no longer the secret agents of a police force but a freely formed collective of citizens intent on the public good. Thus in the very same instant that it discovered the excellence of the individual, Athens also developed a fierce resentment against that excellence. None of the great men of the fifth century B.C. was able to live in Athens without the constant fear of being expelled from the city and condemned to death. Ostracism and the sycophants formed the two prongs of a pincer that held society tightly together. As Jacob Burckhardt was first to recognize, Jacobin pettiness became a powerful force in the *pólis*. The public good was able to claim its victims with the arrogant and peremptory authority that had once been the reserve of the gods. And where a god would speak through soothsayers or a Pythia, chanting in hexameters and using obscure images, the *pólis* could get by with a less solemn apparatus: public opinion, the voice of the people, mutable and murderous as it sped, day after day, through the agoré.

Athens left posterity not only the Propylaea, but political chatter too. The anecdote passed on to us by Plutarch is exemplary: an illiterate man went up to Aristides, who he had never seen before, and asked him to write the name *Aristides* on a potsherd. So he could vote for his ostracism. Aristides asked him: "What harm has Aristides done you?" The illiterate man answered: "None. And I don't know him, but it bothers me hearing everybody call him Aristides the Just." Without more ado, Aristides wrote his own name on the potsherd.

It is a grim irony of history that Sparta continues to be associated with the idea of virtue, in its most rigid and hateful form. It is as if the Equals had placed the hard rule of law above everything else and thus gained themselves a reputation for being tough and cold, yet at the same time noble.

But the truth is that the Spartans had come up with a very different and far more effective way of doing things. They created the image of a virtuous, law-abiding society as a powerful propaganda weapon for external consumption, while the reality inside Sparta was that they cared less for such things than anyone else. They left eloquence to the Athenians, and with a smirk on their faces too, because they knew that that eloquent, indeed talkative nation would be the first to feel nostalgic for the sober virtue of the Spartans, not appreciating that such virtue was nothing more than a useful ploy for confusing and unnerving their enemies. It shouldn't come as any surprise that the Spartans refused to allow strangers to enter their city and were so secretive about what happened within its territories. An accurate report would have exposed their smug insensibility to the very idea of law, which had such a powerful hold over the minds of their neighbors. For the most disturbing examples of indifference toward injustice came not from those animals of passion, the tyrants, but from the cold ephors, supreme guardians of the secret of Sparta. The sad story of Skedasus reveals them to us in all their esoteric ruthlessness.

Skedasus was a poor man who lived in Leuctra. He had two daughters, Hippos and Miletia. He loved to have guests, even though he had little to offer in the way of hospitality. One day he put up two young Spartans. They were both taken by the beauty of the virgin daughters, but because the girls' father was there they restrained themselves and proceeded with their journey to Delphi. On the way back they stopped at Skedasus's house again. But this time he was away. The two daughters took the foreigners in. When the Spartans realized they were alone, they raped the girls. Then, seeing them disfigured by distress, they killed them and threw them down a well. When Skedasus got home all he found was the dog, yelping and running back and forth between his master and the well. Skedasus guessed the truth and pulled out the corpses. His neighbors told him the two Spartans had stopped at his house, and Skedasus realized what had happened, remembering that the two "had admired the girls and spoken warmly of the happiness of their future husbands."

So Skedasus set off for Sparta. He wanted to report the crime to the ephors. One night he was in an inn. Next to him was an old man from Oreos who was complaining bitterly about the Spartans. Skedasus asked him what they had done to him. The old man explained that the Spartans had appointed a man called Aristodemus as governor of Oreos. He had fallen in love with the old man's son and had immediately attempted to abduct the boy from the gymnasium, but the gym teacher had stopped him. The following day he managed to get the boy just the same. He put him on a ship and sailed over to the opposite shore. He tried to rape him. The boy put up a fight. So he cut his throat. That evening, he went back to Oreos and gave a banquet. The old father organized his son's funeral and set off for Sparta. He asked for an audience with the ephors. The ephors didn't even listen to him. Then Skedasus told his own story. When he had finished, the old man told him there was no point in going to Sparta. But Skedasus took no notice. He spoke to the ephors. They didn't even listen to him. So he went to the king, he pleaded with people in the street. It did no good. Finally he killed himself. But history would one day set its seal on the story. Spartan power was broken once and for all at the battle of Leuctra. The fighting took place not far from the tombs of Skedasus's daughters.

For years the wooden image of Taurian Artemis lay hidden in a clump of reeds not far from the river Eurotas. Orestes had stolen it from the sanctuary. He traveled for weeks, holding it tightly in his hands for as long as he felt the madness upon him. Then one day he thought he would try to live without it, and he hid the statue in this wild place. Two young Spartans of royal blood, Astrabacus and Alopecus, came across it by chance when they pushed the reeds aside. Upright and swathed in rushes, the statue stared at them. Not knowing what they were seeing, the two Spartans were seized by madness. Such is the power of the image: it heals only those who know what it is. For everybody else, it is an illness.

Around the small, light statue of Artemis, the Spartans built a temple. They dedicated it to Artemis Orthia and Lygodesma, upright and bound with rushes. People would offer masks to it, horrifying usually, images of the night and the underworld. As once before among the Tauri, when Iphigenia took care of it and washed it, the statue required that young blood be shed. But even the Spartans could sometimes ease up on a harsh custom. They decided they wouldn't kill young people for the statue anymore but just whip them till the blood flowed before the goddess. So now one would see the most insolent of the Spartans, the ones who used to make raids into the countryside to kill helots for fun, for a laugh, agreeing to have themselves thoroughly whipped by other boys. Some of those doing the whipping might hold back a bit, especially when the youth being whipped was very handsome, or belonged to one of the more illustrious families. The statue didn't like this. The priestess held it up beside the boys being whipped. But if the strokes eased off, the statue would begin to weigh more and more, like a meteorite trying to sink into the ground, and the wood would protest: "You're pulling me down, you're pulling me down."

What Plato learned from Sparta was how to get a group of initiates to take over a town's political life without anybody being scandalized. *Éphoroi* and *phýlakes* are very close even from a linguistic point of view: both mean "guardians," "observers from above." "Of a flock," says Plato; "of a territory," says Sophocles; "of children," says Plato again; "of a slaughter," says Euripides. But what do you have to do to become a guardian? Subject yourself to the initiatory torture. The aspirant must be "tried [*basanizómenon*] like gold in the fire." Yet *basanízein*, when removed from the context of noble and inanimate materials such as gold, means "to torture."

The bloody whippings Artemis Orthia demanded of the young Spartans, the *hómoioi*, are only a hint, a small hint, of those "sufferings and pleasures . . . labors, fears, and convulsions" that Plato wanted to impose on his future guardians. And here he reveals his most daring plan: to secularize initiation, to have it pass for something like a good school, a bit tough, along the lines of an English boarding school, but as justifiable as any other kind of training, of soldiers, for example, or artists. While in reality it was far more ambitious, its purpose being to select, once and for all, a group which, purely thanks to its initiatory quality, would be able to run the whole city. "You know I hesitated earlier on to say the rash things I have now said," Plato adds with fake caution, as though his most audacious step had been saying that "truly impeccable guardians must be philosophers." And even as he covers his tracks like this, he is insinuating the real departure: that in order to be "impeccable guardians," the philosophers must be initiated, and hence subjected to those excessive passions that Plato himself had condemned.

But who is an initiate? A person who has experienced a knowledge invisible from without and incommunicable except through the same process of initiation. Inevitably, Plato explains, there can be but "few" initiates. And in fact when compared with the Spartan version, Plato's initiation process is more subtle and more arduous. There are a greater number of trials to overcome and, having survived the last, the initiate may find he is "the only one." Then there may not be enough time for him to pass on his initiation. And there may not be anyone to follow him, with the result that the chain is broken.

So one day Plato began to write the *Republic*. And he wrote the text in the form it is in so that anyone who wanted to understand it might be subjected to that initiatory process of "sufferings and pleasures . . . labors, fears, and convulsions." The many who did not understand, and were not supposed to understand, imagined they were reading a treatise on the perfect State.

Newly born, the boys were washed in wine to see how tough they were. The weaker ones were thrown into the "so-called Dump, a ravine on the slopes of the Taygetus." They used no swaddling clothes and left the babies to cry in the dark. Those boys were "the common property of the city," and hence must be made useful to the city as soon as possible. All their lives they would eat with other males, black broth more often than not. The older men loved practical jokes and war stories. The boys had to learn how to put up with both. They learned to read and write, but nothing more. The notion of anything *more* was abhorred, in everything. Getting married meant leaving the boys' dormitory some nights to see your wife. Sex was furtive and quick, and the couple didn't sleep together. "Some had children without ever seeing their wives in daylight."

Unlike the many fools throughout Greece, they knew right from the start that "all of them, for their whole lives, must wage perpetual war against every city." But the first city they were at war with was their own. They watched the helots, too many of them, working in the fields, and knew that one day they would have to kill one. They also knew that they must always be on the lookout, always carry a weapon. They knew they must close their doors with special keys. They could sense the hatred of the helots. The Equals took pleasure not so much in *pleonexía*, the original sin of lusting for power but, and they were unique in this, in playing police. For it was a more subtle and lasting pleasure: they could feel that other people's lives depended on their decisions, while at the same time remaining anonymous, part of a corps, a wolf pack. We have very little hard information about Lycurgus. But we do know what his name means: "he who carries out the works (or celebrates the orgies) of the wolf."

Sodomized before marriage ("prior to their weddings the rule is that girls should couple in the manner of boys"), visited hurriedly by their husbands at night so that they could conceive and retain "some spark of desire and grace," relieved of the task of bringing up their children, not even interested in weaving, what did the Spartan women do? It is a question that has no answer, like the one the sophists would ask each other over banquets: "What song the *Syrens* sang?"

Plato himself regretted that the lives of the Spartan women were not organized in the same minute detail as those of their men, because this left an opportunity for "license." Athenian malice chose to remember little more of the Spartan women than their naked thighs, which could be glimpsed through a slit down the sides of their tunics. The poet Ibycus calls the Spartan women "thigh flashers." But the Athenians were able to appreciate their strappingly healthy beauty. Lysistrata greets the Spartan woman Lampito thus: "How your beauty shines, my precious. How fleshly and firm your body is. You could strangle a bull." And Lampito answers: "By the Dioscuri, I swear I could. I exercise in the gym and kick my arse with my feet." To which, Cleonice: "What great tits you've got." And Lampito again: "The way you're feeling me up I might be a beast for the sacrifice."

During exercises and games, the Spartan girls went nude beside the nude boys, brought together "out of erotic, not geometric necessity," Plato remarks. If the women speak in public it is only to pontificate in the best civic spirit. Indeed it is to them that we owe the invention of that saddest of figures, the Positive Hero. "We alone generate men," thunders the proud Gorgo, wife of Leonidas, speaking to a foreign woman. She thus does the spadework for Napoleon's quip on his first meeting with Madame de Staël: "Who do you consider the best of all women?" she asks. And he: "The one who bears the most children, madame." But what we would like to know is something quite different: what did these descendants of the Leucippides say to each other amid the clouds of dust they raised as they ran like colts along the banks of the Eurotas, "their hair tossing in the wind like Bacchants waving their thyrsuses." But the Spartan Sirens keep their silence too.

That happiness is an early symptom of misfortune, that "inherent" within happiness is the power to bring on misfortune, above all through the agency of resentment (*phthónos*), whether of men or gods, is a vision that was to persist among the Greeks when almost all others had faded. Yet they did want to be happy. One can appreciate now why it was that the Spartans cut themselves off from the other Greeks, transformed themselves into an unapproachable island. Just as they had perceived the dangers of exchange, so they saw the dangers of happiness. When they weren't sure they could handle something, they preferred to cut loose, to abolish rather than lose control. Thus they chose to put into practice what would later earn them Aristotle's most damning criticism: "they have lost the happiness of living."

Under Lycurgus, Sparta underwent a transformation that condensed into just a few years the whole of political history from sacred kingship right through to the regimes of the present day. Sovereignty passed from a pair of kings, an archaic and obscure institution, to five ephors, a highly innovative expression of absolute power disguised as a judiciary, which in turn was a cover for what was originally a priesthood. The long transition from sacred king to Politburo was thus achieved in one foul swoop. And the fact that this was done while pretending to leave the old institutions intact only added to the audacious modernity of the development. There was no need to cut off the two kings' heads. They could stay where they were, but bereft of power. If they caused trouble, however, the ephors might decide to "kill them without trial." Alternatively, the ephors could take their decision to kill the kings on a starry, moonless night, while silently watching the sky. If a shooting star crossed that sky, it meant that one of the kings had "offended against divinity." Originally no more than observers who kept their eyes on the heavens, the ephors had become supreme supervisors and "guardians," watchful eyes looking down from above. That was how they exploited their priestly past. It offered a sparkling cloak that protected the secret of politics.

On the one hand, a divine king who upholds through his body the attributes of cosmic sovereignty; on the other, a group of mostly faceless, nameless, all-seeing inquisitors: the whole of political history is contained between these two extremes. It is the story of how liturgical power was trans-

formed into invisible power. And that transformation, which
was to go on for centuries right down to the present day,
was achieved in Sparta in almost no time at all, and with
very little effort. The only difficult thing was making sure
that nobody outside realized what had happened. Everybody had to go on believing in those innocuous anecdotes
about the discipline, courage, and frugality of the Spartans.
But there were one or two people who couldn't so easily be
hoodwinked. Thucydides was one. But most perceptive of
all was Plato.

All Plato's political thought is obsessed by one figure: the
guardian, or guardians. Whether they are philosophers, as
proposed in the *Republic*, or men concerned with the Good,
as he likes to pretend in the *Laws*, ultimate power is concentrated in the hands of the guardians. But Plato did not
think of them as hypothetical figures: on the contrary, the
guardians already existed, in the wealthy Peloponnese. They
were the great sophists Socrates had mentioned in *Protagoras*, those who used their sophistry not to show off their
glory but to hide it. They were the ephors, first example of
a wholly godless power. But they didn't let people see that
side of them either; on the contrary, not content with all the
existing cults, they brought in a new one, to which they were
deeply devoted. They built a temple to Fear, close to the
communal dining hall. "They didn't honor her as a dark
demon to be kept at bay, but because they believed that the
State was held together mainly thanks to fear."

The great societies of ancient times were images of something that encompassed them, isomorphs of the cosmos. The
Son of the Sky was the axis of the world before becoming
the axis of the city. It was only with the hubris of the Greeks
that society claimed to be self-sufficient. So the Great Animal, as Plato describes him, was born. From that hubris
sprang all the other repudiations: it was the sign of man's
first move to cut loose from the rest, the human race closed
in on itself, in an attacking formation.

It was Athens: the searing word, cruelty, a play of color. And it was Sparta: slow, circumspect, murderous, seeking to turn everything to its own account. The Spartans even produced a lawmaker, Lycurgus, who committed suicide because he felt it might be useful for Sparta. "So he starved himself to death, reasoning that even the deaths of politicians should be of some value to society, that the end of their lives should not be without its use, but ought to have something virtuous and efficacious about it."

Perhaps Alcibiades penetrated deeper than anyone else into "the secret of the regime" that was Sparta. As an exile, he sought asylum in Sparta, being a descendant of the Eupatrids, who for generations had had links with the family of the ephor Endius. "He shaved his head, washed in cold water, and accustomed himself to eating dry bread and drinking black broth." Although the king of Sparta at the time was not, for once, a puppet of the ephors but a great general, Agis, Alcibiades "seduced his wife Timea and got her pregnant." Thanks to him, even the archaic and somewhat ridiculous regality that remained in Sparta was thus raised to illegitimacy in the person of the bastard child Leotychides, "whose mother, at home, speaking softly before servants and friends, would call Alcibiades, so great was the passion that obsessed her."

Alcibiades left us none of his insights into Sparta, but he did talk to Thucydides. And reading Thucydides one has the impression that the mirage of a virtuous Sparta has entirely dissolved. Thucydides sees and judges the Spartans' actions as though from within, as though the mechanism were there before his eyes, driven by two powerful levers: deceit and brute force. Before being wiped out by the Athenians down to the last man capable of bearing arms, the Melians had hoped for assistance from Sparta. The Athenian ambassadors tried in vain to convince them that such hopes were treacherous, because they depended on those who "more blatantly than any other nation we know of believe that what they like doing is honorable and that what suits their interests is just."

Located on the Asiatic side of the Hellespont, at its narrowest point, Abydos was included in Athens's list of depraved cities. It was here that Alcibiades chose to go for his grand tour. "As soon as you came of age and had got the approval of your tutors, you took your inheritance from them and set sail for Abydos, not in order to recover payment for anything, nor in any consular role, but because you wanted to learn from the Abydian women the sorts of habits congenial to your spirit of illegality and debauchery, so as then to be able to pursue those habits in later life." So says Antiphon in oratorial rage.

But Alcibiades' departure could also claim the right to be recognized by the sophists as one of those passions that flare up at a distance on the basis of a single name, or some story heard from someone else, or some image seen in a dream. The fact is that Alcibiades had heard tell of a legendary courtesan called Medontis, and it was to find her that he left Athens in the company of his uncle and lover, Axiochus. Here Lysias takes over from Antiphon in the assault on Alcibiades, concentrating every possible transgression in a single anecdote: "So Axiochus and Alcibiades sailed to the Hellespont, landing in Abydos, where they both married the Abydian woman Medontis and cohabited with her. She gave birth to a daughter, but neither could be sure who was the father. And when the girl was of marriageable age, they both cohabited with her, and whenever Alcibiades was having his way with her, he would say she was Axiochus's daughter; and when it was Axiochus's turn, he would say she was Alcibiades'."

It is true that Alcibiades would later find occasion to return to Abydos as a military leader, victorious on both land and sea, flaunting his purple sail. But there is nothing to prove that the story of Medontis and her daughter wasn't just an exemplary tale of vice invented by Lysias. All we can say for certain is that right from the beginning Alcibiades' destiny seems to have been marked out by an overriding predilection for prostitution of one form or another. It is as if for Alcibiades prostituting oneself were the secret sign by which strength and excellence are recognized. "Leaving the women of Sparta and Athens behind, he would burst in at the doors of the hetaerae in high spirits." And when, at Plato's symposium, he appeared, "wearing a sort of garland woven of ivy and violets with many ribbons around his head," those flowers were "the first invitation to an encounter and a demonstration of desire . . . for the lure of fresh flowers and fruit demands in exchange the first fruits of the body of the person who picks them." Thus it was a prostitute, Timandra, who recovered Alcibiades' body, riddled by the arrows and javelins of his Spartan assassins. "She wrapped him up in her robes to hide him, then gave him a glorious and honorable burial, using what she could find round about." Shortly before this, in a premonition of death, Alcibiades had dreamt that Timandra was wrapping him in her clothes and making up his face like a woman's.

Almost everything we know about Sparta was written by outsiders. The city's only two poets, Alcman and Tyrtaeus, were probably not Spartans by birth, and in any case they lived before the reforms of the sixth century, which conjured up and froze for all time the mirage that was Sparta. No Spartan ever spoke out, as no priest of Eleusis ever spoke out. Their real legacy was not a concise, sententious morality but silence.

What happened in ancient Greece that had never happened before? A lightening of our load. The mind shrugged off the world with a brusque gesture that was to last a few centuries. When, in the geometric patterns of the vases, we begin to find rectangles inhabited by black figures, those figures already have an empty space behind them, a clearing, an area at last free from meaning. It was perhaps out of gratitude toward this insolent gesture that Greece celebrated in its tragedies the attempt, admittedly vain and doomed to be short-lived, to rid themselves of the consequences of gesture and action.

Then, little by little, the Erinyes darkened the sky ever more rarely, until the most pressing concern became to find a way to control action, as if such control would be sufficient to empty action of its insidious nature, as if control did not itself imply a further action, just as insidious as the first. Anaximander's fragment on *díkē*, the Platonic vision of the meadow, on each side of which yawned four chasms, celestial and terrestrial, with swarms of souls meeting there: these were rare appeals to a rigorous sense of *karman*, appeals that the Hellenic spirit was impatiently stamping out. The Greeks would abandon them, without scruple, leaving them to the sects, the initiates, to Egypt. Like characters on a stage, the now cosmopolitan citizens would soon have no need of anything but jokes and tears. The cosmos was breaking up into Alexandrian chronicle.

Herodotus would have preferred to write about feats of engineering rather than religion, but in Egypt the cults invaded every nook and cranny. In a hasty observation, he pointed to the trait that most sharply divided Egypt from Greece: "The heroes have no place in Egyptian religion." In Egypt the past, like the land, had no ups and downs to it. The only unevenness was that tiny scarp formed by the layers of silt the Nile deposited every year. But, for the Greeks, the progressive deterioration of successive ages, from gold to iron, had at least been interrupted by that hillock, the age of the heroes, to which everything still looked back, even if the period had been nothing more than a capricious wrinkle on the surface of time.

The whole of Greece was strewn with the tombs of heroes, as was Egypt with cat cemeteries. Heroes and animals opened up the path to the dead. And as in Greece the heroes would become confused with the gods, repeating their deeds and taking over their traits, in Egypt the animals that cluttered everyday life reappeared in the heads of those hawks, cats, ibis, and jackals that watched over the soul on its celestial journeys. But there was no call to be overly surprised by such differences. In the end, as Herodotus with his admirable good sense observed, religion is a reality that no one can help but recognize. Which was why, he wrote, "I see no point in reporting what I've been told about Egyptian religion, since I don't believe any nation knows much more than any other when it comes to things like this."

They put earrings on crocodiles. When they died they laid them out in huge subterranean vaults. Cities of the Crocodiles. When there was a fire, the only thing they worried about was saving the cats. And the cats, in turn, threw themselves into the fires. Everything was bigger, longer, and flatter than among other peoples. Numbers were seized by a silent fury of multiplication. Such were the Egyptians. It was a country where all creatures, men and beasts, had barely gasped their last breath before they were being sent to the embalmers—except for the women, that is, who were sent three days later, so that the embalmers wouldn't rape them.

History for the Egyptians was a sequence of statues sitting on thrones. The first series in the sequence was made up of gods. The second series, of men. There wasn't much to distinguish one from the other. Yet the gap between those two series of statues was unbridgeable. Hecataeus, deceitful like all the Greeks, once claimed that his family could be traced back sixteen generations to a god. The priests of Thebes in Egypt humiliated him with a simple gesture. They took him into the nave of the temple and showed him hundreds of wooden statues standing side by side: they were the chief priests to date. All very much the same. Men and sons of men, explained the priests with their measured sarcasm. From other priests Herodotus would hear the list of the three hundred and thirty sovereigns who had reigned over Egypt.

None, they said, had been memorable, except the one queen
Nitocris and the most recent king, Moeris, who had had a
lake built with pyramids.

The Greeks who dropped anchor at Naucratis, at the mouth
of the Nile, were mainly merchants, tourists, or mercenaries.
They would go to the market, which, like Corinth, was famous for its prostitutes ("unusually beautiful," remarks
Herodotus). These Greeks were the first people to settle in
Egypt and go on speaking a foreign tongue. Seven mercenaries from small towns in Ionia carved a few words with
their names on the left leg of a huge statue of Ramses II,
near the second waterfall of Abu Simbel. There were many
such mercenaries: in the reign of Amasis, they formed a Foreign Legion of thirty thousand men.

Charaxus came to Naucratis to seek his fortune, bringing
a ship laden with wine from Lesbos. He was Sappho's
brother. But, instead of making a fortune, he squandered
one on his love for Doricha, also known as Rhodopis, a most
beautiful courtesan. Rhodopis came from Thrace as slave of
a rich man from Samos. One of her fellow slaves was the
storyteller Aesop. Charaxus paid a ransom for Rhodopis and
gave himself over to his passion for her. Back on Lesbos,
Sappho wrote some furious poetry, invoking Aphrodite to
bring her brother back, "unharmed" and with at least some
shreds of his wealth.

Herodotus was shocked when it was suggested that the
Micerine pyramid had been built for Rhodopis. How could
a building "that had cost countless thousands of talents"
belong to a hetaera? But centuries later, when Strabo was
traveling the Mediterranean and saw the heads of the
Sphinxes barely poking up from the desert sand, his guides
pointed out the Micerine pyramid, referring to it as the
Courtesan's Pyramid. They said it had been built by "Rhodopis's lovers." And they told this story. One day Rhodopis
was out bathing. An eagle snatched one of her sandals from
a maid's hands. The bird flew to Memphis, where it dropped

the sandal from high in the air onto the Pharaoh's lap as he was judging people's disputes out in the open. The Pharaoh saw that it was a beautiful sandal. He sent men all over Egypt to look for the woman it belonged to. They finally found her, in Naucratis. She became the Pharaoh's wife. On her death, the pyramid was built in her honor.

Hermes was pining with love for Aphrodite, who paid no attention. Zeus took pity on him. While Aphrodite was bathing in the river Acheloüs, he sent an eagle to snatch one of her slippers (*soccum*). Holding the slipper in her beak, the eagle flew to Egypt to give it to Hermes. Aphrodite followed as far as the city of Amitarnia, where she found both the slipper and the pining god. In return for her slipper, Aphrodite let Hermes make love to her. Hermes showed his gratitude by setting the eagle in the sky, above Ganymede, who had once been carried off by an eagle.

In Plutarch's time, guides in Delphi were still showing people the empty space where the long spears the courtesan Rhodopis had dedicated to the oracle used to be kept. Freed from slavery and having gained great wealth, she had used a tenth of her earnings to "build something the likes of which was never conceived of nor dedicated in any other temple." She did it because she was "eager to leave some memento of herself in Greece." Some said it was a scandal. But the answer to their objections was near at hand: looking up from the space outside the temple, one saw the golden statue of Phryne, which one stoic had disdainfully described as "a monument to Greek debauchery." And, in the end, it was nothing more than Praxiteles' homage to his mistress. Phryne had wanted to offer her golden body as a sort of first fruit, alongside all the other "first fruits and tithes of killings, wars, and pillage," near "this temple bubbling over with all kinds of spoils and loot taken at the expense of other Greeks." Now only the spoils remained. Greece had become just another place to visit, accompanied by a guide, who might just be Plutarch.

Such is the Greek version of events. But the Egyptians, who, as Herodotus remarks, are "the opposite" of the Greeks in all things and always trace everything back to ancient times, tell a different story. In his list of Egyptian rulers, Manetho mentions, as coming at the end of the sixth dynasty, a certain queen Nitocris, "the noblest and most beautiful woman of her time, fair of skin, who built the third pyramid," known as the Micerine Pyramid. Nitocris was also a daring war leader. Her reign ended in upheaval. To avenge her brother's death, she had all his enemies drowned in an underground chamber. Then she shut herself up in a room full of ashes. A surviving description speaks of her as "blond with pink cheeks." And *ródōpis* means "pink-faced."

There were about fifteen hundred years between the life of Nitocris and that of the courtesan Charaxus squandered his fortune on. And about six hundred years between the lives of Sappho and Strabo. That was how long it took for an Egyptian queen to become a blond prostitute arriving in Egypt as a Thracian slave, and for the Greek prostitute to go back to being an Egyptian queen. They are united now in a pyramid. And time has confirmed the truth of the few lines Posidippus wrote for Rhodopis: "Doricha, your bones are adorned by the ribbon tying your soft tresses / and by the perfumed shawl / in which once you wrapped the handsome Charaxus, / flesh against flesh, until the morning cup. / But the white, echoing pages of Sappho's song / remain and will live on. / Most blessed is your name, and Naucratis will watch over it / so long as ships pass by on the still Nile, heading seaward."

For the heroes fighting beneath the walls of Troy, life was not something that asked to be saved. They didn't even have a word that meant "salvation," unless perhaps *pháos*, "light." Salvation was a temporary reassertion of something already there. It didn't mean saving existence, or saving oneself from existence. Existence was beyond salvation. Life: something incurable, to be accepted for what it was, in all its malice and splendor. The most you could hope for was to keep yourself on the crest of the wave a few moments longer, before tumbling back down the steep slope into the darkness of the whirlpool. The word most often used to qualify death was *aipýs*, "steep." Death meant plunging downward, no sooner than you had topped the crest of the world of appearance.

The most terrifying feature of the Homeric afterlife is its apathy, which comes across in the lack of any punishment. Why distinguish between virtue and vice if everybody in the afterlife is to partake of the same helplessness, the same insubstantiality, the same desire to drink blood so as to feed what shreds of soul the funeral pyres have not entirely burned up and stripped from the whitened bones? Such a vision could not last long in an age that was no longer that of the heroes but of the poets who told the stories of heroes past.

Homer's poetry was still buzzing in everybody's ears when the first disciples of a first sect of the Book, the Orphics, began to swarm across Greece. Everything was different now, or at least so the Orphics claimed. Every action, however trifling, set the wheels of cosmic accountancy in motion. All kinds of rewards could be obtained by reciting splendid words, venerating the names of pre-Olympian gods. They knocked on the doors of the rich. They arrived with strange objects—books, a babble of books—and hinted that they were in contact with the gods. If someone felt burdened by a sense of guilt, if another felt an urge to hurt an enemy, the Orphics were ready to help, at a modest price. Sacrifices, charms, purification ceremonies. Until finally they began to turn nasty: anybody who refused their services risked appalling punishments, down there in the bogs of Hades. The men of the sect, the men of the Book, the Orphics with their "bundles of books," and likewise the

Pythagoreans, so intent on listening for fractional variations in sound that they looked as though they were "trying to overhear a conversation next door," were all met with suspicion and impatience. To the heirs of the strong Greece of the past, such as Plato and Aristophanes, there was something irritating and inelegant about their beliefs. Yet it was they, in the end, who won out, thanks, curiously enough, to Plato. For although his style of exposition through dialogue shifted the chiming of obscure poetry onto a stage where all was exaggeratedly clear and rippling with irony, the new doctrine crept in just the same. "To free oneself from that circle which causes weariness and crushing grief," to escape from existence as from a burden, or a crime; this basic Orphic dogma was spread more by Plato's style than by the precepts of the converted, until finally it would become inextricably bound up with the Gospel invitation to reject the Prince of this world.

Only those who have fled the world with pagan or Christian urgency, only those who have retreated into a fragment of soul whose origins lie elsewhere, in the beyond, only those who do not completely belong to this world are in a position to use the world and transform it with such efficiency and ruthlessness. And with that final transition to simply making use of the world we have arrived at an age that is neither pagan nor Christian, but that unknowingly continues to practice the same twin gesture of detachment and flight while sinking its claws into both earth and lunar dust.

One great fault of Homer, for which Plato never forgave the poet, was that he omitted any serious comment on the structure of the cosmos. The heavens were anonymous and superfluous. For the purposes of his narration, he used only three levels: Olympus, high in the ether; the earth, a multicolored disk, a supine body to whose back clung the invisible parasite of Hades; and, finally, the frozen Tartarus. But between Zeus's palace and the earth, and between the earth and the ice of Tartarus, there was simply nothing Homer was interested in talking about.

That immense void yawning beneath the surface of the earth was testimony to a blasphemous euphoria. It was a way of omitting, even obliterating the celestial machinery, the mathematical works of the Artificer. It was a first cataclysm wrought by poetry: the cosmos was made oblivious of itself. But with the Orphics, followers of the Book, and later with Plato, Chaldaean wisdom took its revenge on Homer. The roving islands of celestial bodies, the frayed progress of the Milky Way, the soft sounds of the spheres all regained their privileges. The wonderful flatness of the Homeric vision was lost in the ordered chasms that once again opened up between one heaven and the next. Hades was winkled out from his moldy underworld to be catapulted up into the atmosphere and settled in the cone of shadow between earth and moon, as if the lining of the planet had been turned inside out and shaken skyward, dispatching the multitude of souls it housed out into a turbulent dark. Such was the immense, windblown waiting room of the dead.

There is a radical and shocking divergence between Homer and all later theologians, Hesiod included. Homer, as Plutarch remarks, refuses to distinguish between gods and *daímones:* "he seems to use the two words as equivalents and speaks of the gods as *daímones.*" This makes it impossible to blame the *daímones* for the murkier activities of the gods and precludes any idea of a ladder of being, on which, through a series of purificatory acts, one might ascend toward the divine, or alternatively the divine might descend in orderly fashion toward man. This idea, which forms the point of departure for every form of Platonism, is already implicit in Hesiod's division of beings into four categories: men, heroes, *daímones,* gods.

But Homer ignores such mediation. For him the word "hero" can be substituted more generically with "man," nor did he see any need to introduce a separate class of *daímones.* He thus brought the extremes into immediate contact, leaving nothing to soften the violence of the collision. Yet, as one reads once again in Plutarch, "those who refuse to admit the existence of a class of *daímones* alienate the things of men from the things of the gods, making it impossible for them to mix, and eliminating, as Plato said, 'the interpretative and ministering role of nature,' or alternatively they force us to make a general hotchpotch, introducing gods into our human passions and goings-on and dragging them down to our level whenever it suits us, the way the women of Thessaly are supposed to be able to pull down the moon." Never perhaps as in this passage from the late and knowing Plutarch was the invincible scandal of Homer, the enemy of mediation, so clearly exposed. When the Christian Fathers railed against Homeric debasement, they were really doing no more than dusting off Plato's sense of scandal, and likewise that of his followers, here so lucidly summed up by Plutarch. The course of Greek civilization thus reveals itself as a process in which its founding authority, Homer himself, becomes ever more unacceptable.

Timarchus was a young disciple of Socrates who wanted to "know the power of his master's demon." He was "courageous and had only recently had his first taste of philosophy." So he decided to put himself to a fearful test: he would climb down into Trophonius's cave in Lebadeia, where Kore had once gone to play with the Nymph Hercynia, who kept a goose. When the Nymph was distracted for a moment, the goose disappeared into a cave hidden behind a stone. So Kore went into the cave to look for the bird, caught it, and lifted the stone, upon which a flood of water came rushing from the darkness. Of all the variations of Kore's adventures, this was the most remote and secret, so secret that no one knew about it: the only remaining record of the affair was the statue of a young girl with a goose in her arm in Hercynia's temple.

Having reached Lebadeia, Timarchus spent a few days purifying himself in the house of Good Fortune and Good Spirit. He bathed in the freezing waters of the river Hercynia. He ate the meat of the animals offered up as sacrifices. And every time the priests sacrificed another victim, a seer would read the entrails to see if Trophonius was well-disposed toward the visitor and would receive him kindly. One night Timarchus was taken from the house and led to the river. Two youths washed him with the deference of slaves. Then they led him to some priests, near where the water rose. They told him to drink from two springs. The first they called the water of Forgetfulness. The other was the water of Memory. Then Timarchus set off toward the oracle, dressed in a linen tunic with ribbons. On his feet he wore the heavy local boots. Two bronze poles linked by a chain stood in front of the oracle. Behind was the cave: a narrow, artificial opening, like an oven for baking bread.

Timarchus was carrying a light ladder and some honey cakes for the snakes. He slipped into the opening feet first and immediately felt himself being sucked into the darkness—where the snakes were waiting for him. For a long time he lay in the dark. Then he realized that the plates of his skull were slowly coming apart. His spirit slipped out, breathing freely as though after long compression, and began to rise. It swelled and spread. It was a sail in the sky. The sea it plowed was dotted with "islands sparkling with delicate fire," large islands, though of different sizes, and all round. High above, he saw the face of the moon approaching. Persephone was rushing across the sky with her dogs, the planets, behind her. From beneath, where the earth was, rose a murmur of groans, as though of a never-ending but remote tumult.

On climbing down into Trophonius's cave, Timarchus had imagined he was going toward Hades. But now he realized that Hades had been turned inside out into the sky, become the shadowy cone between the moon and the earth, and the earth was nothing more than the continuation of Hades into the abyss. But then why should the two worlds be so different from each other after all, given that both were places of exile? As the spirit of Timarchus thus reflected, he saw the place, near the moon, where the cone of shadow narrowed to a point, and saw that it was here that the drifting souls were gathering. They were trying to land on that woman's face, the moon, despite the fact that it grew more and more terrifying the nearer they got. The face seemed to be made up with an extremely fine powder, which the dead recognized as the substance of other souls. The moment they tried to grab hold of some wrinkle on the lunar surface, blinded by the white light, many would find themselves dragged back by an irresistible undertow, until they were falling through space again. Yet it was there that salvation lay, and they had come so close. Had they managed to set foot on this outpost of Persephone, they would one day have undergone a second death, more gradual and more delicate than the first. One day Persephone would have separated their minds, *noûs*, from their souls, the way Apollo could prize the armor from a warrior's shoulders. Then, when the substance of their souls had been left behind on the white dust, and keeping only "husks and dreams of life," they would have emerged on the other side of the moon, where the Elysian Fields stretch across a land terrestrial beings have never seen. When Timarchus came back, feet first, from the oracular oven, his body was glowing with light. Three months later he died in Athens.

Plato's attitude toward the myths is one that the more lucid of the moderns sometimes achieve. The more obtuse, on the other hand, still argue around the notion of *belief*, a fatal word when it comes to mythology, as if the credence the ancients lent to the myths had anything to do with the superstitious conviction with which philologists of the age of Wilamowitz believed in the lighting of an electric bulb on their desks. No, Socrates himself cleared up this point shortly before his death: we enter the mythical when we enter the realm of risk, and myth is the enchantment we generate in ourselves at such moments. More than a belief, it is a magical bond that tightens around us. It is a spell the soul casts on itself. "This risk is fine indeed, and what we must somehow do with these things is enchant [*epádein*] ourselves." *Epádein* is the verb that designates the "enchanting song." "These things," as Socrates casually puts it, are the fables, the myths.

In Greece, myth escapes from ritual like a genie from a bottle. Ritual is tied to gesture, and gestures are limited: what else can you do once you've burned your offerings, poured your libations, bowed, greased yourself, competed in races, eaten, copulated? But if the stories start to become independent, to develop names and relationships, then one day you realize that they have taken on a life of their own. The Greeks were unique among the peoples of the Mediterranean in not passing on their stories via a priestly authority. They were rambling stories, which is partly why they so easily got mixed up. And the Greeks became so used to hearing the same stories told with different plots that it got to be a perfectly normal thing for them. Nor was there any final authority to turn to for a correct version. Homer was the ultimate name one could evoke: but Homer hadn't told all the stories.

This flight of myth from ritual recalled Zeus's constant adulterous adventures. Through those incursions, he who was father of Dike, and had her sit on the throne on his right hand as personification of Justice and Order, revealed himself to be "against justice" and to harbor "thoughts opposed to order." The revelation that license was not perennially condemned but might be acceptable, at least if it came from above: that was the gift of the age of Zeus. Divine incursions were an unexpected overflowing of reality. Thus, in contrast to the harsh coercion of ritual, history was a constant overflowing, leaving, visible in its wake, those relics we call characters.

Much was implicit in the Greek myths that has been lost to us today. When we look at the night sky, our first impression is one of amazement before a random profusion scattered across a dark background. Plato could still recognize "the friezes in the sky." And he maintained that those friezes were the "most beautiful and exact" images in the visible order. But when we see a sash of fraying white, the Milky Way, girdle of some giantess, we are incapable of perceiving any order, let alone a movement within that order. No, we immediately start to think of distances, of the inconceivable light-years. We have lost the capacity, the optical capacity even, to place myths in the sky. Yet, despite being reduced to just their fragrant rind of stories, we still feel the Greek myths are cohesive and interconnected, right down to the humblest variant, as if we knew why they were so. And we don't know. A trait of Hermes, or Artemis, or Aphrodite, or Athena forms a part of the figure, as though the pattern of the original material were emerging in the random scatter of the surviving rags.

We shouldn't be too concerned about having lost many of the secrets of the myths, although we must learn to sense their absence, the vastness of what remains undeciphered. To be nostalgic would be like wanting to see, on raising our eyes to the sky, seven Sirens, each intoning a different note around each of the seven heavens. Not only do we not see the Sirens but we can't even make out the heavens anymore. And yet we can still draw that tattered cloth around us, still immerse ourselves in the mutilated stories of the gods. And in the world, as in our minds, the same cloth is still being woven.

For centuries people have spoken of the Greek myths as of something to be rediscovered, reawoken. The truth is it is the myths that are still out there waiting to wake us and be seen by us, like a tree waiting to greet our newly opened eyes.

Myths are made up of actions that include their opposites within themselves. The hero kills the monster, but even as he does so we perceive that the opposite is also true: the monster kills the hero. The hero carries off the princess, yet even as he does we perceive that the opposite is also true: the hero deserts the princess. How can we be sure? The variants tell us. They keep the mythical blood in circulation. But let's imagine that all the variants of a certain myth have been lost, erased by some invisible hand. Would the myth still be the same? Here one arrives at the hairline distinction between myth and every other kind of narrative. Even without its variants, the myth includes its opposite. How do we know? The knowledge intrinsic in the novel tells us so. The novel, a narrative deprived of variants, attempts to recover them by making the single text to which it is entrusted more dense, more detailed. Thus the action of the novel tends, as though toward its paradise, to the inclusion of its opposite, something the myth possesses as of right.

The mythographer lives in a permanent state of chronological vertigo, which he pretends to want to resolve. But while on the one table he puts generations and dynasties in order, like some old butler who knows the family history better than his masters, you can be sure that on another table the muddle is getting worse and the threads ever more entangled. No mythographer has ever managed to put his material together in a consistent sequence, yet all set out to impose order. In this, they have been faithful to the myth.

The mythical gesture is a wave which, as it breaks, assumes a shape, the way dice form a number when we toss them. But, as the wave withdraws, the unvanquished complications swell in the undertow, and likewise the muddle and the disorder from which the next mythical gesture will be formed. So myth allows of no system. Indeed, when it first came into being, system itself was no more than a flap on a god's cloak, a minor bequest of Apollo.

The Greek myths were stories passed on with variants. The writer—whether it was Pindar or Ovid—rewrote them, in a different way each time, omitting here, adding there. But new variants had to be rare, and unobtrusive. So each writer would build up and thin out the body of the stories. So the myth lived on in literature.

The sublime author of *The Sublime* traced literature back to *megalophyía,* a "greatness of nature," which sometimes manages to light up a similar nature in the mind of the reader. But how can nature, which "loves to hide," accept the cumbersome conspicuousness of the rhetorical machine? How escape the ostentatiousness of the *téchnē*? The *chassé-croisé* between Nature and Art, which was to generate comment for two millennia and would be condensed in seventeenth-century capitals, was executed in a single sentence way back at the height of classical decadence: "Only then is art perfect, when it looks like nature, while nature strikes home when it conceals art within itself."

Perfection, any kind of perfection, always demands some kind of concealment. Without something hiding itself, or remaining hidden, there is no perfection. But how can the writer conceal the obviousness of the word and its figures of speech? With the light. The anonymous author writes: "And how did the rhetorician conceal the trope he was using? It's clear that he hid it with light itself." To conceal with light: the Greek specialty. Zeus never stopped using the light to conceal. Which is why the light that comes after the Greek light is of another kind, and much less intense. That other light aims to winkle out what has been hidden. While the Greek light protects it. Allows it to show itself as hidden even in the light of day. And even manages to hide what is evident, made black by the light, the way the rhetorical trope becomes unrecognizable when inundated by splendor and submerged by a "greatness that pours forth from every side." Such was the conclusion the anonymous author's literary analysis brought him to. So he rightly claimed that "judgment about literature is the perfect result of great experience."

.   .   .

Old and blind, Homer spent the winter on Samos. When May came he went from door to door followed by a swarm of children. They each carried an *eiresiōnē*, an olive branch with strips of white and purple wool attached and the first fruits of the season. Homer made his rounds submerged in a buzz of nursery rhymes. They spoke of the *eiresiōnē*, of dry figs and plump bread rolls swinging back and forth, honey and wine. They carried them around, they said, so that the *eiresiōnē* could "fall asleep, drunk."

But why did they have to put this decorated branch to sleep? What kept it so obsessively awake? Followed by the children, Homer went to the houses of the rich Samians. He announced that their doors were about to open of their own accord, that where there was wealth, more wealth would enter, and with it "the blithe spirit and the gift of peace." The bard sang, the wealthy owner appeared and gave something to the old man and his troop of children. And, even if he gave nothing, it didn't matter. Homer would be back, like the swallows. But now it was time to leave the island, because he was a wanderer with no fixed home. One day he left and never returned, and on Apollo's feast days the children of Samos went on acting out his beggar's song outside the houses of the rich.

Whenever the dullness of the profane was left behind, whenever life grew more intense in whatever way, through honor or death, victory or sacrifice, marriage or prayer, initiation or possession, purification or mourning, anything and everything that stirred a person and demanded a meaning, the Greeks would celebrate with fluttering strips of wool, white or red for the most part, which they tied around their heads, or arms, or to a branch, the prow of a ship, a statue, an ax, a stone, a cooking pot. The modern eye encounters these woolen strips everywhere in the fragments that have come down to us but doesn't see them, removes them from the center of attention as mere decorative details, and hence insignificant. To the Greek eye, the opposite was the case: it was those light, fluttering strips of wool that generated meaning, gave it its boundaries, celebrated it. Everything that took place in the soft frame of those woolen strips was different and separate from the rest. What was it those woolen strips, those tassels represented? An excess, a flowing wake that attached itself to a being or thing. And at the same time a tether that bound that being or thing.

Isidore of Seville could still write, *"Vittae dictae sunt, quod vinciant:"* "The woolen ties are so called because they bind." But what was this bond? It was the momentary surfacing of a link in that invisible net which enfolds the world, which descends from heaven to earth, binding the two together and swaying in the breeze. Men wouldn't be able to bear seeing that net in its entirety all the time: they would get caught in it at once and suffocate. But every time someone achieves or is subjected to—but every achievement is subjection, and every subjection achievement—something that uplifts him and generates intensity and meaning, then the woolen strips, the ties, come out. At one end they are bound tight to the body in a knot that may become a noose. At the other they flutter in the air, keeping us company, escorting us, protecting us. The victorious athlete has woolen strips tied to his arms, his torso, his thighs, and they follow him, waving in the air like a triumphant tangle of snakes. Nike, Victory, always carries a bunch of woolen ties to hand out to her chosen favorites. And the initiate keeps the strip of wool he wore on the day of his initiation and preserves it as a relic his whole life long. But woolen strips were also hung from the horns of sacrificial bulls. The girls tied them there carefully before the ceremony, the way the bride's mother tied them around wedding torches of hawthorn wood, and relatives hung them from the dead man's bed.

All these woolen strips, these vain, winged tassels, were nerves of the *nexus rerum*, the connection of everything with everything else, which alone gives meaning to life. We live every moment of our lives swathed in those ties, white because white is the color the Olympians like, or red because blood ties us to death, or purple, yellow, and green. But we

can't always see them, indeed we mustn't, because then we
would be paralyzed, trapped. We feel them blowing about
us the minute something happens to dispel our apathy, and
we become aware of being carried along on a stream that
flows toward something unknown. And just sometimes, but
very rarely, those ties twist and turn and weave around us,
until one loose end becomes knotted to another. Then, very
softly, they encompass us, they form a circle, which is the
crown, perfection.

Heavy with nectar, Poros stretched out in Zeus's garden. He
slept, but in his mind thought was thinking: "What is a garden? The ornate splendor of wealth." Then Aphrodite appeared among beings. She was the daughter of thought.
Soon there would be many copies of Aphrodite everywhere.
They were demons, each one accompanied by a different
Eros, with his buzz of gadflies.

IX

O N ARRIVING AT THE PATRAS ACROPOLIS, Pausanias was told the story of the temple of Triklarian Artemis: "It is said that a long time ago there was a priestess of the goddess called Komaithò, a very beautiful girl indeed. It so happened that she fell in love with Melanippus, who excelled his peers in all things, and, above all, was extremely handsome. When Melanippus had conquered the girl's heart, he asked her father for her hand in marriage. It is natural for the old to oppose the young in many things, and most particularly in matters of love. Thus it was with Melanippus: despite the fact that both he and Komaithò wanted to marry, all they got from both sets of parents was a determined refusal. The unhappy adventures of Melanippus, like those of many others, show how love tends to undermine the law of men and subvert their devotion toward the gods. For, unable to marry, Komaithò and Melanippus slaked the thirst of their passion in the temple of Artemis, then took to using the temple regularly as a nuptial chamber. As a result, Artemis began to wreak her anger on the local inhabitants. The earth ceased to bear fruit, and people contracted strange and fatal diseases. So they fled to consult the oracle at Delphi, where the Pythia laid the blame on Melanippus and Komaithò. The oracle ordered that the lovers be sacrificed to Artemis and that every year the most beautiful young girl and the most handsome young boy be sacrificed to the goddess. Because of this sacrifice, the people dubbed the river near the temple the Merciless. Previously it had had no name. For the young boys and girls who would perish without having committed any crime, and likewise for their families, this was a terrible destiny; but I do believe that for Melanippus and Komaithò it was not a misfortune; only one thing is worth as much as life itself to men: that a love should be successful."

This isn't *Romeo and Juliet* (where the sacrifice to Triklarian Artemis is repeated once again). It isn't Shakespeare who offers us this demonstration, at once so drastic and clear-cut, of a love capable of overturning and trampling on the law in obedience to the "so-called Aphrodite of disorder," which Plato feared. And certainly we wouldn't find the likes of this story in classical Greece, which always had its misgivings about the assaults of the demon. No, the story appears in the autumn of Greece, in the prose of Pausanias, a learned itinerant commentator of ruins that had already been turned over to pastureland. The plot of the story he tells here recalls an Alexandrian romance. But its meaning is a fugitive of the mysteries. It hints at the hidden tension between hierogamy and sacrifice.

If being sacrificed was not, or not only, a "misfortune" for Komaithò and Melanippus, that is because they play a part in the ritual right from the beginning, the most hidden part, the part they have the impertinence to reveal. Eros brings into the open what the law must hide yet nevertheless contains within itself: the fact that the temple is a nuptial chamber. Once again we have to go to an Alexandrian, the disillusioned Lucian, to find in writing that the secret chamber of the "Syriac goddess" was called *thálamos*, the nuptial chamber. Yet that name originated long before Lucian, so long before that people saw no need to mention it in less reckless periods. If hierogamy is the secret of sacrifice, sacrifice will nevertheless serve to hide the fact. It will pile a wall of blood and corpses before the place where Komaithò and Melanippus abandoned themselves to their improbable, "successful love."

The external façade of the temple imposes the "law of men." The nuptial interior subverts it. But if the interior becomes the exterior, the world is threatened by the ado-

lescent *diable au corps* that then invades it. So the world
strikes back and strikes to kill. Sacrifice and hierogamy are
two forces that presuppose each other, are superimposed
over each other and interlocked. They oppose each other,
but they also support each other. Each is the aura of the
other. The girl who is going to be sacrificed seems to be waiting for her spouse. While the background to erotic pleasure
is dark and bloody. Everything that happens is a pendular
motion between these two forces. Facing each other, each,
in its gaze, reflects the other. Hierogamy tends toward the
destruction of the law, whereas sacrifice reconstructs its
bloody base. All it takes to upset this equilibrium is a
"successful love." But history makes sure the equilibrium
survives.

Hierogamy: it was the first way the gods chose to communicate with men. The approach was an invasion, of body
and mind, which were thus impregnated with the superabundance of the divine. But that same superabundance
was already emanating from the eros of the Olympians.
When Zeus and Hera made love on Ida, they were cloaked
in a golden cloud that rained sparkling drops upon the
earth.

Why weren't men able to go on with hierogamy? Because
of a crime, Prometheus's crime. They had to respond to that
invasion, and in so doing they chose their own way of com-
municating with the gods: they would share the same victim, eating its blood and guts and leaving the smoke to the
gods. That was the basis of the "Olympian sacrifice." That
is why *thýein*, "to sacrifice," actually means "to fumigate":
it was a slightly hypocritical homage to the divine. The
crime of Prometheus is the nature of men, which obliges
them to eat, and thus to kill. Hence for men assimilation is
forever bound up with killing.

For all the variegated multiplicity of its forms, the practice
of sacrifice can be reduced to just two gestures: expulsion

(purification) and assimilation (communion). These two gestures have only one element in common: destruction. In each case the victim is killed or devoured, or abandoned to a certain death. We kill to eat, to assimilate; and we kill to separate, to expel. In every other respect the two gestures are different.

The most extreme form of expulsion is stoning, since here those carrying out the sacrifice do not expose themselves to the risk of contact with the victim; the most extreme form of assimilation involves eating the victim's flesh still warm and palpitating. But is it perhaps a mistaken convention, an ancient misnomer, to define both these rituals as *sacrifice*? So it might seem, at least until awareness of another phenomenon behind the two gestures brings them right back together again: hierogamy. Yet hierogamy does not involve any element of destruction, the one thing that kept the two extreme gestures of sacrifice together. How can we explain this? Hierogamy is the premise of sacrifice, but on the part of the gods. It is that first mixing of the two worlds, divine and human, to which sacrifice attempts to respond, but with a response that is merely human, the response of creatures living in the realm of the irreversible, creatures who cannot assimilate (or expel) without killing. To the erotic invasion of our bodies, we reply with the knife that slashes the throat, the hand that hurls the stone.

With time, men and gods would develop a common language made up of hierogamy and sacrifice. The endless ways these two phenomena split apart, opposed each other, and mixed together corresponded to the expressions of that language. And, when it became a dead language, people started talking about mythology.

Hierogamy and sacrifice have in common taking possession of a body, by either invading it or eating it. But, as Prometheus would have it, to assimilate a body men had to kill it and eat its dead flesh. In the meantime the smoke would envelop the gods. And, in reply, the gods would envelop the bodies like a cloud and suck out their juices drenched in eros. Saliva becomes the sacrificial element par excellence, the only one in which the two sides of sacrifice—expulsion and communion—converge. We expel saliva, as something impure, but we also mix it with other like substances and assimilate them, in eros.

For men, hierogamy and sacrifice are superimposed only in the invisible, in the sacrifice of self to the Self, the *coniunctio* between self and the Self. The invisible for man is the visible for the gods. The appearance of the world came about with the copulation of a god with that which was not god, with the laceration and dispersion of a god's body; it was the expulsion into space of a cloud of infected matter, infested by the sacred.

The most discreet and delicate way of having the gods understand the irreversible, scourge of all mortals, was the libation: you poured a noble liquid onto the ground and lost it forever. It was an act of homage, of course: the recognition of the presence and rights of an invisible power. But it was something else as well: an attempt to make conversation. As if men were saying to the gods, Whatever we do, we are this liquid poured away.

The gods too will sometimes appear holding the cup of libation. But who are they pouring their offering to? to themselves? to life? And what is it they're offering? themselves? And how can they pour something away on purpose to lose it, they who can lose nothing, they for whom everything remains forever intact? That gesture of the gods has never been explained. Perhaps it was their way of picking up the conversation, an admiring allusion to the beauty of that gesture that men made so often under the gaze of the gods, and that now the gods chose to imitate.

"Just as their bodies resemble those of men, so too do the lives of the gods." Concise as ever, Aristotle points to that anomalous aspect of the Greek gods, their total anthropomorphism. Total? In every respect but one: food. The food of the gods is different from the food of men, and likewise different is the liquid in their veins. Homer could already explain with perfect clarity that this was because the gods "have no blood and are called immortal." The gods are immortal because they don't eat our food. They don't have blood because blood gets its nourishment from the food men eat. So food carries death within it, our dependence on death, which forces us to kill for more food, so as to keep death at bay. Though never for long.

It was precisely because the Greeks had reduced the difference between gods and men to a minimum that they measured the distance still separating them with such cruel precision: an infinite, unbridgeable distance. And never has that distance been so sharply defined as by the Greeks themselves. No mist hovered about the approaches to death. It was an abyss with razor edges, never crossed. Hence the Greeks were well aware of the powerlessness of their sacrifices. Every ceremony in which a living being was killed was a way of recalling the mortality of all the participants. And the smoke they dedicated to the gods was certainly no use to the divinities as food. The only things the gods ever ate were nectar and ambrosia. No, that smell of blood and smoke was a message from earth, a pointless gift, reminding the Olympians of the consciously precarious existence of all those distant inhabitants of earth, who in every other way were equal to the gods. And what the gods loved about men was precisely this difference, this precariousness, which they themselves could relish only through men. It was a flavor they could never get from their ambrosia or nectar. That was why they would sometimes abandon themselves to inhaling the smoke of sacrifice, breath of that other life which enjoyed the precious privilege of stirring the air of Olympus.

From Iphigenia to the daughters of Erechtheus and the Coronides, it is always a splendid virgin who has to be sacri-

ficed. And the sacrifice is always a pendulum swinging back
and forth between suicide and the wedding ceremony. During the year, by which we mean nature in its totality, there
are "gloomy and ill-omened days," when young girls will
get their throats cut. For this is the way, the only way men
know, to have those girls cross the frontier of the invisible
and so meet the divine avengers waiting for them on the
other side.

These avengers harbor "frenzied, tyrannical desires" for
the girls' bodies and pester them continuously, but they cannot operate in the visible world to the point of being able
"to couple with those bodies and penetrate them." As a result, we men have to find a way of satisfying this angry impotence of the *daímones*, and we do it by abandoning the
lifeless corpses of the girls along that borderline that passes
through the altar. Here lies the origin of every dark eros.

Zeus and Hera had been arguing since time immemorial.
Hera decided to hide in Euboea. When a great goddess withdraws and hides, the world soon falls apart. "Destitute and
lost," Zeus looked for her. He wandered all over Boeotia.
What could he do? How could he get the goddess out of her
hiding place and into the open?

It was a man, Alalcomeneus, who suggested the trick.
Zeus must pretend to marry someone else. The other woman
must be a block of oak carved in the shape of a girl and
draped in veils. Then this rigid bride must be set up on a
chariot and taken to her wedding. They called her Daedala,
which is as much as to say Artifact, because she was the first
creature who embodied art in herself. When the celebrations
had begun and the chariot with Zeus's bashful new bride
was already winding through the streets of Plataea, Hera
could bear it no longer. She jumped up on the chariot in a
rage, looked at her motionless rival, and tore off her wedding veils, meaning to scratch her face to shreds. But then
she realized she was looking at a *xóanon*, one of those endless blocks of wood kept in temples all over Greece. And the

goddess laughed. It was a cruel, ringing laugh, a little girl's laugh. And we owe it to that laugh that the world, at least so far, has not fallen to pieces. But this didn't occur to the women of Plataea at the time. They saw the goddess set herself at the head of the procession, and they strung along after her. First they helped Hera to bathe the statue like a bride in the river Asopus. Then they followed the chariot as far as a clearing topped by oaks on the summit of Mount Cithaeron. The goddess ordered them to build a big bonfire. She placed the statue with its torn veils in the middle. And all around, on the trunks forming the bonfire, the faithful heaped up their animals. The richest even offered cows and bulls. They poured on wine and incense. Then the goddess set it alight.

The statue was reduced to ashes while the shrieks of the animals being burned alive drowned out the crackling of the flames. Many years later, in the same place, the ceremony was still being performed. Pausanias saw the pyre and said: "I know of no fire so high, nor visible from so far off."

In what Plutarch called "ancient physiology" and defined as a "discourse on nature entwined in myths," hierogamy and sacrifice become the two extremes of the respiratory process: air breathed in reaches the blood and nourishes it, becoming unrecognizable in the resulting mix (hierogamy); air breathed out is expelled forever (sacrifice) and mixes with the air of the world. But, even at the point of greatest distance and tension, these extremes were superimposed over each other.

A tall, destructive fire; the penetration of the god in the body of the goddess. Between these two events there turns a hinge: a wooden statue. Hera laughed as she tore the veils from Zeus's inanimate spouse. But that didn't mean she gave up the idea of killing her, of burning the statue to bits like a dangerous rival. As for Zeus, if he wants to lure the goddess out of the darkness, he has to add a copy, an image, to the world. Nothing less than that will suffice to create the hinge that will bring the sovereign couple back together again. A tiny wooden fake is brought into the world, draped in veils, and saves it. But then has to be burned. And the image must be draped in veils because it is itself a veil, a surplus, that hides something else. The bride is draped in veils, as discourse is draped in myth. When the veil is torn away, there is nothing but laughter and flames. First for salvation, then for destruction: but the truth is that the two things are simultaneous. It was all part of those "unspoken things" that are scattered throughout every myth and liturgy and that have always seemed "more suspect than the things one speaks about."

The pagan world was destroyed less by the Christians than by itself. None of the poisoned attacks of the Fathers of the Church had the same destructive power as *Alexander or the False Prophet*, a pamphlet written by a perfect pagan, Lucian of Samosata. It is an unparalleled portrait of a great impostor, model for a civilization that was to produce impostors in plenty. Did Alexander of Abonuteichos ever really exist? Some jewelry, coins, and inscriptions confirm that he did. Yet, apart from those silent witnesses, the only trace of his life that remains is Lucian's violent pamphlet attacking him. Should we believe what Lucian says there? It's hard to say, but the sheer power of literature brushes a question like this aside.

Scornful of anything and everything, Lucian saw in Alexander of Abonuteichos a malignant repeat, an ignominious shadow of that other Alexander, first emperor of the West. Hadn't Alexander the Great set off to conquer the East like a new Dionysus (the fourth, mythographers would say)? Hadn't he been the first to insinuate that a sovereign could also be a god? Well, Alexander of Abonuteichos likewise lived and behaved as if he were a god.

Like Alexander the Great, Alexander of Abonuteichos had grown up in the provinces, in Paphlagonia—but then anywhere that wasn't Athens was the provinces. By the time he died, he was renowned throughout the Roman Empire. As a boy, Alexander of Abonuteichos was extremely handsome, with a clear complexion, a soft beard, and long hair—and if the last wasn't all his own, nobody noticed. "His eyes shone with a divine and compelling enthusiasm." His voice was clear and gentle. He was an amazingly fast thinker. It seemed there was no quality he didn't have. "In fact, on first meeting, all without exception would go away with the impression that they had spoken to the worthiest and most upright man in all the world, and the simplest too, and the least affected. But above all, he had something grandiose about him, as if he would never stoop to worrying about the small things in life, but directed his spirit only to the most weighty of matters."

He immediately began to prostitute his body, which was extremely attractive. And one of his clients was a charlatan, the kind who sold amulets, evil spells, and maps for finding buried treasure. Alexander picked up the trade from him, and just as the charlatan had fallen in love with his body, so Alexander fell in love with the man's tricks. He learned all of them. But his friend soon died, and Alexander's body was now past the point where he could make the best earnings out of prostitution. He decided to change profession and become a charlatan himself. He traveled around selling charms. And on his travels he met a rich Macedonian woman, a bit past it herself but still greedy for sex, so he stayed with her, because she paid well.

The woman came from the once glorious town of Pella, now little more than a handful of dilapidated houses. Here Alexander found a species of snake that were at once very big and extremely tame. They would sleep with children and wouldn't bite you even if you trod on them. Apparently the area was full of them, and Lucian imagined that one of these snakes must have coupled with Olympias to generate Alexander the Great. Now those same snakes would come in useful to another Alexander. He bought some for next to nothing and set off again well contented. With his friend Coccona, a poet who went along with him on his travels (because a con is always better when you have someone to share it with), Alexander came to the conclusion that there was no better way of making money than starting up an oracle. But for an oracle you needed a suitable location. They looked around for the place where people would be most willing to believe absolutely anything. After a lot of discussion, they settled on Abonuteichos. But they must stage-manage their arrival with care: so they buried some bronze tablets in the temple of Asclepius in Chalcedon. Then they dug them out again and read the oracular words inscribed on them: Apollo, father of Asclepius, was about to take up residence at Abonuteichos. The news traveled swiftly to its destination. And the people of Abonuteichos agreed to start building a temple. The god wasn't going to catch them unprepared.

Coccona, in the meantime, was bitten by a viper while practicing his oracles in verse and died. So Alexander turned up on his own. His fake curls came down to his shoulders, and he wore a white and purple tunic with a cloak on top. A curved sword, like the one Perseus had used, hung at his hip, because he was a descendant of Perseus, he said, on his mother's side. Of course the Paphlagonians knew Alexander and his modest parents very well: but when the oracles kept on telling them how, overwhelmed by a frenzy of passion, Podalirius, son of Asclepius, had traveled from as far off as Tricca to make love to Alexander's mother, they gave in. The oracle got into gear. But the fact that Alexander would occasionally have paroxysms and foam at the mouth, with a little help from a root he chewed, wasn't enough. For a proper oracle, snakes were a must. Alexander had brought ten of the Macedonian variety along with him.

One night he went to a spring near the new temple, where he managed to find a goose's egg and a baby snake. He trapped the snake in the shell of the egg and buried it in the mud. The next morning he turned up in the marketplace and, after generally behaving like a maniac and screaming a few words in Hebrew and Phoenician, announced to the amazed citizenry that they were about to receive the god. After that, he ran off to the temple.

He waded into the water of the spring and invoked Apollo.

He asked for a libation bowl and pushed it into the mud. The bowl came up with the goose's egg, which he had put back together with wax. Everybody watched, astonished. Then Alexander broke the shell and let the baby snake wriggle around his fingers. The new Asclepius, he said. The people followed him, brimming with devotion. After which, Alexander took care not to be seen for a few days. Then he waited for the crowd. When they all came running, credulous as ever, Alexander was lying godlike on a bed in a small chamber, his Macedonian snake wrapped around his neck, stretching across his stomach, and then falling in coils to the floor. Beside his beard, Alexander let the onlookers glimpse a dummy head, half snake, half man, which he had stuffed with horsehair. The people thought it was the snake's head. The light was poor, and anyway they were all fighting to get a look at this baby snake that in just a few days had amazingly metamorphosed into a dragon with a human head. People flocked from Bithynia, Thrace, and Galatia, and Alexander always appeared in the same pose. He decided to change his name to Glycon, for reasons metrical. "I am Glycon, grandson of Zeus, light of mankind." At this point the oracle could start making money. People coming to consult it wrote down their wishes on sealed scrolls. Alexander opened the seals with a red-hot needle, then closed them again, exactly as they had been, and produced answers that amazed everybody. Two obols a consultation.

Lucian claims he was earning "between seventy and eighty thousand drachmas a year." Some people were so thirsty for knowledge that they would ask the oracle ten or even more questions. One person who came was Rutilianus, Rome's representative in the region, an experienced man but always ready to worship any old stone so long as it had been anointed and crowned. Alexander soon convinced Rutilianus that he should marry his daughter, telling him she was the offspring of his love for Selene. Yes, Endymion's good fortune had been his too; it had happened one night when the moon had shone down on his white and sleeping body. Thus the sixty-year-old Rutilianus turned up as the groom, offering huge sacrifices to the moon, whom he imagined was his mother-in-law. Alexander loved faking religious mysteries in the sanctuary, his favorite being his own birth. On the third day of the wedding celebrations, he organized a show of his lovemaking with Selene. He pretended to be asleep in front of the crowd, while from the ceiling, as though from the sky, the attractive Rutilia, wife of one of his administrators, was lowered onto him. Alexander and Rutilia were lovers, and now they had the chance to fondle each other with impunity in front of an audience that included Rutilia's husband. Every now and then, apparently by chance, Alexander would let the crowd get a glimpse of one of his thighs, which glittered with gold. So people began to whisper that the soul of Pythagoras must have transmigrated into him. By now he had scores of people working for him. Groups of young choirboys were drafted in from Paphlagonia for long periods of service in the sanctuary. He called them "the ones within the kiss." But he made a point of not kissing any of them once they were over eighteen. Thanks to his good relations with the Emperor Verus, he was able to have coins minted with a design showing himself with Asclepius's bands and the sword of Perseus, a tribute to his ancestors. On the other side of the coin was a snake with a human head.

Alexander had prophesied he would live to be a hundred and fifty and die only when struck by lightning. In the event, he died before he was seventy when a leg turned gangrenous and became infested by worms. To anoint his head with balsam, the doctors had to remove his wig. Who would inherit the sanctuary now? The ever faithful Rutilianus decided that no one should take the prophet's place. Before his death, Alexander had managed to get the authorities in Rome to change the name of Abonuteichos. Now it was to be known as Ionopolis. People went on practicing Alexander's cult there for about a century. Even today the city is called Inebolu. We shall never know if Alexander was really the sordid con man Lucian describes, or a wise man who in latter days chose to reenact the primordial scene. There where pagan self-parody and Christian inquisition rage, where the shameful and the ridiculous reign supreme, the most ancient secret will often lie concealed.

In the solitude of the primordial world, the affairs of the gods took place on an empty stage, with no watching eyes to mirror them. There was a rustling, but no clamor of voices. Then, from a certain point on (but at what point? and why?), the backdrop began to flicker, the air was invaded by a golden sprinkling of new beings, the shrill, high-pitched cry of scores of raised voices. Dactyls, Curetes, Corybants, Telchines, Silens, Cabiri, Satyrs, Maenads, Bacchants, Lenaeans, Thyiads, Bassarides, Mimallones, Naiads, Nymphs, Titires: who were all these beings? To evoke one of their names is to evoke them all. They are the helpers, ministers, guardians, nurses, tutors, and spectators of the gods. The metamorphic vortex is placated; once surrounded by this noisy and devoted crowd, the gods agree to settle down into their familiar forms. Sometimes that crowd will appear as a pack of murderers, sometimes as an assembly of craftsmen, sometimes as a dance troupe, sometimes as a herd of beasts.

That worshiping crowd was the first community, the first group, the first entity in which one name was used for everybody. We don't even know whether they are gods, *daímones*, or human beings. But what is it that unites them, what makes them a single group, even when different and distant from one another? They are the initiated, the ones who have seen. They are those who let themselves be touched by the divine. Which of them came first? We don't know, since for every god there is always a corresponding god or goddess— in Asia, or Thrace, or Crete—who predates them and who likewise surrounds himself with such beings. But of all of them we could say that they were *honey thieves*.

"People say there is a sacred cave in Crete, a cave inhabited by bees, where, as myth would have it, Rhea gave birth to

Zeus. There is a sacred law that no one, whether man or god, may set foot there. Every year, at a certain time, a dazzling flame flashes from the cave. The myth says this happens when the blood Zeus spilled at birth periodically boils. The cave is inhabited by the sacred bees who fed Zeus as a baby. Laius, Celeus, Cerberus, and Egolius took the risk of going into the cave in the hope of stealing a big store of honey; they had protected themselves with bronze armor and began to take the honey; then they saw Zeus's swaddling clothes and their armor began to split across their bodies. Zeus thundered and brandished his lightning bolt, but the Moirai and Themis held him back; the holiness of the place would have suffered had someone died there; so Zeus turned the intruders into birds; and they became the progenitors of those species which bear omens: the solitary sparrow, the green woodpecker, the cerberus, and the barn owl. When any of these birds appear, they offer truer and better omens than other birds, because they have seen the blood of Zeus."

Zeus's birthplace, the Cretan cave, was thus out of bounds to both gods and men. And it was the place where one could not die. That cave held a secret beyond any other. When a rite is secret, it is so because in this way it "imitates the nature of the divine, which eludes our perception." But here the divine wished to elude even the perception of the gods. What was it that Zeus had to conceal from the other gods at all costs? The four young Cretans stepped into a dark space dripping with sweetness. The rock was spread thick with honey. The honey stuck to the rock the way their bodies stuck to their bronze armor. In the shadows they noticed some bloody swaddling clothes. When he opened his eyes at birth, these same rocks had been the first thing Zeus saw. He was like any baby then: "stained with blood and with the waters of his mother's womb, more like someone just killed than someone just born." The four young Cretans were thinking about this, about those bloodstains in the honey—might there have been a murder?—when they felt their bronze armor splitting apart. Zeus thundered. There was a great light.

In Crete the secret had always been there for everybody to see. Up on a mountain they would show people Zeus's tomb. They told the truth one must not tell. No one believed them. Ever after, people would say: Cretans, liars all.

What Zeus let us know about his life were the wars and the amorous adventures. But not much else. He divided his secrets between his two sons, Apollo and Dionysus, who would one day rise to sovereignty. Every era lives out, without knowing it, the dream of the era that came before. Just as Zeus had found himself thinking what his father, Kronos, dreamed, so Dionysus and Apollo would suffer what Zeus had already experienced, in secret. To Dionysus and Apollo the world would attribute deeds and passions that had their origin in the most hidden recesses of their father's life.

But Zeus cannot have secrets. Zeus simply is. "You are always," says a late poet. And in Dodona, the first women ever to chant poetry would say: "Zeus was, and is, and shall be, oh great Zeus." And now the secret of Zeus was to go and reside in the dark, impenetrable area where the two flourishing young gods had to come to terms with and suffer death. The secret of Zeus was made up of two parts: his having killed Typhon; and his having been killed, as an infant, in the Cretan cave. Zeus transferred the first secret to Apollo: Apollo killed Python. And the second to Dionysus: the baby Zagreus was killed by the Titans. Dividing himself up into his two sons, Zeus reproduced wholeness in each of them. For Apollo and Dionysus include their opposites within themselves and swing back and forth between the two extremes. Just as Dionysus is the tearer apart and the torn apart, so Apollo is both the hunter and the quarry.

The Delphic youth who every eight years at the Stepteria festival fled from Delphi without looking back, while a hut he had just set alight burned behind him, was imitating the flight of Apollo from Delphi when he went to purify himself in Tempe after killing Python. But he was also recalling the hunting of Python, wounded by Apollo's arrows. The god chased the snake along the same road, "which is now called the Sacred Way," only to arrive too late, albeit "by very little," to put him out of his agony. The son of Python, Aix, the Goat, had already buried his father, this huge snake who had dragged himself, dying, from Phocis to Thessaly.

Dactyls, Curetes— and then, at night, the Titans: they are the first *koûroi*, nimble dancing fingers, echoing bronze shields, sharp flute. The Curetes are the "instants, the herdsmen of time," transfixing the continuum. They dance in a circle, waving spears and toys. Hidden in the center of that circle is a defenseless child: Zeus—or Zagreus. Are they protecting him? Are they about to kill him? They save him with the terrifying clamor of their weapons, and they trick him with toys, before burying their knives in his flesh. The initiated aren't just those who know how to shake off guilt but those who more than others have reason to be guilty. The complicity between initiates has to do with a shared knowledge, but likewise with a crime. However much we try, we can never quite sever the bond that links the initiated with the gang of criminals.

Before the knife came down, the infant Zagreus saw those pale figures surrounding him, offering him toys, as his friends and guardians. Curetes? Titans? Such distinctions could only be of use to mythographers. In the dark, Zagreus saw that these strangers (or did he know them?), their faces smeared with chalk, were led by a more attractive figure, tall and white, with a whiteness that came not from chalk but from some natural luminosity. And Zagreus had seen that same being (a woman perhaps? but what was a woman?) leading his guardians, the Curetes, before. Silent and armed, Athena presided over the torture about to be performed on her brother Zagreus.

The boy touched his face and felt the soft chalk the Titans had daubed there. Now they went round and round him, as though moving to some nursery rhyme, and Zagreus knew perfectly well that they were waiting for the right moment to kill him. He looked at the toys all around him: a top, dolls with jointed limbs, golden apples, a pinecone, a mirror. He reached for the little mirror and looked at himself. He saw an "alien image," another white face. And recognized the very person about to kill him.

As though it were a duty, the knife already sparkling in a Titan's hand, Zagreus turned himself into a young Zeus, into the old Kronos, into a baby, into a youth, into a lion, into a horse, into a snake, into a tiger. And finally into a bull. At which, out of nothing, came the booming sound of Hera, lowing. Amazed, the bull froze in that form for a second too long. Long enough for the knife to plunge. The bull crashed down. Streams of blood spurted out onto the white faces of his killers as they passed the knife from hand to hand to strike and strike again.

When they had boiled up Zagreus, roasted him on spits, and devoured him, the Titans were themselves shriveled up by Zeus's thunderbolts. Nothing was left but a black film of soot amid the grass and thorns of the Cretan mountains. Then Athena looked around in the sultry air and saw, on the ground, a pulsating piece of flesh that had been tossed away. It was Zagreus's heart, and it seemed not to care about having been torn from his chest. It sucked from an invisible lymph and pumped it away again into the invisible. Athena was fascinated by that trembling red blob. Something in the shapeless shred of flesh was speaking to her, as she stood detached from all else, gray, blue, and sharply outlined in her armor. Something was announcing her name. *Pállein* means "to pulse"; Pallas, "pulsating"; such was Athena beneath the cold exterior of her weapons, where the hard surface met the indivisible mind, which she saw outside herself for the first time now in that dirty piece of red flesh tossed to the dogs. Delicately, she picked up the heart and laid it in a basket, closed the lid. Then she went off. She was going to give the "thinking heart" to her father, Zeus.

For a long time Zeus was overcome by grief. He recalled how Hera had mocked him for his inaction while his son was being torn to shreds. When Zeus saw his pain wasn't getting any relief, he took some plaster and began to shape the statue of a *koûros*, like a shining white suit of armor. The era of metamorphoses having come to an end, the era of the statue had begun. And, once again, Zeus was the beginning: he erected the first statue for his dead son. As soon as he'd finished, the god slipped Zagreus's heart through a hole in the plaster so that it was inside the statue. In the dark cavity of the artifact, the heart reawoke. It thought: white all around me again, like the waxy faces of my murderers, and the night too. But now the dance is over, the whiteness is still, like a sky, like the lid of a sarcophagus. Seen from outside, the statue looked like the funeral stone of a beautiful young man. Inside, Zagreus's heart went on silently beating, and thinking.

In the *Etymologicon Magnum*, the name Zagreus is explained as "the Great Hunter." But there were other Great Hunters among the gods too. Zeus is the Great Hunter. And Hades is the Great Hunter. A plumb line comes down from the ether, passes through the earth, and reaches right to the very depths of the underworld: it is the Great Hunter. There is no part of his being where the divine will renounce the gesture of following a prey. At no height or depth, whether it be the glass-clear air of Olympus, the swirling air of earth, or the perennially gloomy air of Hades, does the sharp profile of the Great Hunter ever fade.

A Maenad had a fawn tattooed on her soft, bare right arm. She was breast-feeding a fawn, stroking and playing with it. Then she grabbed it, tore it to pieces, and sank her teeth into the still pulsing flesh. Why this sequence? And why must this sequence forever take the form of a sudden raptus, when really it was a ceremony? What went on inside the Maenad? Dionysus tormented her with pleasure in every vein. The Maenad ran, didn't know how to respond. The sacrifice, that slow, solemn butchery, wasn't enough to quell her frenzy. The only thing that would work was "the pleasure of eating live flesh." Altarless, she wandered through the trees. Dismembering the fawn, the Maenad dismembered herself, possessed by the god. Hence, in devouring the fawn, she devoured the god, mixed in its blood. She who was possessed thus tried herself to possess a part of the god. But what happened afterward? A great silence. The sultry heat of the woods. Strips of bleeding flesh glimpsed through the leaves. The god wasn't there. Life—incomprehensible, opaque.

For the shortest of times Zagreus, the boy king, sits on the throne Zeus has left vacant to go off on a journey (where to?). Then he will be the first prey. He will be torn to pieces. Then he will lead his own initiates off to tear others to pieces, others like him, his priests perhaps. He who has the shape of the bull leads the band that devours the bull, alive. Dionysus Zagreus: in him we have the most violent of identifications, that of the hunter with the prey.

The *páthē* of Osiris and of Christ are captured and stilled in the images of the victim torn to pieces or nailed to the cross. But with Dionysus Zagreus, the circle immediately begins to turn again. Driven by the god, the Maenads will repeat the very gestures that killed the god himself. And most of all they will kill whoever tries to stop the circle turning.

Orpheus broke away from the cult of Dionysus like the renouncer from the Brahminical cult. Before withdrawing into the forest to live among the wild beasts, he too had experienced "the pleasure of eating live flesh." Now the new element in his thinking could be summed up in two words: *phónōn apéchesthai,* "refrain from killing."

In every other respect, just as the renouncer still bowed down before the structure of Vedic metaphysics, so Orpheus still observed the Olympian theology. But he knew that this new precept of his was enough to undermine its order. He knew he had interrupted the back-and-forth of killing and being killed. The sun rose through a bright, unsullied air, and Orpheus, dressed in white, greeted it from a mountaintop in Thrace. Behind him, in the wood, he heard a roaring noise. The Bassarids, the women who had once been his companions, were approaching, coming to tear him to shreds. Of Orpheus's body, only the head was left; it bobbed away on the swirling surface of the river that flowed down the valley, still singing.

In Aristophanes' time, someone might refer to the feast of the Bouphonia as one speaks of a relic of times past, something vaguely incongruous, like the golden cicadas eminent Athenians had once worn in their hair as clasps. The texts that have come down to us about Athenian festivals, the admirable tradition that gave rhythm to the seasons and the key moments in people's lives, are few and fragmented. But, by a stroke of luck, we do have a passage about the Bouphonia that Porphyry copied from Theophrastus, a passage that offers the noblest and clearest Mediterranean formulation of the metaphysics of sacrifice.

"In olden times, as I said before, men would sacrifice the fruits of the earth to the gods, but not the animals. Indeed, they didn't even eat animals. The story goes that during a public sacrifice celebrated in Athens, a certain Sopatrus, who wasn't originally from the area but was farming some land in Attica, had placed some bread and other cakes on the table to sacrifice them to the gods, when an ox on its way back from work came up to the table, ate part of the offering, and trod on the rest. Seized by rage at what had happened, and seeing somebody nearby sharpening an ax, Sopatrus grabbed it and struck the ox. When he had killed the animal, his rage subsided and he realized what he had done. Upon which he buried the ox, then fled to Crete, where he remained in voluntary exile, as if guilty of a wicked crime. A drought followed and there was a terrible scarcity of food. A delegation went off to consult the god, and the Pythia told them that the exiled man now in Crete would put an end to the drought: if they punished the killer and got the victim back on its feet in the course of the same sacrifice in which he was killed, and if they ate some of the victim themselves without being squeamish, then things would improve. So off they went to look for Sopatrus, who was the cause of the trouble. Sopatrus reckoned he might escape the dire straits his impurity had placed him in if he could get all the others to behave as he had. So when the delegation came for him, he told them that an ox from the city must be killed. Given that the others were nervous when it came to choosing which of them should actually kill the animal, he offered to do it himself, on the understanding that they would accept him as a citizen and agree that the killing was the responsibility of the group. They agreed and, on returning to the city, arranged matters in the following way, which has never changed to this day.

"They chose some girls as water bearers: water was brought to sharpen the ax and the knife. When they had been sharpened, one of them handed over the ax, another struck the ox, and another cut its throat; then some others skinned it and they all tasted it. When all this had been done, they sewed up the ox's hide, filled it with hay, and put the animal back on its feet in the same position it had been in when it was alive. They even yoked it to a plow as if it were working. Then they held a trial to judge the killing, and all those who had taken part were called upon to justify themselves. The girls who'd brought the water pointed to those who had sharpened the blades as being more guilty than themselves, while those who had sharpened the blades pointed to the person who had held the ax. He pointed to the one who had cut the ox's throat, and he pointed to the knife. Because the knife had no voice to speak, it was accused of the killing. From that day to this, during the Dipolia held on the Athens Acropolis, an ox is sacrificed in the same way. Having placed bread and other cakes on the bronze table, they walk the chosen oxen around it, and the one that eats the offerings is killed. Those who perform these rites are now divided up into families. All the descendants of he who first struck the ox, Sopatrus, are called *boutýpoi* (those who strike the ox); the descendants of the person who led the oxen around the offering are called *kentriádai* (the ones with the goad); and the descendants of the man who cut the ox's throat are called *daitroí* (those who celebrate), because of the celebrations that follow the distribution of the meat. Having stuffed the ox's hide and appeared at the trial, they throw the knife into the sea."

Those who first laid down the rules of sacrifice were too subtle as theologians to claim that guilt only manifested itself with the killing of a living being: that notion they left to future tribunals who would know only the limited order of men. If it were enough just to abstain from killing, life could indeed become innocent. But guilt resides in the veins—and can only move from one place to another, transform itself, reveal itself, celebrate itself.

The primordial crime is the action that makes something in existence disappear: the act of eating. Guilt is thus obligatory and inextinguishable. And, given that men cannot survive without eating, guilt is woven into their physiology and forever renews itself. But then who is at the origin of the guilt? The ox, the working ox, man's companion, the ox who one day ate the bread and cakes offered to the gods. That gesture, obtuse and meek, was the first lesion in the realm of the existent, and every later lesion was implicit in it: it was the gesture that steals away something that exists, as Hades stole away Kore. From that gesture, bound together in a single chain, come all the other crimes. Guilt is so deeply embedded in existence that all it took to usher it into consciousness was for a farm animal to stretch out its snout toward a country pie.

But whom do we find at the other end of the chain of guilt? The knife that "has no voice" (*áphonos*). The only two things condemned, the ox and the knife, cannot speak. He who cannot speak is condemned at once. He who can speak—and is guilty just the same—lives under a perpetually suspended sentence. Between them, between one end of the chain and the other, the ox and the knife, are all the rest of us: the charming water bearers, who remind us of the fifty Danaids, spurts of lymph and death; the cold instigators who use their goads to point the ox to the cake so as to have it unknowingly make the guilty gesture that will single it out as the victim; then those who spend their lives absorbed in sharpening the sacrificial axes and knives; those who are happy just to offer the ax to whoever is going to strike the blow; he who brings down the ax, as the women break the silence with a shrill cry (*ololugḗ*) of joy and horror; those who cut the animal's throat after it is down, because if blood doesn't flow the death is pointless, the animal can't be eaten; those who use the same knife that slit the throat to divide the meat into portions for each and every citizen; and, last of all, those who watch the killing and eat the animal's flesh: everybody.

The Delphic priests were guardians not only of the *lógos* but also of the doctrine of sacrifice. When the Athenians consulted the oracle after Sopatrus's cruel gesture, the Pythia answered with the brutal words that would make it possible to found the city, to found any city, because cities can only be founded on guilt. *Eat the victim's flesh and don't be squeamish:* with these words civilization was born. All the rest is honey and acorns, the Orphic life, nostalgia for a pure beginning. But not even that life could ignore the fact that the world is waste and dissipation. On the bronze table lies the bread. Then it is gone. Absence, sudden and irreversible absence, the sign that dissipation is at work. And each person, every being—the dumb beast of burden and the man who kills and the metal blade likewise—all play their part in that work. Guilt pervades everything that acts. Everything will be judged. But not so that, after the judgment, the guilt can be put aside, dissolved. On the contrary, guilt was imposed on us by the gods, even before the law.

The Pythia offers the Athenians an enigma composed of five fragments: the Stranger must be called back from exile; the crime must be repeated, and hence exalted; the killer must be judged; the victim must be "put back on its feet, in the course of the same sacrifice in which it was killed"; the men must eat the victim's flesh and not be squeamish about it. Only if all five of these conditions are simultaneously met, then "things might improve." The Pythia's answer bristles with contradictions. The Stranger is guilty but must be called back from exile; indeed, he is the essential element in any possible salvation. The ox is guilty, because it ate the offerings made to the gods, but it must reappear, set on its feet once more and stuffed with straw. (And for those moderns who tend to be overamenable to any possibility of resurrection, it should be said that the stuffed ox beneath the bloody hide is *not* a resurrected ox: it is merely the ox *present*, "in the same position it was in when it was alive," brought back, that is, to remind us that the true offense, even before death, is disappearance.) Everybody must be committed to trial for the killing of the ox, but everybody must also, indeed immediately, eat its meat, and "without being squeamish."

What is all this about? The gods aren't content to foist guilt on man. That wouldn't be enough, since guilt is part of life anyway. What the gods demand is an awareness of guilt. And this can only be achieved through sacrifice. On its own the law will serve to punish guilt but certainly not to make us aware of it, which is far more important. Sacrifice is the cosmic machine that raises our guilty lives to consciousness. After Sopatrus brought down the ax on the ox's nape, he woke up from his rage as though from a dream

and "became aware of [*sunephrónēsen*] what he had done."
He threw down the ax and fled far away. But Sopatrus was
acting alone at this point; his was the action of one individual. And he was fainthearted. He buried the ox instead of
eating it. His guilt took on no resonance; he didn't go all the
way.

The Pythia demanded that Sopatrus's ax go on striking
for all time and that everyone, the whole community, the
pólis and every single member of it, participate in that act
and be aware of committing it. Nor was that all: the community must also welcome Sopatrus into its midst—Sopatrus the Stranger—and welcome him precisely because he
had committed that act, that furious slaying of a working
ox that had gobbled up the bread so that it disappeared in
its mouth.

Kore and Demeter are a dual being, even in name (Deó). In
a dazzling transposition, every gesture made by one corre-
sponds to a gesture of the other. When their stories approach
a stasis that would prove fatal—Kore sitting on Hades'
throne in funereal immobility and Demeter sitting on "the
stone that does not laugh"—something happens to dispel
that rigidity: Kore, distracted by what Hades is saying, eats
a pomegranate seed; Demeter, distracted by Baubo's ob-
scene dance, eats the initiates' broth like a hungry traveler.
It was from these two gestures that the mysteries arose. By
accepting and assimilating foods that were neither nectar
nor ambrosia, Demeter and Kore shared in that guilt peculiar to men, exposed themselves to that special weakness
the gods had always mocked: that submission to time that
causes living beings to disappear, and at the same time the
complicity of those beings with their own destroyer, since
man cannot live without himself making something else disappear. The mysteries are the wound that opens in the
hitherto intact Olympic epidermis, a wound which then tries
in vain to heal itself in ceremony after ceremony. That that
wound may never heal is the hope of the initiates.

The *palaiòn pénthos*, the "ancient grief," persists undiminished across time and demands that men take some liberating action. Isn't that what the mysteries are? For we live surrounded, in the invisible air, by wandering avengers who never forget the "ancient contaminations." It is an Olympian paradox that this oppressive vendetta affects gods as well as men. Thus, when Apollo committed his primordial crime by killing Python, we find this proudest and most distant of gods humbly imitating men, offering libations and going into exile, as would Oedipus one day and Orestes.

When the gods come into contact with guilt, they lower their gaze toward men and begin to copy their gestures so as to free themselves from it. A parallelism thus develops between the way men imitate gods and vice versa. Men, writes Strabo, "imitate the gods chiefly when they are doing good; or rather, when they are happy." The gods, in contrast, imitate men when they do or suffer evil (and for the Greeks the two things were bound by the same knot: *adikeîn, adikeîsthai*) or, rather, when they are unhappy. We have evidence of such unhappiness on the part of the gods in "what we hear tell of the gods in the myths and hymns—their abductions, secret wanderings, exile, servitude." It was precisely with these elements, these precious clues, indeed the only clues to the experiences of the gods on earth, that men composed the mysteries. Here every gesture achieves its maximum density and enjoins us to silence: in the mysteries men repeat the gestures the gods made as they imitated men in order to free themselves from divine guilt. Hence the vertigo of the mysteries. More even than in their happiness, men approach the gods in their celebration of the gestures the gods made when they were unhappy.

For those not initiated in the mysteries, they seem to have to do with the immortality of men; for the initiates, the mysteries are a moment when the gods become tangled with death. "Many things related to death and mourning are to be found mixed together in the initiation ceremonies," says Plutarch. But that most dangerous turncoat of the pagan world, Clement of Alexandria, is even more precise, indeed brutal: "The mysteries can be summed up in just two words," he says, "killings and burials."

It is not the men who pass through the mysteries who are immortal but the mysteries themselves. When, in Smyrna, the public speaker Aelius Aristides hears that a raid by Costobocis has devastated Eleusis, he says: "The battles on sea and the battles on land and the laws and the constitutions and the arrogance and the tongues and all the rest have melted away: only the mysteries remain."

Pelasgian: thus the Greeks designated the erratic block of their origins. There were Pelasgians on Samothrace: they celebrated mysteries with cranes and pygmies; they were the first to square stones from which young heads and erect phalluses would protrude. There were Pelasgians in Arcadia, Aeolis, Lemnos, Imbros, Argos, Athens. For thousands of years, from Ephorus right through to Klages, scholars have been obsessed by the quest to identify the Pelasgians. But Pelasgian man is elusive. You can never pin anything on him: he is always the mute "neighbor" (*pélas*), the thing language and history have split away from. Without dwelling on the point, Herodotus remarks that, "being Pelasgian, the Athenians changed their language when they were absorbed into the Greek family." Thus the Athenians made two claims about themselves: that they were autochthonous, born from the soil, because they were Pelasgian; and at the same time that they had rejected the language of the soil, the lost Pelasgian language, which Herodotus himself already found incomprehensible.

What importance this might have had, Herodotus doesn't say. But when, as a curious traveler, he arrived in Dodona, this is what the three priestesses of the sanctuary, Promeneia, Timarete, and Nicandra, told him. Long before, at a certain moment in the ancient history of the sanctuary, a group of Pelasgians arrived at Zeus's oak (but did they call him Zeus? or was he just *theós*?). They had come to consult the oracle. Hitherto, the Pelasgians had "offered sacrifices of every kind to the gods and prayed to them, but without distinguishing between them with names and titles, because they didn't know that any such things existed." Now some sailor or other had come back from Egypt bringing the names of the gods with him. But was it right to use them? And were these unknown names the correct ones? The oak tree told them that the names were right and that it was right to use them. Zeus is the god who allows the other gods to be named. Zeus is the god who allows things to appear.

The story the three priestesses of Dodona told Herodotus is also the fable that ushers in the opposition and superimposition of *nómos* and *phýsis*, law (or convention) and nature, and hence the underlying structure of all thought from then on. Only that day, in Dodona, did the Greeks become Greek: if by Greek we mean nothing more than the coexistence of a dark, obscure background, like the rustling of a tree, dedicated to any and every power, with a sound that comes from a foreign land and forever superimposes on that background the sovereign caprice of a name. The Pelasgians went from a mute homage to the gods to an homage in which they evoked those gods with foreign names they knew nothing about. Thus did the Greeks tense their metaphysical bow; such was their style as they raised it to their shoulders.

Zeus was not to have a temple in Dodona, the most ancient of oracles, until the fifth century. The center of the sanctuary was an oak, protected by a circle of tripods. It looked out over a broad, flattish valley. At each side of the valley rose long, rolling hills, hills like so many others, their slopes mottled with green patches that grew thicker and thicker until they formed a solid green carpet at the bottom of the valley. Dodona was not a prominent, strategic, exposed place, like Delphi; nor was it a blissful place, like Olympia. Dodona had no profile, whereas Delphi was nothing but. But Delphi was Apollo. And everything that is not Apollo is an enemy of Apollo. By contrast, Zeus is flat, accepting and welcoming everything.

Zeus has no character, he is the support beneath every character. Just as his statue in Olympia was the support for all the shapes and parasites on it, his place admits of every other place. And his voice, the rustling of the oak, is the closest thing imaginable to undifferentiated sound, a voice that more than any other on earth recalls the sea. Only Zeus is able to transform the flat background of existence into something marvelous. All the other gods have their shapes, their signs, their profiles. Zeus has the background, and the background noise. Zeus is the commonplace supporting the unique. The unique cannot exist without that support. But the support can exist alone. The unique tends to be jealous, because there are things that don't belong to it. The support tends to be indifferent, because everything rests upon it.

On the small lead plates people would use to consult the oracle at Dodona, we read: "Did Pistus steal the wool from the mattress?" "Eurydamus would like to know where he might find his lost cup." But, alongside these trivial requests referring to everyday objects, we also find a quite different kind: "Which god should I ask to help me do what I have in mind?" "Peithione would like to know whether he would do well to pray and offer sacrifices to Asclepius." "Hermone the Corinthian would like to know what god he should invoke to have good children by his wife Cratea."

In Delphi, people consulted the Pythia to find out what Apollo thought about something. In Dodona, they consulted the oak to have Zeus guide them through the tangle of the gods. Those coming to the oracle weren't anxious about whether they should make a sacrifice or not. They were anxious because they were afraid of making their sacrifice to

the wrong god. And there is nothing as sad as a sacrifice
made to the wrong god. So much of our lives is made up of
them. It was precisely to avoid mistakes of that kind that
people followed the footsteps of the Hyperboreans to Dodona. Like some supreme post office, Zeus sorted their requests and sent off the supplicants to this or that Olympian
or hero, suggesting into which vein of the invisible their offerings should be poured. No matter was too small, no question too big to be put to Zeus. Apollo wove conspiracies with
those who came to him, greeted them in a temple crammed
with spoils. Zeus resided in the trunk of an oak tree, and
from there, with the neutrality of a guide, pointed the way
to recovering the lost cup, the way to gaining the favor of
the god most suitable for the occasion.

Among the many acacias and poplars, there is only one
oak tree left in Dodona, and not a particularly big one at
that. But such is Zeus: any old oak tree. Only Zeus can sustain the wonder of normality.

The hymn etched in the stele of Palaikastro describes Zeus
as the *mégistos koûros*, "the greatest of the *koûroi*." As
though he had only just detached himself from his identical
companions, and so become the sovereign, the unique Zeus;
as though the god were born from a projection of the initiates' gaze. They see themselves in the one *koûros* who steps
forward from the ranks of the others. They are the Curetes
who danced around the infant Zeus, clashing their shields.
Now they are ready to follow him through the mountains,
vagabonds and wizards and assayers of metals. On the stele
of Palaikastro, Zeus is also invoked as *pankratès gánous*,
"sovereign of the liquid splendor." But *gános* is something
no one can circumscribe. The *Etymologicon Magnum* attributes to it the following sequence of meanings: *hýdōr
chárma phòs lípos augè leukótēs lampēdón:* "water joy light
fat brilliance whiteness flash." And then adds these words,
ignored for centuries, words that mark the point where, in
the waters of the Mediterranean, the essences of Athens and

Jerusalem meet: "*Gános,* to the Cypriots, means paradise (*parádeisos*)."

Gános is a substance, a feeling, a radiance. Zeus is made of *gános*; the Twelve Olympians are made of *gános*. Zeus is sovereign of the radiant material with which he shapes himself and with which the circle of the Twelve is shaped round about him. A reflection of that substance shone in the statue that Zeus fashioned to hide the heart of Zagreus.

X

FROM TIME TO TIME THE HEROES WOULD get together for some common adventure: a hunting party, a conquest, a war. The prey might be a fabulous animal, or an image, a statue: the Calydonian boar, the Golden Fleece, the Trojan Palladium. They are a magnificent sight, the heroes, lining up in disciplined ranks on the benches of the Argo, muscles glistening like flames. And all the Olympians watch them, from the balconies of heaven. Or there's that moment when Jason shoulders his way through the throng of the Magnetes before setting out on his travels, and the priestess of Artemis kisses his hands and stares at him with such feeling she can't say a word, and Jason leaves her behind him, as the young leave the old. Or the moment when Pollux, Zeus's boxer son, gets ready to face Amycus, king of the Bebryces, and radiates strength, although his cheeks are barely downed with hair and his eye is wet and glistening like a child's. It is at such moments, and not in their shrewder gestures, that the splendor of the heroes shines through. Apart from Theseus and Odysseus, whose greatest adventures were solitary, the heroes reveal something about themselves when they're together, something that was already there and oppressing them when they were alone: a sort of dark curtain weighs on their minds, a noble obtuseness dogs them.

Before setting out, Jason is immersed in gloomy reflections. He feels he is not in control of the adventure. There is so much enthusiasm for it, so much noise, even nature is joining in, with a cry raised by the harbor of Pagasae and another by the Argo itself, a cry that comes from the "divine beam," which crossed the ship from stem to stern and had grown as an oak in Dodona. And indeed at the beginning of their adventure the Argonauts act like so many sleepwalkers, as if blindly obeying a mechanism that makes fools of them. Seized by lust, they all, without exception, throw themselves on the women of Lemnos. One night they perpetrate a massacre by mistake, killing the best of the Doliones, who had received them with friendship. Another day they set sail and only discover they have left Heracles and Polyphemus behind when it is too late to turn back. Little by little, one begins to appreciate why the greatest heroes were so stubbornly determined to become initiates, as Heracles and the Dioscuri finally did at Eleusis, or the whole party of the Argonauts at Samothrace: they know there is something essential that they haven't got and need; they know they are not perfect.

In the beginning, the hero's intelligence is intermittent and limited to his role as a slayer of monsters. But when he manages to break the frame of this role, without abandoning it, when he learns to be a traitor, a liar, a seducer, a traveler, a castaway, a narrator, then the hero becomes Odysseus, and then, to his first vocation of slaying everything, he can add a new one: understanding everything.

The Argonauts had just landed at Thynias, an uninhabited island off the Pontus. They were exhausted, having rowed nonstop for a day and two nights, sweating like oxen in the yoke. Now it was almost dawn. A figure appeared, a huge figure. Ringlets of blond hair dangled on his cheeks. Gripped in his left hand, a silver bow gleamed in the first light. Suddenly the sea grew wild, the earth shook, and angry waves crashed on the beach. That was the only sound. The Argonauts fell to the ground in helpless bewilderment, none of them daring to look the figure in the eyes as, ignoring them, he passed. Only when the god's feet had left the island

and begun to tread the air, suspended above the water, did
they realize it was Apollo on his way to the Hyperboreans.
The Argonauts kept their heads bowed. Finally Orpheus
said: "It was Apollo of the Dawn, let us raise an altar to him
on the beach."

The Argonauts lay in ambush, invisible among the reeds.
Jason was grim. He was strong, but strength lives in the fear
of coming up against another and just slightly greater
strength, which will destroy it. And perhaps he had finally
found such an adversary, right here in Colchis: a sleepless
monster keeping guard over the Golden Fleece where it
hung from the branches of an oak tree. Jason knew that the
moment had come when he must unleash the goddess in
himself or die.

On high, in a bedroom in Olympus, Athena and Hera got
together. They thought: where there's a monster, there's a
woman, and where there's a woman, there's Aphrodite.
They would go and see her, although it had been a long time.
Aphrodite had just remade Hephaestus's bed. He'd gone off
to work far away, on a wandering island. In the half dark
of the room, she was smoothing out her long hair with a
golden comb. She shifted the cloak covering her shoulders
so as to plait it in tresses. Then she started. Aphrodite didn't
have any woman friends; she was aware of spending most
of her time with men. And she wasn't used to getting visits
from two powerful goddesses, who quite probably envied
her, and certainly considered her incapable of understanding anything really important. She immediately guessed
what they were after: they wanted her to send her son Eros
off into the world yet again. For a moment she let her guard
slip and started telling them the truth: that her son respected her even less than he did other women, because they
were two of a kind, she and her son. In fact he laughed in
her face; he wasn't ashamed of anything with her. But as
soon as she started talking about her own troubles, Athena
and Hera exchanged an irritating look of complicity.

Enough of that then, Aphrodite thought, since nobody's interested. Still, she wanted to show how efficient she could be this time. She caught up with Eros in Zeus's orchard. The "ineffable rascal," *áphaton kakón*, was playing dice with Ganymede, cheating and winning. Aphrodite knew that nothing grabbed his attention better than certain types of toys: golden dice, spinning tops, balls. This time she would bribe him with something that had been Zeus's, something his nurse Adrasteia, one of the women of fate, had given him: a golden ball, with lots of circles etched into it and an enamel spiral that cut across them. When you threw it up in the air, it left a flaming wake. Describing the toy to Eros, she immediately saw that the boy would agree to the deal: the golden ball in return for an arrow in Medea's heart, right up to the feathers if possible. So Eros, the perennial, ruthless youthfulness of the world, he who strikes but is never stricken, once again came down from Olympus. He was already thinking of when he got back, of playing with the golden ball, crossed by that deep enamel spiral.

There is a misunderstanding between hero and princess that will go on and on repeating itself in relationships between men and women, at least for as long as the man thinks of himself as the hero and the woman as the princess, which is to say almost always. The night Jason turned up at the court in Colchis, Princess Medea dreamed that the hero had come not to kill the monster but to carry her off. Jason knew that, to beat the monster guarding the Golden Fleece, he must get Medea's help. And, if the princess helped him, she would be carried off. It was a game of silences, of things understood but unspoken: both hero and princess wanted to make it look, he to her and she to herself, as if the slaying of the monster were only a pretext for her being carried off.

When Jason had taken the Golden Fleece and the Argo was sailing off toward Greece with Medea on board, it seemed as though the princess's dream had come true. Right from the beginning Medea had thought of Jason as a nocturnal vision, when "creeping like a dream, her mind followed his marching footsteps." So who remembered the monster now? But for the hero there is never just the one monster. Hence it cannot be forgotten. For every monster is the forerunner of the next. It is far more likely that it will be the princess who is forgotten. The identity of the monster is diffuse, it reappears and repeats itself in every fragment of monster; but each woman is a profile, and at any moment a new profile may blot out the earlier ones. So it is that stories of heroes and princesses tend to end badly. Perhaps in this regard, as in others, Theseus was the most clear-sighted and tactful of the heroes; at least he abandoned Ariadne on an island, before arriving home.

Gifts from the gods are poisoned, stamped with the ill-omened sign of the invisible become palpable. Passing from hand to hand, they ooze poison. Aphrodite's necklace and Athena's golden tunic, both given to Harmony on the occasion of her marriage to Cadmus, lead to a slaughter of heroes that will go on for two generations, from the expedition of the Seven against Thebes to the revenge killings of the Epigoni. It was the same with the sacred purple tunic Dionysus fell asleep in, his head resting on Ariadne's fair breasts. The purple was bright on the sands of Naxos. But one day that fabric, drenched with happiness as it was, would become the banner of desertion, betrayal, murder. Yet the fragrance of Dionysus never left it, and the "sweet desire" to touch and stare at that tunic would never fade. The Charites had woven it for Dionysus; Dionysus had wrapped himself in it with Ariadne. Then he gave it to his son Thoas. Thoas gave it to his daughter Hypsipyle, who gave it to her lover Jason before he abandoned her. And the purple tunic of Dionysus was the gift Jason and Medea chose for Apsyrtus, Medea's brother, when they decided to kill him.

It all happened without witnesses, on the dark little island in the Danube estuary where the Brygi had raised a temple to Artemis. There was no other trace of a human presence. Medea waited for her brother on the temple porch. Jason crouched in the darkness. Medea looked away and covered her eyes with a white veil as Jason struck Apsyrtus with the gesture of a butcher dispatching cattle. Apsyrtus fell to his knees like a huge-headed bull. Before dying, he scooped up some black blood in his hands and managed to smear it on his sister's white veil. Jason went around the corpse, cutting off the hands, feet, and ears. The first fruits. Three times he licked the dead man's blood and spat it into his mouth. Medea raised a torch, the sign agreed on with her lover's friends.

Granddaughters of the sun, it was immediately obvious that Ariadne and Medea were related. They both had a sort of golden light spreading outward from the eyes. They were born far apart, in the far south and the far north of the earth. Both helped a foreigner, were carried off by him, by him abandoned. They never met. But they touched each other through a fabric. Each had fingered that purple tunic, woven for a god and still fragrant with his vanished body.

Oistrus, the gadfly who torments the cattle, is the most elusive and at the same time the most omnipresent of the powers that governed the Greeks. Ate, that infatuation that includes its own punishment, is the equivalent figure among the women of destiny, the Fates. But Oistrus is a boy and rarely shows himself. In the sultry mythological heat their seminude bodies inhabited, gods, heroes, and the sons and daughters of gods moved about with moist, bright eyes, until a buzzing approached them from the invisible. A sting pricked them to their very souls, and thus were events unleashed. In the beginning it was difficult to tell erotic and murderous frenzies apart. Both arose from that intermittent buzzing, the incursions of that small, malicious creature. Only once, on the wonderful Canosa wine bowl, now in Munich, does Oistrus appear in all his majesty. It is a synchronic vision of the last convulsion of the tragedy of Medea. The characters are arranged on three levels. Above, as always, are a few distracted divinities: the Dioscuri are looking at each other, maybe talking quietly. Athena is seated, one arm resting on her shield, the other holding her helmet. Heracles, naked and armed, is watching her. The next level shows Creon's palace. Creontea is lying across the throne, on her head the poisoned crown, gift of the sorceress Medea, crazed with jealousy: "*coronam ex venenis fecit auream.*" Her brother, Hippotes, is running to snatch the murderous crown from her head, while Creon, her father, clutches his hair in desperation. Other people are running to help too, even an old man with a stick. And they all know there's nothing they can do. On the lowest level we find Medea, Oriental granddaughter of the Sun. She is wearing the most sumptuous, ornate clothes, which hide everything but her beautiful, staring face and her hands, the right gripping a big sword while with the left she grabs the hair over her son's forehead from behind. He is on tiptoe, as though dancing, on an altar stone. Another second and the sword will plunge into his naked chest. Jason bursts into the picture from the right, Jason the betrayer, the hero who has been overwhelmed. His body is tense and powerful, more so than Heracles', an expression of furious impotence on his face. Farther to the right, and motionless, stands another Oriental figure, solemn this time. The painter of the bowl has written around his head: "phantom of Aeetes."

The ghost of Medea's father, who had always been against her passion for Jason, thus watches the denouement he had foreseen. Then there are two objects as well, strewn like toys on a dark background: an open box in which Medea had put the poisoned crown; a nuptial basin, knocked over, forgotten. And in the center of it all, firm and erect between Medea and Jason, a young man with long hair and a smooth chest holds a torch in each hand. He is standing on a light-wheeled chariot, driven by two long snakes, which rise in flowing spirals, turning their forked tongues toward Medea.

That young man on the chariot is Oistrus, and it is he who is directing events; he is the prompter, the archon who just this once shows himself in the splendor of his person. But elsewhere, even in the element where he resides, the invisible, Oistrus is the companion of all excesses, all cravings, all the passions with which for centuries the Greeks wove their stories.

One of the most charming enigmas of the ancient world is the life of Nonnus. Almost nothing is known about him with any certainty, except his place of birth: Panopolis, in Egypt. As to the date of that birth, scholars have varied embarrassingly, but it now seems generally accepted that it must have been in the fifth century A.D. The enigma, however, has to do with the order in which he wrote his works: Nonnus left us the *Dionysiaca* in forty-eight books (a number equal to the sum of the books in the *Iliad* and the *Odyssey*) and a *Paraphrase* of St. John's Gospel.

This great writer, who has often been disparagingly dubbed "baroque," but in the same spirit could equally well be described as rococo, encrusted his poetry with voluptuous idylls and cosmological secrets. The *Dionysiaca* are an overflowing summa of the pagan world, a world that should have been on the brink of extinction but that here opens up before our eyes like a meadow of narcissi. What bothers people, though, is the fact that the only other work by Nonnus, his *Paraphrase* of St. John's Gospel, presupposes a Christian author. Yet there is nothing that would allow us to claim that the *Paraphrase* was written after the *Dionysiaca*. This raises the following questions: did Nonnus celebrate the last, and truly dazzling, lights of the pagan world with his poem on Dionysus, then convert to the new and already dominant faith and write the *Paraphrase*? Or was it the other way around: Nonnus, a Christian, was quite suddenly struck by the pagan vision, as though by lightning, and thus went from the *Paraphrase* to the tidal wave of the *Dionysiaca*? Or could one offer a third hypothesis: that

Nonnus wrote the *Dionysiaca* and the *Paraphrase* at the same time. With one hand he described the adventures of Dionysus while the other evoked the trial of Jesus. His mind was moved by both these divine beings. And perhaps he didn't even need to ask himself whether he believed in both, because he was writing them.

There are no demonstrable facts to help us solve the enigma. All we have are the texts, the style. And here the rhetorical ploy that most immediately strikes us in all Nonnus's writing is his redundancy. The *Dionysiaca* are the most sumptuous celebration imaginable of the redundant variant and the rampantly superfluous. But behind Nonnus the poet lurks Nonnus the theologian. This churning variegation, vain as nature itself, in fact alludes to the ultimate truth of the tale he is telling: that it is precisely those endlessly and meaninglessly shifting colors that lie at the heart of the divine. Nor does the vision change when Nonnus abandons the many gods to tell the story of the only son of the one God. The form he chooses this time is not the epic poem broken into a multitude of idylls but the paraphrase, which is to say redundancy reduced to its essence, so that each of the bare phrases of the Gospel is blown up and up as though by the action of an irrepressible breath and a good dose of yeast.

It is in this choice of style that we may glimpse something of Nonnus's faith: before being either pagan or Christian, it is a faith in redundancy as the way in which the cosmos makes itself manifest. And if we go on to examine the details of the narrative, there is at least one that would lead us to plump for the most improbable of our hypotheses: that Nonnus wrote the *Dionysiaca* and the *Paraphrase* at the same time, or at least without seeing any discrepancy between them. The *Dionysiaca* are dominated by Oistrus. Time and time again we see him at work, and some of the most torrid erotic scenes begin with the buzzing of that gadfly. But now let's turn to Palestine, according to Nonnus. The Jews accuse Jesus. And where St. John's Gospel says: "Say we not well that thou art a Samaritan and hast a devil [*óti daimónion écheis*]?" Nonnus paraphrases: "and now the wandering and vengeful gadfly [*alástoros oîstros*] of the demon Lyssa [Madness] goads you on." It is a delicate and precise pointer to Nonnus's consistency: impartial to Dionysus and Christ alike, he constantly finds the same demonic gadfly in both their stories, goading them on to intoxication, frenzy, delirium, illumination.

Fifteen centuries have passed, and the number of readers who have understood Nonnus could be counted on the fingers of one hand. Giovan Battista Marino, who read Nonnus in Eilhard Lubin's Latin translation (Hanau, 1605), had no doubt about it: Nonnus was the only one who could compete with Homer, the only poet who could empty his work of all heroic sobriety and encourage every possible twirl and caprice while still preserving a quite vast frame all around. This was just what Marino needed for his own *Adonis*: an ancient authority for at last departing from all those liberations of the Holy Sepulcher and other such bold and noble deeds. With Nonnus behind him, the poet could abandon himself to a project that until now had seemed blasphemous: the weaving together in a massive epic of garland upon garland of erotic verse.

Thus Marino frequently pays Nonnus the supreme homage that one writer can pay to another: theft—and the sweetest of thefts at that, the kind that remains a secret, shared in complicity by the two authors, because no one else notices. With a note of defiance Marino wrote to Achillini: "they [other literati] do not ply the sea where I fish and trade, nor will they ever catch me with my prey, unless I reveal it to them myself."

As early as 1817, in his essay *Nonnos der Dichter*, dedicated to Goethe, the learned young Ouvaroff of St. Petersburg, friend of the Senator, i.e., Joseph de Maistre, could justly complain that: "The flowery field of Greek poetry has been so thoroughly tilled that it would be hard indeed to find a poet who has not been appreciated and studied with care, not to say love; Nonnus alone pays for the sins of his age; for centuries his poem has been condemned to being a lumber room invaded by dust and corrosion where only the most zealous mythographer might penetrate. It would be hard to name but a few who have read him for the quality of his poetry, and harder still to name any who have been sufficiently bold to declare that Nonnus was truly a poet, in the full sense of the word." Another hundred and fifty years would have to pass before Giorgio de Santillana, speaking at a conference, would point to Nonnus's *Dionysiaca* as the "blossoming" of that "Japanese flower" that was for him "the archaic myth."

Jason would have preferred to live a bourgeois life at home, just as Nietzsche would have preferred to be a professor in Basel, rather than God. "I would be happy enough living in my home country, if Pelias would give his consent. May the gods see fit to free me from my labors," says Jason to Hypsipyle. And his voice is at once that of the ever hypocritical lover trying to soften the cruelty of his desertion and that of the hero who looks, weary and detached, over the scene where he is obliged to kill, cheat, travel, desert, and finally be killed, with any luck by a rotten timber while sleeping in the shade of his ship. The fable's happy ending is not an option for the hero. His part was written before he was born; his labors predate him: they are never chosen but come to meet him, like a towering wave.

Jason never managed, not even for the briefest of moments, to go beyond his role as hero. He soon realized this and clammed up in gloomy silence. He worked at his adventures: but that was precisely the point, he worked. Even the women he came across, who usually fell in love with him, were part of that work. He abandoned Hypsipyle because he had to press on with his expedition. He promised Medea he would marry her because he had to get hold of the Golden

Fleece and needed her help. Then he did marry her, because King Alcinous forced him to; the Golden Fleece was their shining nuptial pallet in the cave of Macris. Then he abandoned Medea, because he had to unite his family with that of the reigning house of Thebes. Everything he did was done to achieve something else, and always in obedience to orders from above. There were days when this made the memory of his cruelest deeds easier to bear: he had done them because they were his destiny. He had traveled far and wide, visited the remotest of peoples, yet had always lived like a donkey plodding around the same well.

Right from the start, beautiful as she was, Jason felt a strange repulsion for Medea. She was a woman who knew only two states: either hopeless unhappiness, desertion, lonely misery, helpless rejection; or dazzling, lightning-swift power. It was conceivable that one might go through all kinds of adventures with such a woman (and she could be pretty useful too, more so than many a hero); but could you live with her day in day out? Jason was old now, shunned by everybody. People told his adventures to their children, with the result that he couldn't find anyone to tell them to himself. He went back to Corinth, where he had witnessed horror upon horror, where he had even reigned as king. There, pulled up onto dry land, lay his ship, the Argo. It was his first, his last, his only true companion. And he couldn't say it had been a silent companion either, because its main beam had a voice, a sound unlike any other and one Jason would always remember. Once it had frightened him; now it pricked him with nostalgia, like the voice of an old nurse. He looked at this ship, which he had loved more than any woman, and certainly more than Medea, that fake savage, who always seemed to be on the brink of disaster but at the end of the day did nothing but slip from one palace to the next, one kingdom to the next, sowing calamity everywhere she went and always saving herself, along with her chariot and her snakes. The charms of the Argo were rarer and nobler. Jason thought the Argo might grant him a last favor: he would hang himself from the wooden bowsprit. Then he lapsed back into his thoughtful brooding, his back resting against the keel. A rotten timber fell from the deck, struck him on the head, and killed him.

The appearance of the heroes covers a very brief period in Greek history. They all knew one another, or had heard stories about the others from people who had known them. Like links in a bracelet, the Cretan cycle, the Argonauts' cycle, the Theban cycle, and the Trojan cycle are all connected. And the whole phenomenon burned itself out in just a few years. Between the killing of the Minotaur and the killing of Agamemnon, there were only two generations. Theseus buried his sword in the Minotaur, and his son Acamas was one of the Achaeans who lay in ambush in the Trojan horse. The fall of Crete, the fall of Mycenae, the fall of Troy, the rise of Athens: the heroes put their seal on the key events, then disappeared. Swiftness was of their essence. It is as if the Greeks had wanted to concentrate all the stories whose consequences they would live among into the shortest possible time. The age of the heroes was brief, overcrowded, cruel. And the earth groaned: "oppressed by the weight of humankind, while there was no devotion left among them."

If, in Greek eyes, the origin of all historic crimes could be traced back to the Trojan War, the origin of the war itself was far from clear. Helen, who was the only witness to the whole thing and the pivot of the scales, attributed the cause to a double-edged plan of Zeus: to unburden the earth and give glory to Achilles. These goals are seemingly unconnected: on the one hand, we have the slaughter of hundreds of heroes, as if they were a mere nameless number, an excess ballast of feet trampling the belly of the earth; on the other, the exaltation of a single person, likewise a hero, and not so much his strength, which was brief and thrust upon him, but his name pure and simple, the sound of his glory. And all this was to be achieved via a single artifice: Helen, and not even Helen herself but her "breathing phantom," her "name." By examining the nature of this fatal artifice, we begin to see the unity of Zeus's design, how it converges on a single goal: to scoop out a vacuum in the material world, to lighten its density, to fashion a sounding box between skin and shade. The fullness of the Homeric word, effortlessly bringing into existence whatever it names, is the last heritage of an earth filled and oppressed by the heroes, by their amorous and cruel trampling. What follows is a new story, in which something has been taken away from the density of the body to house the vacuum of the word.

Zeus decided to do this because he knew that the appearance of Achilles hailed nothing less than a new era: the posthumous era of Zeus, an era in which Achilles came to substitute, albeit only for a short time (but as a sign it was valid forever), for the son of Thetis who was to have overthrown Zeus. Even if Zeus's sovereignty remained intact, and that son was never born, the change had somehow come about: a god can only shift the meaning of what is predestined, not cancel it out. Thus, as it first appears, the symbol is a tool the gods use to defend themselves from destiny. By forcing the earth to swallow up the innumerable bodies of the heroes, Zeus accepted that his own body be lessened too. He thus opened the space for the word, a hollowness in the body of the god himself, a memory of that other Zeus, who had existed before Achilles and whom now the poets celebrated in their songs, insofar as he allowed them to celebrate Achilles.

What we call Homeric theology was a reckless interval in the lives of the gods. For a brief period the world accepted the supremacy of the visible. Not so that the power of the invisible might somehow be diminished. Nobody imagined power could reside anywhere else. It was just that for the first time the invisible agreed to fashion itself in every tiny detail according to the rules of the visible, as though deeply attracted to that precarious way of being.

Considered from the heights of the divine home, life on earth opened out in a vast and trembling fan: its value was intrinsic to itself and lasted only as long as it did, standing out sharply against the light. After that life came neither punishment nor reward but the same suffering for all: the protraction, beneath the earth, of an enervated existence, in which mental powers were reduced to a subdued muttering, the body to an impalpable shade, the voice to the squeak of a bat. Only in Homer's Greece does the cry of the warrior who begs Zeus that he may be killed in the light make any sense: "Destroy us in the light, since such is your pleasure." The light will serve not to escape death but to usher it in. A death in the gloom of the fog would already be a fragment of the sorrowful afterlife, all weakness and vacillation, whereas a death in the light is a last instant of clarity. The light the hero invokes has nothing to do with Mazdean photism, forerunner of every internal and transfiguring light. It is an external light, almost solid, the light in which things, all things, stand out in radiant profile. Such a vision of life, and of the afterlife that mockingly follows it, amounts to an unparalleled cruelty. All the more irresistible then must one's brief spell in the light have appeared. But it was not a tension man could bear for long.

The heroes wiped one another out beneath the walls of Troy, not just because Zeus wanted to lighten the earth but because they themselves could no longer bear this form of life and thus, with silent assent, chose to seek their deaths together. The battles beneath Troy were, among other things, a bloody banquet of farewell.

Neoptolemus was a young man when he raised his sword above old Priam's head, a boy even, you might have said, were it not for the weapons weighing him down. He planted his feet firmly on the ground, tensing the big adult calves that bulged in their shin guards, before bringing down his heavy blade on the bald, already blood-bespattered head leaning toward him and partly covered with desperate hands. Between the fingers of those hands, a few wisps of hair peeped out, like white grass. Priam was sitting on the hollowed stone of the altar of Zeus Herkeios, where for years blood had flowed in streams, forming long streaks and dark stains. On his knees he cradled a body not unlike Neoptolemus's, but naked and with deep wounds to chest, stomach, and one thigh: it was Astyanax, Hector's son. Thus on Priam's body the old blood of the sacrifices, the still gushing blood of Astyanax, and that of his own head and shoulder wounds were all mingled together.

The hour of the heroes' children had come—now they were killing and getting themselves killed just as their fathers had, but quicker, without tears, without divine frenzy, without stirring words: the stories were complete now; all that remained was to put the last seal on them. As Neoptolemus lifted his thin, sinewy arm, the fronds of the palm beside the altar bent in the night wind, thus opening up the space the metal had to pass through to split Priam's head. And, to hold that head still, like a chunk of wood, Neoptolemus's left hand gripped the old man's shoulder through his blood-soaked tunic.

At the very same moment, another hand was reaching out to another body in the smoky darkness of Athena's temple. The hand of Ajax Oïleus closed on the short hair that barely covered the nape of Cassandra's neck. Powerful fingers followed the direction of his inflamed and lustful gaze. Like her father, Priam, Cassandra was pressing her body against something sacred: not the stone of Zeus but the Palladium. That small, stiff statue, that Athena with shield and raised spear, was the guardian of Troy. The city could only exist where that statue was, as a language only exists where its poet is. Cassandra forced her soft body against the statue. She was completely naked but for a little cloak knotted beneath her chin and falling down behind her shoulders to form a sort of backdrop to her high breasts, the nipples pointing sideways, as if wanting to flee in opposite directions. Ajax Oïleus tightened his fingers on her hair, while her fingers clutched at the flank of the Palladium. A shock

of violence went from the warrior's fingers, through those
of Apollo's priestess, to the statue. Her father, Priam, had
covered his eyes with his arms; round about, some Trojan
women crouched down weeping and terrified, their heads
in their hands; but Cassandra's gaze was steady and calm
as she watched Ajax Oïleus's armor bearing down on her:
indeed with her free hand she seemed to be egging her assailant on, opening her fingers between the hero's sword and
thighs, drawing him to her, urging him to strike.

All along their roads the Greeks raised stones to the dead.
But what did those stelae remind them of? Of Achilles'
horses weeping hot tears on the death of Patroclus. They laid
their heads on the ground "like a stele that stays planted in
the earth," says Homer. Around them, the clash of arms.
The Greeks and Trojans were fighting over Patroclus's
corpse, tugging at it as though at a bull's hide. Sweat and
fatigue turn flesh to water. But sorrow petrifies it. In the
stelae they raised for their dead, the Greeks captured the
absorbed, translucent life of those immortal horses, weeping. Looking down from on high, Zeus didn't feel compassion on seeing the warriors fall in battle, but he did when
he saw the tears of the horses as they looked on their fallen
driver and master's friend. Zeus felt closer to those animals
than to any man. Like him they were immortal. Yet now
they abandoned themselves to something that was forbidden to immortals: tears.

After the death of Patroclus, when Achilles goes back to the
battlefield, gritting his teeth, a light as though from a distant
beacon flashing from his shield, Zeus once again calls the
gods to an assembly. This time the minor Nymphs are there
too, and the rivers. They all wait for a sign. But for the moment there is nothing to decide, no divine intrigue to slip in
among the warriors. Everybody, gods and men alike, knows
what is about to happen. Achilles is going to die. Xanthus,

the immortal horse, is already mourning his master. Achilles himself senses his death as something palpable, like a helmet thrust on his head. And then Zeus chooses this of all moments to loose the whole pack of the gods onto the battlefield. "Thus they went to war, god against god." All of them. Even those who, like Hephaestus and Leto, have so far kept out of the struggle.

Why did Zeus throw them all into the fray? We are closing in on the nerve of Homeric theology here. In the maximum pointlessness lies the maximum splendor. And the real never shines so brightly as when its reality is duplicated, when for every hero's arm there is a god's arm coming to meet it, to guide it, when two scenes, one visible, the other invisible, because dazzling, are one inside the other, so that every joint is doubled. Achilles is denied any chance of putting off his end, which must happen, for so it has been decreed, in a certain way, at a certain moment. But destiny does hold out one last honor for Achilles, and Zeus has no desire to deprive him of it, because this honor is his pleasure: it is that the last battle be hard, uncertain, furious.

At the same time Zeus has something else on his mind: he must see that no one on the earth can ever, by mere dint of force, do anything that goes "beyond destiny," that no one ever manage to postpone his own death. Achilles' fury might allow him to conquer those walls that are destined to fall at a later date. This would put a crack in the order of things. So now, with the intervention of the Olympians, the tension on the battlefield is raised to something almost unbearable and at the same time placed in a new equilibrium. The clashing swells, indicating that an unprecedented concentration of forces is at work. Indeed the noise even has Hades starting nervously. The only one of the gods not on the battlefield, he senses the excess of tension on the earth and gets up from his throne, fearing that the grassy mantle above him may be about to break up and expose to the light the endless mold of his subterranean world, abhorred by gods and men alike.

. . .

In the *Iliad*, all living things, even the horse Xanthus, even
the river Scamander, tell us that they are not the "cause,"
not responsible for anything. But they don't say this in order
to lay the blame on someone else. No, that recognition is the
supreme act of Homeric devotion, a stepping aside before
overwhelming power. Every affirmation of an ego would be
crude, here where the distinction between how much each
person may do alone and how much a god allows him to do
or gives to him is so subtle. The merest breath decides everything, a change in the rhythm of the massacre grants the
upper hand to one side or the other.

There is something that distinguishes Homeric characters
from everything that was written before or would be written
after. They behave like those perfect atheists who have
never existed and who are convinced that life is coterminous
with breath. After death, for the science-bound atheist,
there is but a vague nothingness. For the Homeric character,
there is a long torment, a craving without mind or memory.
Not another life, and not even a punishment for their lives,
but an enervated and delirious physiology, which stops
short of life.

Yet for as long as they drew breath, everything was full
of gods. Thinking of Achilles, who every day at dawn
dragged Hector's corpse around Patroclus's pyre, Hecuba
says: "But not for this was he [Patroclus] brought back to
life." No artifice, no rite, no merit can alter this fact. The
gods "are always," as the formulaic tags unceasingly tell us;
those who recognize the gods live but a brief space. In their
modesty, the atheists are full of vainglory. For the brief span
of their lives they are convinced they are in control of something, an island of independence later to be dispersed into
blind atoms. The Homeric heroes allowed themselves no
such consolation: while they lived they were aware of being
sustained and imbued by something remote and whole,
which then abandoned them at death like so many rags.

.   .   .

CHAPTER X

The *Iliad* is the world of brusque, precipitous passages from
one state to the other. Its consummate expression is Achilles.
Achilles weeps with Priam, his enemy's father, then looks
at him with admiration, then, just a few moments later, has
to stop himself from killing him. The intensity is extreme in
each phase. And each phase lives by and for itself, nor is it
concerned with what came before or will come after. Why
should things be consequent upon one another? Is a motionless, bleeding body consequent upon a body tense in the
chase? These states follow each other like stretches of a
giant wall, reduced to stumps. Marooned in the powerful
isolation of each separate block, we must always try to remember that those walls form a single line. When Thetis
visits her son, Achilles, wallowing in grief for Patroclus, she
doesn't try to lead him slowly out of his suffering, step by
step. Thetis looks at him and reminds him of the existence
of bread and bed. Then adds: "It is a good thing to unite
with a woman in love."

When the Christians built churches on the sites of pagan
sanctuaries, incorporating the old capitals and columns in
their naves, they were behaving as Heracles had with the
Nemean lion, or Athena with Gorgon. In the hero's relationship with the monster, what matters is this: that the
monster possesses, or protects, or even is the treasure. To
kill the monster means to incorporate it in oneself, to take
its place. The hero becomes the new monster, clothed in the
skin of the old and decorated with some metonymic trophy.
Thus Heracles will no longer show his face, except through
the motionless jaws of the lion he has killed.

The monster is the most precious of enemies: therefore it
is the enemy one goes and looks for. Other enemies might
simply attack us: the Giants, for example, or the Titans, rep-
resentatives of an order in the process of being replaced, or
looking for revenge for having already been replaced. The
monster is quite different. The monster waits near the well-
spring. The monster *is* the spring. He doesn't need the hero.

It is the hero who needs him for his very existence, because his power will be protected by and indeed must be snatched from the monster. When the hero confronts the monster, he has as yet neither power nor knowledge. The monster is his secret father, who will invest him with a power and knowledge that can belong to one man only, and that only the monster can give him.

In the beginning the monster was in the center, the center of the earth and the heavens, where the waters rise. When the monster was killed by the hero, his dismembered body migrated to recompose itself at the four corners of the earth. Then it embraced the world in a circle of scales and water. It was the composite margin of all there was. It was the frame. That the frame is the home of the monster, the artisans of the Baroque knew only too well, and the frames they made were far more intricate, far denser, far more archaic than all the idylls they enclosed—and perhaps would one day suffocate. Then came the moment when people didn't want frames anymore. The museums hung pictures without frames, which looked as though they'd been stripped bare. The frame is not the antiquated, but the remote. With the frame gone, the monster loses his last home. And returns to wander where he will.

The Greeks were drawn to enigmas. But what is an enigma? A mysterious formulation, you could say. Yet that wouldn't be enough to define an enigma. The other thing you have to say is that the answer to an enigma is likewise mysterious. This is what distinguishes the enigma from the problem, although at the beginning of Greek civilization the two categories were confused. When a problem is resolved, both question and answer dissolve, are absorbed into a mechanical formula. Climbing a wall is a problem, until you lean a ladder against it. Afterward, you have neither problem nor solution, just a wall and a ladder. This is not so for the enigma. Take the most famous one of all, the Sphinx's: "What is the being that has but one voice and yet sometimes has two feet, sometimes three, sometimes four, and is progressively weaker the more feet it has?" Oedipus answers: "Man." But if we think about that answer, we realize that precisely the fact that "man" is the solution to such an enigma suggests the enigmatic nature of man. What is this incongruous being that goes from the animal condition of the quadruped through to the prosthesis (the old man's stick), all the time preserving a single voice? The solution to the enigma is thus itself an enigma, and a more difficult one.

Resolving an enigma means shifting it to a higher level, as the first drops away. The Sphinx hints at the indecipherable nature of man, this elusive, multiform being whose definition cannot be otherwise than elusive and multiform. Oedipus was drawn to the Sphinx, and he resolved the Sphinx's enigma, but only to become an enigma himself. Thus anthropologists were drawn to Oedipus, and are still there measuring themselves against him, wondering about him.

Oedipus was the unhappiest of the heroes and the most vulnerable, but he was also the one who took a step beyond the other heroes. The hero's relationship with the monster is one of contact, skin against skin. Oedipus is the first not to touch the monster. Instead he looks at it and speaks to it. Oedipus kills with words; he tosses mortal words into the air as Medea hurled her magic spells at Talos. After Oedipus's answer, the Sphinx fell into a chasm. Oedipus didn't climb down there to skin it, to get those colorful scales that allured travelers like the rich clothes of some Oriental courtesan. Oedipus is the first to feel he can do without contact with the monster. Of all his crimes, the most serious is the one no one reproaches him with: his not having touched the monster. Oedipus goes blind and becomes a beggar because he doesn't have a Gorgon on his chest to defend him, doesn't have the skin of a wild beast over his shoulders, doesn't have a talisman to clutch in his hand. Words grant him a victory that is too clean, that leaves no spoils. And it is precisely in the spoils that power resides. The word may win where every other weapon fails. But it remains naked and solitary after its victory.

With Oedipus, monster slaying splits in two: on the one hand, we have a perfectly conscious slaying, that of the words that destroy the Sphinx; on the other, a perfectly unconscious slaying, when Oedipus kills Laius in a brawl between travelers. From then on the lucidity we associate with consciousness is turned inside out in a way that can only bode ill. This is the monster's revenge. The monster can pardon the hero who has killed him. But he will never pardon the hero who would not deign to touch him.

XI

THE LONG CHAIN OF THOSE STORIES THAT predate history, and of which the *Iliad* and the *Odyssey* form a number of links, opened with the copulation of Uranus and Ge and closed with the death of Odysseus. The circle opened with the mingling of earth and sky and closed with a paltry brawl, a fatal accident, as, in a foreign land, the young Telegonus unknowingly kills his father, the old Odysseus, with the sting of a devilfish. After Odysseus, our life without heroes begins; stories are no longer exemplary but are repeated and recounted. What happens is mere history.

Partly because he is so near the boundary, so near the point where the circle closes, Odysseus is the hero who most often tells stories. The circle began with the majestic and suffocating obscurity of the world's origins, commanding silence; it ends with this warrior disguised as a Phoenician merchant, who some suspected of being a Phoenician merchant disguised as a warrior. Odysseus invited irreverence, insinuation. Certainly he inspired less respect than any other hero. There were even rumors that he had been Homer's lover. That was why, detractors said, the poet treated him so well, concealing many of his worst traits and even removing the figure of Palamedes from the *Iliad*, so as to leave no clue that might point us to his treacherous murder, set up by Odysseus. That was why he said that Odysseus had defeated the Sirens, whereas in fact—some sneeringly maintained—it was the Sirens who disdained this sailor, with his "squashed nose," as being "past it, erotically speaking." When, at the end of the *Odyssey*, Zeus has a temporary harmony descend upon Ithaca to wind up the poem, it does seem that the curtain is being hurriedly lowered before too many questions can be asked. But in the centuries after Homer, people would go on wondering about Odysseus, and question and answer would pass from mouth to mouth, as if in a long stubble fire.

It is part of the essence of Odysseus that he be the last of the heroes, the one who closes the cycle. Being the last, Odysseus is the closest to the life that will follow, a life never more to close in any cycle. His foot treads the boundary line. Thus it was not the *Iliad*, that erratic rock abandoned on the plain, that bequeathed us the multiform novel but the sinuous *Odyssey*: "a private not a public affair," as Telemachus says of his search for his father. And yet, last among the heroes to return, Odysseus is also the one who right up to the end maintains his contact—and what an intimate contact it was—with the primordial powers who appeared in the first phases of the cycle. His wanderings were partly a compendium, a roll call, of all those beings and places that were already growing confused in many a memory, already being removed to the realm of the fabulous. With Odysseus they are present, powerful and whole for one last time, and in Odysseus they salute the last traveler able to see them with his own eyes and bear witness.

While Odysseus was still sailing laboriously back to his island, in the halls of the palace of Ithaca the bard Phemius was already celebrating the deeds of the warriors he had fought with beneath the walls of Troy. Almost everything was already words. Only one blank remained to be filled: the deeds of Odysseus himself, the buckle that would close the cycle. Odysseus, master of the word, was the last to have us believe that not all was words, for as long, that is, as his own sparkling haul of stories was still missing. After his return to Ithaca, after the *Odyssey*, man's approach to primordial beings and places could only take place through literature.

Alone among the Achaean leaders, Odysseus keeps his eyes down. But not out of fear. While his gaze is lowered, Odysseus concentrates his mind, isolates it from all around in a way his companions are not used to doing, weaves a plot, gives shape to a *mēchanē*. He is the opposite of the man who is continually caught between the forces, machines, and *mēchanaí* of nature and of the gods. To their invisible tangle, Odysseus adds new *mēchanaí*, ones that he has elaborated himself. Now he has the secret, he need not merely submit to it. Thus he adds to the confusion of elements at play, then takes advantage of that confusion to elude the various traps. The frontal approach of the hero holds no attraction for him. Odysseus takes one step back toward the tortuous mind of Kronos, to get the run-up he needs to leap beyond the heroes. When the heroes are dead, or obsolete, Odysseus will still be looking out to the sea he expects will be the death of him, still dreaming of setting sail again, perhaps toward that land where men know nothing of the sea.

Odysseus and Oedipus, the most intelligent of the heroes, killed and were killed by mistake. Odysseus was killed by his son Telegonus, who didn't recognize him; Oedipus killed his father, Laius, without recognizing him. In both cases the deaths were the result of a pointless brawl: over who should go first at a crossroads, over a squabble between the Ithacan palace guards and a stranger. The lucidity of Odysseus and Oedipus releases a murky, murderous smoke round about them.

Socrates was not the first just man among the Greeks to be killed because he was just. During the Trojan War the same fate befell Palamedes, although he was not yet a just man but a wise one. Those ten years beneath the walls of Troy were only occasionally taken up in skirmishes and the dust and clash of conflict. More than fear, the warriors' most constant companion was boredom. Having set up their huts on a dull Asiatic plain, they watched the horizon. There were no women, and even passions between men could grow wearisome. As year followed year, they had just one precious resort: a man like themselves, a warrior, Palamedes, had taught them how to play with dice, checkers, astragals. Staring at those small rolling objects, at their checkered boards, they managed to forget time. It was said that Palamedes invented other things too: some of the letters of the alphabet, the length of the months, beacons. But for the common soldier he was the inventor of the game, of a motionless, endless spell. Apart from which, Palamedes was a prince like any other. His only distinguishing feature was that he didn't have a beard. And yet there was someone powerful who hated him: Odysseus.

One day, in Ithaca, when he was pretending to be crazy so as not to go to Troy, Odysseus saw Agamemnon, Menelaus, and Palamedes heading toward him across the fields. He went on plowing. He tossed handfuls of salt in the furrows, and he had yoked together an ox and an ass. He tossed the sea, which knows no harvest, into the hollow of the fertile earth; he who one day, after seeing the whole world, would take his salty skin to a place where people knew nothing of the sea. But it was too early for Odysseus to appreciate that he was representing his own life in this gesture. On his head, to add insolence to pretense, he wore a pointed hat, the kind Cabirian initiates wore. Only another initiate would be able to understand his game. Palamedes watched him. Then, quite suddenly, he snatched the baby Telemachus from Penelope's arms and threw him down on the ground in front of the plow. At which Odysseus stopped. He was beaten. Palamedes had forced him up against the limits of simulation. There was nothing Odysseus loathed more, even if he knew that this wasn't quite how it was, for simulation must know no limits for him. That was his secret, that was what separated him from the vigorous simplemindedness of

all the Ajaxes. Simulation meant gliding down from high
above, commanding everything with one's eye, without ever
being commanded by another eye even higher up. Palamedes was that other eye.

Odysseus said nothing and followed him. Locked away in
his heart, he nursed a hatred no enemy would ever rouse.
They were to fight side by side for years. Compared with
Odysseus, Palamedes was "mentally quicker, but not so
good at helping himself." His inventions enchanted the soldiers but didn't achieve anything. They obeyed the power
of abstraction and at the same time mimicked the course of
nature. Palamedes knew that. He dedicated the dice he had
invented to Tyche, in her sanctuary in Argos. Tyche was not
a popular divinity at the time. But one day everybody would
recognize her as the image that most closely resembles nature. When life strips off all her finery, what remains is fortune. Everything that happens is a constant collision of
tossed dice. One day this image became fixed in people's
minds, never to be replaced. But Palamedes was the only
one of those beneath the walls of Troy who saw this truth
in all its starkness. That was why Odysseus hated him, that
was why he felt that this man was too close to himself for
comfort. His own intelligence needed solitude and distance
from others. He could not accept a complicity he hadn't
sought.

When the Achaeans needed to find Achilles to take him
to Troy, Odysseus immediately thought of the trick Palamedes had used to unmask him. He went to Scyros disguised
as a merchant and got himself taken to the women's quar-
ters. He had brought a crate of precious goods, and now he
laid them out on the floor. Immediately, girlish hands were
fingering the fabrics, searching among the jewelry. But there
was a shield and spear in the heap too. And a redhead
grabbed them at once, as if she'd spent her whole life sling-
ing such things over her shoulder. It was Achilles. Odysseus
knew then that he had won the war, using Palamedes' trick.
With Achilles on their side, Troy had already fallen. Now all
he had to do was take his revenge on Palamedes.

He mulled over it for years. And in the end he chose the

trick that was at once the most cowardly, the most sure to work, and the most philosophical. In unmasking Odysseus's fake madness, Palamedes had demonstrated the existence of a truth behind the simulation. A truth of gesture. Odysseus responded by demonstrating the opposite: that the truest of gestures could be judged a perfect pretense. He took a Trojan prisoner and gave him a forged letter, ostensibly from Priam, to take to Palamedes. The letter spoke of gold in return for an understanding between them. Then he killed the Trojan prisoner and contrived to have the letter discovered as if by chance. In the meantime he had hidden some gold under Palamedes' bed. When the letter was discovered and Palamedes declared himself innocent, Odysseus suggested people look under his bed. Upon which Palamedes was unanimously condemned by his companions, and they stoned him. Every one of the dice players threw a stone at him, and likewise the Achaean leaders, and Odysseus, and Agamemnon. The only thing Palamedes said before dying was that he mourned the passing of the truth, which had died before him. Those words were his answer to Odysseus. Palamedes' enemy had shown that a total agreement between the world and the mind could be falseness itself. All had been sincerely indignant in their condemnation of Palamedes. All had seen the gold under his bed. The lie was more consistent than the truth. Odysseus could feel alone again at last, in the rapturous gliding of his intelligence.

The ranks of the dead appeared to Odysseus in Hades as a throng of women. Their queen, Persephone, spurred them on. But how did she spur them on? What goad did she use to rouse them from their cold thickets, to assemble them before the black blood and before that man with the sword hanging from his powerful thigh? Those women had been the daughters and bedmates of the heroes. Some of them, of gods. They all wanted to drink the blood and talk at the same time. That throng of women is memory in its natural

state: all alike, all particles of the same cloud. The mind is
terrified by this cloud, which is always with it. And the
strength of the mind lies in the cleverness with which it
manages to separate those particles from one another and
then question them one by one.

Odysseus drew his sword and threatened them. The
women got into line. One by one they drank the blood and
spoke. Odysseus wanted to hear them all. He was hearing
knowledge in its primordial form: genealogy. One spoke of
the "amorous works" of Poseidon: she had been bathing in
the river when a wave rose above her high as a mountain.
Another spoke of a hanging. Another of precious gifts accepted in return for betrayal. Another of a hunt for some
elusive cows. And, as Odysseus listened, the intricate cobweb
of descendances settled over his mind: the Deucalionides,
the Inachides, the Asopides, the Atlantides, the Pelasgides.
Not all the threads came together again in that web. Some
became superimposed over each other, knotted together;
others made fragile shapes that turned in on themselves,
others trailed in the darkness, abandoned.

The age of Odysseus, the hybrid age of the heroes, was all
there in the intersecting of those names, those births, those
deeds. If he could have listened for time without end to all
those women's voices, one after another, he would have
known what no man knew: the course of history, the history
of an age that would die out with his death. But soon, or
perhaps after a very long time, Persephone dispersed her
throng of women in a squeaking of bats.

After the age of the heroes, the Greeks measured time by the
succession of priestesses in the sanctuary of Hera in Argos.
During the age of the heroes the passing of time took its
rhythm from the succession of divine rapes. The anonymous
author of the *Catalogue of Women* lists sixteen for the house
of the Deucalionides alone, and eight for the Inachides.
Whereas among the Pelasgides they were rare. In those races
where divine rape was frequent, so was contact, exchange,

and interbreeding with remote and fabulous lands. It was among these peoples that sea routes were opened, kingdoms rose and fell, dynasties migrated. In those races where divine rape was rare, events remained circumscribed and trapped, as the Pelasgides were trapped in the mountains of Arcadia.

È̱ hoíē: "Or like she who . . .": such was the recurrent formula in the *Catalogue of Women,* for centuries attributed to Hesiod, and then lost. Thus, time after time, the story of another woman in the catalogue would begin. Thus was each new link in the chain of generations opened, as though, for the Greeks, the only form in which the heroic past, from beginning to end, might be recorded was not that of a genealogy of kings but this linking together of scores of girls and their stories in monotonous and stupefying succession. In the end, the *Iliad* and the *Odyssey* recounted only a few days and a few years of the story, the last throes of the heroic age. While the age as a whole could only be told as a sequence of women's tales, as though turning page after page of a family album. For those learned genealogists whose supreme ambition it was to map out the tree of time through all its branches, the only frame that could contain the age of the heroes was there in those two words: *È̱ hoíē . . . ,* "Or like she who . . ."

Unlike the peoples of the ages that preceded them—the golden age, the silver age, the bronze age—the heroes had no metal upon which to model themselves and their world. Their physiological composition was hybrid but impalpable, because half of their being was made up of the substance of the gods. And their appearance marks a break in the order of descendances, which until now had merely degenerated from one metal to the next.

Quite suddenly, when the people of the bronze age, a race of muscled armed warriors, went under the earth again, leaving only silence behind, having killed one another off without the name or glory of even one of them surviving—

quite suddenly, Zeus had the fanciful idea of breaking the chain of peoples for a while and so allowed the gods to follow what was first and foremost his own example and couple with the daughters of men. It was a brief and dangerous attraction, out of which history was born. It was the age of the heroes. Only then did Names emerge that would outlive the race that bore them. Until one day, when Helen had just given birth to Hermione in Sparta, and with the other gods quarreling furiously round about him, Zeus began to think. And what he thought was that this breed must die out like the others. The time had come. The heroes, this parenthesis in the affairs of the world and the succession of metals, must be wiped out. The age of black iron was approaching, age of a people who would live in the memory of the heroes. Zeus thought, and round about him none of the rest of the Twelve realized what was happening. They had become so used to the heroes, so involved with them, they thought they would go on forever, as if it were quite normal for the Olympians to have these charming mobile toys down on earth, toys they quarreled over every day now.

The climate began to change. Camped in Aulis, the Greeks were astonished by unseasonal storms, endless, unremitting gales that prevented them from sailing. Like the gods, they didn't realize that these unusual storms marked the beginning of the end for their age. There were only a few years left now, just long enough to kill off all those who were setting out to fight on the plains of Troy. The events of those years would be told in detail as none had ever been told before, as if a huge lens had come down from the sky to magnify every tiny gesture. If time speeded up toward the end, the focus certainly broadened: in that last generation of the heroes, even the names of those who lived in the shadow of glory, the names of the cupbearers, the helmsmen, the serving maids, would be etched in the air for the first time.

Why did Zeus decide to wipe out the heroes? A thousand tribes trod the soil and, "seeing this, Zeus felt pity in the depths of his thoughts." So says the poet of the *Kypria*. But why did Zeus, who wasn't easily stirred to pity, feel concerned for the vast body of the earth, on which, when seen from on high, the race of heroes, however numerous, couldn't have looked very different from all the other clinging parasites?

The crime of the heroes, perhaps, lay not so much in their treading the earth but in their detaching themselves from it. The heroes were the first to look at the earth before them as an object. And seeing it as an object, they struck out at it. Their model was Apollo, who loosed his arrows at Python's scales, mottled as the slopes of Delphi were mottled with shrubs. He who strikes the snake strikes the earth on which it slithers and the water that springs from the earth. Now the heroes were imitating Apollo, and Apollo had imitated Zeus. Imitation is the most dangerous of activities for world order, because it tends to break down boundaries. Just as Plato wanted to banish the poets, whom he loved, from the city, Zeus wanted to see the heroes, whom he loved, wiped off the face of the earth. They had to go, before they began to tread that earth with the same heedlessness with which the Olympians had trodden it before them.

But Zeus didn't just want the heroes dead: "he forced the land of the Greeks and the hapless Phrygians to go to war so that Mother Earth might be lightened of the mass of mortals and so that the strongest of the Greeks might be made famous." Here Zeus's plan seems appalling. The extermination of a whole race turns out to be a necessary step in exalting the glory of a single person, Achilles—and this in a world that had still to discover what glory was, in the sense of a power that goes beyond the race. To bestow glory on a hero means to bestow it on all the heroes. It means to evoke glory itself, something unknown to the peoples of the golden, silver, and bronze ages. Glory is a pact with time. Thanks to the death of the heroes, men would win themselves a bond with time. The most arduous of bonds and metaphysically superior to all others. Zeus wanted the death of the heroes to be a new death. What had death meant until now? Being covered once again by the earth. But, with the heroes, death coincided with the evocation of glory. Glory was something you could breathe now. The men of the iron age would not be composed in body and mind as the heroes had been, but they moved in an air that was drenched with glory, as their predecessors had lived among the "mist-clad" *daímones*, the thirty thousand invisible "guardians of men" into whom the beings of the golden age had been transformed.

How did the heroes explain this plan of Zeus that condemned them to extinction? They didn't explain it, they submitted to it. But there were two people living among them who dared to posit the motives behind that plan: Helen and Alcinous. Just a few words, almost the same in each case. Speaking to Hector and having twice referred to herself as a "slut," Helen concludes: "Zeus has prepared a woeful destiny for us so that in the future we might be sung of by the bards." Alcinous, king of an intermediate realm, of a race of ferrymen who go back and forth more through time than on the water, catches Odysseus trying to hide his tears on hearing the story of the sack of Troy and says: "This is the work of the gods: they brought about the ruin of men so that others might have song in the future." Alcinous, like his people, loves parties, seafaring, and song. He loves "frequent changes of clothes, warm baths and beds." Nothing else. And his near-perfect, marginal world is at a good safe distance from all the others. Helen is the opposite: the center of the exterminating storm that swirls around her body. But does her body exist in the same way other bodies do? And what is going on in Helen's mind, that mind that nobody pays any attention to?

The immense scandal of Homer lies first and foremost in his allowing Helen to survive the fall of Troy. Telemachus reached Sparta to find Helen sitting beside Menelaus on an inlaid seat, her feet resting on a stool. She had a golden spindle in her hand and looked like Artemis. Many years before, another guest—Paris—had found her in the same pose. The only difference seemed to be this: that now there were stories to tell, stories that demanded to be told. Even before Helen came into the room, Menelaus had begun to talk to the two strangers about the long and tortuous return from Troy.

Helen had barely sat down, and already she was looking straight at Telemachus. She recognized him immediately: he must be Odysseus's son. A few moments later they were all crying, Helen included. They had been seized, all at the same time, by "the desire to sob." Each of them had his or her dead to mourn. And all those dead belonged to the same story, which had begun in that very room, when another stranger and guest had been shown hospitality and Paris had looked at Helen. The first to dry his tears was the young Peisistratus, offspring of the happy stock of Nestor, who was traveling with Telemachus. He hadn't been at Troy, but he had lost a beloved brother there. With the mollifying good nature typical of his family, he suggested that they postpone their tears till the following morning. Menelaus approved. And they went back to enjoying their party.

But let us leave the men for a moment and look into the mind of Helen, the most inscrutable of them all. A thought crossed that mind. She picked up a bowl for mixing wine and poured in a drug. It was opium, dried lymph of poppies grown from an earth rich with enchantments. Queen Polydamna had given it to her when she was in Egypt. Helen knew that the drug would prevent a person from crying for a whole day, even if "he were to see a brother or beloved son put to the sword before his very eyes." She waited for the men to drink the drugged wine. Then she invited them to abandon themselves to "the pleasure of talk" (*mýthois térpesthe*). And she decided to start the ball rolling herself. With something "suitable," she added. Odysseus, said Helen, loved to dress up as a beggar. And on one occasion he tried the trick on the streets of Troy. No one recognized him, except Helen. They had an argument because Odysseus didn't trust her. Then he decided to follow her. Helen washed Odysseus, dressed him again, and assured him he could count on her loyalty as a traitor. Upon which, Odysseus drew out a long blade and set about massacring Trojans. Later, when she heard the women mourning over the bleeding bodies, Helen exulted. Aphrodite's *átē*, that infatuation which had dominated her life, seemed to have subsided. "Her heart turned and longed for home."

That night, Odysseus managed to get hold of the Palladium in the temple of Athena. Helen knew, being herself a phantom, an idol, that the life of a city resides in an image and that, when the image deserts it, the city is lost. Helen had told the story to celebrate one of the many deeds of their young guest's father. Menelaus gave her a happy, misty look. He approved of the story, he told her, and called her "dear," as if they were having an evening together after a day's hunting and everybody were waiting his or her turn to recount some highlight of the day's doings.

But if it was stories about Odysseus they wanted, there were plenty of others. For example, Menelaus said, what the hero did the night Troy was sacked. When the Phaeacian court hard, Demodocus, evoked that night in verse, Odysseus hadn't been able to hold back his tears. And for Demodocus it was mere literature and recent history. But now Menelaus wanted to tell the story of that night, a story both he and Helen had been personally involved in. He told it so as to recall, before the hero's son, the great deeds of a lost friend.

The heroes were all crouched down in the smooth belly of the horse. Throughout the day, in the stale dark, with only a breath of air filtering down from an opening in the beast's mouth, they had heard a constant din of voices. The horse had been drawn right up to the walls of Troy, like a big toy on wheels. Then, heaving away, they had pulled it as far as the Acropolis. And meanwhile the argument went on and on. Some were for disemboweling it, some for burning it, some for guarding it as a sacred statue. Seen from the outside, the horse inspired feelings of "terror and beauty." Its mane was golden, its eyes flamed with beryl and amethyst. The Trojans wreathed the animal's neck with garlands of fresh flowers. On the ground before it they had laid a carpet of roses. Children screamed and shouted round about.

All of a sudden Cassandra's shrill voice rose above the others. She spoke of Athena, scourge of cities, and said the goddess had prepared this trick. She saw blood. She told the truth. But then they heard old Priam's voice, and he spoke of dances, of honey, of freedom. And he told his daughter to go away. Night fell, and hidden in the horse the warriors no longer heard the sound of voices arguing. Instead there was the hubbub of a party. Then the hubbub faded. The party was coming to an end. Shuffling footsteps, voices growing fainter. It was then that Helen arrived, escorted by Deiphobus, her new husband.

She stopped in front of the horse. Complete silence now. She went around it, slowly. Then, with her hand, she began to touch that belly packed with warriors. And all of a sudden, as Helen's hand slid over the wooden planks, knocking softly as though at a lover's door, they heard her voice. She was calling names. She called Menelaus, Diomedes, Odysseus, Anticlus. For each name she found a different voice. In the darkness, careful not to bang their shin guards together, some of the heroes began to get excited. There was a chorus of suffocated groans. It was the least appropriate time and place for nostalgia and desire. Yet Menelaus and Diomedes were on the point of getting to their feet. Anticlus couldn't help himself and opened his mouth to answer Helen's voice. But Odysseus stopped his mouth and tightened strong hands around his neck. Helen's voice went on calling names as Anticlus slowly expired, strangled. There was a last convulsion; then, moving carefully, the other heroes laid him down on the wood and stretched a blanket over him.

Menelaus fell silent, still absorbed in the pleasure of telling the story. Telemachus looked at him and said a few sober words. Yes, it was true, his father, Odysseus, had "a heart of iron." Yet he too had come to a wretched end, heaven knew where. It was time to go to bed, he said. They deserved "to enjoy their sweet sleep." Helen had already told the servants to prepare beds for the guests in the porch. Then she went off in her long tunic toward the rooms deep inside the house where Menelaus would lie down beside her.

Menelaus didn't tell Telemachus how that night in Troy had ended. When Helen had gone, the Acropolis was shrouded in a silence unbroken even by a dog's bark. The heroes got ready to swarm to the ground, "like bees from the trunk of an oak." Then the voiceless slaughter began in the Trojan bedrooms. Menelaus and Odysseus didn't even watch their backs. They rushed into Deiphobus's house. They found him on his bed, still warm from Helen's embrace. Menelaus was determined to perform a systematic mutilation on the man. He hacked off his hands and ears, split his temples, and cut his head in two along the line of the nose. Then he went deeper into the huge house. And at the back of the last room he found Helen. He advanced without a word, his sword, bespattered with blood and gore, pointing at her belly. Helen looked at him and bared her breast. Menelaus let his sword drop.

According to Stesichorus and Euripides, Helen was *a* phantom. According to Homer, Helen was *the* phantom, *eídōlon*. The Homeric vision is by far the more thorny and frightening. Dealing with a phantom while knowing that there is a reality to counter it doesn't involve the same kind of tension as dealing with a phantom and knowing that it is also a reality. Helen is as gold to other merchandise: gold too is merchandise, but of such a kind that it can represent all the others. The phantom, or image, is precisely that act of representation. While Troy burned, Menelaus found himself confronted by Helen's bared breast. He could have smothered it in blood, repeated what he had just done to Deiphobus. But how can one kill gold? Helen would have gone on breathing in some niche of her murderer's mind, and likewise in the minds of all the other warriors who had wanted to respond to the lure of her voice when they were shut up in the horse's belly. Helen was a reflection on water. How can you kill a reflection without killing the water? And how can you kill water? Menelaus didn't actually think any of this as he let his sword drop, but it was this that made him drop it.

Meanwhile, he was thinking of something completely different. He was thinking of Agamemnon. He was afraid his brother would take him for a coward or a weakling once again. So he decided to get smart, the way the others had. He gripped Helen's wrist and dragged her along as though to the slaughter. And at last Agamemnon turned up. Menelaus had to pretend to have his brother convince him not to kill Helen. Agamemnon unwittingly played the part he was supposed to. Words that had once been Priam's sprang to his lips: "Helen isn't the cause of this." Menelaus wasted no time agreeing. Now there was one last problem: the army of warriors. Once again, Menelaus decided he would have to present himself in the role of the avenging husband. He approached the Achaean camp holding Helen tightly by the wrist, his face grim. The crowd parted before them. They all had stones in their hands. They had chosen them carefully to stone Helen. Menelaus pressed on, dragging his faithless wife, and, as the warriors formed a semicircle around them, he heard the dull thud of stones falling thick and fast to the ground, already forgotten.

In the deep calm of the opium, Menelaus managed to recall, without so much as a quiver of resentment, how Helen had tried to the very last to bring ruin upon the Greeks. It was thanks to her that Anticlus had been strangled. But if Odysseus hadn't strangled him, if one of the heroes had answered her alluring voice, they might all have been burned alive in the belly of the horse. Or the Trojans would have thought up some other horrible death for them. Yet Menelaus recounted the episode, in front of Helen and their guests, as though it were an image of glory, to be savored with pleasure.

Twenty years later, Menelaus had understood a thing or two about the woman beside him. He no longer thought of punishing her, as he had for so many years and so obsessively fantasized. He was happy to have understood of her what amounted to no more than the hem of her tunic. And this, among other things, was what he had understood: that for Greeks and Trojans alike Helen had posed the danger of the phantom, the image. Living with the phantom is ruinous, but neither of the two sides had wanted to live without. It was over the phantom they had fought. And now the phantom went on threatening and enchanting life in Greece.

The night Troy was put to the torch, Helen had pushed the danger for both Greeks and Trojans to the limit, for this was of her essence. She insinuated her voice into the seething dark of the horse, shaking the soul of the Achaean warriors. Then, just a few moments later, while dancing on the Acropolis with the other Trojan women, she waved the torch that was to signal to the other Achaeans waiting on their ships that it was time to attack. Two incompatible actions, one right after the other. Helen performed them both with the same serenity. Those two actions were Helen. Never as on that night did Helen reveal herself so completely, a great, intoxicating moon radiating its light impartially on all.

What is the evil of exile? "One and terrible," claims Polynices: "not having freedom of speech [*parrēsía*]." And his mother, Iocasta, adds: "Not to say what one thinks is the way of the servant." Frankness, that first feature of the aristocratic ethic, becomes secularized with democracy into freedom of speech. Odysseus steered clear of both. He renounced the frankness of the warrior when he pretended to be crazy so as not to sail for Troy; he renounced freedom of speech when he played the part of the wandering beggar who could be told to shut up and sent packing by the merest servant.

Odysseus was the first to have mediation triumph over the immediate, postponement over presence, the twisted mind over straightforwardness. All the character traits that would be assigned over the centuries to the merchant, the foreigner, the Jew, the traveling player were coined by Odysseus in himself. He looked ahead to a human condition in which neither aristocratic frankness nor democratic freedom of speech would be enough. Many centuries later, that condition seems normal, but in Odysseus's time it was a foresight granted only to one who had traveled a great deal between earth and heaven. So, whereas Achilles and Agamemnon stand out in our memories as leftovers of another creation, consumed by catastrophe, Odysseus is still familiar to us, a sort of invisible companion. The presence he renounced in its immediacy is redeemed in the stream of memory and history. Achilles has to be evoked; Odysseus is already at our side, wherever we are, whatever the circumstances.

Throughout Odysseus's life, and above all during the long years of the voyage back from Troy, there was a constant whispered exchange between himself and Athena. Nothing happened to the hero without that whisper being part of it. Only once did it peter out altogether. Then Odysseus had to find his way back to another female voice, even more remote, a voice beyond which all voices fall silent. He was clutching the raft he'd built with his own hands on Calypso's island. Huge waves battered the mast. Naked, clinging to a few planks of wood, he might have been the first or last man on the waters of the flood. He couldn't hear Athena's voice. Then, looking up amid the whirling foam, he saw a white sea gull on the top of the mast, and in its beak it held a purple ribbon.

That ribbon, incongruous in the storm, reminded him of something. It was absurd trying to remember what, when at any moment a wave might submerge his raft forever. But Odysseus was determined he would remember. One day, in

Samothrace, when he had been initiated into the mysteries of the Cabiri, some nameless person had come up to him and tied a purple sash around his waist, the *krédemnon*. And that sash now seemed to be fluttering in the sea gull's beak. Odysseus realized that only a veil lay between him and death, and that veil was initiation. When everything is reduced to its most basic and is about to be swallowed up, there is still a ribbon fluttering in the dark.

Instead of protecting himself from the waves, Odysseus exposed himself by reaching out an arm to take the purple ribbon from the sea gull's beak. Then he tied it around his waist. He repeated the ritual of Samothrace, but this time the nameless person's hands were his own. For years that purple ribbon that saved Odysseus from shipwreck had been tied around the hair of Leucothea, the White Goddess. And before becoming the goddess who rises from the watery depths to rescue sailors, Leucothea had been a poor mad woman who drowned herself, throwing herself into the sea from a cliff, her infant child in her arms. At the time her name was Ino; she was one of the four daughters of Cadmus and wife of King Athamas. During her mother Harmony's lifetime, and perhaps partly because Harmony "knew of many crimes committed in the past by barbarians and Greeks," the most heterogeneous and remote elements had agreed to submit to the same yoke. Afterward, during the lifetime of her daughters, every unity was torn apart and dismembered, as if the gods had wanted to have everybody appreciate, and fast, that the harmonious yoke that binds disparate elements is the most precarious form of all.

Ino was the last of Cadmus's daughters to go crazy and kill. She had seen her mother reduced to ashes, had seen Agave cut her son Pentheus to pieces, had seen Autonoë pick up the remains of the stag that had been her son Actaeon, torn apart by Artemis's dogs. All these horrors had been reflected in Ino's eyes before being repeated one last time with herself when she plunged the little Melicertes into a caldron of boiling water, while her other son, Learchus, was run through by his father, Athamas. Yet this princess who committed suicide was saved, and became herself a savior. Why? She had shown kindness to the orphaned Dionysus; she had disguised him as a little girl in her palace; she had given him her white breast just as she did to her own son Melicertes; she had hidden him in a dark room wrapped in a purple veil while Mystis the serving maid gave him his first taste of the sound of the cymbals and tambourines and offered him his mystical objects as toys. But it wasn't only Dionysus who remembered Ino. Aphrodite remembered her too. *"Spuma fui,"* "I was foam myself," the goddess said to Poseidon, encouraging him to accept Ino among the divinities of the sea. That foam was the ribbon in Leucothea's hair; it was the veil around the hips of the initiates in Samothrace; it was the slow upward spreading of the light as the hidden is made plain in the dawn; it was the whiteness of appearance itself and the sovereign purple of blood; it was the only veil that is laid over the shipwreck.

The veil, or something that encloses, that wraps around, or belts on, a ribbon, a sash, a band, is the last object we meet in Greece. Beyond the veil, there is no other thing. The veil is the other. It tells us that the existing world, alone, cannot hold, that at the very least it needs to be continually covered and discovered, to appear and to disappear. That which is accomplished, be it initiation, or marriage, or sacrifice, requires a veil, precisely because that which is accomplished is perfect, and the perfect stands for everything, and everything includes the veil, that surplus which is the fragrance of things.

No one was ever lonelier than Calypso. From the mouth of her cave she watched the violet waves, knowing that none of the other gods was interested in her. Behind her she heard the whirlpool bubbling deep underground, throwing water up to the surface in four directions. Divine hostess, time denied her any guests. But why was the sea around her so empty, why didn't the smoke of sacrifices rise to her from the lands of the earth? Calypso's distance from the world wasn't only to be measured across the huge expanse of the waters but first and foremost across time. Like her father, Atlas, "who knows all the depths of the sea" and watches over the great columns that separate earth and sky, Calypso lived at a point of cosmic intersection: Ogygia was a primordial island, not to be confused with any other, just as the water of the Styx, which dissolved any and every material and frightened even the Olympians, was not to be confused with any other water. But no one paid any attention to these places. They were orphans of a lost era, of the usurped realm of Kronos. These days the gods sat on a mountain and sparkled in the light.

Calypso means "She Who Conceals Things." Concealment was her passion, cloaking something in a veil, like the veils she sometimes wore around her head. But she was given nothing to conceal, apart from the constant mingling of the heavenly and earthly waters beneath her cave, a dull roar she could perfectly well distinguish from that of the sea before her. As a little girl she had played on flowery meadows with Persephone and other Nymphs. Now the only beings she ever saw were the two maids who served her and the birds perched on the dark trees around her cave. Toward Calypso, Odysseus felt the same attraction Gilgamesh had felt for the barmaid Siduri, for the woman who pours drinks behind a counter and talks, listens. What did that attraction conceal? Odysseus knew what would later be forgotten: it concealed the woman who welcomes us at the entrance to the kingdom of the dead.

In that world between worlds, suspended, the only place one might delude oneself, one was beyond life and beyond death, one drinks and plays dice. The conversation with the woman who pours the drinks goes on and on through an endless night, unthreatened by any dawn on the windowpanes. After Odysseus, men would forget: but they still felt an obscure attraction to hostesses, barmaids, as if every counter where drinks are poured were the threshold to another world.

Odysseus spent seven years with Calypso, long enough for

many of his subjects to decide to consider him lost. They were years when time sucked him backward into a fabulous prison that was also a floating sepulcher. If he looked at the ground he saw violets and lovage, plants usually strewn about the dead. If he raised his eyes he saw alders, cypresses, black poplars, willows: the trees of the dead. And everything had a primordial beauty that left even the gods amazed. Talking to Achilles in Hades, Odysseus had come up against the horror of death. Now, all around him, he found another death, one that presented itself in the uncertain guise of a better life but was in fact a static wallowing in time. For Odysseus knew that there was no better life. Like the Elysian Fields and the garden of the Hesperides, Ogygia was a place to acquire knowledge but not a place where you could live. Day after day, crouching on the beach, Odysseus told Calypso about the Trojan War. With a stick, he drew the positions of the camps and the armies in the sand. Every time he spoke, he changed the story or the way he told it. Calypso sat next to him, silent, concentrating. Then a wave bigger than the others would erase the lines in the sand. Once Calypso said to him: "You see, that's what the sea does. And you want to trust your life to the sea?" After that Odysseus didn't go to the beach with her anymore. Now he sat alone, on a rock, the most exposed rock of all, and wept. At sundown he returned to the cave as if after a day's work. And every evening it was the same. Sitting on his golden stool, Odysseus would reach across the table for his human food. It had been placed next to the ambrosia and red nectar Calypso ate as she sat opposite, watching him. Every evening for seven years Calypso hoped Odysseus would try her food. Then he would become immortal, ageless, a semigod lost at the boundaries of the world. But Odysseus never touched it. Later they would twine their bodies together in the bed at the back of the cave, and on those nights Calypso would feel she was truly alive, because she was concealing Odysseus between her big body and the bedclothes. The rest of the time she was oppressed by melancholy and doubt, as if her life were no more real than the names of the warriors Odysseus spoke of, names that had now become familiar, impalpable presences for her.

When Calypso told him she was going to let him leave, Odysseus suspected her words might conceal some other trick to trap him there, "some other evil." They were enemies fighting it out to the last with their respective weapons, in silence and without witnesses. Feeling a stab of tenderness, Calypso called Odysseus *alitrós*, "rascal," and "she caressed him with her hand." Odysseus would never hear another woman use a word at once so intimate and so accurate.

A cousin of Helen, Penelope was given as a bride to the swift, sturdy suitor who had raced faster than all the others, Odysseus. Her father, Icarius, wasn't happy with the marriage. He followed the couple and stopped them when they were already some distance from Sparta. But Penelope stood her ground. She was a stubborn duck.

Years later, when Odysseus was still fighting beneath the walls of Troy, somebody arrived claiming he was dead. Penelope in desperation threw herself into the sea, but a flock of ducks followed her beneath the water and pulled her up, gripping her sodden clothes in their beaks.

Pan, the wildest and most bestial of the gods, Pan the masturbator, the terrorizer, chose as his mother the woman who for centuries people would point to as an example of chastity and faithfulness: Penelope. There are two versions of the story of Pan's birth. Some claimed that when Odysseus got back to Ithaca he found "his house infested from top to bottom by lecherous thieves of women." In the middle of them was Penelope, "the Bassarid, the whorish fox, who majestically keeps her brothel and empties all the rooms of their riches, pouring away the wretched man's wealth in her banquets." The wretched man was her husband, Odysseus. So the hero threw her out. She'd have to go back to the father she had once been happy to leave, clinging to her spouse. Thus it was that Penelope saw the Spartan plain again and the mountains that encircled it. On the highlands of Mantinea she made love with Hermes. And, after giving birth to Pan, she died. Pan has run about playing his pipes on the crags of Arcadia ever since.

Others said that, when Odysseus got back to Ithaca, Penelope had already let all one hundred and eight suitors have their way with her. And they were the fathers of Pan. Odysseus's footsteps echoed in the desolate corridors of the palace, as the suitors lay drenched in blood and Penelope slept on. He opened the door to a room he didn't remember being there. It was completely empty. In the darkness a child with a sly look on his face was watching him. Two delicate horns sprouted from his curls, and his feet were like a goat's. Two shiny hooves poked out from the hare's pelt the baby Pan was wrapped in. Odysseus immediately closed the door. Without saying a word, he went down to the harbor and once again set sail from Ithaca. He didn't know where to, and this time he was alone.

The suitors' bodies made a carpet of flesh, blood, gore, and dust. Outside the palace hall, in the courtyard, the twelve unfaithful serving maids swung in the wind, hanged. Everything else was still, save for the jaws of the dogs fighting over Melanthius's testicles and penis.

Penelope slept on. Her sleep this morning was the sweetest she'd had in twenty years. She sank into irresponsible pleasure, let a weight force itself down on her eyelids, while from behind the door and through the thick walls came the thud of falling bodies and the high-pitched twang of the bow. When Eurycleia woke her, saying that Odysseus had come back and killed the suitors, Penelope was scornful of the old woman's excitement and dishevelment. For Penelope immediacy was an evil. All her life had been a shrewd avoidance of immediacy. And just as her husband, Odysseus, used to lower his eyes so he could think, his face hidden from all around him, so Penelope, on coming down the big stairway, would lift her tunic up over her cheeks so as to give nothing away in her expression. But now she must go down there again, to greet—they said—the newly returned Odysseus.

The hall was empty and smelled of sulfur. The men had been using sulfur and fire to try to hide the stench of slaughtered flesh. Penelope and Odysseus found themselves sitting down face to face in the glow of the fire. Once again Odysseus lowered his eyes. Penelope's gaze ran over him feature by feature. In that moment of mute tension they were at once close and hostile as never before. They were two "hearts of iron," two beings walled up behind the defenses of the mind, occasionally using the weapons of strength and beauty but then immediately withdrawing to their invisible fortresses. Long used to the solitary life, they were reluctant to recognize someone with whom to share their own monologues. Penelope is described as *períphrōn, echéphrōn*; Odysseus as *polýmētis*—all words that suggest the supremacy of mind: as artificer of a shrewd control, in Penelope's case, of constant and complex invention in Odysseus's. More than the complicity of the flesh, they shared the complicity of intelligence. But intelligence is isolated and distrustful; thus, before recognizing each other, they clashed.

Their son Telemachus couldn't understand this. He was angry with his mother for being so cold. Penelope answered that she would only feel able to recognize Odysseus if he gave her one of the "signs that only they knew about." Upon which, a small smile crossed Odysseus's face. Yes, Penelope too wanted to "put him to the test." That, in the end, was the one constant in his life. Even Athena, the goddess who protected him, had allowed the suitors to insult him so that "sorrow might bite even deeper into the heart of Odysseus, son of Laertes." And right to the end, when the battle with the suitors had already begun and in the form of a swallow the goddess was perched on a beam to watch the massacre, even then she had chosen to "put his strength and courage to the test." One after another, favors and desertions formed an unending series of ups and downs in his life, the only link between the two being Odysseus's capacity to endure both good fortune and bad. Every good and bad fortune is a test: the sovereignty of the mind lies in recognizing them, in dealing with them as such, in getting through them with the secretly indifferent curiosity of the traveler.

Odysseus rose from his seat and began to give out orders. It was as though the clock had been turned back twenty years. Still Penelope said nothing. Odysseus had his servants wash him and rub him with oil. Athena appeared to him again, "pouring down grace on his head and chest." And now Penelope recognized him. But, before letting her knees go weak, she wanted to wring at least one of their secret signs out of him. With an authoritative tone to her voice, she ordered Eurycleia to move Odysseus's bed. And just this once Odysseus rose to the bait. No one could move his bed, he said, unless they chopped it in two first. He had made it with his own hands from a huge olive trunk. The bedroom had been built around the trunk.

It was the sign Penelope was waiting for. And now she let her knees give and, embracing Odysseus, wept. Odysseus wept too, for a long time. When he started talking again, he said nothing of the house and the woman he had come back to. He spoke of tests again, of one last test that loomed in the future. "Woman, we haven't reached the end of our trials; a great, hazardous, and extraordinary task still awaits me, and I will have to see it through." Odysseus's first words to Penelope after she recognized him thus looked forward to a new test and a new desertion. But tests were also their secret language. What separated them in life brought them together in the mind. Penelope was already prepared to look to the future again. She asked for details about this trial. Odysseus spoke of new wanderings, of having to travel from city to city until he reached, alone as ever, the people "who know nothing of the sea." Penelope merely said in her sober way: "If the gods plan to grant you a better old age, then you may hope that there will be a way out of your troubles." Eurynome came forward with a torch and led them off to their bed with its mighty roots.

XII

ZEUS IS NEVER RIDICULOUS, BECAUSE HIS dignity is of no concern to him. *"Non bene conveniunt nec in una sede morantur / Maiestas et amor,"* says Ovid, master of matters erotic. To seduce a woman with a bundle of lightning bolts in one's hand would be injudicious, and not even very exciting. But a white bull, an eagle, a swan, a false satyr, a stallion, a stream of gold, a blaze of fire: these are divine. Only when he assumes these forms does Zeus manage to "leave aside his very being Zeus." Thus when the god came down from Olympus to seduce some mortal woman, the lightning was left behind, forgotten. Zeus preferred to be unarmed when he exposed himself to the amorous gadfly that tormented and aroused him just as it did the lowliest of his subjects. Eros is the helplessness of that which is sovereign: it is strength abandoning itself to something elusive, something that stings.

Zeus was seducing the Nymph Pluto when Ge, avenger of all the victims of the Olympian age, nodded to her son Typhon, as one assassin giving the go-ahead to another. A huge body stretched across heaven and earth: an arm, one of the two hundred attached to that body, reached out to Olympus, the fingers searching behind a rock from which rose rags of smoke. Typhon's hand closed around Zeus's bundle of thunderbolts. The sovereign god had lost his weapon. Olympus was terror-struck. The gods fled like a stampeding herd.

They shed the human forms that made them too recognizable and unique. Trembling, they camouflaged themselves
beneath animal skins: ibis, jackals, dogs. And they flew toward Egypt, where they would be able to blend in among
the hundreds and thousands of other ibis, jackals, and dogs,
the motionless, painted guardians of tombs and temples.

Europa's fine hair was still shrinking to a speck that
would lose itself in the wide expanse of sea when King Age-
nor called together his sons Cilix, Phoenix, Cepheus, Thasus,
and Cadmus. He commanded them to go and find their sister. They were to never show their faces in Sidon again unless they had Europa with them. The sons had already
traveled for years with their father through Egypt, Assyria,
and Phoenicia. Now they had to set out again, and this time
alone. Thus began the long wanderings of Cadmus. His
brothers set out too but were soon distracted from the quest
that had driven them from their home. Cadmus thought of
the bull, the bull "that no mortal can find."

Still wandering about in search of his sister, he reached
the Cilician mountains. He was walking through dense
woodland when a flock of birds flew over his head with a
convulsed whirring of wings, heading south. Cadmus sensed
a sudden emptiness above and beneath him. He didn't know
that that flock of birds were the Olympians, fleeing to Egypt.
Olympus was uninhabited now, a museum in the night. And
in a cave a few yards from Cadmus, although he hadn't
found the place yet, lay Zeus, helpless. Wrapping himself
around the god's body, Typhon had managed to wrench his
adamantine sickle from him and had cut through the sinews
of his hands and feet. Now, drawn out from his body, Zeus's
sinews formed a bundle of dark, shiny stalks, not unlike the
bundle of lightning bolts that lay beside them, although
these were bright and smoking. Zeus's body could just be
glimpsed through the shadows, an abandoned sack. Wrapped
in a bearskin, his sinews were being guarded by Delphine,
half girl, half snake. And out from the cave drifted the
breath of Typhon's many mouths, Typhon with his hundred
animal heads and the thousands of snakes that framed

them. The Olympians were routed. Already nature was slowly degenerating. And the only witness to the scene was that traveler lost in the woods dressed as a shepherd.

Cadmus felt a loneliness no one had ever felt before. Nature's soul was fading, order gasped its death rattle, destiny shrank to a single point, in that wood, before the mouth of that cave, where a Phoenician prince was about to take on a primordial and evil creature, Typhon. Cadmus had no weapons, bar the invisible resources of his mind. He remembered how in his childhood, when he used to follow his father on his travels, the priests of the Egyptian temples had squeezed into his mouth "the ineffable milk of books." And he remembered the most intense joy he had ever known: one day Apollo had revealed to him, and him alone, "the just music." What was the *just music?* No one else would ever know, but Cadmus decided to play it to the monster now, a last voice from the deserted world of the gods. Hiding in a thicket of trees, he played his pipes. The notes penetrated Typhon's cave, rousing him from his happy torpor. Then Cadmus saw some of Typhon's arms slithering toward him. Head after head rose before him, until the only human one among them spoke to him in a friendly voice. Typhon invited Cadmus to compete with him: pipes versus thunder. He spoke like a bandit in need of company who grabs at the first chance to show off his power. With the bluster of the braggart, he promised him marvelous things, although in this particular moment that braggart really was the sole master of the cosmos. And, as he spoke, he was struggling to imitate Zeus, who he had long observed with resentment. He told Cadmus he would take him up to Olympus. He would grant him Athena's body, untouched. And if he didn't like Athena he could have Artemis, or Aphrodite, or Hebe. Only Hera was out of bounds, because she belonged to him, the new sovereign. Never had anyone been at once so ridiculous and so powerful.

Cadmus contrived to look serious and respectful, but not frightened. He said it was pointless him trying to compete with his pipes. But with a lyre, maybe. He made up a story of his once having competed with Apollo. And said that, to save his son the embarrassment of being beaten, Zeus had burned his strings to ashes. If only he had some good, tough sinews to make himself a new instrument! With the music of his lyre, Cadmus said, he would be able to stop the planets in their courses and enchant the wild beasts. These words convinced the ingenuous monster, who enjoyed conversation only when it centered on power, immense power, the one thing he was interested in. He agreed. His many heads went back into the cave and then emerged again. In one hand he was holding the shining bundle of Zeus's sinews. He handed them to Cadmus. He said they were a gift for his guest. He thought this was how sovereigns behaved. Cadmus began to finger the divine sinews like a craftsman examining his materials before getting down to work. Then he went off to build his instrument. He hid Zeus's sinews beneath a rock. Then he pressed on into the thicket and, skillfully sweetening the tone of his pipes, began to play a tune.

Typhon strained hundreds of ears to listen. He heard the tune and didn't understand it. But harmony was working on him. Cadmus told him he had invented the composition to celebrate the flight of the gods from Olympus. Typhon wallowed in self-gratification. The music pricked him with its sweet goad. He ventured outside the cave to hear it better. For the first time he felt he understood how Zeus must feel when his eye settled on the breast and hips of a woman about to yield to him. That sensation had always been obscure and impenetrable to Typhon. But now he must learn all about it, if he was to take Zeus's place. Typhon was immersed in the music, every one of his hundred heads distracted. Zeus took advantage of the situation to sneak out of the cave. Dragging himself across the ground with great effort, he found his sinews behind the rock. A few moments later the bundle of lightning bolts was back in his hand. He had seen the smoke rising from them in the darkness. When Typhon roused himself and went back to the cave, he found it empty.

.   .   .

Before Cadmus embarked on his musical competition with Typhon, Zeus appeared to him in the shape of a bull. He was full of anguish, fearing defeat and ridicule. He was afraid the cosmos might break its sudden silence with a roar of mocking laughter from his old father, Kronos. And he was afraid that "Hellas, mother of myths," might rearrange all her fables, transferring to Typhon all those gratifying epithets of sovereignty that he himself had enjoyed until now. So it was that the bull, like Typhon, solemnly promised Cadmus a woman, and something else as well: he would sleep with Harmony and be "savior of the cosmic harmony."

Thus, when Cadmus had tricked Typhon and when Zeus, thanks to the thunderbolts he'd retrieved, had hurled the monster into the depths below Etna, the Phoenician traveler set out once more, except that now he was looking not for one woman but two: Europa and Harmony. Winter was nearing an end, and Orion was rising. Cadmus came down from the Taurus Mountains, following the swift streams of Cilicia, banks bright with saffron. And he took to the sea again. Zeus's "prophetic breezes" blew him along. He didn't know where, only that he was going toward Harmony. Cadmus's sailors lay down to sleep on the beach in Samothrace. The waters were still beneath a windless calm that seemed as though it would last forever.

Toward dawn, Cadmus was awakened by strange sounds. The resonant skins of drums, measured steps, the rustling of oaks, voices behind the leaves. He left the coast behind him, heading inland. Approaching the city, he came across some washerwomen treading their dirty laundry in the water and singing. Cadmus watched, intrigued, amused, as if in no hurry to arrive in the town. But he was already wandering through the narrow streets now, and came out in front of the palace. It looked new, sparkling, smothered with decorations. Doorways featuring historical scenes, pale stuccos, a dome, palms, and hyacinths. In the middle of the garden was a fountain surrounded by gold and silver statues of young men and women. And statues of dogs: except that, as Cadmus approached, these dogs spoke with the voices of automatons and wagged their tails. Struck by his beauty and the expression in his eyes, Haematius, king of the city, welcomed Cadmus as a guest.

At the end of the banquet, Cadmus told, as all visitors must, his story. The opening words were not very different from those Odysseus would one day use in the court of King Alcinous. Then he went back over his intricate genealogy, beginning with Io, the cow who wandered from sea to sea, and ending with the bull that rose from the sea to carry off his sister, Europa. "It is on her account, traveling without cease, that I have arrived thus far." As he spoke these words, Cadmus knew he was leaving out the most important thing. That while looking for his abducted sister, he had in fact come to Samothrace to win another girl, who was now listening to him in suspicious silence.

At the end of the banquet, the queen mother, Electra, who had been sitting next to the foreign guest, saw a young man with curly hair hanging down over his cheeks coming to speak to her. It was Hermes. The god took the queen to one side and explained that Zeus, her first lover, was ordering her to grant her daughter Harmony to the foreigner. And for once Hermes assumed a solemn tone: "This man defended your lover in his moment of grief, this man ushered in the day of liberation for Olympus."

Electra reflected: she remembered her childhood with her six sisters, the Pleiades. Zeus had seduced her young. Haematius was born. One day, while she was still nursing him, Aphrodite had appeared, bringing a baby girl in her arms. That was when Electra first saw Harmony, love child of Aphrodite and Ares. The girl's mother had smuggled her out of Olympus and wanted to entrust her to Electra. Electra pressed Harmony's mouth to her breast and from that moment on treated her as if she were her own daughter. But just as she had quite suddenly appeared one day, so one day this "maiden descended from heaven" was destined to disappear.

It wasn't easy to get Harmony to agree. Locked in her girlhood bedroom, she wept tears of rage, touching all the things that were dear to her and that she didn't want to leave behind. Why had her mother decided to give her to this stranger who told tall tales and had nothing to offer but the tackle of his ship? He was a drifter, a fugitive, a sailor, a man with neither hearth nor home. It wasn't Electra who finally convinced Harmony but the girl's friend Peisinoe. She came and shut herself in Harmony's room with her. She wanted to confess, she had this sensation of emptiness just above her stomach, of burning, and she couldn't stop thinking of the handsome stranger. With a little girl's infatuation, she described Cadmus's body, fantasized his hand boldly touching her round breasts, fantasized herself uncovering the nape of his neck. Harmony listened and realized that something was changing inside her: she was falling in love with her friend's desire, and at the same time she went on looking around in desperation, because she knew that, if once she left, she would never see this room again.

For the first time she felt pricked by a goad that would not leave her be. In her mind she began to say words of farewell. She said good-bye to the caves of the Cabiri and the shrill voices of the Corybants, she said good-bye to the palace she had grown up in and the rugged coasts of Samothrace. And all at once she understood what myth is, understood that myth is the precedent behind every action, its invisible, ever-present lining. She need not fear the uncertain life opening up before her. Whichever way her wandering husband went, the encircling sash of myth would wrap around the young Harmony. For every step, the footprint was already there. And Harmony was surprised to find herself saying these words: "I'll follow this boy, invoking the marriages of the gods as I go. If my lover leads me across the sea to the East, I'll celebrate the desire of Eos for Orion, and I'll remember the nuptial beds of Cephalus; if I go toward the misty West, my comfort will be Selene, who suffered likewise for Endymion on Latmon." When she went back to meet the others in the halls of the palace, Harmony had a feverish look in her eye. She ran her fingers along the doorposts, embraced the maids, then went back to her room and stroked the bed, the walls. She picked up a handful of earth and raised it to her lips.

It was time to go. Cadmus and Harmony stood at the prow, like a double figurehead, exposed to the wind that lifted and mingled their hair. Around them were a swarm of passengers they didn't know, merchants for the most part, paying their way from the coasts of Asia to Greece. All of them looked on the two youngsters, dreamily facing out to sea, as just two more fellow travelers, the sort you meet on a journey and never see again. But such was the halo of beauty around them that the others could not help but see it as a good omen for the crossing.

Many days would pass, and Cadmus and Harmony would have to survive many an adventure before they could celebrate their marriage. At the head of a crowd of wayfarers, carts piled with belongings, they arrived in Delphi. And there Cadmus heard the Pythia pronounce the words that were to decide the course of his life: "In vain, Cadmus, do you plant your wandering footsteps far and wide; you seek a bull never born to any cow; you seek a bull no mortal can find. Forget Assyria; take an earthly heifer as your guide and follow it; do not seek the Olympian bull. No herdsman could lead Europa's spouse; he treads neither pastureland nor meadow, nor is there any goad that he obeys. That bull has chosen the tender bonds of Aphrodite, not the yoke and the plow. To Eros only does he bow his neck, not to Demeter. Put your longing for Tyre and for your father behind you. Settle in a foreign land and found a city that will bear the name of your homeland, Thebes of Egypt. Found it in the place where the heifer, by divine inspiration, falls to the ground, stretching out her weary hooves."

The heifer's fetlocks buckled under her in the valley of Tanagra. Immediately Cadmus began looking for a spring to purify himself before sacrificing the heifer. He found one. But, coiled around the crystalline water, the huge snake of Ares was waiting for him. Many of Cadmus's companions would have their bones crushed in the snake's coils before the hero was able to attack it. He could already feel his legs being trapped in the monster's grip when Athena came to spur him on with some rousing words. Then the goddess disappeared, leaving the print of her heel in the air. Cadmus felt a new strength fill his breast: he lifted a rock and smashed it down on the snake's head. Then he pulled out the sacrificial knife that hung at his thigh and buried it in the beast. His companions watched as he turned the knife around the snake's head with the deftness of a practiced butcher. Finally he managed to cut the head off and raise it in the air, while the snake's coils went on writhing in the dust.

Now Cadmus must found his city. In the center he would put Harmony's bed. And around it, everything would be modeled on the geometry of the heavens. Iron bit into soil, the reference points were calculated. Stones of different colors, like the signatures of the planets, were taken from the mountains of Cithaeron, Helicon, and Teumesus, and arranged in piles. The seven gates of the city were laid out to correspond to the seven heavens, and each one was dedicated to a god. Cadmus looked on his finished city as though it were a new toy and decided that their wedding could now go ahead.

The many halls of the palace of Thebes were filled with an incessant chatter, a rustle of light feet, melodious meetings and greetings. All the gods had come down from Olympus for the marriage of Cadmus and Harmony. They wandered through the rooms, busy and talkative. Aphrodite took care of the decorations for the marriage bed. Inane and jolly, Ares unbuckled his weapons and tried out a dance step or two. The Muses offered the full range of song. Amusing herself playing maid, Nike's wings brushed against those of the darting Eros.

Finally the bridal pair arrived, standing straight as stat-

ues on a chariot drawn by a lion and a boar. Apollo played
the cithara beside the chariot. No one was surprised to see
those unusual animals: wasn't that what Harmony meant,
yoking together the opposite and the wild? As dusk fell,
thousands of torches flared. Zeus walked the streets of
Thebes. He liked the town. It reminded him of the heavens.
It was like a dance floor. They all got together for the banquet, on seats of gold. Zeus and Cadmus laid their hands
on the same table, sat next to each other, poured out wine
for each other. Zeus looked at Cadmus with the eyes of a
friend who has kept a secret promise. When the Dragon
flickered in the sky, the moment had come to accompany
the bride to her bed. And now the Olympians stood in line
to offer their gifts. The most mysterious, and the grandest,
was Zeus's. He gave Cadmus "all perfection." What did that
mean? Cadmus bowed his head in gratitude.

Aphrodite came up to her daughter Harmony and fas-
tened a fated necklace around her neck. Was it the wonderful necklace Hephaestus had wrought to celebrate the
birth of Eros, the archer? Or was it the necklace Zeus had
given to Europa, when he laid her down beneath a plane
tree in Crete? Harmony blushed, right down to her neck,
while her skin thrilled under the cold weight of the necklace.
It was a snake shot through with stars, a snake with two
heads, one at each end, and the heads had their throats wide
open, facing each other. Yet the two mouths could never bite
each other, for between them, and caught between their
teeth, rose two golden eagles with their wings outspread.
Slipped into the double throat of the snake, they functioned
as a clasp. The stones radiated desire. They were snake,
eagle, and star, but they were the sea too, and the light of
the stones trembled in the air, as though upon waves. In that
necklace cosmos and ornament for once came together.

Among the guests was Iasion, Harmony's brother, who
had hurried over from Samothrace. Demeter glimpsed him
through the crowd during the preparations for the feast and
immediately desired him with that vehement passion of hers
the Olympians knew so well. Everybody was milling toward
the marriage chamber now. Looking around, Zeus realized

that Demeter and Iasion had disappeared. He went out into the night. The din of the party faded in the distance. He crossed the threshold of one of the city's seven gates. Now the empty fields were all around, dark against the glow of the torches and the palace behind. In a deep furrow in the black soil, he saw two bodies tight together, furiously clasping each other and mixing with the earth. He recognized Iasion and Demeter's cry.

After that remote time when gods and men had been on familiar terms, to invite the gods to one's house became the most dangerous thing one could do, a source of wrongs and curses, a sign of the now irretrievable malaise in relations between heaven and earth. At the marriage of Cadmus and Harmony, Aphrodite gives the bride a necklace which, passing from hand to hand, will generate one disaster after another right up the massacre of the Epigoni beneath the walls of Thebes, and beyond. At the marriage of Peleus and Thetis, failure to invite Eris leads to the Judgment of Paris in favor of Aphrodite and against Hera and Athena, and thus creates the premise for the Trojan War. Lycaon's banquet, where human and animal flesh are served together, brings about the Flood. Tantalus's banquet, where little Pelops is boiled in the pot, marks the beginning of a chain of crimes that will go on tangling together ever more perversely right up to the day when Athena casts the vote that acquits the fugitive Orestes.

What conclusions can we draw? To invite the gods ruins our relationship with them but sets history in motion. A life in which the gods are not invited isn't worth living. It will be quieter, but there won't be any stories. And you could suppose that these dangerous invitations were in fact contrived by the gods themselves, because the gods get bored with men who have no stories.

The gods didn't realize, nor did men, that that wedding feast in Thebes was the closest they would ever get to each other.

The next morning, the Olympians had left the palace. Cadmus and Harmony woke up in the bed Aphrodite had made for them. Now they were just a king and queen.

They had four daughters: Autonoë, Ino, Agave, and Semele. Cadmus's hair had turned white and woolly on his bony head when one day, years later, he stopped in front of his daughter Semele's tomb immediately outside the palace. It was an area of rubble with thin plumes of smoke rising from the place where Semele's bed had been when Zeus came to make love to her. Vine shoots twisted around the crumbling stones. In that scene of devastation and luxuriance, Cadmus saw the image of his life. The plume of smoke was the sign Zeus's thunderbolt had left, the thunderbolt Zeus had recovered from Typhon's cave thanks exclusively to Cadmus. But Cadmus couldn't tell anyone about that. That story of long ago was sealed up inside him. It would hardly have seemed proper that Zeus had once been saved from defeat by the merest Phoenician traveler. And it would have been even less proper to have spoken of the sinews stolen from Zeus's body. No one would ever know anything about it. Cadmus went on looking at Semele's tomb. The broken columns were covered by a thin layer of ash. Who could guess what part of Semele's tender body had been transformed into that gray dust—Semele, the youngest, the most beautiful of his daughters, envied from birth by the others, although they too were very beautiful. Just as Europa had disappeared across the water, so Semele had vanished in the flames. Zeus, always Zeus, the encircling one. But that was another story that couldn't be told. Cadmus's other daughters, who hated their sister passionately, said she had coupled shamelessly with a stranger and then begun to tell lies about Zeus having come to her bed. Semele's sisters were happy she had been reduced to a handful of ashes. And Cadmus couldn't even mourn her, or adore her as mother of a new and ancient god, the god who announced his presence in the vine shoots twisting among the broken stones and who was, in the end, his grandson: Dionysus.

Cadmus went on staring at Semele's tomb. The tempest

of calamities wasn't over yet. When he had married the young Harmony, the opposite extremes of the world had come together in visible accord for one last time. Immediately afterward they had separated, torn apart. Semele was reduced to ashes; all her sisters, at some point of their lives, were either cut to pieces or cut someone else to pieces. Nobody ever inflicted or endured laceration as much as Harmony's daughters. Actaeon, Autonoë's son, was torn to pieces by Artemis's dogs. Learchus, Ino's son, was run through by the spit of her father, Athamas. And time held still other lacerations in store. Cadmus was no longer king of Thebes. He had given up his throne to his grandson Pentheus, Agave's child. And this grandson of his, who looked on him as a more or less good-for-nothing old man, had chosen to quarrel with Dionysus, the new god, of whom he knew nothing and understood less. Cadmus was obliged to play the part of the rather undignified old man who lifts his thin legs in a dance with the thyrsus. Pentheus watched him with scorn. Pentheus thought he was the city. He refused to remember how Thebes had been nothing more than a hillside of wild grass before Cadmus sunk his plow into the earth. One old man leaning on another, Cadmus and Tiresias set off for the mountains where the delirious Maenads lived. Lost among them, unrecognizable amid those sleeping or ecstatic bodies, were the three princesses: Autonoë, Ino, Agave. Step by wary step, Cadmus and Tiresias climbed on into the woods. They knew that one does not quarrel with a god.

Cadmus was back in Thebes in time to pick up the shreds of Pentheus's body, torn to pieces on the mountains by his mother's own hands. He called his old wife, Harmony, and told her to get ready to leave, one last time. He had been a wanderer when she met him, and as wanderers they would end their days. Shortly afterward, Dionysus appeared in Thebes. He took possession of the city and expelled Agave, Cadmus, and Harmony. After Pentheus's atrocious death, they were all contaminated. Helped by his servants, Cadmus loaded a few sacks on a big cart. Harmony already had the reins in her hands. Dionysus pointed the way. They must head for the western boundaries of the earth, the mists of Illyria.

On their wedding day, young and radiant, Cadmus and Harmony had arrived standing on a chariot drawn by a lion and a boar. Now, thrown out of their own home, these two old exiles climbed on a cart pulled by a pair of simple oxen and loaded with memories. When the cart rolled off, Cadmus and Harmony sat down side by side, and the Thebans saw the couple's backs knot together in the scales of a single snake. Cadmus and Harmony rode away, twined snakes below, heads held high. Thus we may still see them today on the stone that marks their tomb, "by the edge of the black gorges of the Illyrian river."

As he drove his cart westward, knotted to his spouse, like some stubborn emigrant still seeking a new city long after it is too late, Cadmus thought about the past. What was left of it? A few bundles of things on a cart, and behind them a city Dionysus had shaken with an earthquake. Cadmus had saved Zeus, but this hadn't saved him from life's precariousness. He had set out to find his sister Europa and had won the young Harmony. A traveler had told him that Europa had become queen of Crete. Harmony was at his side, an old snake. He felt as he had when he climbed off his ship in Samothrace: a man without gifts, because everything he had was on the cart. But Cadmus's gift was impalpable.

Another king from Egypt, Danaus with his fifty bloodthirsty daughters, had brought Greece the gift of water. Cadmus had brought Greece "gifts of the mind": vowels and consonants yoked together in tiny signs, "etched model of a silence that speaks"—the alphabet. With the alphabet, the Greeks would teach themselves to experience the gods in the silence of the mind, and no longer in the full and normal presence, as Cadmus himself had the day of his marriage. He thought of his routed kingdom: of daughters and grandchildren torn to pieces, tearing others to pieces, ulcerated in boiling water, run through with spits, drowned in the sea. And Thebes was a heap of rubble. But no one could erase those small letters, those fly's feet that Cadmus the Phoenician had scattered across Greece, where the winds had brought him in his quest for Europa carried off by a bull that rose from the sea.

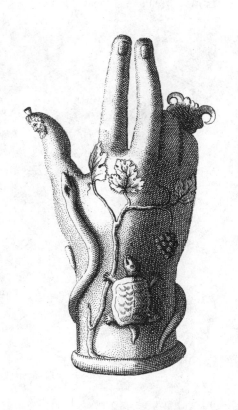

SOURCES

(Note: The first number refers to the text page, the second to the line on which the quotation ends.)

4,4   *Homeric Hymn to Demeter,* 5.

8   Ibid., 10–11.

7,7   Lycophron, *Alexandra,* 1293.

12   Ibid., 1297.

8,12   Herodotus, *Historiae,* I, 4, 2.

15   Ibid., I, 4, 3.

9,14   G. Moreau, *Pasiphaé,* in *L'assembleur de rêves,* Fontfroide: Fata Morgana, 1984, p. 69.

27   Diodorus Siculus, *Bibliotheca historica,* V, 77, 3.

12,19   Plutarch, *Life of Theseus,* 19, 6.

14,33   Virgil, *Aeneid,* VI, 397.

19,32   Ovid, *Fasti,* III, 498.

20,8   Chaeremon, *The Centaur,* 71 F 11, in *Tragicorum Graecorum Fragmenta (TrGF),* vol. 1, ed. B. Snell.

22,14   Plutarch, *Life of Theseus,* 20, 8–9.

18   Euripides, *Hippolytus,* 339.

23,27   *Iliad,* XIV, 296.

30   Callimachus, *Aetia,* II, fr. 48 (Pfeiffer).

24,11   *Iliad,* XIV, 349.

28,27   Nonnus, *Dionysiaca,* XLVIII, 372.

31,31   Ibid., XV, 409.

34,33   Ibid., X, 339.

38,1   F. Solmsen, *Eratosthenes' Erigone: A Reconstruction,* in "Transactions of the American Philological Association," 78, 1947, p. 262.

2   Hyginus, *Astronomica,* II, 4, 2.

22   Ovid, *Metamorphoses,* VI, 123.

39,27   Eratosthenes, *Erigone,* fr. 22, in I. U. Powell, *Collectanea Alexandrina.*

34   R. Merkelbach, *Die Erigone des Eratosthenes,* in "Miscellanea di studi Alessandrini in memoria di A. Rostagni," Turin, 1963, p. 472.

41,21   *Rig Veda,* VII, 87, 5.

42,4   Nonnus, *Dionysiaca,* XLVII, 135.

21   Ibid., XLVII, 190, 249.

44,20   Diodorus Siculus, *Bibliotheca historica,* II, 65, 2.

26   Plutarch, *Isis and Osiris,* 364 d.

28   Nonnus, *Dionysiaca,* XVI, 229, 252.

44,29 Ibid., XVII, 184; XXXVI, 469.

31 Clement of Alexandria, *Hortatory Address to the Greeks*, II, 39, 3.

33 Ibid.

53,23 Nicola Damasceno, H 90 F 38, in F. Jacoby, *Die Fragmente der griechischen Historiker (FGrH)*, II, A, p. 345.

56,30 Hyginus, *Fabulae*, CCII, 1.

32 *Catalogue of Women*, fr. 60 (Merkelbach-West).

57,18 Hesiod, fr. 298 (Merkelbach-West).

22 Isyllus, *Stones of Epidaurus*, in I. U. Powell, *Collectanea Alexandrina*, p. 134, v. 47.

29 *Odyssey*, XI, 581.

33 Pausanias, *Description of Greece*, X, 4, 3.

58,1 Ibid., X, 4, 1.

29 Munich, Museum antiker Kleinkunst, 2309 (in *Corpus Vasorum Antiquorum*, Munich, col. IV, bearbeitet von R. Lullies, plate 161).

36 Pindar, *Pythian Odes*, III, 15.

59,1 Ibid., III, 20.

5 Ibid., III, 21–23.

19 Apollonius Rhodius, *Argonautica*, IV, 612–614.

60,14 Plutarch, *Life of Theseus*, 6, 9.

17 Ibid., 6, 8.

61,33 Ibid., 6, 4.

36 Isocrates, *Eulogy to Helen*, 23.

62,2 Pausanias, *Description of Greece*, I, 39, 3.

62,22 J. J. Bachofen, *Das Mutterrecht*, in *Gesammelte Werke*, Basel: Schwabe, vol. II, 1, 1948, p. 271.

34 Diodorus Siculus, *Bibliotheca historica*, IV, 28, 4.

63,5 Plutarch, *Life of Theseus*, 30, 5.

6 Ibid., 29, 3.

22 Tzetzes, *Scholium to Aristophanes' Pluto*, 627 b, 1–4, in *Scholia in Aristophanem*, pars IV, ed. L. M. Positano, Groningen: Bonma, 1957.

26 Plutarch, *Life of Theseus*, 35, 7.

64,36 Aeschylus, *Supplices*, 9.

66,20 Pindar, *Pythian Odes*, IX, 114.

67,12 Strabo, *Geography*, VII, 6, 8.

20 Aeschylus, *Choephori*, 631.

68,29 Aeschylus, *Danaids*, fr. 44, in *TrGF*, vol. 3, ed. S. Radt.

69,5 Aeschylus, *Supplices*, 291.

9 J. J. Bachofen, *Das Mutterrecht*, vol. II, 1, pp. 288–89.

70,32 Aeschylus, *Myrmidones*, fr. 136, in *TrGF*, vol. 3, ed. S. Radt.

71,23 Pseudo-Lucian, *Loves*, 48.

72,2 Callimachus, *Hymns*, II, 49.

16 Plutarch, *De genio Socratis*, 591 b.

19 Euripides, *Alcestis*, 147.

73,19 Plutarch, *On Love*, 768 e.

35 Plato, *Symposium*, 179 c.

74,4 Ibid., 179 d.

35 Herodotus, *Historiae*, VII, 129, 1.

75,27   Hesychius, Lexicon, A 1156.

33   Plutarch, *On Love*, F61 e.

76,32   Aeschylus, *Supplices*, 214.

77,11   Euripides, *Alcestis*, 147.

30   Plato, *Symposium*, 182 a.

78,12   Ibid., 182 d.

19   Ibid., 183 b.

33   Theocritus, *Idylls*, XII, 13.

35   Plato, *Symposium*, 184 e.

79,2   Ibid.

7   Ibid.

17   Anacreon, fr. 125 (Gentili).

20   Pseudo-Lucian, *Loves*, 42.

25   Ibid., 39.

30   Achilles Tatius, *The Adventures of Leucippe and Cleitophon*, II, 38, 3–4.

80,6   Aeschines, *Against Timarchus*, 185.

14   Pseudo-Lucian, *Loves*, 41.

81,24   Plutarch, *Amatorius*, 750 c.

29   Pseudo-Lucian, *Loves*, 1.

82,22   Ibid., 5.

36   Ibid., 12.

83,32   Ibid., 16.

84,1   Ibid., 17.

29   Theocritus, *Idylls*, XVI, 108–9.

85,1   Simonides, in *Anthologia Palatina*, VII, 25, 3.

5   Plutarch, *Amatorius*, 751 d.

21   Strabo, *Geography*, X, 4, 21.

32   Plutarch, *Amatorius*, 751 c.

36   Aristophanes, *Clouds*, 978.

86,12   Xenophon, *Symposium*, VIII, 21.

24   Plutarch, *Amatorius*, 751 e.

31   Plato, *Symposium*, 180 b.

89,6   Herodotus, *Historiae*, II, 53, 1.

89,10   Ibid., II, 53, 2.

15   Hesiod, *Theogonia*, 885.

90,25   *Iliad*, I, 184, 323, 346.

27   Ibid., I, 143, 310, 369.

28   Ibid., I, 298.

91,3   Ibid., I, 304.

4   Ibid., I, 13.

4   Ibid., I, 23, 111, 377.

6   Ibid., I, 447.

14   Thucydides, *Historiae*, I, 11, 1.

17   M. Parry, *The Making of Homeric Verse*, Oxford: Clarendon Press, 1971, p. 97.

29   Apollonius Rhodius, *Argonautica*, IV, 794–95.

32   Ibid., IV, 799.

92,2   Ibid., IV, 796.

8   Aeschylus, *Prometheus Bound*, 768.

8   Pindar, *Isthmian Odes*, VIII, 36.

13   Apollonius Rhodius, *Argonautica*, IV, 804.

23   *Iliad*, I, 395.

93,6   Aeschylus, *Prometheus Bound*, 762.

19   Ibid., 768.

33   *Iliad*, III, 164.

94,21   Sophocles, *Antigone*, 613–14.

95,30   *Iliad*, III, 394.

36   Ibid., I, 599.

96,2   Ibid., VI, 138.

7   Lucian, *Images*, 21.

23   *Iliad*, XIX, 125.

97,2   Pausanias, *Description of Greece*, II, 4, 7.

11   *Iliad*, XIII, 359–60.

25   Parmenides, fr. 8, 30–31 (Diels-Kranz).

28   Plato, *Republic*, 616 c.

34   *Iliad*, IX, 337–38.

SOURCES

98,4   R. B. Onians, *The Origins of European Thought*, Cambridge: Cambridge University Press, 1951, p. 333.

9   P. Chantraine, *Dictionnaire étymologique de la langue grecque*, Paris: A.-K. Klincksieck, 1968, p. 83.

14   Sophocles, *Trachiniae*, 831–32.

36   Arrian, *Anabasis*, II, 3, 6–7.

99,2   Ibid., II, 3, 7.

5   Ibid., II, 3, 8.

6   *Iliad*, XIII, 359–60.

16   Macrobius, *Saturnalia*, I, 19, 17.

20   Simia, *The Wings of Love*, in *Anthologia Palatina*, XV, 24, 3–4.

21   Ibid., XV, 24, 12.

22   Ibid.

100,15   *Iliad*, XIV, 214–17.

33   Sophocles, *Trachiniae*, 443–44.

101,9   *Iliad*, XVI, 433.

10   Ibid., XVI, 441.

13   Ibid., XVI, 436–37.

22   Ibid., VII, 58–62.

34   Ibid., V, 593.

35   Philostratus, *Images*, II, 29, 2.

102,9   Callimachus, *Hecale*, fr. 238, 15–16 (Pfeiffer).

103,25   *Iliad*, X, 247.

32   Ibid., X, 246–47.

104,26   Ibid., X, 280.

31   Ibid., X, 272.

35   F. Hölderlin, *Letter to Böhlendorff of 4 December, 1801*.

105,4   F. Hölderlin, *Über Achill*, II.

105,34   Philostratus the Younger, *Images*, 392, 2.

106,11   Euripides, *Iphigenia in Aulis*, 959–60.

18   Ibid., 987–89.

107,18   Ibid., 1083.

19   Ibid., 1083–84.

108,2   Ibid., 1318.

3   Ibid., 1378.

5   Ibid., 1400–1401.

6   Ibid., 1401.

109,2   Ibid., 1218–19.

5   Ibid., 1250–51.

19   Pliny the Elder, *Naturalis Historia*, XXI, 8, 11.

110,7   Aeschylus, *Sphinx*, fr. 235, in *TrGF*, vol. 3, ed. S. Radt.

14   Hyginus, *Astronomica*, II, 15, 4.

26   Aeschylus, *Prometheus Unbound*, fr. 202, in *TrGF*, vol. 3, ed. S. Radt.

35   Athenaeus, *Deipnosophists*, XV, 674 c.

111,9   C. Daremberg and E. Saglio, *Dictionnaire des antiquités grecques et romaines*, Paris: Hachette, 1887, vol. 1–2, p. 1524.

10   Chaeremon, *The Centaur*, 71 F 11, in *TrGF*, vol. 1, ed. B. Snell.

17   Aristotle, *Symposium*, fr. 101 (Rose).

19   *Iliad*, I, 470.

25   Athenaeus, *Deipnosophists*, XV, 674 f.

28   Lucian, *On Sacrifice*, 12.

112,3   Sappho, fr. 81 b, 1–4 (Lobel-Page).

23   Sappho, fr. 58, 25 (Lobel-Page).

114,12 Athenaeus, *Deipnosophists*,
VI, 233 a.

14 Diodorus Siculus,
Bibliotheca historica, XVI,
64, 2.

36 Plato, *Republic*, 493 c.

115,4 Plato, *Laws*, 967 a.

15 Aeschylus, *Agamemnon*,
923–24.

22 Euripides, *Iphigenia in
Aulis*, 10.

116,6 *Iliad*, I, 277–81.

20 Ibid., IX, 665.

25 Ibid., IX, 637.

26 Ibid., IX, 638.

117,1 Ibid., IX, 406–9.

23 *Odyssey*, XI, 476.

25 Ibid., XI, 483.

26 Ibid., XI, 485.

31 Ibid., XI, 488–91.

119,15 Aeschylus, *Agamemnon*,
231–47.

29 Euripides, *Hecuba*, 553–
54, 557–70.

33 *Scholium to Hecuba*, 574.

121,6 *Iliad*, XIX, 325.

8 Lycophron, *Alexandra*,
171–73.

122,1 *Etymologicon Magnum*,
328, 7.

12 Euripides, *Andromache*,
598–99.

18 Ovid, *Heroides*, XVI, 149–
52.

123,6 Ibid., XVI, 250.

124,15 Ibid., XVI, 101.

33 *Iliad*, IX, 571; XIX, 87.

125,31 *Kypria*, fr. 6, 5 (Kinkel).

32 Ibid., fr. 6, 10.

126,1 Ibid., fr. 6, 3.

5 Ibid., fr. 6, 5–6.

127,26 Theocritus, *Idylls*, XVIII,
24.

129,4 Herodotus, *Historiae*, II,
113, 2.

129,19 *Iliad*, VI, 289–92.

131,3 Herodotus, *Historiae*, II,
116, 1.

3 Isocrates, *Eulogy to Helen*,
49.

6 Ibid., 53.

14 Ibid.

24 Ibid., 68.

28 Ibid., 18.

132,3 Ibid., 16.

7 Ibid., 25.

8 Ibid., 37.

13 Ibid., 59.

16 Ibid.

18 Ibid., 60.

20 Ibid.

28 Ibid., 16.

35 Ibid., 65.

133,5 Athenaeus, *Deipnosophists*,
XIII, 592 b.

13 Plutarch, *Vitae decem
oratorum*, 838 b.

134,12 Stesichorus, fr. 46, 4–5
(Page).

18 Aeschylus, *Agamemnon*,
62.

19 Euripides, *Troades*, 936.

33 Dares of Phrygia, *Excidio
Trojae Historia*, XII.

135,5 Aristophanes, *Lysistrata*,
155–56.

14 Horace, *Satirae*, I, 3, 107–8.

15 Athenaeus, *Deipnosophists*,
V, 191 b.

16 Ibid., V, 190 f.

38 Euripides, *Cyclops*, 179–
81.

138,14 Ammianus Marcellinus,
History, XIV, 11, 26.

16 Ibid.

139,14 Pausanias, *Description of
Greece*, VII, 5, 13.

143,7 Ibid., X, 5, 5.

9 Ibid., X, 12, 2.

143,16	Ibid., X, 12, 6.	172,13	Ibid., V, 7, 3.
144,34	Ibid., X, 7, 2.	14	Ibid., V, 13, 11.
146,10	Pindar, *Paeans*, VIII, 65–67 (Snell).	24	Ibid., VI, 22, 9.
		26	Ibid., VI, 22, 10.
13	Ibid., 68–71.	174,4	Ibid., V, 7, 2.
16	Pausanias, *Description of Greece*, X, 5, 12.	16	Ibid., V, 7, 3.
		182,20	Ibid., V, 13, 1.
26	Pindar, *Pythian Odes*, IV, 216.	36	Ibid., V, 20, 1.
		183,34	Ibid., V, 13, 5–6.
147,15	Ibid., IV, 213.	186,18	*Odyssey*, I, 29.
151,6	Museum of Olympia, B 4422.	193,13	Herodotus, *Historiae*, I, 67, 4.
		200,30	*Fragmenta Orphicorum*, 82 (Kern).
152,23	Apollonius Rhodius, *Argonautica*, II, 501–2.		
		32	Ibid.
23	Plato, *Phaedrus*, 75 d.	204,17	Euripides, *Helen*, 1307.
156,9	Euripides, *Ion*, 505.	205,8	Arnobius, *Adversus Nationes*, V, 20.
157,4	Ibid., 1013.		
8	Ibid., 1615.	10	Ibid.
25	Herodotus, *Historiae*, I, 47, 3.	19	Ibid., V, 21.
		30	Ibid.
28	Ibid., I, 48, 2.	31	Ibid.
159,34	Ibid., I, 30, 1.	35	Ibid.
161,18	Euripides, *Andromache*, 1092–93.	206,23	Anonymous Tarentine quoted in Clement of Alexandria, *Hortatory Address to the Greeks*, II, 16, 3.
23	Pausanias, *Description of Greece*, X, 21, 3.		
162,3	Ibid., X, 22, 4.	34	*Fragmenta Orphicorum*, 31, 24 (Kern).
35	Ibid., X, 23, 7.		
163,3	Ibid., X, 23, 8.	209,12	Plato, *Alcibiades*, 133 a.
32	Plutarch, *Quaestiones Graecae*, 293 e.	14	Ibid.
		210,1	Virgil, *Georgics*, 1, 37.
164,10	Plutarch, *On the Principle of Cold*, 953 d.	1	Lucan, *Pharsalia*, VI, 740–41.
34	Plutarch, *De E apud Delphos*, 387 a.	211,4	*Homeric Hymn to Demeter*, 10–11.
166,3	Plutarch, *Quaestiones Graecae*, 293 b.	6	Ibid., 403.
169,19	Pausanias, *Description of Greece*, V, 8, 5.	213,25	Clement of Alexandria, *Hortatory Address to the Greeks*, II, 34, 3–4.
23	Ibid., V, 8, 6.	29	*Scholium to Aristides*, 22, 4.
25	Ibid., V, 8, 7.		
170,4	Quintilian, *Institutio oratoria*, XII, 10, 9.	31	Ibid.
172,12	Pausanias, *Description of Greece*, V, 7, 1.	35	Gregory of Nazianzus, *Orations*, 39, 4.

214,1   *Orphic Hymns*, 41, 9.

215,10   Plato, *Symposium*, 187 d–
    e.

23   Pausanias, *Description of
Greece*, I, 37, 2.

216,2   Hyginus, *Fabulae*, CCLI.

19   Euripides, *Hippolytus*,
1013.

20   Ibid., 957.

22   Ibid., 1080.

23   Ibid., 1006.

39   Rufus, *On Denomination*,
112 (Daremberg-Ruelle).

217,9   Euripides, *Hippolytus*,
1352.

17   Ibid., 1333.

19   Ibid., 1438.

21   Oppian, *On Fishing*, II,
488.

218,11   *Iliad*, V, 395.

22   *Homeric Hymn to Demeter*,
344–45.

27   Ovid, *Fasti*, IV, 555.

219,2   *Homeric Hymn to Demeter*,
350.

230,25   Sophocles, *Ajax*, 764–65.

28   Ibid., 767–69.

231,3   *Odyssey*, XIII, 313.

8   Aeschylus, *Eumenides*, 737.

9   Ibid., 738.

232,2   *Chaldaean Oracles*, 34, 2
(Des Places).

11   Aeschylus, *Eumenides*,
827–28.

234,1   Callimachus, *Hecale*, fr.
260, 19 (Pfeiffer).

29   Euripides, *Ion*, 22.

237,9   Pausanias, *Description of
Greece*, I, 27, 3.

14   Ibid.

27   Aristophanes, *Lysistrata*,
640.

33   Ibid., 641–47.

238,6   Thucydides, *Historiae*, VI,
54, 2.

238,10   Ibid., VI, 59, 1.

16   Ibid., VI, 31, 6.

32   Herodotus, *Historiae*, I, 60,
5.

36   Ibid., I, 60, 3.

239,11   G. De Sanctis, *Atthis*,
Florence: La Nuova Italia,
1975, p. 348.

22   Ibid., p. 347.

36   Aristotle, *The Athenian
Constitution*, XIV, 4.

241,4   Iamblichus, *Introduction to
the Arithmetic of
Nicomachus*, 38.

12   Lucian, *Images*, 7.

243,5   Sophocles, *Ajax*, 383.

244,17   Pindar, fr. 140 (Bowra).

22   Hippolytus, *The Refutation
of All Heresies*, 5, 40, 8.

23   Aristophanes, *Ranae*, 395.

29   Ibid., 396.

33   Euripides, *Bacchae*, 194.

245,2   Aristophanes, *Ranae*, 389–
90.

4   Ibid., 392.

7   Ibid., 410–12.

12   *Scholium to Pluto*, 485.

36   Herodotus, *Historiae*, I,
153, 1.

246,2   Euripides, *Rhesus*, 355.

4   Cornutus, *Summary of the
Traditions Concerning
Greek Mythology*, 32,
p. 67, 3–4 (Lang).

21   Herodotus, *Historiae*, I,
131, 1–2.

25   Berossus, fr. 11, in Jacoby,
FGrH, III, C, p. 394.

29   J. Burckhardt, *Griechische
Kulturgeschichte*, in
Gesammelte Werke, Basel:
Schwabe, 1978, vol. V,
p. 93.

248,35   Plato, *Protagoras*, 342 a–d.

SOURCES

249,3 Plato, *Laws*, 686 d.
27 Plutarch, *Life of Lycurgus*, 28, 3–5.
33 J. Burckhardt, *Griechische Kulturgeschichte*, vol. V, p. 9.
250,16 Thucydides, *Historiae*, IV, 80, 3–4.
18 Herodotus, *Historiae*, IV, 146, 2.
251,11 Plato, *Hippias Major*, 285 c.
16 Pausanias, *Description of Greece*, II, 8, 2.
19 J. Burckhardt, *Griechische Kulturgeschichte*, vol. V, p. 110.
252,13 Plutarch, *Life of Lycurgus*, 16, 10.
20 Ibid., 22, 5.
23 Ibid., 22, 1.
25 Ibid.
27 Tyrtaeus, *Elegies*, 7, 31–32 (Gentili-Prato).
253,1 Plutarch, *Life of Lycurgus*, 29, 1.
14 Thucydides, *Historiae*, I, 10, 2.
22 Plato, *Alcibiades*, 122 e.
24 Plato, *Laws*, 641 e.
254,15 Plato, *Republic*, 548 a–c.
32 Isocrates, *Panathenaicus*, 178.
255,13 Ibid., 181.
16 Plutarch, *Life of Aristides*, 7, 7.
257,26 Plutarch, *Amatorius*, 773 e.
259,16 Plato, *Republic*, 459 e.
17 Sophocles, *Oedipus Coloneus*, 145.
17 Plato, *Phaedrus*, 265 c.
18 Euripides, *Rhesus*, 30.
21 Plato, *Republic*, 503 a.
27 Ibid.

259,36 Ibid., 503 b.
260,3 Ibid.
11 Ibid.
15 Ibid., 540 d.
23 Ibid., 503 a.
28 Plutarch, *Life of Lycurgus*, 16, 2.
30 Ibid., 15, 14.
261,6 Ibid., 15, 9.
9 Ibid.
26 Athenaeus, *Deipnosophists*, XII, 602 e.
28 Plutarch, *Life of Lycurgus*, 15, 10.
262,1 Plato, *Laws*, 637 c.
4 Ibycus, fr. 65 (Edmonds).
13 Aristophanes, *Lysistrata*, 79–84.
16 Plato, *Republic*, 458 d.
19 Plutarch, *Life of Lycurgus*, 14, 8.
29 Aristophanes, *Lysistrata*, 1312–13.
32 Aeschylus, *Agamemnon*, 832.
263,9 Aristotle, *Politica*, 1333 b.
24 Plutarch, *Life of Cleomenes*, 10, 6.
28 Plutarch, *Life of Agis*, 11, 5.
30 Plutarch, *Life of Cleomenes*, 9, 2.
264,27 Plutarch, *Life of Lycurgus*, 29, 8.
265,9 Thucydides, *Historiae*, V, 68, 2.
16 Plutarch, *Life of Alcibiades*, 23, 3.
19 Ibid., 23, 7.
24 Ibid.
266,2 Thucydides, *Historiae*, V, 105, 4.
12 Antiphon, fr. 67 (Blass).
31 Lysias, fr. 30 (Gernet-Bizos).

267,7 Athenaeus, *Deipnosophists,* XIII, 574 d.
10 Plato, *Symposium,* 212 e.
13 Athenaeus, *Deipnosophists,* XII, 554 a.
18 Plutarch, *Life of Alcibiades,* 39, 7.
268,25 Herodotus, *Historiae,* II, 50, 3.
269,11 Ibid., II, 3, 2.
270,7 Ibid., II, 135, 5
24 Sappho, fr. 5, 1 (Lobel-Page).
28 Herodotus, *Historiae,* II, -134, 2.
34 Strabo, *Geography,* XVII, 1, 33.
271,10 Hyginus, *Astronomica,* II, 16, 2.
23 Herodotus, *Historiae,* II, 135, 3.
24 Ibid.
28 Plutarch, *De Pythiae oraculis,* 401 a.
32 Ibid., 401 c.
34 Ibid.
272,4 Herodotus, *Historiae,* II, 35, 2.
9 Manetho, *A History of Egypt,* fr. 20 (Waddell).
15 Ibid., fr. 21 b.
31 Posidippus, quoted in Athenaeus, *Deipnosophists,* XIII, 596 c–d.
273,9 *Iliad,* XVII, 365; XVIII, 129.
38 Plato, *Republic,* 364 e.
274,3 Ibid., 531 a.
12 *Orphic Tablet from Thurii,* 6 (Colli 4 /A 65/).
275,23 Plutarch, *De defectu oraculórum,* 415 a–b.
276,9 Ibid., 416 f.

276,19 Plutarch, *De genio Socratis,* 590 a.
21 Ibid.
277,23 Ibid., 590 c.
278,18 Plutarch, *De facie in orbe lunae,* 994 f.
279,1 Plato, *Phaedon,* 114 d.
24 Nonnus, *Dionysiaca,* XXXI, 87.
25 Ibid., XXXI, 95.
280,2 Plato, *Republic,* 529 c.
3 Ibid., 529 c–d.
282,5 *Upon the Sublime,* 13, 2; 36, 4.
7 Heraclitus, fr. A 92 (Colli).
15 *Upon the Sublime,* 22, 1.
22 Ibid., 17, 2.
32 Ibid., 17, 2–3.
35 Ibid., 6, 1.
283,9 Plutarch, *Life of Theseus,* 22, 7.
15 Pseudo Herodotus, *Life of Homer,* 17.
284,8 Isidorus, *Etymologiae,* XIX, 30, 4.
290,6 Pausanias, *Description of Greece,* VII, 19, 1–5.
12 Plato, *Laws,* 840 e.
36 Lucian, *De Syria Dea,* 31.
293,33 Aristotle, *Politica,* 1252 b.
294,6 *Iliad,* V, 342.
295,4 Plutarch, *De defectu oraculorum,* 417 c.
9 Ibid., 417 d.
12 Ibid.
20 Plutarch, *Moralia,* fr. 157, 1 (Sandbach).
296,19 Pausanias, *Description of Greece,* IX, 3, 8.
20 Plutarch, *Moralia,* fr. 157, 1 (Sandbach).
21 Ibid.
297,12 Ibid.
298,5 Lucian, *Alexander or the False Prophet,* 3.

298,14 Ibid., 4.
300,21 Ibid., 18.
28 Ibid., 23.
301,18 Ibid., 41.
303,19 Antoninus Liberalis,
Metamorphoses, XIX.
24 Strabo, *Geography*, X, 3, 9.
35 Plutarch, *On the Love of Offspring*, 496 b.
304,18 Callimachus, *Hymns*, 1, 9.
20 Pausanias, *Description of Greece*, X, 12, 10.
305,6 Plutarch, *Quaestiones Graecae*, 293 c.
7 Ibid.
13 Porphyry, *On the Images of the Gods*, fr. 8 (Bidez), quoted in Eusebius, *Praeparatio Evangelica*, III, 11, 37.
306,10 Nonnus, *Dionysiaca*, VI, 173.
307,4 *Fragmenta Orphicorum*, 210 (Kern).
308,9 Euripides, *Bacchae*, 139.
309,1 Ibid.
3 Aristophanes, *Ranae*, 1032.
311,16 Theophrastus, *On Devotion*, fr. 18 (Pötscher), quoted in Porphyry, *De Abstinentia*, II, 29–30.
315,1 Pindar, fr. 133, 1 (Snell).
5 Plutarch, *De defectu oraculorum*, 418 c.
16 Strabo, *Geography*, X, 3, 9.
22 Plutarch, *De defectu oraculorum*, 417 e.
316,2 Ibid., 415 a.
6 Clement of Alexandria, *Hortatory Address to the Greeks*, II, 19, 2.
13 Aristides, *Eleusinian Oration*, XXII, 8 (Behr).
27 Herodotus, *Historiae*, I, 57, 3.

317,7 Ibid., II, 52, 1.
318,24 Ioannina Museum, M 34, M 42.
30 Ibid., M 21, M 31, M 12-2941.
319,20 *Hymn of Palaikastro*, 2.
30 Ibid., 3.
34 *Etymologicon Magnum*, 223, 47–48.
320,2 Ibid., 223, 48.
324,3 Apollonius Rhodius, *Argonautica*, I, 526.
325,5 Ibid., II, 129.
327,2 Ibid., II, 446–47.
27 Ibid., IV, 429.
329,10 Hyginus, *Fabulae*, XXV, 2.
332,1 John 8: 48–49.
3 Nonnus, *Paraphrase of St. John's Gospel*, VIII, 158–59.
30 G. B. Marino, *Letter to Signor Claudio Achillini*, in *Epistolario*, Bari: Laterza, 1911, vol. I, p. 260.
333,8 S. Ouvaroff, *Nonnos der Dichter*, in *Etudes de philologie et de critique*, Saint Petersburg: Imprimerie de l'Académie Impériale des Sciences, 1843, p. 248.
12 Giorgio de Santillana, *Les grandes doctrines cosmologiques*, in *Reflections on Men and Ideas*, Cambridge, Mass.: MIT Press, 1968, pp. 281–82.
17 Apollonius Rhodius, *Argonautica*, I, 902–3.
335,21 *Kypria*, fr. 1 (Kinkel).
336,1 Euripides, *Helen*, 34.
2 Ibid., 43.
337,11 *Iliad*, XVII, 647.
339,14 Ibid.

340,5   Ibid., XX, 75.
23   Ibid., XX, 30.
341,2   Ibid., XXI, 370; II, 164;
XIX, 86; XIX, 410.
26   Ibid., XXIV, 756.
27   Ibid., XXI, 518; XXIV, 99;
Odyssey, I, 263; I, 378; II,
143; III, 147; IV, 583.
342,18   Iliad, XXIV, 130–31.
350,1   Philostratus, Heroics, 11.
2   Ibid.
15   Odyssey, II, 82.
353,9   Ovid, Metamorphoses, XIII,
37–38.
355,10   Odyssey, XI, 246.
357,38   Kypria, fr. 1, 3 (Kinkel).
358,26   Euripides, Helen, 38–41.
359,6   Hesiod, Opera et Dies,
255.
7   Ibid., 253.
15   Iliad, VI, 344, 356.
17   Ibid., VI, 357–58.
22   Odyssey, VIII, 579–80.
24   Ibid., VIII, 249.
360,10   Ibid., IV, 183.
29   Ibid., IV, 225–26.
31   Ibid., IV, 239.
33   Ibid.
361,6   Ibid., IV, 260–61.
14   Ibid., IV, 266.
36   Tryphiodorus, The Capture
of Troy, 103.
362,37   Odyssey, IV, 293.
363,1   Ibid., IV, 295.
9   Tryphiodorus, The Capture
of Troy, 534.
364,17   Quintus Smyrnaeus,
Posthomerica, XIII, 412.
365,27   Euripides, Phoenissae, 391.
29   Ibid., 392.
367,24   Pausanias, Description of
Greece, IX, 16, 4.

368,10   Ovid, Metamorphoses, IV,
538.
369,4   Odyssey, I, 52–53.
371,5   Ibid., V, 179.
8   Ibid., V, 182.
9   Ibid., V, 181.
29   Lycophron, Alexandra,
770–71.
33   Ibid., 771–73.
373,13   Odyssey, XXIII, 172; IV,
293.
28   Ibid., XXIII, 109–10.
30   Ibid., XXII, 114.
34   Ibid., XVIII, 347–48.
38   Ibid., XXII, 237.
374,11   Ibid., XXIII, 162.
27   Ibid., XXIII, 162.
35   Ibid., XXIII, 248–50.
38   Ibid., XXIII, 286–87.
377,3   Ovid, Metamorphoses, II,
846–47.
9   Lucian, Charidemus, 8.
378,18   Nonnus, Dionysiaca, IV,
295.
379,12   Ibid., IV, 267.
15   Pindar, Hymns, fr. 2
(Puech).
381,6   Nonnus, Dionysiaca, I,
385.
11   Ibid., I, 396–97.
20   Ibid., III, 12.
382,12   Ibid., III, 319.
25   Ibid., III, 440–41.
36   Ibid., III, 376.
383,37   Ibid., IV, 191–96.
384,32   Ibid., IV, 293–306.
386,15   Ibid., V, 127.
390,16   Apollonius Rhodius,
Argonautica, IV, 516.
31   Nonnus, Dionysiaca, IV,
260.
33   Ibid., IV, 263.

ILLUSTRATION CREDITS

A NOTE ABOUT THE AUTHOR

Roberto Calasso was born in Florence in 1941. He lives in Milan, where he is publisher of Adelphi Edizioni. The Marriage of Cadmus and Harmony, *his third book, has been translated into twelve languages.*

A NOTE ON THE TYPE

This book was set in Bauer Bodoni, a typeface named after Giambattista Bodoni (1740–1813), a printer of Rome and Parma and an innovator in type design. Bodoni's faces were drawn with a mechanical regularity that is readily apparent when compared to the less formal old style. This version is perhaps the most faithful to the spirit of the original Bodoni types.

Composed by Brevis Press, Bethany, Connecticut

Designed by Anthea Lingeman